PRAISE FOR
*ON VIOLENCE AND ON VIOLENCE
AGAINST WOMEN*

"No stone goes unturned in Rose's exhaustive inquiry into the enduring global crisis of sexual violence . . . Rose's framework examines how systemic power structures reinforce themselves, and how sexual violence intersects with gender, sexuality, race, and class."   —Adrienne Westenfeld, *Esquire*
(Best Book of Spring)

"[Rose] has the gift that the greatest expounders of psychoanalysis share, of compressing difficult theoretical ideas and making them immediately applicable and illuminating . . . The more I read her, the more I see the world through her questions . . . Rose's careful attention to detail, her power as a close reader, yields startling insights . . . Her real power, what makes her necessary as well as unique, may be how she teaches readers to ask probing questions on their own."
—Christine Smallwood, *The New York Review of Books*

"Provocative and generative . . . Rose recombines the philosophical DNA of her greatest influences . . . *On Violence and On Violence Against Women* is a work of intellectual virtuosity and moral vigor."   —Judith Levine, *Boston Review*

"These provocative essays probe assumptions that both fuel and mask violence in Western culture."   —*The New Yorker*

"A thinker with an uncanny ability to write in a spirit of feminist solidarity without repressing either difference or discomfort,

Rose has always been willing to investigate the darkest corners of the human psyche . . . She writes beautifully, especially considering her subject, and offers penetrating insights into the effects of violence as well as ways to find inspiration in those who are fighting the structures that enable it."

—Cora Currier, *The Nation*

Mia Rose

JACQUELINE ROSE

ON VIOLENCE
AND ON VIOLENCE
AGAINST WOMEN

Jacqueline Rose is one of the world's leading feminist literary and cultural critics. She is the codirector of the Birkbeck Institute for the Humanities, a cofounder of Independent Jewish Voices, and a fellow of the British Academy. Rose is a frequent contributor to the *London Review of Books* and *The Guardian*, among many other publications. She is the celebrated author of *Sexuality in the Field of Vision*, *The Haunting of Sylvia Plath*, *Women in Dark Times*, and *Mothers: An Essay on Love and Cruelty*.

Also by Jacqueline Rose

The Case of Peter Pan;
or, The Impossibility of Children's Fiction

Sexuality in the Field of Vision

The Haunting of Sylvia Plath

Why War?:
Psychoanalysis, Politics, and the Return to Melanie Klein

States of Fantasy
(Oxford University's Clarendon Lectures in English Literature)

Albertine

On Not Being Able to Sleep:
Psychoanalysis and the Modern World

The Question of Zion

The Last Resistance

Proust Among the Nations:
From Dreyfus to the Middle East

Women in Dark Times

Mothers:
An Essay on Love and Cruelty

ON
VIOLENCE

AND

ON
VIOLENCE
AGAINST
WOMEN

JACQUELINE ROSE

Picador / Farrar, Straus and Giroux / New York

For Braham Murray
1943–2018

Picador
120 Broadway, New York 10271

The Library of Congress has cataloged the Farrar, Straus and Giroux
hardcover edition as follows:
Names: Rose, Jacqueline, author.
Title: On violence and on violence against women / Jacqueline Rose.
Description: First American. | New York : Farrar, Straus and Giroux, 2021. |
    Includes bibliographical references and index.
Identifiers: LCCN 2020057030 | ISBN 9780374284213 (hardcover)
Subjects: LCSH: Violence. | Women—Violence against.
Classification: LCC HM1116 .R667 2021 | DDC 362.88082—dc23
LC record available at https://lccn.loc.gov/2020057030

Paperback ISBN: 978-1-250-84937-3

Our books may be purchased in bulk for promotional, educational, or
business use. Please contact your local bookseller or the Macmillan
Corporate and Premium Sales Department at 1-800-221-7945, extension 5442,
or by email at MacmillanSpecialMarkets@macmillan.com.

For book club information, please visit facebook.com/picadorbookclub or
email marketing@picadorusa.com.

picadorusa.com • instagram.com/picador
twitter.com/picadorusa • facebook.com/picadorusa

1 3 5 7 9 10 8 6 4 2

CONTENTS

INTRODUCTION

ON VIOLENCE AND ON VIOLENCE
AGAINST WOMEN

> The evil that is in the world almost always stems from
> ignorance [. . .] the most hopeless vice being ignorance
> which believes it knows everything and therefore grants
> itself the right to kill. The soul of the murderer is blind
> and there is no true kindness or loving and being loved
> without the utmost far-reaching vision.
>
> ALBERT CAMUS, *THE PLAGUE*, 1947*

> We're going to tackle the virus,
> but tackle it like fucking men.
>
> JAIR BOLSONARO, PRESIDENT OF BRAZIL, PUBLIC
> STATEMENT ON COVID-19, 30 MARCH 2020

It is a truism to say that everyone knows violence when they see it, but if one thing has become clear over the past decade it is that the most prevalent, insidious forms of violence are those that cannot be seen. A group of identical-looking white men in dark suits are photographed as their president signs an executive order banning US state funding to groups anywhere in the world offering abortion or abortion counselling.[1] The passing of this 'Global Gag Rule' in January 2017 effectively inaugurated the Trump presidency. The ruling means an increase in deaths by illegal abortion for thousands of women throughout the developing world. Its effects are as cruel as they are precise. No

*Translated by Stuart Gilbert, Penguin, 1960; translation modified.

non-governmental organisation (NGO) in receipt of US funds can henceforth accept non-US support, or lobby governments across the world, on behalf of the right to abortion. A run of abortion bans followed in conservative Republican-held US states. In November 2019, Ohio introduced to the state legislature a bill which included the requirement that in cases of ectopic pregnancy, doctors must reimplant the embryo into the woman's uterus or face a charge of 'abortion murder' (ectopic pregnancy can be fatal to the mother and no such procedure exists in medical science).[2] At a talk in London in June 2019, Kate Gilmore, the UN deputy commissioner for human rights, described US policy on abortion as a form of extremist hate that amounts to the torture of women. 'We have not called it out in the same way we have other forms of extremist hate,' she stated, 'but this is gender-based violence against women, no question.'[3] The resurgence of hate-fuelled populism has become a commonplace of the twenty-first century. But it is perhaps less common to hear extremist hate, notably against women, being named so openly as the driver of the supreme legal machinery of the West.

Judging by that original photograph – which has become iconic of twenty-first-century manhood in power – the White House officials might just as well have been watching the president sign off on anything. They looked as bland as they were ruthless, mildly complacent and bored. No shadow across their brow, no steely glint in the eye or pursing of the lips to suggest that their actions were fuelled by hatred. Doubtless, they believed that their motives were pure, that they were saving the lives of the unborn. It is a characteristic of such mostly male violence – 'violence regnant', as it might be termed, since it represents and is borne by the apparatus of state – that it always presents itself as defending the rights of the innocent. These men are killers. But their murderousness is invisible – to the world (illegal abortions belong to the backstreets) and to themselves. Not even in their wildest dreams, I would imagine, does it cross their minds that their decisions might be fuelled by the desire to inflict pain. Neither the nature nor the consequences of their actions is a reality they need trouble themselves about. With their hands lightly clasped or hanging loose by their sides, what they convey is vacuous ease. Above all, they brook no argument. Their identikit posture allows no sliver of dissent (not amongst themselves, not inside their own heads). It is the central premise of this book that violence in our time thrives on a form of mental blindness. Like a hothouse plant, it flourishes under the heady steam of its own unstoppable conviction.

I start with this moment because it stands as one of the clearest illustrations of the rift between act and understanding, between impulse and self-knowledge, which for me lies at the core of so much violence. We can name this male violence against women, as the UN commissioner did without reserve, but men are not the only human subjects capable of embodying it. Women throughout history have wrapped themselves in the mantle of state power. And men are also the victims of violence – the most prolific serial rapist in UK history, sentenced to life in January 2020, had preyed consistently upon vulnerable young, heterosexual men.[4] But, in response to the crisis of the hour, the increasing visibility of gender-based violence, this book tilts towards male violence against women, and towards one deadly mix in particular: the link between the ability to inflict untold damage and a willed distortion – whether conscious or unconscious – in the field of vision. Violence is a form of entitlement. Unlike privilege – which can be checked with a mere gesture, as in 'check your privilege', and then left at the door – entitlement goes deeper and at the same time is more slippery to grasp. As if hovering in the ether, it relies for its persistence on a refusal to acknowledge that it is even there.

To take another iconic moment of the last few years: Prince Andrew's infamous BBC television interview of November 2019, when he tried to explain that his visit to the home of child trafficker and abuser Jeffrey Epstein in 2010, barely months after Epstein's conviction for sexual assault, arose from his tendency to be too 'honourable' (staying with a convicted sex offender was the 'honourable' thing to do). He was floundering in the dark. His denials that he had ever met or had sex with Virginia Giuffre, formerly Roberts, who states that she was coerced into sex with him when she was a seventeen-year-old girl, were the subject of ridicule. It was an extraordinary display of blindness: to the young women victims, trafficked by Epstein – allegedly with the support of Ghislaine Maxwell, who is now awaiting trial – not one of whom got a single mention; to the self-defeating farce of his own case (unlike Oedipus, his blindness was atoning for nothing). But he was also revealing a chilling truth, which I suspect played its part in the speed with which he was summoned by the Queen and dismissed from his royal duties without ceremony, despite the fact that he is reputed to be her favourite child. Honour, here in its royal incarnation, revealed its true colours as the right to violence with impunity (in the UK any investigation into Epstein has been summarily dropped). For that very reason Virginia Woolf warned women in the 1930s not to be tempted by the panoply of power and the trappings of national honour which would suck them into war.[5] But the shiftiness is not an afterthought. It is hardwired into the whole process, the chief means whereby

4

entitlement boasts its invincibility and hides its true nature from itself.

o   o   o

In one of his best-known formulas, Freud wrote of 'His Majesty the Baby', by which he meant the will to perfection and the burden of adoration which parents invest in their child. Narcissism starts with the belief that the whole world is at your feet, there solely for you to manipulate. Beautifully self-serving, its legacy is potentially fatal – as in the myth of Narcissus, who drowned in his own reflection in a pool – since it makes it well-nigh impossible for the human subject to see or love anyone other than themselves. Aggressivity is therefore its consequence, as the child struggles with the mother or whoever takes her place against the dawning recognition that they are as helpless as they are dependent on others to survive. 'Every injury to our almighty and autocratic ego', Freud writes in his essays on war and death, 'is at bottom a crime of *lèse-majesté*' (in the unconscious we are all royalty).[6] But for those at the top of the social pecking order, narcissism mutates, not into loss, not into something you have at least partly to relinquish, but into an accursed gift, one which too easily leads to violence. No human, however powerful, is spared confrontation with the limits of their own power, with those realms, in the words of Hannah Arendt, 'in which man cannot change and cannot act and in which, therefore, he has a distinct tendency to destroy'.[7] Arendt was writing in the 1950s about the forms of murderous totalitarianism that had spread over the earth, but her prescient words are no less relevant now, when dictatorships are on the rise, we face the destruction of the planet, black men are being shot on the streets of America, and the rates of death from austerity, rampant inequality and impoverishment are increasing by the day. When the pandemic started to break across the globe from the end of 2019, it soon became clear that one of its most striking features would be the way it accentuates the racial and economic fault lines of the world – from the fact that BAME (black, Asian and minority ethnic) citizens in the UK are four times more likely than whites to die of Covid-19, to the killing of George Floyd which, mid-pandemic, repeated and underscored a historic context of violence. At the same time, the conduct of dictators and would-be dictators (or close) – Bolsonaro, Trump, Erdoğan – in their boastful and death-dealing defiance of the virus, has given Arendt's idea of 'impotent bigness' a whole new, chilling dimension. Her concept will reappear in what follows as one of her most eloquent and suggestive (Arendt shot into the US bestsellers list on the election of Trump in November 2016).

Who decides what is called out as violence? Who determines the forms of violence we are allowed, and permit ourselves, to see? Not naming violence – its often undercover path of destruction, its random disposal of the bodies it needs and does not need – is one of the ways that capitalism has always preserved and perpetuated itself.[8] In one of her sharpest insights and most trenchant ripostes, socialist revolutionary Rosa Luxemburg cautioned against the charge that the 1905 Russian Revolution had spilt blood by pointing out that the level of suffering was nothing compared with the indiscriminate, mostly unremarked, cutting down of lives by the brute machinery of capital which had flourished up to then. 'Abroad the picture created of the Russian Revolution is that of an enormous blood-bath, with all the unspeakable suffering of the people without a single ray of light,' she stated at a rally in Mannheim in 1906. 'The suffering during the revolution is a mere nothing compared to what the Russian people had to put up with before the revolution under so-called quiet conditions.'[9] She then listed hunger, scurvy and the thousands of workers killed in the factories without attracting the attention of the statisticians. 'Quiet conditions' is key – she is referring to the skill with which capital cloaks its crimes.

In January 2019, Conservative ministers in the UK recommended that grant allocations to local authorities no longer be weighted to reflect the higher costs of deprivation and poverty so that money could be redirected to the more affluent Tory shires (a move variously described as a 'brutal political stitch-up' and 'an act of war').[10] These moments of violence move silently, as do the women today who are so often the most affected: threatened by Brexit with the loss of equality and human rights protection, including employment rights and funding for women's services, notably in relation to sexual violence where the level of reporting amongst survivors is around fifteen per cent, with prosecutions falling; or forced into sex work as a result of the Universal Credit system, part of a Conservative overhaul of benefits for people on low household income which is now acknowledged as catastrophic for the most socially vulnerable (six previous benefits rolled into one, with payment delays threatening many with destitution). When Iain Duncan Smith, architect of the policy, was knighted in the 2020 New Year's Honours List, 237,000 people signed a petition objecting to the award for a man 'responsible for some of the cruellest, most extreme welfare reforms this country has ever seen'.[11] The Department for Work and Pensions denies any link between the new credit system and survival sex, dismissing the tales of women as 'merely anecdotal'.[12]

Today the concentration of wealth in the hands of the few has never been so high. From the time of the Conservative government's first election in 2010 (in coalition) up to 2020, tax cuts for the rich have been accompanied by the slashing of public spending in the UK. As a direct consequence, thousands of people were left to die on beds in the corridors of NHS hospitals over the three years from 2016 to 2019.[13] It is generally recognised that the spending 'free-for-all' inaugurated by Boris Johnson after his 2019 election victory is intended to secure a further electoral term but will have no effect on the basic gulf between the rich and the dispossessed (the monies released for the NHS are a fraction of what is needed). Nor is there any confidence that the flurry of NHS spending brought on a year later by the pandemic will be significantly sustained. The pay increase announced in July 2020 for NHS staff excludes nurses; there is no increase mooted for workers in care homes. Meanwhile, Johnson refuses to sack Robert Jenrick, his minister for housing, communities and local government, despite troubling allegations of corruption in his dealings with the former porn baron, publisher and property magnate Richard Desmond, who boasts that Johnson promised to change the gambling rules on his behalf.[14]

Why, I once asked someone whose opinion I valued, do millionaires like Richard Branson, Robert Maxwell and Rupert Murdoch go on accumulating past the point at which their riches could possibly serve any tangible, let alone benign, purpose? His reply was as instant as it was illuminating: because they only feel powerful in the act, only in the very moment when they accumulate; and because they cannot take their wealth with them when they die. For Arendt, such grandiose, ultimately self-defeating behaviour would fall under the rubric of the 'impotence of bigness', words which might help explain, for example, why the level of sexual abuse in Hollywood and in the corridors of Westminster is so high and persistent – as we will see, the public fight against sexual harassment in the US and UK has significantly increased awareness, but we cannot be sure of its long-term effects. These places are full of men who have been led to believe they rule their domain, but who somewhere know they are deluded, since even the wildest success, the most obscene wealth, does not spare anyone from potential humiliation, or from the perils of life and death, although it can cushion you for a while. Abuse is the sharpest means, the one most readily to hand, to repudiate such knowledge with hatred.

This book is not exhaustive. It makes no claim to cover violence in all its forms or violence everywhere. Its focus is mainly on male violence. But it is central to my argument that the masculinity enjoined on all men, and paraded by so many, is a fraud. Throughout, I take my distance from radical feminism, notably of the influential school of Catharine MacKinnon and Andrea Dworkin, which sees violence as the unadulterated and never-failing expression of male sexuality and power, a self-defeating argument if ever there was one (if true, then men will rule the world for ever).[15] Instead of which, it is crucial for me that, even while calling out masculinity in its worst guise, we allow to individual men the potential gap between maleness and the infinite complexity of the human mind. How can we as feminists make that gap the beating heart of women's fight against oppression, against the stultifying ideology of what women are meant to be, and not allow the same internal breathing space to men? Surely it is on the ability of all of us to stop, think and reject the most deadly requisite behaviours that our chance of a better world relies? No man comfortably possesses masculinity (any more than, other than by killing, one person is in total possession of anyone else). Indeed such mastery is the very delusion which underpins the deranged and most highly prized version of masculinity on offer. Prowess is a lie, as every inch of mortal flesh bears witness. But like all lies, in order to be believed, it has to be endlessly repeated.

One of the most striking aspects of the saga of Hollywood producer and sexual abuser Harvey Weinstein, as told by Jodi Kantor and Megan Twohey who broke the story in the *New York Times*, is that he seems to have been at least as keen on the slow burn of coercion and resistance, which would sometimes go on for hours, as on any act of so-called consummation. Rowena Chiu, for example, describes how, shortly after being hired as his assistant, she endured four hours of threats, cajoling and bribes. At the end, 'He parted her legs, and told her that with one single thrust it would all be over.'[16] She managed to get out of the room. (What exactly, we might ask, was in it for him?) Emily Nestor, a temporary receptionist in Weinstein's Los Angeles office, described him as 'very persistent and focused, though she kept saying no for over an hour'. (Nestor chose not to file a complaint so these words come from a first-hand account by someone in whom she confided.[17]) Clearly, for Weinstein, the revulsion he provoked was a core component of his pleasure, which is not to say that he did not also wish to get his way with these women. 'If he heard the word "no",' commented one of the key witnesses in the February 2020 New York rape trial, who chose not to be named, 'it was like a trigger.'[18] For Zelda Perkins, another assistant who was subjected to his assaults, he was 'pathologically' addicted: 'It was what got him out of bed in the morning.'[19]

If sexual violence always tends to spiral out of control, it is because the agent of that violence must know deep down he is on a losing wicket (an English cricket term which means your turn at batting will fail). Jessica Mann, one of the two main witnesses in Weinstein's rape trial, stated that he lacked testicles, appeared to have a vagina and was therefore inter-sex – to the objections of Weinstein's lawyers, sketches of his anatomy were then distributed to the jury.[20] The point is not whether the claim was correct but the unstable, sexually uncertain image of the human body which had suddenly erupted in the courtroom. Seen in this light, Weinstein's physical collapse after his arrest should be read not just as a staged plea for sympathy – a day after photos were released showing him using a Zimmer frame on his way into court in December 2019, he was seen walking around a supermarket unaided – but also as an inadvertent display of the fragility and eventual bitter truth of the human body, a truth which his predatory behaviour was designed to conceal from the women he abused, from the world, and from himself. In which case, for him at least, the party is truly over. ('I feel like the forgotten man,' he said in a December 2019 interview with the *New York Post*.[21]) This suggests to me that one reason why he got away with it for so long, why so many people in the profession chose to turn a blind eye, was not only brute negligence towards women, nor fear of the career-destroying consequences for anyone who dared to speak out, but also because no one wanted to open the Pandora's box of a man like Weinstein's inner world, to look too closely at his greatest fears, any more than they wanted to recognise what, given half a chance, such a man might be capable of. 'The #MeToo movement', writes novelist Anne Enright, 'isn't just a challenge to male entitlement; it may also pose a general question about male sanity.'[22] Although not the sanity of all men, as she is careful to qualify.

In 2012, Jimmy Savile, British TV comedian, charity entrepreneur and chat show host, was found to have run a regime of systematic sexual abuse for most of his fifty-year career, including the abuse of patients at Leeds General Infirmary ranging in age from five to seventy-five. Savile had been the cherished mascot of two of the UK's most venerable and prized institutions, the National Health Service and the BBC, though many people – myself included – had always found him repellent (and not just with hindsight). Pretty much everyone he worked with, certainly at the BBC, had had some inkling of his crimes and misdemeanours, a fact which suggests that the worse, and more blatant, the offence, notably in the domain of sexual life, the more the blindness seems to increase. Like Weinstein's, Savile's acts of violence had hovered for decades on the threshold of the visible world. He had been hiding in plain sight.

o   o   o

This puts anyone seeking to combat these forms of violence in something of a double bind, or at least imposes on us the need for special vigilance. If, as I argue here, sexual violence arises from a form of tunnel vision, on burying those aspects of the inner life that are most difficult to acknowledge or see, it is also the case that raising violence to the surface of public consciousness is not always transformative in the ways we would want it to be. Perhaps nowhere so much as in the field of sexual oppression does the adage apply that recognising an injustice, bringing it to the world's attention, does not mean in and of itself that the offence will be obliterated and justice prevail. Despite the sea-change of

#MeToo for the film industry, across the run of the 2019 festivals, there was still a palpable 'predatory vibe' (Roman Polanski was welcomed and awarded the Grand Jury Prize in Venice while Weinstein awaited trial).[23]

Meanwhile, from the summit of English sport, another of the UK's celebrity-packed and most venerated institutions, cricketer Geoffrey Boycott, who had been convicted in a French court of assaulting his girlfriend in 2014, was knighted in Theresa May's 2019 resignation Honours List. The French judge responded that she stood by her decision to find him guilty. When told that a leading domestic violence charity in the UK had condemned the award, Boycott replied that he did 'not give a toss'.[24] The sporting world would seem to be another domain with a special proclivity to sexual abuse, which cannot be unrelated to the superhuman prowess that athletes are meant to have on permanent display. Certainly this expectation, compounded by his disability, was central to the life and stellar sporting career of Oscar Pistorius, whose killing of Reeva Steenkamp in 2013 and the trial that followed is the subject of a chapter here. In April 2018, Paddy Jackson and Stuart Olding, defendants in the notorious Belfast rugby rape trial, were acquitted, to the consternation of many who had watched the sustained ritual humiliation of the plaintiff in court, and listened to the verbal violence of the defendants towards her (in their shared messages, they boasted of having 'pumped' and of 'spit-roasting' a bird). According to journalist Susan McKay, 'they had been treated like young gods' from the moment they showed signs of real talent on the playing fields. 'All of them had the macho swagger that goes with it.'[25]

Harvey Weinstein's February 2020 conviction for criminal sexual assault in the first degree and rape in the third degree, together with his jail sentence of twenty-three years the following month, are a victory for women. He was, however, cleared on the two most serious charges of predatory sexual assault, which means that one of the women – the actress Annabella Sciorra, who had been the first woman to testify against him in a criminal court – was not believed. The suggestion by Weinstein's lawyer, Donna Rotunno, that she would be an 'excellent witness' as she had spent her whole life 'acting for a living' appears to have been effective, as if only liars make acting their career. The idea that this trial dismantled once and for all the image of the 'perfect' rape victim – unknown to the assailant, certainly not in a relationship with him that continued after the rape, able to recover and recount her experience with perfect clarity almost from the moment it happened – might also have been premature. There is also the risk that the celebrity which put him under the spotlight might turn out to have served as a distraction from the perennial, 'mundane', nature of sexual crime.

In this case, revulsion against a sexual felon – the revulsion that also appears to have fuelled his own desire – and the law were on the same side. But time and again in what follows, we will see the legal struggle for redress against sexual assault brought up against the most stubborn forms of resistance and sidelining, due at least in part, I suggest, to the fact that human subjects can be roused by what disgusts them, that licentiousness, even in the political order which is meant to tame and subdue it, can be a draw. This certainly seems to have played a part in the 2016 election of Donald Trump, when his ugly misogyny was either dismissed as mere masculine playfulness or else championed, and positively fired up his base (in the same way as the charge of sexual assault against Brett Kavanaugh did nothing to damage, and may indeed have increased, his chances of being elected to the US Supreme Court in 2017). Chelsea Clinton has described such misogyny as 'the gateway drug', a soporific which lulls the senses and opens the door to greater nastiness to come.[26] Permission granted to a vicarious frisson of erotic pleasure and rage, so often directed towards women, which no one is in a hurry to admit to. In her article on the Belfast trial, McKay describes how much she enjoyed watching, as a form of 'light' relief, the popular Irish TV drama *The Fall*, notably the episode in which the main detective, played by Gillian Anderson, undresses for the camera unaware – unlike the viewer – that she is being watched by the serial killer she is hunting and who has just rifled through her clothes: 'I hated the show's pornographic gender politics, the way it made me feel like a voyeur, but did not miss a single episode.'[27] She is trying to understand why the trial had become a major tourist destination, the vicious communal sexism of the defendants seeming to have been part of the appeal.

By common assent, Trump is a law-breaker: two rape charges, one made and then withdrawn by his first wife, Ivana, and one from the journalist E. Jean Carroll, who has sued Trump for defamation on the grounds of his denials and aspersions; multiple cases of sexual harassment, by his own boastful acknowledgement; numerous alleged illegal and exploitative hiring and financial practices swept under the carpet or settled out of court, but still publicly known; not to mention the grounds for his impeachment in 2019 – abuse of power for political gain (passed by the House of Representatives and then blocked in the Senate). 'Obstruction of justice as a way of life' is how his conduct is described by former national security adviser John Bolton, who alleges that Trump promised to halt criminal cases against one Turkish and one Chinese company to placate Recep Tayyip Erdoğan and Xi Jinping.[28] Likewise Boris Johnson: there is the strongest evidence that on one occasion in 1990, he agreed to provide the address of a journalist to a friend who wanted to arrange for the journalist to have his ribs cracked as revenge for investigating his activities. In the transcript of the conversation between them, Johnson asks, 'How badly hurt will he be?' He then insists, 'OK . . . I've said I'll do it. I'll do it, don't worry', when he is reassured that it won't be *that* bad. (The journalist's requests for an apology from Johnson have so far been without effect.[29])

To say they get away with it is therefore misleading. In the case of Trump's impeachment, for example, it was not that his supporters even necessarily agreed with him that the charges were a 'hoax', as he repeatedly claimed in the face of mounting evidence against him. Or even that he could do no wrong. But rather that he was adulated in direct proportion to the wrong which he clearly could do. It is because he was transgressive – because, in the words of US TV host Rachel Maddow, he could be relied upon to do something 'shocking, wrong or unbelievably disruptive' – that it became 'a rational newsworthy assessment to put a camera on him at all times'.[30] A law-breaker at the summit of politics is enticing. Arendt wrote of the danger to the social fabric posed by a world in which state authority and its laws have degenerated to the point where it is civil order and democracy, or even mere decency, that come to be felt as treacherous: 'Evil in the Third Reich had lost the quality by which most people recognise it – the quality of temptation.'[31] A lawless regime relies on the hidden guilt of human subjects, drawing them into the illicit, dissolute world to which everybody already at least partly belongs in the unconscious (no one is fully innocent in their heart of hearts; forbidden thoughts are the property of every-one). Or, in the words of a Southern Baptist woman, asked on BBC television how she could vote for Trump given his moral failings, 'We are all sinners.'[32]

'Why', asked German columnist Hatice Akyün in the news-paper *Der Tagesspiegel*, after the murder in June 2019 of Walter Lübcke, a member of Angela Merkel's Christian Democratic Union party (CDU), 'are the people of my country not flood-ing to the streets in disgust?'[33] Lübcke had been killed by a neo-Nazi as revenge for his sympathetic stance on migration. In October 2019, a video was released by a pro-Trump group with connections to the White House which showed Trump killing opponents and political journalists (in one sequence, the faces of all those shot, stabbed and punched were covered with the logo of CNN). When challenged, the organiser of the website insisted that the video was merely 'satirical': 'Hate-speech is a made-up word. You can't cause violence with words.'[34]

o o o

There is a poison in the air and it is spreading. This world of sanctioned violence, violence elevated to the level of licensed pleasure, is by no means exclusive to Trump and Johnson, even if, by general recognition, they uniquely combine the quali-ties of self-serving autocrat and clown – the glow of attraction between them now rivalling that between Reagan and Thatcher, whose belligerent neo-liberalism in the 1970s prepared the ground for so much of the destructive global order that has followed. But the rise of dictators across the world who boast of their prowess and nurse their distastes – in Hungary, Turkey, Poland, Brazil, India – suggests that we are living, or may be on the verge of living once more, what Arendt described as temptation gone awry. In Brazil, President Bolsonaro has proclaimed that he will finish the task of the military regime that ruled Brazil for two decades from 1964 to 1985 – 'if a few innocents get killed, that's OK'; he states openly that he is in favour of torture (only acknowledged by the military in 2014).[35] In 2003 he told Maria do Rosário, a fellow member of Congress, that he could not possibly have raped her because 'you do not deserve it' (shades of Trump telling E. Jean Carroll that he could not have raped her as she was not 'his type').[36] Perhaps most telling of all, he once quipped that only a 'moment of weakness' can explain why one of his five children 'came out a woman'.[37] The formula 'came out a woman' is the real giveaway, as if an infant's sexual destiny as woman were fixed from the beginning and she has no right to any other ideas. His words resonate with potential sexual violence, not just because he clearly holds all women in such brazen contempt. Ensuring that women will be women and nothing else, pinning them down as women, can be seen as one of the core motives of rape, which is why all rapes, not only those which are targeted at lesbian women, should be defined as 'corrective' (in Brazil, a woman is the victim of physical violence every 7.2 seconds).[38] All of which makes the struggle for redress against injustice, especially when charged with sexual valency, more pressing – even though, or rather because, it has another hill to climb.

In what follows, trans experience will be central as it crystallises so many of these concerns, and clearly binds the issue of sexuality to that of political struggle – freedom achieved and withheld. Despite being far more widely accepted than ever before, trans people are still the target of violence for daring to present the world with the mostly unwelcome truth that sexual identity is not all it is cut out to be. Not everyone comfortably belongs on the side of the inaugurating, sexual divide where they originally started, or to which they were first assigned. Some cross from one side to the other, others see themselves as belonging on neither side, others on both (these options are by no means exhaustive). Sexuality creates havoc. Kicking it back into place – a doomed project – is one way in which an oppressive culture tries and fails to lay down the law. Bolsonaro has explicitly stated that removing 'gender theory' from the university curriculum is a chief objective of his educational reforms (cutbacks to the cultural humanities in favour of increased spending on national history subjects in schools). For 'gender theory', we can read a reference to the work of philosopher Judith Butler, who argues that our polarised gender identities are as unstable as the performance we muster to sustain them.[39] Just over a year before Bolsonaro's election, at the end of 2017, Butler visited São Paulo for an international conference she had co-organised, where effigies of her were burned on the streets to the chant: 'Take your ideologies to hell.'[40] In fact, the conference was not on gender but on the topic of democracy, which indicates how hard and fast political freedom under threat slams up against virulent sexual hatred.

Repeatedly we see what intimate companions political and sexual coercion can be. In Poland, the Law and Justice Party placed the demonisation of LGBT people at the centre of its 2019 election-winning campaign, together with an assault on the independent media and judiciary, the cornerstones of liberal democracy. In October 2019, Marek Jędraszewski, Archbishop of Krakow, issued a pastoral letter – one of many such interventions on his part – describing LGBT 'ideology' as a 'new form of totalitarianism', which required parents who truly love their children to protect them from falling victim (there could be no greater tragedy).[41] In São Paulo the demonstrators attacked the conference agenda as 'Marxist', and as supported by foreign money, while holding up placards inscribed with the words 'family', 'tradition' and 'In favour of marriage as God intended, 1 man, 1 woman'. In Spain, the ultra-right Vox party made huge gains in the April and November 2019 elections (in November it entered the Congress of Deputies for the first time). Visiting Madrid in April that year, I was handed one of its flyers, which specifically targeted 'supremacist feminism', 'radical animal rights activists' and the LGBT lobby. 'Supremacist feminism' is the sister term to 'feminazis', coined by the US right-wing radio host Rush Limbaugh to describe radical feminists – by which he means militants and extremists – who, he claimed, 'want to see as many abortions as possible'.[42] In March 2019, the ultra-right Catholic organisation Hazte Oír – 'Make Yourself Heard' – campaigned for the repeal of Spain's laws on gender violence by driving through cities in buses sporting a picture of Hitler and the hashtag #Feminazi painted underneath. (A Barcelona judge rejected a call for the buses to be banned.)[43]

In fact, the rise of Vox in Spain was propelled by the increased visibility of feminist protest against sexual violence, notably the nationwide demonstrations following the infamous *manada* or 'wolf-pack' rape of a young girl at the annual Pamplona festival of the running of the bulls in 2016 and the trial that followed two years later. When two of the judges ruled that the men were not guilty of rape as there had been no violent coercion and a third absolved the defendants completely of the charge, thousands of protesters filled the streets ('Spain's largest spontaneous feminist uprising in living memory').[44] A year later, in September 2019, protesters in more than 250 towns and cities across Spain declared a 'feminist emergency' after a series of high-profile rape cases and a summer in which nineteen women were murdered by current or former partners (the worst figures for more than a decade). Similar demonstrations have taken place across the world, in countries including Mexico, India, Italy, France, South Korea and South Africa, in each of which the incidence of violence against women over the past couple of years has visibly increased and is being recognised like never before.[45] Addressing the protesters in Cape Town, Cyril Ramaphosa acknowledged that South Africa was one of the 'most unsafe places in the world to be a woman', one reason why the country will provide a test case for this book.[46] In Seoul, South Korea, at a rally to legalise abortion in April 2019, most of the women wore black surgical masks (before Covid-19) in order to prevent identification. Isabel Cadenas, one of the organisers of the annual march on International Women's Day in Madrid, praised a younger generation of feminists – sixty-five per cent of Spanish women under thirty describe themselves as feminist: 'They know violence for what it is, in a way that we didn't.'[47]

This is the context in which Vox agitates for the repeal of laws passed in 2004 tackling gender-based violence, for the removal of all sex change and abortion procedures from public health services, and for the dissolution of all federally funded feminist organisations. They have also called for the abolition of the Law of Historical Memory, which was designed to ensure that the legacy of Franco is not forgotten, to be replaced by a ministry to protect the rights of the 'natural family' as an institution prior to the state, and for the building of a frontier wall to halt illegal immigration 'encouraged by globalist oligarchies' – child migrants were presented as a special menace.[48] Each one of these is an unabashed incitement to violence – against women, migrants, and historical memory which is being wiped off the page. Each one will appear in what follows, as we slowly move from violence at the apex of the West to the countries (South Africa) and the places (the shores of Europe and the border with Mexico) which have been, and continue to be, where some of the clearest targets of such incitement are to be found.

A staple of right-wing discourse, hatred of migrants is something which every single one of the leaders so far mentioned shares. In Hungary, Prime Minister Orbán has been accused by the Helsinki Committee, the human rights organisation, of systematically denying food to failed asylum seekers held in detention camps on the border, a human rights violation it described as 'unprecedented in twenty-first-century Europe'.[49] In the past decade, ten thousand child refugees have risked their lives to get into Britain. One of the first moves of the newly elected Conservative Party in January 2020 was to remove the clause protecting child migrants from the EU withdrawal bill.[50] Donald Trump routinely refers to migrants at the Mexican border as 'bad hombres', 'thugs' and 'animals' (in the first nine months of 2019, only eleven out of ten thousand asylum applications were granted in the US).[51] In December 2019, the advocacy group Human Rights First accused his administration of exposing asylum seekers to 'life-threatening dangers' after documenting 636 cases of violence against those who had been returned to Mexico under the new policy 'Migration Protection Protocols' or 'Remain in Mexico'. These numbers included a nine-year-old girl and her mother who had been kidnapped and raped in the border town of Tijuana.[52] The ways in which anti-migrant hatred is specifically targeted against women is the subject of the final chapter here.

Far-right parties do not all hold the levers of power, but they stalk its corridors, releasing their ugly permissions into the mental and social atmosphere. 'We're only saying what everyone is thinking' is the common justification and refrain. They wrap themselves in the mantle of redemption, as if they were saving the world from burning injustice (righteousness raised to the pitch of frenzy is the particular skill of the far right). 'Hate can exist without any particular individuals,' comments the narrator of Edouard Louis's bestselling 2016 *History of Violence*, which narrates the story of his rape after a casual encounter on the Paris city streets; 'all it needs is a place where it can come back to life.'[53] This too leads to a quandary, one which, in writing this book, I have had to confront at every turn. How to convey the psychic intensities released by the subject of violence without fanning the flames, adding to the spectacle, making the analysis complicit with the crime? 'Even writing about sexual violence', writes Anne Enright in the middle of her own article on sexual violence, 'is a kind of complicity. You must have the fantasy in order to refuse it, because once a thing is named or imagined, it exists – if only as aversion.'[54] There is always a risk – one which I have tried to avoid, though I am sure not always successfully – of turning sexual violence into the crime we love to hate.

If violence is so rousing, it would seem to be in direct proportion to its ability to suspend anything vaguely resembling thought, to release the rush of blood that gives you no time to pause. No introspection, even though – or because – violence plunges so deeply into who we are (the claim that violence is declining in our times, which is presumably intended to make us all feel better about ourselves, drastically misses the point, sidestepping the key moment of recognition that violence requires permanent vigilance in so far as it is a potential for everyone).[55] 'Violence', observes novelist Graeme Armstrong, who was involved in gang culture from a young age, 'is very, very quick, and afterwards, you don't always remember things . . . You remember what happens to you afterwards, the injuries or whatever, but the violence itself is often just a blur.'[56] As if it is only in a state of blindness that violence can bear to conduct itself. The aim of this book is, therefore, to slow the pace, to resist the will to action at any price, to create the space for reflection. It is a paradox of human subjectivity that knowing you are capable of violence – recognising it as your problem, instead of blithely assigning it to someone else (race, class, nation or sex) – reduces the chances of making it happen. The idea of crushing violence – stamping it out or eradicating it from the earth – simply increases the quotient of violence we have to face. We have seen this before at the centre of twentieth-century Europe, in the belief that the First World War would be the war to end all wars, a delusion which allowed that same war and its aftermath to carry on silently laying the groundwork for the next.

o o o

A key focus of this book is post-apartheid South Africa, because it is the place where all these forms of violence – historic, intimate – coalesce and rearrange themselves, spread throughout the social fabric and intensify. If South Africa feels so urgent in this context, it is because of the acute contradictions of its history: crucible of apartheid, one of the deadliest embodiments of state violence in the twentieth century, and of the steadfast political passions that succeeded in bringing it to an end. During the Rhodes Must Fall student uprising of 2015–17 – which will be the focus of a chapter here – the country was also the site of one of the most eloquent and far-reaching social protest movements against injustice which the past decade has seen. The urgency of that protest could not be more resonant today. In May 2020, in the midst of the pandemic, protesters against the US police murder of George Floyd tore down the statue of slave dealer Edward Colston from the city centre of Bristol and dumped it in the harbour. The link to Rhodes Must Fall was explicit. Weeks later, Oxford University students secured approval from the governors of Oriel College for the removal of the statue of Cecil Rhodes from the facade of the building, having failed to do so two years before. (It is still unclear whether the university will finally concur with the college governors.)

Rhodes was a mining magnate, Prime Minister of the Cape Colony from 1890 to 1896, founder of the Southern African territory of Rhodesia; he believed the Anglo-Saxons were the 'first' race, with the God-given right to rule the world. In her study of totalitarianism, Arendt explains how it was Rhodes who propelled the British into the African continent, persuading the British government that 'expansion and export of the instruments of violence was necessary to protect investments, and that such a policy was a holy duty of every national government.'[57] For violence, read subjugation and exploitation of the native people. '"Expansion is everything,"' he once said, but then, she elaborates, he 'fell into despair, for every night he saw overhead "these stars [. . .] these vast worlds, which we can never reach. I would annex the planets if I could."'[58] Impotent bigness which, given half a chance, will stop at nothing.

Today South Africa has one of the worst rates of sexual violence across the world: a woman murdered every three hours, more than a hundred rapes reported every day (Cape Town is known as the 'rape capital of the world'). 'It began', writes journalist and crime writer Margie Orford, 'with a new flag, a new anthem and a new constitution and it was lost [. . .] to corruption and a plague of gendered violence.' Violence against women and girls she describes as the 'collateral damage' of a society whose ongoing inequality and injustice have snatched away the dream.⁵⁹ In September 2019, partly fired by the boldness of the Rhodes Must Fall campaign, thousands of women demonstrated on the streets of Cape Town against such violence. When Cyril Ramaphosa addressed the protesters, he was handed a memorandum with a list of demands, including the demand that a state of emergency should be declared. The protest had been called in response to the death of Uyinene Mrwetyana, a nineteen-year-old Cape Town student who was raped and murdered by a post office worker who had tricked her into returning to the office after closing time. At the funeral, her mother, dismayed at having been unable to protect her daughter, said that the post office had never figured on her list of places she needed to be wary about (Mrwetyana being a student and the fact it happened at a post office were seen as the unexpected stand-out features of this case). In the same month, police reports had included a woman killed by her husband, who set fire to her body after a marriage-counselling session; a former boxing champion shot dead by her ex-boyfriend, who was a policeman; four young girls hanged by their father/stepfather after he was handed divorce proceedings by their mother. 'There are many stories like these,' South African journalist Rosa Lyster wrote in the *New Yorker*, '[but] there is no template for how to proceed after you have reached the conclusion that what is happening is not normal.' Or isn't it rather, as she also suggests, that we need to acknowledge just how 'distorted our definition of "normal" has become'?[60] Days before the killing of Reeva Steenkamp by Oscar Pistorius, a seventeen-year-old black girl, Anene Booysen, was gang-raped and disembowelled in Bredasdorp on the Western Cape. She died a few hours after being found by a security guard. Although she told the police before she died that several men had been involved in the attack, only one stood trial (he was given two consecutive life sentences). The case provoked a national outcry – though it is little known outside South Africa, and even inside the country it gained a fraction of the attention accorded to the killing of Steenkamp. 'It sometimes feels', Lyster wrote on her Twitter account with reference to the death of Mrwetyana, 'like you can't tell people who aren't South African about what happens to women and girls here because they find it too upsetting, but I hope that people read this story.'[61] The day before she died, Steenkamp had been preparing a talk in honour of Booysen to be delivered in a school in Johannesburg in support of the Black Friday campaign for rape awareness.

In South Africa, the slogan of the campaign against sexual violence is not #MeToo or #TimesUp but, far more chillingly, #AmINext. Like Steenkamp's act of race solidarity and gender empathy, it cuts through racial boundaries to make violence against women the responsibility and possible destiny – or rather the responsibility *because* it might be the destiny – of anyone (although Steenkamp can hardly have known that it was about to be her own). While both lay claim to a common experience, #MeToo focuses on the woman making her claim, whereas #AmINext strikes me as stronger because of the way it creates a community of potential targets, alerting the world to a continuum, not only of violence which has already happened but of violence to come. Indiscriminately, the hashtag draws everyone, regardless of race, class or status, into its net. To this extent, #AmINext oddly echoes the 'veil of ignorance' posited by legal theorist John Rawls as the sole precondition for justice: only if individuals have no idea of where they are likely to find themselves in the final dispensation will they contemplate for a second the possibility that they might land up amongst the most destitute, and cast their die on the side of a fairer world.[62] By being so inclusive, #AmINext stands as a one-line answer to the continuing divisions of the nation.

South Africa's first racially democratic elections, in 1994, heralded an unprecedented constitutional and legal transformation, but the forms of racial and economic inequality which that moment was supposed to bring to an end continue to seep through the social fabric of the nation, a cruel rebuke to the belief and hope that everyone would now be living in a just world. Hence the euphoria when the Springboks, South Africa's national rugby team, won the 2019 Rugby World Cup, a victory which, in the words of veteran anti-apartheid activist Archbishop Desmond Tutu, had restored the faith of 'a self-doubting nation' (even though the victory would be powerless in the face of widespread corruption, soaring joblessness, patchy delivery of basic services and power cuts which have pushed the country close to recession).[63] Once again, we see an impossible burden of idealisation laid on the heroes of the sporting world, who are raised to the status of gods and burdened with the task of redemption. Likewise, the stellar career of Oscar Pistorius was held up as proof that the fight for social justice had been won. If a disabled man could succeed in the new South Africa, then, whatever the odds stacked against them, so could anyone.

South Africa presents us with the problem of what happens to a legacy of violence and an ongoing history of injustice that cannot bear fully to acknowledge itself. It brings us up against another version of how violence enters, and is rebuffed by, the human mind. What happens to violence in a world where it is meant to have been transcended? Where does violence lodge itself in the social, physical and mental body of a nation? When the students erupted in protest in March 2015, they were telling the universities, telling the whole world, that the project of equality was not working and the process of 'decolonisation' – shedding the debris of a colonised history – had barely begun. Rhodes Must Fall, and then Fees Must Fall, had two core demands: rejection of the emblems of the colonial past – the same demand that erupted in the US and around the world after the killing of George Floyd – and free education for all. It stretched back into the history of colonialism and forward into what was felt by this young generation to be a betrayal of the radical promise of 1994.

In 2017, I visited Cape Town in an attempt to understand these protests, whose energies I knew were at least partly directed at the cruel colonial legacy of Britain. My sense of responsibility for that legacy as a British subject, even though I come from a Polish-Jewish émigré family, has fuelled a special interest in South Africa that goes back decades. I was the awkward guest of the university which had sparked the protests. They had not subsided; if anything positions were becoming more entrenched. On the plane, I found myself sitting next to a black South African woman who worked in the Land Registry Department and asked her what she thought. I was not expecting a sympathetic reply. The students, she said, were 'alerting' the nation. I was struck by 'alerting', the idea that the students were warning the nation of a hidden danger yet to come.

South Africa has taught me that violence never belongs solely in the present tense, that it cannot be severed from the historic legacies of oppression which so often trail behind it. It was the 1913 Natives Land Act, enacted by the British colonial power, which laid the ground for racial segregation and eventually apartheid. It was Ronald Reagan and Margaret Thatcher who made the decision to allow multinational corporations, without let or hindrance, into the global south, a decision which made possible the racialised economic injustices which continue to scar the nation. This would be an example of violence in so-called 'quiet conditions', as Rosa Luxemburg put it, an economic order fostering brute forms of social inequality, which formed the steady, unerring backdrop to the more visible atrocities of apartheid.[64] In such circumstances, a nation invested in the belief that it has left violence behind, that it has 'done' with violence, is all the more likely to find itself confronted with violence once more: in the intimacies of domestic life, in the shadows of the cities, in the anger of the young who were tasked with escaping it, and deep inside the corridors of power.

If South Africa brings this reality into such sharp focus, it is also because the country staged a unique public confrontation with the legacy of violence in the shape of the Truth and Reconciliation Commission set up in 1995, an unprecedented experiment in listening, where the victims and perpetrators of apartheid were summoned to tell their stories in a bid to lay the past to rest. For today's students, the process has failed because it traded racial and economic justice for truth, and decolonisation for democracy. The Commission was, for example, powerless to impose reparations for violence or to guarantee the more equitable distribution of resources in the new South Africa; whites still dominate the universities in terms of who teaches and the content of what is taught. But there is another way of seeing it, that such a process could only be interminable (the project of justice is endless). There can be no 'being done' with violence. Reckoning with violence has to be enacted over and over again. This at least is the wager of the Historical Trauma and Transformation Centre, based at the University of Stellenbosch, founded in 2006 by Pumla Gobodo-Madikizela, psychologist and participant in the Truth and Reconciliation Commission, which I visited in 2018 and which forms the subject of one of the final chapters here. In Stellenbosch, the widow of Fort Calata, murdered by the apartheid state, and the grandson of Hendrik Verwoerd, one of the chief architects of apartheid, told their tales (the grandson had spent his adult life struggling against the legacy of his grandfather). It was precisely because the project of reconciliation is now seen to be faltering that their doing so under the same roof felt so urgent.

o o o

Throughout this book, fictional writing plays a central role. It is for me one of the chief means through which the experience of violence can be told in ways that defy both the discourse of politicians and the defences of thought. As will be clear in what follows, one of the greatest challenges I see in the fight against violence today, notably sexual violence, is to expose it, to call for legal redress, without sacrificing the ungovernable aspects of human sexuality, not least because bringing sexuality to heel would be a pretty accurate descriptor of sexual violence itself. All the writers presented here upend the clichés which imprison, dislodge the stereotypes which bind identities to the floor. Haitian-American writer Roxane Gay, Temsula Ao in Nagaland, Virginia Woolf and Daisy Johnson in England, Eimear McBride and Anna Burns from Belfast, Han Kang from South Korea and Hisham Matar from Libya. Each one moves across myriad forms of violence, from the struggle for secession in post-Independence India as met by the violent barrage of the new state, to military massacres by dictators in South Korea and Libya, to sexual violence in Haiti, Belfast and in the heartlands of middle England, to Britain basking in false innocence on the threshold of the Second World War.

In every case, the writing takes us deep into parts of the world crying out unambiguously for justice while refusing to reduce by one iota the contrary pathways of the mind. An old man in Nagaland who had been a fighter in the secessionist war against India remembers the violence of his own actions at the risk of his heroic pride. A young man searching for the truth about his father's political murder finds himself, despite his strongest impulses, recoiling against the knowledge he desperately seeks because he knows it might defeat him. A young woman subjected to sexual violence goes looking for the violence which has scarred her; another, also damaged by assault, embraces her own capacity for bloody violence as deepest pleasure. Both these stories turn the tables on the accusation that women sometimes ask for the violence they suffer, since in each case violence went after them long before they made the vocation of violence their own (the argument that women 'ask for it' fatally mistakes symptom for cause). These stories have inspired me. Their willingness to go so deep into the entrails of violence I see as grounds for hope. Like, for example, the story of a state massacre of students whose spirits, against all human and inhuman odds, lift themselves out of the bodies in the morgue into the shadows of a new communal world.

My sister, the philosopher Gillian Rose, wrote of 'the equivocation of the ethical', by which she meant the importance of not assuming that ethical rightness is something that anybody ever completely owns. We are all subjects of violence, not least because we are embedded in a violent social world.[65] There is always a point in any ethical position or turn – the struggle against injustice, the fight for a better, less violent order – where it starts and stutters, trips and breaks, before setting out on its path once more. At the beginning of *The Human Condition*, Hannah Arendt writes: 'What I propose, therefore, is very simple: it is nothing more than to think about what we are doing.'[66] If there is one thing of which writing about violence has convinced me, it is that if we do not make time for thought, which must include the equivocations of our inner lives, we will do nothing to end violence in the world, while we will surely be doing violence to ourselves.

1

I AM A KNIFE

Sexual Harassment in Close-up

Given the media coverage, not to say frenzy, it might seem as if the sexual harassment of women had never been in the public eye before. At the very least we need to question why it took the fall of a powerful media mogul to turn the story into front-page news, and whether the endless photo spreads of his female targets weren't designed to provoke not just outrage and a cry for justice, but the pleasure of the voyeur. This of course is the pleasure on which the cinema industry thrives and which had made these women vulnerable at the outset. Past pictures of actresses smiling with Harvey Weinstein, his arm proprietorially around various parts of their bodies, only repeated the offence, since everyone looked as if they were having such a good time. Later these images would be used by Weinstein's lawyer to undermine the charges against him, as if the photos 'were proof that nothing untoward had happened'.[1] More institutions and public figures were to follow – from news anchors and comedians to MPs, celebrity chefs, financiers, billionaire businessmen, cult gurus, schoolteachers, cardinals and Benedictine monks – with less screen potential, one might say. But I could never quite get out of my head the feeling that these women were once again being asked to audition for their parts or were being paraded across the red carpet on Oscar night.

This is just one reason why celebrations of #MeToo as a historic breakthrough in attitudes towards harassment should be viewed with caution. Remember the images of Angelina Jolie walking across the international stage, arm outstretched to greet William Hague as part of their 2014 London 'summit' (*sic*) against rape as a war crime? It struck me then that she was being offered as a trade-off or collateral damage – woman as bait served up to the fantasy life of everyone – as the price for bringing such violence to an end. The initiative is now seen as a costly failure since the number of rapes recorded in the eastern Democratic Republic of the Congo, on which they focused their attention, rose in the following year and has shown no signs of any significant decrease since then. It is just one facet of this ugly reality – one more thing to contend with – that, while attention to violence against women may be sparked by anger at harm and a desire for redress, it might just as well be feeding vicariously off the forms of perversion towards women that fuel the violence in the first place.

Sexual harassment has existed ever since there has been a world of work, while sexual violence against women goes back way before then. Feminists have long insisted that harassment occurs whenever women find themselves in the vicinity of men in positions of power. It also takes place on the street. Vanessa Grigoriadis of the *New York Times Magazine* had often been whistled at and catcalled as she walked through the city, but when researching her book on campus sexual harassment in 2016, she noticed that men seemed to be stopping and harassing her even more than usual.[2] Her father was dying at the time. It was not exactly that these men could read her thoughts, but certainly she felt that they were picking up on her vulnerability, seizing their moment to probe into what was already an open wound. They were excited by her distress (just as one target of Weinstein's advances said he was clearly roused by her fear[3]). The aim of harassment, this would suggest, is not only to control women's bodies but also to invade their minds. Grigoriadis's experience is telling. Though the modern city is scarred by dereliction and poverty, it can also be a place of relative freedom where a woman can muse and fantasise (the great thing about fantasy as inner freedom is that it interferes with no one other than yourself). Harassment is always a sexual demand, but it also carries a more sinister and pathetic injunction: 'You will think about me.' Like sexual abuse, to which it is affiliated, harassment brings mental life to a standstill, destroying the mind's capacity for reverie.

As far back as 1982, in their pamphlet *Sexual Harassment at Work*, the UK National Council for Civil Liberties (NCCL), which became Liberty in 1989, described harassment as an 'intentional assault on an individual's innermost privacy'.[4] Ironically, in the light of recent developments, it also noted that a 'moral complaints bureau' had been set up by the US Screen Actors' Guild to deal with 'casting couch complaints'. In October 2017, a Hollywood Commission on Sexual Harassment and Advancing Equality in the Workplace opened its inquiry, chaired by Anita Hill, famous for having brought sexual harassment charges against US Supreme Court nominee Clarence Thomas in 1991. We can only hope that this enquiry will be more effective (two years later, in October 2019, industry experts were reporting that the pace of change had been 'glacial').[5]

In the past years, our understanding of what constitutes sexual harassment has been put under considerable strain. For all the remonstrations of the accused – 'You are making a fuss about nothing', 'Things were different back then' – the reality is crystal clear. Sexual harassment consists of unwelcome sexual advances which, *pace* the mostly – though not exclusively – male protests, are never innocent, a mere trifle, playful or a joke. And that is because however minimal the gesture, it nearly always contains the barely concealed message: 'This is something which I, as a man, have the right to do to you.' Women of course can also harass, but it is comparatively rare (the glee with which such examples are jumped on by those wanting to downplay the issue as a feminist issue is worth noting in itself). Sexual harassment, we might then say, is the great male performative, the act through which a man aims to convince his target not only that he is the one with the power, which is true, but also that his power and his sexuality are one and the same thing. As Judith Butler has argued, the performative always veils a hidden melancholia since, as the word suggests, performing, far from expressing a true, deep, essential self – something sacred and untouchable – is no more than skin deep ('melancholia' also because of all the other buried and unconsciously grieved sexual lives one might have led).

To this extent, a feminism which takes harassment as the unadulterated expression of male power and authority is in danger of colluding with the very image of masculinity which it is protesting against. These men indeed hold the power, but they do what they do – advance and insult in one and the same breath – precisely because they are anything but cocksure (like the Wizard of Oz behind the curtain with precious little to show for himself). 'Combine male fragility with white fragility and the perennial fear of falling,' writes Dayna Tortorici, 'and you end up with something lethal, potentially.'[6] As psychoanalysts have pointed out, the idea of the phallus is a delusion, above all for any man who claims to own or embody it, since there is no such thing as an ever-ready penis that is permanently erect (a truly uncomfortable prospect, I am told). Harassment is ruthless, but it also carries a whiff of desperation about it, as if the one harassing knows somewhere that their cruelty, like all human cruelty in a precarious world, is sourced in a fraudulent boast. Not that this makes it any less of a threat. As Hannah Arendt argued, it is illegitimate and/or waning power that turns most readily to violence.

But if we all now know exactly what harassment looks like – 'in your face' as recent coverage has sometimes felt to me – on the other hand, the borders around what constitutes harassment are blurred. Is harassment a form of violence? I have lost count of the number of times people have expressed outrage at the merest suggestion of an affinity between harassment and violence on the grounds that it tars the innocent (at worst thoughtless) and the guilty (at worst serial predators) with the same brush. It is true that the two should not be equated, but they are surely connected, like siblings or bedfellows. At the very least, they belong on a sliding scale since a sense of entitlement ready to turn nasty underpins both (Weinstein appears to have moved effortlessly along the spectrum). When Matt Damon insisted that some cases were really not so bad, Minnie Driver suggested men might not be the best judges of the issue: 'We need good intelligent men', she responded, 'to say this is all bad across the board.'[7]

Towards the end of her tribute to Fezekile Ntsukela Kuzwayo ('Khwezi'), who brought rape charges against South African President Jacob Zuma, Redi Tlhabi writes:

> She fought for every one of us – every woman who has been too afraid to say, 'I was raped,' too afraid to say, 'That man groped me' or 'He demanded sex in exchange for the job, the lift, the favour.' She fought for all the women whose bodies have been

appropriated by men, known and unknown, through lurid descriptions and graphic imagery, men who whistle and undress women with their eyes in public and private spaces. Uncles who wink at them when their parents are not looking, the managers and senior colleagues who, in a handshake, quickly turn their index finger to circle their palms, knowing that they will not call them out. That they are too paralysed to react. That, even when they are being disrespected, they will pull away quietly and carry on as if nothing had happened.[8]

Khwezi was eventually driven into exile after her case had been mangled to pieces in the courts and her house burnt down.

o   o   o

In April 2011, the Assistant Secretary of the Department of Education under President Obama issued a 'Dear Colleague' letter on college harassment which became the defining document for policy in the US. The letter is a directive to universities on how to implement Title IX, originally part of the 1972 Education Amendments to the Civil Rights Act, which prohibits sex discrimination in education. Harassment is seen as a form of discrimination because it creates a hostile environment which impedes a student's educational progress. Schools are required 'to take immediate action to eliminate the harassment, prevent its recurrence, and address its effects': investigate the complaint, appoint at least one Title IX co-ordinator, provide training for all campus law enforcement employees, publish grievance procedures and issue guidelines on what constitutes sexual harassment (a college where students are deemed in ignorance on this matter is automatically in violation of Title IX). Although it would be revoked under Donald Trump, it remains, in the words of Grigoriadis, 'the era's seminal text on college sexual violence'.[9] 'It is hard to overstate', Jennifer Doyle writes in *Campus Sex, Campus Security* (2015), 'the impact of this nineteen-page document.'[10]

Sexual violence is upfront from the first page. Rape, sexual assault, sexual battery and sexual coercion are all included in the same category: 'All such acts of sexual violence are forms of sexual harassment under Title IX', although the use of the conjunctives – 'harassment *and* violence' here, 'harassment *or* violence' later in the letter – suggests a less steady link. This has been decisive. During her interviews with student activists against harassment, Grigoriadis found that refusal to define 'assault' as 'sexual violence', for example, was seen as a cop-out, immediately identifying the speaker as not aligned with 'the radical cause'. (Though clearly on the activists' side, she chooses to use 'assault' throughout her book.) 'It's all violence,' one of them told her passionately.[11] Likewise, calling out harassment as violence, they felt, was the only way to ensure that it would not be dismissed as petty interference or minor assault. This makes sexual harassment a safety issue: 'The Department is committed to ensuring that all students feel safe in their school.' In the 1982 pamphlet, the NCCL too defined harassment as a health and safety concern. Any university in 'violation' of the Department of Education directive – not enacting due process for the protection of its students and the pursuit of their claims – is considered 'non-compliant' and faces the possibility of having its federal funding withheld, a potentially catastrophic financial outcome which has never taken place. This made Grigoriadis wonder whether the Obama administration had not initiated a 'political dance'.[12]

Title IX was a breakthrough, but it is also flawed. Legal critics have claimed that it ignores 'due process': acting as a court of law while neglecting protections such as the right to an attorney, or full advance notification of charges against the accused. They also disapprove of the standard of evidence used in sexual misconduct cases: a 'preponderance of evidence' – meaning fifty-one per cent – rather than the higher standard of 'clear and convincing' evidence ('hunting for a feather', in the words of Brett Sokolow, introduced by Grigoriadis as 'the nation's top university sexual-misconduct adviser').[13] At moments, it is also unclear in these cases who is acting on behalf of whom. In one of its most striking clauses, the letter states that where confidentiality is requested or where there is a request not to pursue, the college concerned must take all reasonable steps to investigate and respond to the complainant, consistent 'with the request not to pursue an investigation'. This is a rare moment when the possible human cost of assault, how it might silence someone who has been the target, is allowed to show through the legalese. In fact, this clause echoes anti-rape activists who have long insisted that no woman should ever feel obliged to make a formal complaint. 'What', asks Roxane Gay, 'if she doesn't want to tell her story?'[14]

To which we might add: 'What if she can't?' In May 2015 at Liverpool Crown Court, Farieissia Martin was convicted of murdering her partner after years of physical and mental abuse. Everything hung on how convincingly she could tell her story in the witness box. Sobbing and barely able to speak, she failed to persuade the jury that she was not guilty (for some reason, in their eyes, her vulnerability made her more likely to have been a cold-blooded killer rather than less). As Sophie Elmhirst asks in her investigation of the case, 'how do you perform the story of your own abuse?'[15] 'Perform' should give us pause, since it is so at odds with the legal priority of establishing the unvarnished truth. 'I'd have to act the part, or no one would believe me,' states the narrator of Louis's *History of Violence*, as he explains his reluctance to press charges against his rapist – he wants to send no one to prison – or even to file a report with the police: 'Being allowed to speak of a thing, and being obliged or summoned to speak, are entirely separate things.'[16] Telling also takes time. 'A big part of the problem', actress Helen Hunt remarked in an interview about #MeToo in September 2019, 'is that if a woman is assaulted, by the time they feel they can get the words out of their mouth there are statute of limitation laws that say "too late".'[17] How can you be expected to get the words out of your mouth when the very act of recall makes you choke? 'That's what they keep saying,' the narrator protests in *History of Violence*, 'file a report because that's what they want, they want you to bear witness, they want you to bear it on your back [. . .] and tough luck if the story is too much to bear, tough luck if it cracks my ribs, splits my skin, tears my joints, and crushes the organs inside me.'[18]

Look back over the objections to the 'Dear Colleague' letter and you can see that in each instance the letter was trying to facilitate the path for women plaintiffs notoriously let down by the system whenever they bring legal charges or try to press a case. What, for example, would count as 'clear and convincing evidence': that the woman wrote it in her diary? That she told her best friend? Or perhaps that she went straight to the police or to the hospital for a medical test? One of the main difficulties is that the letter obliges universities to adjudicate disputes and impose penalties but gives them no legal power to summon witnesses – who in any case are not to be found, since the only witnesses in such cases tend to be the plaintiff and the accused. This is just one reason why women who report harassment and assault have historically been so vulnerable: 'Your word against his,' as one British college adviser put it to a young undergraduate friend of mine who had been raped by another student, to discourage her from going to the police: 'I am dealing with two traumatised, vulnerable people,' the adviser said. (The student turned out to be a serial rapist who was eventually convicted and barred from the legal training which, unbelievably – or perhaps not – he had been pursuing since completing his undergraduate degree.) To say the absence of witnesses can be exploited is an understatement. In December 2018, four women in the US revived sexual allegations against Donald Trump first made during the 2016 presidential campaign, when Trump had immediately tweeted that they were part of a Democratic conspiracy. Pressed to produce evidence, White House Press Secretary Sarah Sanders said: 'The president has first-hand knowledge of what he did and didn't do' (as if the women did not).[19] As Grigoriadis puts it, sexual assault is at once 'the problem from hell' and 'the perfect crime'.[20]

One perhaps unanticipated consequence of Title IX has been that the university itself has started to feel under threat: 'Anxiety about legal exposure', writes Doyle, 'registers on every campus as a background hum.' As a result, administration and bureaucracy in American universities have swelled (as have the salaries of investigators), while Title IX cases take on 'a mind-numbing fractal complexity'.[21] At exactly the same time, across the US, university management has been increasingly aligning itself with campus security – hence 'campus sex, campus security', the title of Doyle's book, although she is careful to insist that there is no seamless line that runs between the two. At Arizona State University, a campus police officer was recorded violently arresting a black woman faculty member, Professor Ersula Ore, who had refused to show her ID on the street (she was shoved up against a car, thrown to the ground and handcuffed). In November 2011, at the time of the Occupy movement, police pepper-sprayed students as they protested silently against higher tuition fees at UC Davis. A subsequent investigation, forced on the authorities because a student's photo of the scene had gone viral, established that the police had been sent in by the university's chancellor, Linda Katehi. In a subsequent statement, Katehi explained she had acted out of concern that the campus was under threat of outside infiltration – an age-old ploy to discredit and quash political protest. These vocabularies have chilling resonance across the globe. Note, for example, how effortlessly harassment – 'groping' – can slip into far-right discourse about the threat posed by migrants: 'Our authorities submit to imported, marauding, groping, beating, knife-stabbing, migrant mobs,' Alice Weidel, joint leader of the German AfD in the Bundestag, tweeted in January 2018 (a tweet eventually blocked by Twitter).[22] Katehi feared the consequences for the university if 'anything happens to any student while we're in violation of policy'.[23]

Who, we might ask, is violating whom? Who or what exactly is in danger? A student's 'experience of vulnerability', Doyle writes, 'has translated into a sense of the university's impending doom, to which it responds with a militarization of all of its processes'.[24] This was just one of several worrying moments I encountered while researching the topic of harassment, because it demonstrated the speed with which a progressive cause can be complicit with, or co-opted by, nasty political agendas (I realise that should hardly have been a surprise to me in the age of Brexit and Trump). Likewise Katehi's suggestion of 'outside infiltration'. Since 'outsider' usually means 'foreigner', danger to women, not for the first time, is being sidelined by a felt racial threat, another example of the short time span in which women's issues are ever allowed to be the main event. There is an irony in this resurgence of racist tropes given that Obama saw the issue of campus assault as belonging to the agenda of civil rights. 'There's a reason the story of the civil rights movement was written in our schools,' he stated at the 2009 NAACP Convention. 'It's because there is no stronger weapon against inequality.'[25] 'Education has long been recognized', the Department's letter states in its opening line, 'as the great equalizer in America.' Sexual harassment harms students. But I also wonder if it would be the focus of such official concern were it not seen to be chipping away at national pride, tarnishing what – for most US citizens and certainly for students burdened with crushing debt – has always been, and is even more today, the ever-retreating vision of the American dream (the debt part applying equally to students in the UK).[26]

o o o

From the very beginning there has been one particular feminist subtext to this story. Catharine MacKinnon was one of the earliest campaigners for the inclusion of sexual harassment in universities under Title IX.[27] In her first book, *Sexual Harassment of Working Women*, published in 1979, she argued that harassment was a form of discrimination arising from inequality. Inequality is crucial, as distinct from difference. Case after collapsing case in the courts had shown that if you take as your starting point the idea of a pre-existing, God-given difference between the sexes, then it becomes much more difficult to prove discrimination, even in cases of harassment. Because men are different, you will be told, they are just behaving as normal (they cannot help helping themselves). Instead she insisted, in what is for me one of her strongest arguments to date, that only if such behaviour is seen to stem from unequal power relations, rather than expressing the natural order of things, can it be classified as illegal under discrimination law. Forms of behaviour 'that would not be seen as criminal because they are anything but unusual may, in this context, be seen as discriminating for precisely the same reason'.[28] The 'usual' – what passes as the norm for men – being precisely what anti-harassment activists consider themselves to be fighting against.

As the pay gap in the UK widens, notably for young women entering the workforce for the first time, we should take note.[29] In a special Channel 4 News report on harassment in December 2017, Maryann Brandon, one of Hollywood's most successful film editors and producers – her list includes *Star Wars* – stated that as long as there is unequal pay, harassment will continue. I am less sanguine than Brandon that equal pay in and of itself would bring sexual harassment to an end (in April 2019, ten women filed a lawsuit against Disney for gender pay discrimination).[30] When the NCCL published its pamphlet on sexual harassment, with specific reference to US civil rights legislation, it too defined harassment as unlawful discrimination and placed it firmly in the world of work, as a trade union matter. But, although it made reference to US legal recommendations, it was far more wary of the likely success of women having recourse to the law. MacKinnon, on the other hand, has spent much of her life trying to bring sexuality within the law's remit. If sexuality were separated from gender inequality, she writes in the final pages of the book, then the risk is that sexuality 'would become a law unto itself'.[31]

Although I am sure MacKinnon did not intend it in this way, 'a law unto itself' might, however, be a perfect description of exactly what sexuality is. For psychoanalysis, sexuality is lawless or it is nothing, not least because of the way it plunges its roots into our unconscious lives, where all sexual certainties come to grief. In the unconscious we are not men or women but always, and in endlessly shifting combinations, neither or both. This is where I have from the beginning parted ways with MacKinnon and more generally with radical feminism which, brooking no ambiguity on such matters, sees masculinity as perfectly and violently in control of itself, whereas for me it is masculinity out of control – masculinity in a panic – that is most likely to turn ugly. 'Toxic masculinity', comments writer and hip-hop artist Jordan Stephens, 'is being championed by men who are so terrified of confronting any trauma experienced as children that they choose to project that torture onto others.'[32] Student-on-student harassment can be a way for anxious young men to launch themselves into a form of power which, they realise, just might be beyond them. For more than a decade now, male students in the US have consistently been getting lower grades than women.[33] Across the US as a whole, the proportion of men earning BAs is declining, at thirty per cent of men between the ages of twenty-five and thirty-four, compared with thirty-eight per cent of women. Women also gain more doctoral degrees than men and are now more likely to enter medical and law school. In high schools boys are also consistently under-performing girls, as indeed they are in the UK.[34]

This of course exempts harassers from nothing – even if some of those busily collating these statistics are using them to excuse male violence, at the same time as they target women's advancement, not to say feminism, as the cause. But it does allow to (some) men a glimpse of their own imperfection. It opens up a gap between men who brook no challenge to their authority and those for whom such authority is nothing to be proud of, not least because they understand that one person's power is always exercised at somebody else's expense. If this were not the case – and all men were by definition exactly who they are – then feminism is on a hiding to nothing. The mind, with no mercy, shuts down on itself with no get-out clause, no room for psychic manoeuvre for either sex (a feeling I always have when I read MacKinnon and her followers on these matters). None of which is to underestimate how unremitting masculinity can be, even when a man is convinced he is reformed or, to use the current term, 'woke'. This is how a student at the University of Austin, Texas, described to Grigoriadis, without a trace of irony, his new ethos – 'good words to live by' – now he had come to understand that 'pushing' girls into sex was wrong: 'Shave with the grain the first time, always buy tools you don't have to replace, don't aim a gun at someone unless you intend to shoot them. Don't have sex with anyone who doesn't want to have sex with you.'[35]

We need, then, to acknowledge the strange vagaries of human sexuality, which has always felt emancipatory to me; recognise its stubbornness once it has been locked into place (what feminist psychoanalyst Juliet Mitchell has described as the heavy undertow or drag of sexual difference); insist that harassment is unacceptable and must cease. Holding these apparently contradictory ideas in mind at the same time, moving on more than one front: for me this presents the greatest challenge raised by the present crisis. The tension between these components of the issue perhaps helps us to understand why legal attempts to curtail harassment, as they have incrementally spread across campuses in the US, might also seem to be ineffective, to go awry, even to defeat themselves. At the end of her book, Grigoriadis cites statistics which suggest that efforts at legal redress, and other measures, over the past decade appear not to have reduced the incidence of harassment on campus. She is, incidentally, scrupulous in her use of statistics: the *New York Times* had to issue a public apology for a review which wrongly suggested she had overlooked US Department of Justice figures indicating that women students were less likely than other women of the same age to be the target of sexual assault (as if this somehow made campus rape less of a big deal). But even if Title IX has not produced the sought-for result – the elimination of campus harassment or even a change in attitudes – Grigoriadis concludes that on balance it has been a good thing.[36] The fact that she has to spell this out indicates how far her own journey has taken her from certainty on the matter.

Her book, however grim, is a carnival of characters. There is no one she declines to talk to, no place she will not go. Talking to college guys late at night is not something she enjoys. More than once I found myself asking how on earth she could bear to carry on some of these conversations (a question she also asks of herself). Not altogether willingly – appropriately, we could say, for her topic – she immerses herself in the college fraternity scene where male students, notably in their first term, set out to prove they have arrived by grabbing as much sex as they can, their unbridled misogyny seeming to be the source of most assaults. ('Last night I should have gone to jail' is a popular response when she asks them about consent.[37])

Her description of frats, which makes Hollywood sound comparatively progressive, matches that documented from 2008 to 2018 by photographer Andrew Moisey, whose pictures of fraternity life uncovered ritual humiliation, homoerotic bonding and animal cruelty from men 'destined to be America's future leaders'. These rituals can start even earlier. In November 2018, a 'hazing' video emerged capturing a young student in Toronto being pinned down by schoolmates in a locker room and sexually assaulted with a broom handle; up to then, the all-boys Catholic school had long been known as a 'beacon of tradition, Catholic faith and elite hockey'.[38] In the course of one year, 2017, four freshman students died as a direct result of hazing rituals during initiation ceremonies (around a hundred thousand young men choose to undergo these rituals every year).[39] Drawing on historian Nicholas Syrett's 2009 study of fraternities, *The Company He Keeps*, Grigoriadis tracks this behaviour to the 1950s when GI Bill undergrads came back from foreign wars 'with notches on their belts to face Eisenhower's moral strictures at home'.[40] None of this changes the reality that all-male fraternities are surrounded with an aura of the sacred (indeed the ugliness of the rituals may be the reason why). In 2016, the North American Interfraternity Conference joined with the National Panhellenic Conference and agreed to spend $300,000 on lobbying, amongst other things, against fraternities going coeducational, as those at Harvard and Wesleyan had done. They were also calling for congressional nullification of the 'Dear Colleague' letter (on this they would get their way).[41]

Grigoriadis listens to young women who, while entering freely into the campus hook-up culture of casual sex, also describe themselves falling into alcoholic stupor and waking up to find they have had sex they knew nothing about and were certainly not in any position to enjoy. Alcohol on campus plays a key role, but that is most often turned against women, as if the problem was their being out of it, rather than the fact that someone took advantage of their state. A woman having been intoxicated is, of course, precisely what the accused, the police and the counsel for the defence in rape cases use to discredit her evidence and get a case dismissed. In a recent survey, seven per cent of women students answered yes to questions about whether they had been penetrated while asleep, unconscious or incapacitated by alcohol or drugs.[42] When serial 'black cab rapist' John Worboys was released on parole in the UK after serving nine years and nine months in prison, one of his many accusers described how she had been laughed at by the police: '[The police officers] said I must have been drunk and fallen over. I was not believed.' (She woke up bruised after Worboys had persuaded her to have a drink and forced a pill into her mouth.)[43]

Grigoriadis also talks to a group of young women whose casual attitude to sex extends to assault, which, like many of the women who voted for Trump in 2016, they dismiss, while rolling their eyes at male boorishness. Yet they too describe the 'weird' things that happened to them at the start of their freshman year, and find themselves wondering whether encounters meant to be sex might in fact have been rape. She talks to the mothers of boys who feel they have been wrongly accused, some of whom have been sent down from college, their educational ambitions and future prospects in shreds: 'to hell with the university's bullshit due process,' one of the mothers says. She talks to one boy who genuinely seems to believe that he 'accidentally' had anal sex with his girlfriend. She talks to abusers and rapists who are proud of what they have done, and then lists their truly sickening comments about women, which I have chosen not to reproduce here. She listens as one student first denounces Trump as most likely 'terrible' for his country, then triumphantly proclaims '*the bitch is dead*': 'We're back, we won, and we're mad.' She describes cases where it felt to her, as she got deeper and deeper into their complexity, that the facts had begun to 'blow away'.[44]

Hesitantly, Grigoriadis admits to not believing every student plaintiff, although she has no doubt that the call to believe women has brought about a welcome sea-change.[45] She allows for mixed motives and confused memories – blurred lines – in which both plaintiff and the accused might genuinely feel they are telling the truth, where what one student genuinely experiences as unwelcome may not have 'knowingly' stemmed from an intent to harm. 'Unknowingly' on the other hand brings us slap-bang up against the unconscious where all hues darken and blur. (Freud used the blurred outlines and colours of modern painting as an analogy for the unconscious.[46]) The *Blurred Lines* of her title is an allusion to the title of a popular song by Robin Thicke, which includes the line 'Must wanna get nasty' and repeats 'I know you want it' at least six times. The song is also the basis of an essay by Roxane Gay in her bestselling *Bad Feminist*, one of the reasons she is a 'bad' feminist being that she finds herself wanting to sing along.[47]

Blurred Lines starts and ends with the case of Emma Sulkowicz, who, having unsuccessfully brought a rape charge against a fellow undergraduate at Columbia University, politicised a whole generation of students on sexual harassment with her *Mattress Performance (Carry That Weight)*, a work of endurance art and political protest whose self-imposed 'rules of engagement' required her to carry a dormitory mattress everywhere she went on campus for nine months. 'That image', Hillary Clinton said in her speech to the Democratic National Committee's Women's Leadership Forum in 2015, 'should haunt all of us.'[48] By the end of her book, Grigoriadis believes Sulkowicz's account of what happened, despite its having been challenged down to every last detail by Paul Nungesser, the student she accused. Nungesser went on to file his own complaint against the university for violating his Title IX rights by allowing Sulkowicz to continue with her protest piece, for which she received academic credit (Columbia settled with him out of court). Nungesser's case is not helped when his mother alludes to women Nazi perpetrators in his defence. Grigoriadis continues to believe Sulkowicz after hearing released messages in which she appears to be appealing for the anal sex which is at the basis of the charge of rape. And when, in a gesture Grigoriadis sees as verging on a 'retraction', Sulkowicz writes in a note accompanying a later piece based on her experience: 'I do not mean to be prescriptive, some people find pleasure in feeling upset.'[49] The sentiment comes dangerously close to suggesting that women enjoy experiences they later complain about.

One thing, however, is absolutely clear, and that is the energy, commitment and imagination of the students who have launched and are struggling to keep up the anti-harassment campaign. For the past decade, the US alt-right have been baying at 'rape-culture panic' and targeting universities. A culture of grievance, they claim, is spreading from colleges across the whole of the US, as if educational institutions were worst exemplar and cause of the 'nanny state' (as so often in the discourse of the right, the greatest danger is presented as a heady combination of money, aka welfare, and sex). In September 2017, Betsy DeVos, Trump's Education Secretary, announced that she was rescinding the Obama-era 'Dear Colleague' guidance on Title IX. The new guidance describes the letter as 'well-intentioned' but 'stacked against the accused', with no reference to the historic backdrop which made the strongest possible support for complainants essential. 'In the forty-five years since the passage of Title IX,' it asserts, 'we have seen remarkable progress toward an educational environment free of sex discrimination.'[50] Anti-harassment activists might disagree. Even before the 2016 election, it was clear that DeVos would do 'her damnedest' to roll back measures which, however flawed, young women students see as progress.[51] In June 2020, eighteen Attorneys General lost their case when they brought a lawsuit against DeVos and the US Department of Education to block the final rule which limits Title IX to cases of sexual misconduct that occur within 'an educational program or activity', on the grounds that it will 'reverse decades of effort to end the corrosive effects of sexual harassment on equal access to education' and will require institutions to 'completely overhaul' their current systems for addressing sexual misconduct in less than three months amid the coronavirus pandemic.[52] This is the world in which anti-harassment activists – 'fierce, ruthless, determined' – have been making, and continue to make, their case. In their bid for 'sexual empowerment', writes Grigoriadis, they have 'cast off the language of victimhood'. They want a world in which rape will no longer be what historically it has been: 'a property crime, the woman's fault, or a man's privilege'.[53] They want to be listened to and believed; they want an end to sexual harassment.

o　o　o

It would be wrong to assume that all self-defined feminists believe that Title IX, and the struggle against harassment it represents, has been unequivocally emancipatory for women. If #MeToo has acted as a great unifier of women, the responses to it have laid bare some of the most prominent fault lines inside feminism itself. Though covering the same terrain as *Blurred Lines*, Laura Kipnis's *Unwanted Advances – Sexual Paranoia Comes to Campus* feels as if it comes from another planet. Grigoriadis mentions it once in parentheses as an 'anti-Title IX manifesto'. She is being measured; I would call it a tirade. Kipnis sees herself as belonging on the side of freedom, which now has to fight back against a repressive, stultifying, molly-coddling administrative world (the echoes of the alt-right critique of Title IX are striking). There is a feminist back-story to this argument. Twenty years ago, in *Feminist Accused of Sexual Harassment*, Jane Gallop had made a plea for the erotics of teaching – a case which had in fact been made more effectively by bell hooks in *Teaching to Transgress* three years before. hooks had been careful to place her argument for the thrill of learning in the context of the US history of racism. All her teachers at Booker T. Washington Elementary had been black women who, although they never stated it in such terms, were fired up by a 'revolutionary pedagogy of resistance'.[54] For these women, rousing their students was to transgress a racial heritage that did everything it could to suppress black thought and desire. Later, in hooks's case, after she became a teacher herself, such transgression went on to include at least one sexual liaison with a student. All this changed with racial integration. Black children bussed to white schools quickly discovered that their passionate enthusiasm in the classroom was seen as a threat to white privilege. They were cut down to size. This – hooks is citing Buddhist Pema Chodron – could, I think, fairly be called a manifesto:

> My models were those who stepped outside of the conventional mind and who could actually stop my mind and completely open it up and free it, even for a moment, from a conventional, habitual way of looking at things . . . If you are really preparing for groundlessness, preparing for the reality of human existence, you are living on the razor's edge, and you must become used to the fact that things shift and change. Things are not certain and they do not last and you do not know what is going to happen. My teachers have always pushed me over a cliff.[55]

Likewise – though not exactly – Kipnis is arguing for the myriad, uncontrollable and often sexual nature of human behaviour and thought. Grigoriadis is there to remind us, however, that you can be on the side of the complexity of life and mind without, as Kipnis does, turning against Title IX as the devil's work (I barely exaggerate).

Unwanted Advances opens with the moment when Kipnis found herself charged under Title IX for writing an article in which she had opposed a new directive banning all sexual relations, even if consensual, between undergraduates and faculty. She was seen as taking the wrong side, encouraging discrimination and betraying the progressive cause. Gallop had been treading similar ground when she argued that all teaching relationships were in effect 'consensual amorous relations'. As a student, Gallop had seduced a number of her teachers and come to no harm. She viewed the experience as a 'conquest', which made her feel 'cocky' and in touch with her own 'power'. She was most excited by students who wanted to be like her (perhaps not something to boast about). She announced at a conference that graduates were her 'sexual preference', which unsurprisingly did not go down very well. The charge of harassment was brought against her after she passionately kissed one of her graduate students in a crowded room; she admits she got off on the spectacle.[56] Gallop, Kipnis and Jennifer Doyle have in common that they all find themselves embroiled in university statutes on harassment, although in the case of Doyle the comparison stops there, as she was the one bringing a case under Title IX against a student who had been harassing and stalking her.

Sexual harassment comes mainly from men to women, faculty to student – recently there have been a flood of cases in academia, both in the UK and in the US, which include some of today's most illustrious male intellectuals. We should not, however, lose sight of the fact that neither women nor men automatically pitch up in the most obvious place. In August 2018, Avital Ronell, distinguished professor of German and Comparative Literature at New York University, was found guilty of harassment against a male graduate student (Judith Butler, one of a group of academics who had written in her support when the story first broke, apologised after the finding and the release of the legal transcript). Likewise in the movie industry: Asia Argento, the Italian actress and director, and one of the first women to publicly accuse Harvey Weinstein, reportedly paid off a young actor who accused her of sexual assault when he was seventeen (in the US eighteen is the age of consent). Such stories must be acknowledged, though feminism surely needs to be wary of the uses to which they are put, as if their mere existence lets the men involved in the preponderance of cases off the hook. As I read *Unwanted Advances*, I could not help asking: whose side does Kipnis think she is on? She would probably see that as a compliment.

Kipnis's previous book, *Men – Notes from an Ongoing Investigation* (2014), opens with a paean to Larry Flynt, the editor of *Hustler*, a magazine she considers disgusting – 'it grossed me out' – but finds herself celebrating for its pornographic assault on American prudery and social hypocrisy which she places in the tradition of Rabelais.[57] When she accepts an invitation to meet Flynt, he is in a gold-plated wheelchair, the result of an assassination attempt years before by a white supremacist enraged by *Hustler*'s interracial slant. She is not, therefore, wrong that there is a progressive stripe embedded in the monstrosity of the magazine, although to find it you have to dig deep. Kipnis is open about the pleasure she gets as a woman writing about men: 'potency', 'a bit of lead in your pencil' (rather like Gallop's language of sexual conquest).[58] In an earlier book, *Bound and Gagged – Pornography and the Politics of Fantasy in America* (1996), she opened with the case of Daniel DePew, stung by a San Jose police undercover officer who lured him to a hotel room and got him enthusiastically to engage with the idea of a snuff movie in which he would play executioner and which would involve the kidnapping and murder of a child. As Kipnis saw it, DePew, who was sentenced to thirty-three years in prison, had been arrested for a fantasy – 'a crime that never happened'. It sounded more to me as if he had been caught making a plan.

Whether today's focus on harassment is making people afraid of their own thoughts seems to me a fair question. But, already twenty years ago, this strikes me as an odd use, or misuse, of fantasy. For psychoanalysis, unconscious fantasy, as distinct from conscious fantasy or daydream, is not something you want to happen; indeed it is often something that would horrify you if it came to pass in real life. This is an easier idea to grasp than it might first appear. One student told Grigoriadis that he understood that women's rape fantasies are not real because 'men don't want their penises cut off but dream about it anyway.'[59] For any such fantasies, you cannot and should not be punished – most often the voice chastising you in your head for even having such a thought is punishment enough. Men in a hotel room discussing how to murder a child would not make the cut (fantasy would be no excuse).

This may feel far from Title IX, but I think it is central. By her own account, Kipnis's strongest identifications are with men – 'lead in my pencil', 'daddy's girl' – especially those she feels have been targeted by injustice: Larry Flynt, Daniel DePew and, at the heart of *Unwanted Advances*, Peter Ludlow, a philosophy professor at Northwestern University. Ludlow was the subject of Title IX complaints from two students concerning inappropriate sexual behaviour, in one case rape. He was found guilty of sexual misconduct and resigned on the point of termination. One of his accusers had been a freshman major in his class, the other a postgraduate student – in the book, they are given the pseudonyms of Eunice Cho and Nola Hartley. Kipnis has written the case for the defence. You could argue that she is trying to redress the balance, a term I have always considered to be corrupt in an unbalanced world (I have also noticed that the demand for balance only ever arises when you clash with the official position or are seen to be on the wrong side of a debate, never when your views are welcome).

For Kipnis, the administrative behemoth which is Title IX is part of a backlash against the intellectual and sexual freedoms seized over decades by feminists, and is endangering student autonomy, intellectual spirit and the impulse to learn. A mental and sexual straitjacket is turning women students into passive victims, who are, or see themselves as, totally the prey of men. (Isn't being the prey of men precisely what anti-harassment activists most hate?) She wrote her book when, having expressed sympathy with Ludlow, he gave her access to a stash of over two thousand emails and messages between himself and Hartley, with whom he had been in a relationship for more than a year. When she is critical of Ludlow, it feels like a concession: 'Let me be honest: you are not going to find me arguing that Ludlow showed fantastic judgement' (independently of the main charges against him, he admits that during his career he had two undergraduates in his bed).[60] She also fairly demonstrates that the Title IX investigators in this case, and not only this case, are heavily inclined towards the plaintiff. But, as I see it, she makes the fatal error of confusing her critique of what have clearly been injustices under Title IX with tearing the woman complainants' evidence to shreds. Even allowing that Kipnis is driven by the wish for women to claim back their sexual agency over their own lives, the feminist aspect of this way of proceeding escapes me. Challenged on Facebook, Kipnis responded that *Unwanted Advances* is 'a polemic, not journalism. It's a work of opinion. It's based on reporting, and a close reading of the available documents, but the heart of the book is my interpretation of that material.'[61] The Philosophy Graduate Association had accused her of 'unauthorised exposure of private material and of reckless unfounded speculation' against Nola Hartley.

One of my key questions in this book is what role psycho-analysis can play in opening up our understanding of the complexities of our inner, sometimes violent, sexual worlds.

One of the most humane aspects of psychoanalysis is the way it brings mental life, however troubled, out of its dark shameful corners and into the light. Psychoanalysis does not judge. Its findings cannot be adduced in a court of law (which has not prevented lawyers invoking the idea that women might have unconscious rape fantasies to get a rape charge dismissed). In *Unwanted Advances*, terms like hysteria, projection and paranoia – paranoia in the title – are thrown around, alongside 'witch-hunt', as if they could be used to settle political debate, with no regard for the way they have classically been used to persecute, insult and silence angry women. And other oppressed groups. 'I am thinking of paranoia,' writes Sara Ahmed on her Feminist Killjoys blog, in relation to racism, 'and the good reasons for bad feelings.'[62] (In a racist world, 'paranoia' on the part of racial minorities might just make perfect sense.) It is also worth remembering that psychoanalysis began by listening to the voice and stories of the hysteric, who had previously been dismissed as insane (at the turn of the twentieth century in France, hysterics were being incarcerated as 'the dregs' of society in the Paris asylum La Salpêtrière).[63]

Faced with contradictory behaviour on the part of one of Ludlow's two main accusers ('both flinging herself at Ludlow in a sexualised way and also feeling victimised'), Kipnis does not hesitate to offer a wild diagnosis of borderline personality disorder, a serious condition which means that the patient, instead of being happily, or rather unhappily, neurotic more or less like everybody else, sits on the boundary between neurosis and psychosis. One of its components, we are told, is 'provocative or seductive behaviour', at which point I find myself wanting to evoke Jane Gallop as an ally.[64] Victimised and seductive – far from being the sign of mental disturbance, this might instead be grounds for hope. It suggests that a woman's ability to seduce has not been completely quashed by ambient violence. Is it disordered, in a sexually disordered world, for a woman to feel something of both?

As for the rush to mental casualty, I was once stopped in the mid-1970s by a colleague in the car park at Sussex University – an important detail because the car park was some way from the Arts Building so always allowed time to talk. Laughingly, he told me that a woman student, who was of course clearly disturbed, had brought a charge of sexual misconduct against him. 'Laughingly' because he said he happened to be innocent in this one case. Adding insult to injury, he was therefore boasting of all the rest. This moment came to mind when I read Jodi Kantor and Megan Twohey's account of their first meeting with Harvey Weinstein, on the eve of their exposé in the *New York Times*. Weinstein denied having done the dreadful things to women of which he was being accused: 'He wasn't that bad. He then smiled sardonically: "I'm worse."'[65]

At Sussex, I subsequently discovered, my colleague was known as 'the groper'; all the new women students were forewarned. By the time we got to the building, I had managed to expostulate that the charge of mental disorder should never be brought against a woman making a sexual complaint – the idea of setting yourself up as judge in your own case being even more unacceptable in the sphere of psychic and sexual life. Later, when I confronted a second colleague on behalf of a student who had appealed to me, he was simply enraged that I did not unequivocally support his denials (he too turned out to be a serial offender). Needless to say, there were no official procedures anywhere in the system for dealing with such cases. But it is only now, looking back on these moments, that I realise just how inadequate was my response.

o o o

Like Paul Nungesser at Columbia, Peter Ludlow had been named and shamed. This can indeed be seen as summary justice, which is one of Kipnis's main charges against Title IX. The same case can be made in relation to Liam Allan, a Sussex student accused of rape, against whom all charges were dropped in December 2017 when previously undisclosed evidence was released to the court (he had been on bail and banned from campus for a year). Citing senior barristers, *The Times*'s headline described the 'scandal' as 'the tip of the iceberg'; police and prosecutors are now, according to one QC, biased in favour of women rape plaintiffs; a subsequent letter suggested we are living in a 'culture of victim belief'.[66] Given the obscenely low, indeed rapidly declining, level of rape convictions in the UK, that would be something of a turnaround in itself (nor, to my knowledge, has the systematic discrediting and disbelief of women who bring rape charges to court ever been graced with the term 'culture'.) 'Scandal' and 'tip of the iceberg' sound to me like the language of backlash. An analysis of rape cases in September 2019 uncovered systematic police flaws at the expense of the most vulnerable, with rape regularly recorded as an incident rather than a crime, resulting in no investigation taking place.[67] One result of the Liam Allan case was to make confiscation of a plaintiff's phone and disclosure of private messages a central part of rape investigations (children reporting rape are being told to hand over their phones).[68]

Harassment on campus needs to be seen in this broader context. In March 2017, the *Guardian* chose to headline assault across UK campuses as an 'epidemic'.[69] As early as 2004 in the US, *The Encyclopedia of Rape* had described rape as arising 'most often where there is social hierarchy: men in prison, men in marriage, soldiers in war, those who have enslaved another group, adults who control children, those preying upon people with mental and physical disabilities.'[70] 'It is absolutely true – and absolutely absurd,' Grigoriadis comments, 'that we could add the modern campus college to that list.'[71]

In British universities, those accused of harassment in whatever form tend not to be named, on the grounds of confidentiality. Cases rarely proceed to court as universities do all they can to avoid adverse publicity (this can also include rape cases, as the advice given to my friend not to go to the police after she had been raped makes clear). In June 2016, Sara Ahmed resigned from her post as director of the Centre for Feminist Research at Goldsmiths, University of London over the university's treatment of harassment: 'I have resigned from a college', she wrote on Twitter, 'that uses my labour to deny what I show #sexual harassment'.[72] The work she was doing to expose the issue was being taken as evidence that the issue did not exist: 'We don't have a problem of sexual harassment because there are people in our college who show there is a problem of sexual harassment.'[73]

Expressing its solidarity with Ahmed, a student blog reproduced sixteen repeated images of the title pages of books by a Goldsmiths faculty member, each one scrawled with accusations naming the author as a serial harasser who they stated had been suspended but allowed to resign before a full disciplinary hearing could be held.[74] The outcome they describe – hushing up, discreet departure, financial settlements or non-disclosure agreements with students – is not uncommon, both here in the UK and, despite Title IX, in the US. When nine women at Dartmouth University brought charges of abuse – including one allegation of rape – against three prominent professors in 2018, the college encouraged them to continue working with the professors for several more months. In the case of Todd Heatherton, one of the accused, instead of 'responding appropriately', it promoted him. The women brought a lawsuit against the college which eventually came to a $14 million settlement.[75]

If the accused is not formally charged, this means amongst other things that he can more or less seamlessly move on to another institution, safeguarding, indeed advancing, his career. When Carole Mundell spoke out in 2017 against her boss at Liverpool John Moores' Astrophysics Research Institute for writing a glowing reference for a serial harasser, she was branded a whistleblower and had a libel claim made against her by the college (it was thrown out by the High Court).[76] The harasser had been able to leave the university without charge and take up a prestigious academic position in South Africa. By contrast – and this is one of the least noted aspects of campus sexual harassment – women graduate students who have been on the receiving end, as often as not, fall by the professional wayside. 'I am leaving academia because of what happened,' one woman stated to the *Guardian* in response to their call-out. 'I'm going to do my PhD, and then that's it.'[77] Another example would be the woman who gave up an MA place at Warwick when students who had discussed her as one of a group of potential sexual targets returned to the campus.[78] Already in 2004, an independent report on the philosophy department at the University of Colorado Boulder described how, as a result of the atmosphere of sanctioned and/or ignored sexual harassment, young women philosophy graduates were leaving academia in disproportionate numbers.[79] 'Get used to it or get out of it,'

Ahmed writes in *Living a Feminist Life*. 'No wonder if these are the choices, many get out of it.'[80]

Goldsmiths subsequently revised its policies on sexual harassment and created a management post to improve its practices. An earlier statement issued in response to Ahmed's resignation by Jane Powell, then Deputy Warden, opened: 'We take sexual harassment very seriously and take action against those found to be acting in ways incompatible with our very strong values . . .' (no problem, then). 'Non-performativity given new meaning!' Ahmed tweeted. 'One of the most embarrassing institutional speech acts ever!'[81] The new plan includes a single policy on sexual harassment, violence and misconduct; a partnership with Rape Crisis in South London; more robust co-ordination of records; training/induction for all staff. Critics responded that insufficient attention had been paid to the overall culture that allowed things to go so wrong in the past. Goldsmiths' aim is to make its policies 'exemplary' – an acknowledgement of the fact that there is no co-ordinated policy on harassment across the UK. When I spoke to Lisa Blackman, co-head of Media and Communication at Goldsmiths, about what had happened and what the college was doing in response in 2017, she commented that as a sector, 'we don't have the measure of the problem.' (She was not speaking in any official capacity, and is herself centrally involved in sexual harassment policy initiatives across the sector in the UK.)[82]

According to a survey published by the *Guardian* in December 2017, almost two thirds of universities had no harassment advisers or sexual violence liaison officers; nearly a quarter no designated point of contact for anyone wanting to bring a complaint; over a third were not training staff on any form of misconduct and/or gender violence, this despite a 2016 recommendation from Universities UK, the representative body for higher education, that a centralised reporting system for all such cases should be established. A 'shocking and depressing complacency,' commented Rachel Krys, co-director of the End Violence Against Women coalition.[83] Since then, progress has, to say the least, been slow. In June 2019, a new report commissioned by the higher education regulator for England urged universities to hire specialist staff to investigate hate crimes and sexual harassment committed against their students. Outside a relatively small number of pilot schemes, reports of incidents were being neither collected nor analysed. In particular, black and ethnic minority students lacked confidence in existing complaints procedures, to which they were unlikely to appeal.[84] A month later, Warwick University was accused of negligence and discrimination, and of not being a safe place for women and minority students, when no action was taken against a group of men who had been exchanging violent sexual comments about them (the university subsequently apologised).[85] In November of the same year, it emerged that the University of Birmingham was refusing to investigate any alleged rape that took place off campus premises, even in privately rented student accommodation, or any assault 'unrelated to university activity',[86] the same criterion now included under Title IX. (Presumably it would have done so if the act had taken place in a lecture hall?)

Perfectly consistent with the behaviour expected of women on the receiving end of harassment, most UK universities have been turning a blind eye. 'Not addressing the problem of sexual harassment', Ahmed blogged shortly after her resignation, 'is reproducing the problem of sexual harassment.' Her response is to make a virtue of 'snapping': 'By snapping, you are saying: I will not reproduce a world I cannot bear, a world I do not think should be borne.'[87] All of which might serve as a caution to anyone wanting to put the clock back on Title IX (not to speak of the problem of landing on the same side as Betsy DeVos and the North American Interfraternity Conference). Laura Kipnis, asked whether she wanted Title IX rescinded – a fair conclusion for anyone reading *Unwanted Advances* – suggested that this on its own would not be enough to turn the tide. The solution, she believes, will only come from the civil courts when those like Ludlow, who have fallen foul of Title IX, sue institutions for lost reputations and livelihood.[88] As I cast my eyes from the UK to the US and back again, it strikes me that in relation to harassment, there is no legal or procedural middle ground. Sexuality collides with the law. The only available options, at least to date, seem to be too much legal intervention or not enough.

For Kipnis, the atmosphere around Title IX meant that the critical, enquiring spirit of women students was being suppressed. For the Goldsmiths students, on the other hand, it was the crushing of curiosity about sexual harassment, the quiet disappearance of the accused and the lack of transparency that threatened bodies and minds alike. As far as they were concerned, they were just reaffirming the impulse that brought them to university in the first place: 'We are at university because we are curious and we want to learn . . . Clearly something is being covered up, which makes our desire to learn even stronger.'[89] Despite the vast distance between the way campus harassment is treated in the UK and in the US, this is what unites the student activists across the board: 'fierce, ruthless, determined, they have cast off the language of victimhood.'

Like the million and more voices in the #MeToo campaign, these women are fired up with rage. They are not passive, nor are they 'damsels' laid out on the railway tracks – to cite just one of the images used by Kipnis to describe the way women students are being portrayed under Title IX. Perhaps, compared with the sisters turned on by feminist teaching in the 1970s and 1980s, today's feminist students are excited by different things. Why – in an era where misogyny and assault against women show no signs of diminishing – would they not be a little more cautious about sex? Grigoriadis's book is littered with stories of women students who look back on their willing participation in hook-up culture with regret, not least because of the dire sex. Or because it took them time to realise fully what had happened. 'It took me a while', one woman comments to the *Guardian* in response to their call-out on harassment, 'to realise that he shouldn't have done that.' She is not denying responsi-bility: 'I thought . . . that's OK, I put myself in that situation. I took a while to realise what he did was wrong.' None of this, it should be said, says anything about a woman's pleasure and agency during a freely engaged sexual act. Nor indeed about so-called passivity, a term that could itself do with some undo-ing. As Freud once observed, striking a blow against the active/passive distinction as one of the most misleading and sexually discriminating binaries of them all, it can take 'a large amount of activity . . . to achieve a passive aim'.[90] Kipnis reads this as passivity's bad faith; I take it as a sign of its latent energy.

o   o   o

Evidence is always key, especially in a disputed case. But evi-dence is not neutral. 'The evidence we have of racism and sex-ism', writes Ahmed in her essay-length blogpost on the topic, 'is deemed insufficient *because* of racism and sexism.'[91] Evidence has

to be interpreted. When a student in a long-term consensual relationship with a tutor messages him to apologise for hurting his
feelings and tells him that she loves him, someone has to decide
that her subsequent claim that he had raped her the day before
was a lie. Someone has to decide that the delay, possibly a long
delay, between an event and feeling upset means that your claim
to have been disturbed by the event is false (this again would
be news for psychoanalysis, which takes delayed effectivity, the
mind's reluctance to register what is happening at the time it is
happening, to be one of the hallmarks of trauma). Someone has
to decide that a student who messages a hook-up inviting him to
have anal sex must have really wanted it, or that if she had wanted
it at that time, she could not have changed her mind, and could
not, therefore, have been anally raped. Someone has to decide
that a woman student whose messages establish that she wanted
sex with a male student who was rejecting her advances, that she
even mused on the pleasures of violence – 'It is always nice to
be sexually assaulted without breaking the law' – could not have
been raped.[92] They asked for it, no? I take these examples from
the cases of Ludlow (the first two), Sulkowicz and Allan respectively. Each one opens a door into the murky world of sexuality
where all bets are off, where desire and a change of heart can
persist in one and the same breath. These moments may indeed
give us pause. But it is the elation with which they are seized,
the unseemly haste with which they are used to bludgeon the
complainant's case, that I find so chilling. A woman starts down,
even initiates, a sexual path, which for whatever reason she no
longer wants to continue. She tries to bring it to a halt. If the
man does not stop – and please don't tell me that he might fail
to understand the message, or that once he gets going no man
can control himself – then it is rape.

To which we must surely add that a woman can be driven to co-operate in a violent sexual act, or seem to be co-operating, out of fear. This is common in cases of rape. 'Judges and juries are more convinced if they can see torn knickers and proof that the victim was beaten,' human rights QC Helena Kennedy has said about the 'ideal' victim in rape trials in the UK, but:

> even the signs of resistance have to be more than the odd bruise, which defendants explain away as the result of vigorous sex-play and playful pinching. The paradox is that the requirement to show that they put up a fight flies in the face of everything we are told about self-protection. As one victim said when interviewed about her experience, 'Everything I did right to save my life is exactly wrong in terms of proving I was telling the truth.'[93]

In which case, the 'evidence' will be fake.

And what of the strange idea that loving or caring for an abuser, even the next morning, rules out a claim of abuse? Jennifer Marsh is vice president of the US national support service for abuse victims, RAINN (Rape, Abuse and Incest National Network), founded in 1994 with Tori Amos as its first spokesperson. They take on average 266 calls a day. 'One of the first things that our users say is "I don't know what happened to me." . . . It's not uncommon for them to say things like, "I woke up the next morning and cooked him breakfast."'[94] 'As in all things shitty,' Hartley messaged Ludlow the morning after the alleged rape, 'this too shall pass. I love you.'[95] Women's refuges across the UK are packed with women who have entered, willingly and lovingly, into intimate relationships that turn violent. The enduring nature of the attachment is one of the reasons it can be such a struggle to stop them from returning home.

This did not prevent the Conservative government in the UK in 2017, at the exact moment when sexual harassment and assault had hit the news like never before, from ending guaranteed funding for refuges, a move that was predicted to leave stranded around four thousand women and children in flight from domestic abuse. The government also slashed legal aid, which disproportionately affects abused women who are left with no choice but to represent themselves in court, often face to face with their abusers.[96] In October 2018, twenty men were found guilty of belonging to a gang that had raped and abused girls as young as eleven in the West Yorkshire town of Huddersfield over several years. Nazir Afzal, the Crown Prosecution Service's former lead on child abuse and violence against women and girls, accused government-driven austerity of undermining local attempts to protect victims. In 2013 the government had introduced a fee of £1,200 to go to tribunal; since then there has been a seventy-one per cent drop in the number of discrimination cases brought on grounds of sex.

All this has been brought to a head by the surge in domestic violence which was unleashed during the pandemic (similar surges have been reported across the world, for example in China and in Spain).[97] At the height of the lockdown, calls to refuge centres rose dramatically as women found themselves trapped in their homes with abusive partners. Between 23 March and 12 April 2020, the project Counting Dead Women identified sixteen domestic abuse killings; the average for the same period over the previous year had been five.[98] Offers from hotels to house women in flight from domestic violence were refused by the UK government on the grounds that the women would be too easily traced. The Mayor of London stepped in with a £1.5 million emergency fund to rehouse such women. In

May, the government pledged £76 million to provide services for the most vulnerable, including victims of domestic violence, a move that was welcomed, although it was the prior slashing of funds by Conservative governments which had made the need so pressing; resources for the longer term were not guaranteed.

In October 2017, when the #MeToo movement spread to the corridors of Westminster, Prime Minister Theresa May made a commitment to create 'robust' policies which would protect staff from sexual harassment. By November, the Speaker of the House was demanding that the proposals for handling allegations should be made public, while members of the cross-party working group were complaining that the plan was simply being transferred from the procedure for dealing with employment grievances, and would not offer sufficient protection since it would remain within the hands of MPs: like foxes 'talking about how to make the hen-house safer'.[99] A year later, a proposed new government code for employers on sexual harassment in the workplace was met with criticism for not going far enough: 'Failing to introduce a new duty on employment to prevent harassment', Sam Smethers, chief executive of the Fawcett Society, commented, 'is a missed opportunity and leaves women dealing with the problem alone.'[100]

And in perhaps one of the most unbelievable (or almost unbelievable) cases of them all, MP and former minister Andrew Griffiths, who had bombarded two young women with over two thousand lewd text messages, was cleared of wrongdoing by the parliamentary standards watchdog in September 2019, on the grounds that he had not sent the messages when he should have been engaged in parliamentary activity, which presumably carried on regardless. Allegations that he had breached the House of Commons Code of Conduct had not been upheld. 'However damaging these events have been for Mr Griffiths personally,' the watchdog's resolution letter stated, 'I am not persuaded that the texts he exchanged with the two women have caused significant damage to the reputation of the House of Commons as a whole, or of its members generally.'[101] Personal damage to the MP, reputational damage to the House of Commons and/or its members. Am I missing something? Not even a hint that the most significant damage might have been inflicted on the two young women themselves.

All of which, once again, might make us wary of the idea that, in relation to sexual harassment and violence, a corner has at last been turned. If we are dealing with the drag, the ugly undertow, of sexual difference in a toxic world, then institutions can only do so much (though genuinely getting on the case and doing something would surely help). We also need to look beyond the plush corridors and gilded cages of Westminster and Hollywood. According to a 2017 TUC report, more than half of women in the workplace experience sexual harassment, most of whom do not report it or fail to achieve a positive outcome when they do (which more or less takes us back to the 1970s where we started).[102] Today, women who are casually and precariously employed are the most vulnerable, their numbers steadily rising in an economy in the relentless grip of profit. #MeToo was founded in 2007 by Tarana Burke, an African-American woman, as a grassroots movement for women, particularly women of colour, in underprivileged communities, with the motto 'Empathy stamps out shame.'[103] At the height of the Weinstein scandal, although it received comparatively little attention, seven hundred thousand women farmworkers sent a joint letter in solidarity to the most prominent figures to have spoken out in Hollywood, protesting against the constant harassment they experienced at work.[104] It would take two more years, however, before the systemic and violent harassment of workers in the garment industry – fashion's 'dirty secret' – was even acknowledged let alone redressed: the 2019 Lesotho Agreement threatens loss of contract with international firms such as Levi's to any factory not implementing a zero-tolerance policy on harassment (although these hard-won gains are now threatened by job losses following the pandemic).[105]

o   o   o

I have never so regretted agreeing to write on a subject. But as I have sunk deeper into the morass, Roxane Gay is the writer who more than once has come to my aid. Gay rose to fame as the 'bad' feminist who sang along to Robin Thicke's lyrics, had fantasies about Bill Clinton and likes to wear pink. She has also made assault against women more or less her life's writing work. Reading the tales of sexual harassment both here and in the US, I have started to feel that all the attention has served not only as an urgent call for a better world but, oddly and at the same time, as a diversionary tactic to help us avoid having to think about sex. Or to put it another way, if harassment and sexual violence are the whole story of human sexuality, then we may as well lock the door on who we are and throw away the key. How, then, can we acknowledge sexual harassment for the vicious endgame it is, while leaving open the question of what sexuality, at its wildest – most harmful and most exhilarating, sometimes both together – might be?

Gay was gang-raped at the age of twelve. The gang included a boy she loved who set the whole thing up and whom, although he had treated her badly, she had more or less trusted until then. The legacy of that moment – above all a manic appetite that turned her body into a fortress against pain – is the subject of her memoir, *Hunger*, which was published in 2017: 'If I was undesirable, I could keep more hurt away [. . .] My body could become so big it would never be broken again.'[106] She also recounts the episode towards the end of *Bad Feminist* but it was not the part of the book to receive most attention nor, I suspect, what led to its huge success. Amongst other things, *Hunger* is a one-woman riposte to those who find it odd that a woman could go on loving a man who treated her with unforgivable violence ('I woke up the next morning and cooked him breakfast'; 'As with all things shitty, this too shall pass. I love you'), or that it might take a very long time for what happened to fully register, for the experience to break the threshold of its own anguish and pass into speech. Gay does not shy away from the word 'victim'. She prefers it to 'survivor': 'I don't want to pretend I am on some triumphant, uplifting journey.' Far from rendering her passive or pathetic, naming herself in this way is a form of agency that fuels her capacity to live and to write: 'I am stronger than I am broken.'[107] Even if she also pays a price: 'Writing that kind of story requires going to a dark place. At times, I nauseated myself in the writing and by what I am capable of writing and imagining, my ability to *go there*.'[108]

At the same time as telling this gruesome story perhaps more graphically than anyone I have read, Gay also explores the furthest limits of a woman's imagination, the lengths to which she can be driven, or choose to go, in the domain of love and intimacy. This is especially true of her second collection of short stories, *Difficult Women*, also published in 2017 but which received less attention than *Hunger*. Critics seem to have greeted *Difficult Women* with either disappointment or false cheer (in tune with the options available to many women in a heartless world). Gay has been accused of exploitation. She has also been praised for having 'fun' with her 'ladies': 'no shrinking violets', they give 'as good as they get'.[109] She is, I suggest, a borderline writer, a term I intend not as diagnosis but as praise. Despite, or perhaps because of, what happened to her, Gay is always on the side of the untamed. *Untamed State* is the title of her first novel. It too tells the lurid story of a rape which – and this is one of the strengths of her writing – is given its fullest race and class dimension: the daughter of a rich arriviste Haitian businessman is kidnapped, held to ransom and repeatedly raped by a gang of men who roam and spread fear on the streets.

In *Hunger*, revulsion towards fat people is seen as fuelled by anxiety at unruly bodies, bodies whose outlines stretch to infinity and which break all the rules: 'My body is wildly undisciplined' – 'undisciplined' and 'unruly' are a refrain.[110] A fat person stands as a terrifying rebuke to those who foolishly believe that their mortal body, not to speak of their inner life, could ever be truly under control or in shape. Hence the 'strange civic-minded cruelty' with which Gay, like all fat people, is greeted, as if such cruelty were the only way the people hurling the insult or turning away in disgust can feel confident of keeping their place in the ranks of the civilised.[111] 'My wife and I', explains the narrator of the short story 'Florida', in *Difficult Women*, 'watch documentaries about the lives of extraordinarily fat people so we can feel better about ourselves.'[112] Despite the ugly beginnings, *Hunger* – which portrays appetite as uncontrolled, unruly, untamed – slowly but surely becomes a testament not only to trauma but to the intensity and breadth of human desire, for which the word hunger becomes the drive and metaphor: 'I often tell my students that fiction is about desire one way or another [. . .] We want and want and oh how we want. We hunger.'[113] This is for me what Gay does so brilliantly: point the finger without reserve at male violence and its deadly aftermath for women, while exuberantly – and some would say perversely – keeping open all the pathways of the mind.

'There's a lot to love about breaking things,' observes the narrator of 'North Country', another story from *Difficult Women*, and then to her new lover, the first man, we are told, who has ever said that he likes her, 'You don't have to be soft with me.'[114] This story also includes a fleeting episode of sexual harassment at the University of Michigan, where Gay herself studied for a PhD. The narrator is the only black person and the only woman in her department – which may well also have been the case. She is seduced by her dissertation adviser, who endlessly promises her marriage and then takes up with his new lab assistant – she finds them having sex in the lab – when she fails to move on after the death of their unborn child. Babies who have died recur in Gay's stories. They are often, but not always, the cause of the agonised pleasure her protagonists take in psychic and physical pain: 'At a bar I found a man who would hit me [. . .] I used one hurt to cover over another [. . .] I tried to lose myself in my bruising.'[115] She would be a much less interesting writer if that were always the explanation, as if there must be a get-out clause for women who travel to the most tortured places of the heart (violated virtue as a woman's only possible route to vice). Gay sits on a border between a space in which trauma is the sole cause of anguish: 'look what has been done to me', and that of a mind which, in spite of trauma – thumbing trauma, one might say – takes flight: 'see how far I can go'. A mind that does not shy away from deploying the full psychic palette in its most raucous and bloody hues (think 'bleeding heart' with a twist).

Perhaps the most disturbing story opens: 'My husband is a hunter. I am a knife.' She likes him to mark her body and takes pleasure in skinning and disembowelling his prey. Long ago, when her sister lay dying by the roadside after their car was hit by a drunk driver, she used her knife to cut out the heart 'he did not deserve' and placed it inside her sister's chest, until the two hearts 'started beating as one'. At the end of the story, she delivers her sister's unborn child, and then loses her own: 'I wish I could carve the anger out of my body the way I cut everything else.'[116]

To borrow the title of psychoanalyst Jessica Benjamin's 2018 book, Gay's characters are 'beyond doer and done to', or more precisely they participate in both.[117] They are violated, but they are also agents as they proceed, with exceptional energy and cutting determination, on their way through their lives. As a writer, Gay shunts between the acuity of her rage and the creative mess of her mind. In the world of sexual harassment, the idea of fiction or fabrication is, as we have seen, almost invariably bad news for women, as in 'She made the whole thing up.' Gay is there to remind us that fiction, rather than being suspect or fraudulent, is an imaginative tool that belongs at the centre of these debates. It can depict damage as well as freedom, seized from a wretched past. In her hands, telling stories – her own story, the stories she invents – is the place where impossible paths meet.

2

TRANS VOICES

Who Do You Think You Are?

Some time in the 1970s, in the home of the feminist film theorist Laura Mulvey, I found myself in the company of another distinguished cinema critic, who had just returned to London from the Berlin International Film Festival. Over dinner he took pleasure in regaling us with stories of male-to-female transsexual prostitutes he had met on the city streets, and how difficult it was to 'complete' the transaction since the body interprets the surgically created vagina as a wound, which it attempts to close. I could not tell if he had persisted down this path, but his delight in telling the tale of sexual encounters which, by his account, could only be sadistic for the man and painful for the women involved was repellent. He was boasting. I had no doubt that he thought he was promoting their case. He registered my disapproval. Twice I declined when he offered to refill my glass with red wine. Faced with his persistence, I put my hand over the glass to make myself clear. Refusing to take no for an answer, he proceeded to pour the wine over the back of my hand. It was my first inkling, at a distance, of what transsexual people, even from those purportedly on their side, might be up against.

Just a few years before, one of the most renowned instances of transsexuality in the UK had been in the news. In 1969, Arthur Corbett, first husband of the famous male-to-female trans-sexual April Ashley, sought an annulment of their marriage on the grounds that at the time of the ceremony, the respondent (Ashley) was 'a person of the male sex'. In the course of the proceedings, Corbett – or 'the Honourable Arthur Cameron Corbett', as he introduced himself to Ashley after initially using the alias 'Frank' – presented himself as a frequenter of male brothels and a cross-dresser who, when he looked into the mirror, never liked what he saw: 'You want the fantasy to appear right. It utterly failed to appear right in my eyes.' He then explained how, from their first meeting at the Caprice, he had been mesmerised by Ashley. She was so much more than he could 'ever hope to be': 'The reality [. . .] far outstripped any fantasy for myself. I could never have contemplated it for myself.'* It took a while for Ashley, along with her medical and legal advisers, to realise what Corbett was up to (no fewer than nine medical practitioners gave evidence in court). He was, in her words, portraying their marriage as a 'squalid prank, a deliberate mockery of moral society perpetrated by a couple of queers for their own twisted amusement'.[1]

Corbett's ploy was successful. The marriage was annulled, in a case that is commonly seen as having set back the cause of transsexual women and men for decades. Transsexual people lost all right to marry for more than thirty years. The decision ruled out any change to their birth certificates, a right they had

---

* Throughout this chapter I use 'he/she' and 'his/her', selected to reflect the post-transition identity, rather than 'ze', 'sie', 'hir' as advocated by some transsexual writers, and as approved for example by the Harvard Faculty of Arts and Sciences for use by students in September 2015. In all other cases I have used 'they', as has become increasingly accepted usage. I have also used the more familiar term 'transsexuality' rather than 'transsexualism', and 'sex or gender reassignment surgery' rather than 'gender confirmation surgery'. Unless quoting, I have avoided 'sex change', which today is considered to be denigrating.

enjoyed since 1944, thereby denying them legal recognition of their gender. In 1986, female-to-male transsexual Mark Rees, in the first challenge to the ruling, lost his case at the European Court of Human Rights against the UK government for its failure to recognise his male status, entailing loss of privacy and barring his marriage with a woman.[2] Only with the Gender Recognition Act of 2004, which introduced the requirement of a Gender Recognition Certificate, was the law changed to permit transsexual people to marry as their chosen gender. The January 2016 UK parliamentary report *Transgender Equality* noted that the medicalised certificate pathologises transsexuality and 'is contrary to the dignity and personal autonomy of applicants'. Describing the Act as pioneering but outdated, it called for a further change in the law.[3] In 2018, it was recommended that the law be changed to make gender a matter of self-recognition, a change that has provoked intense controversy, which will be discussed later in this book. But Corbett vs Corbett cast its shadow over public understanding of trans experience for a very long time. 'Not since the Oscar Wilde trial', Ashley comments in her 2006 memoir, *The First Lady*, 'had a civil matter led to such socially disastrous consequences.'[4]

For Justice Ormrod, the case – 'the first occasion on which a court in England has been called on to decide the sex of an individual' – was straightforward.[5] Because Ashley had been registered as a boy at birth, she should in perpetuity be treated as male. Suggestions of intersex were dismissed on the grounds of medical evidence attesting that she was born with male gonads, chromosomes and genitalia. Although there had been minimal development at puberty, no facial hair, some breast formation and what Ashley referred to as a 'vestigial penis' because of its diminutive size, the judge also ruled out intersex or hermaphroditism as a consideration. Nor did the fact that Ashley had undergone full surgical genital reconstruction, and that there had been some penetrative sex, albeit unsatisfactory, between her and Corbett, make any difference: 'the respondent was physically incapable of consummating a marriage as intercourse using the completely artificially constructed cavity could never constitute true intercourse' (what would constitute 'true intercourse' is not specified). Ashley was not, to his mind, a woman. For Ormrod, this was a more correct way of phrasing the issue in relation to the validity of the marriage than in terms of whether or not she was still a man. At the outset he had been sympathetic towards her, but as the hearing proceeded, he became progressively less persuaded: 'Her outward appearance, at first sight, was convincingly feminine but on closer and longer examination in the witness box it was much less so. The voice, manner, gestures and attitude became increasingly reminiscent of the accomplished female impersonator.' Her femininity was pastiche – in the words of one of the expert witnesses, her 'pastiche of femininity was convincing' (although you might argue that a convincing pastiche is a contradiction in terms).[6]

If the judge found for the plaintiff on the grounds that Ashley could not fulfil the role of a wife ('the essential role of a woman in marriage'[7]), it is nonetheless obvious from Corbett's statements that this was never exactly what he had had in mind. For Corbett, Ashley was never an object of desire, but of envy. He coveted her freedom, her scandalous violation and embodiment of the norm. She was someone he wanted to emulate. Corbett's wording is precise. Ashley was his fantasy or dream come true, the life he most wanted, but could not hope for, for himself: 'The reality [. . .] far outstripped any fantasy for myself. I could never have contemplated it *far myself*.' He did not *want* her, as in desire; he wanted to *be* her, as in identification (for psychoanalysis this is a rudimentary distinction), or rather the first only as an effect of the second. In this, without knowing it, he could be seen as coming close to obeying a later transsexual injunction, or piece of transsexual worldly advice. As Kate Bornstein, one of today's most celebrated and controversial male-to-female transsexuals, puts it towards the end of her 2012 account of her complex (to say the least) journey, *A Queer and Pleasant Danger, A Memoir – The True Story of a Nice Jewish Boy Who Joins the Church of Scientology and Leaves Twelve Years Later to Become the Lovely Lady She Is Today*: 'Never fuck anyone you wouldn't wanna be.'[8]

One of the challenges mounted by transsexual people to the popular image of human sexuality is to insist, in the words of author and political activist Jennifer Finney Boylan, that: 'It is not about who you want to go to bed *with*, it's who you want to go to bed *as*' (she was explaining the difference to Michael Cashman, co-founder with Ian McKellen of Stonewall).[9] This, it can be argued, is the province of gender – how you see yourself and wish to be seen. In fact the term gender with reference to transsexuality was first used by the psychiatrist and psychoanalyst Robert Stoller, a matter of months before the Corbett/Ashley case, in his 1968 study *Sex and Gender*, the second volume of which was called *The Transsexual Experiment*. For Stoller, gender was identity, sex was genital pleasure, and humans would always give priority to the first – many transsexual people today say the same thing.[10] To talk of a 'gender dysphoria syndrome' was therefore as inappropriate as to talk of 'a suicide syndrome, or an incest syndrome, or a wanderlust syndrome'.[11] Stoller's best-known transsexual case was Agnes, who had secured genital reassignment surgery having duped

Stoller and his associate Harold Garfinkel into believing that her female development at puberty was natural (they diagnosed her as having a rare condition of intersex in which an apparently male body spontaneously feminises at puberty). Eight years later, she returned to tell them that since puberty she had in fact been regularly taking oestrogens prescribed for her mother: 'My chagrin at learning this', Stoller wrote, 'was matched by my amusement that she had pulled off this coup with such skill.'[12] Stoller was always careful to insist that his own category of gender identity was not sacrosant: 'With *gender* difficult to define and *identity* still a challenge to theoreticians, we need hardly insist on the holiness of the term "gender identity."'[13]

Before meeting Ashley, Corbett had been paying boys in the brothels to dress him up and masturbate him, but once he started seeing her and learned her back-story, he stopped. She 'cured' him, allowing him for the first time to feel that his life had slotted into place: 'You've stopped my pendulum swinging.' (Ashley helpfully explains that Corbett had been brought up in a world of grandfather clocks.)[14] Not that Corbett's fantasies of being a woman stopped there. According to Ashley, he had a second, 'vile' persona who during their relationship would regularly appear on the scene without warning – 'She Who Must Be Obeyed', whose voice would rise in pitch, whose suddenly crossed legs would become terribly exaggerated and who would accuse Ashley of being a whore: 'A bitchy accusing edge came into her voice, the mouth pursed, his bottom squirming among cushions.'[15] None of this is mentioned in court. There is a limit to how far Corbett will go in his attempt to screw Ashley (he brings the case primarily to avoid any financial obligation towards her). Corbett is after all an English peer. Ashley is convinced that she loses the case at least partly through snobbery, the sheer affront of someone born into a Liverpool slum marrying into the aristocracy.[16]

Cruel and outdated as this case may be, it nonetheless makes a number of important things clear. The transsexual woman or man is not the only one performing; she or he does not have a monopoly on gender uncertainty; what makes a marriage is open to interpretation and fantasy – for better or worse, couples can want to change places, to be each other, as much as anything else. There is strictly no limit to what two people can do to, and ask of, each other. Above all, perhaps, this case suggests that the enemy of a transsexual person might be their greatest rival, embroiled in the deepest unconscious identification with the one they love to hate; while the seeming friend, even potential husband, might be the one furthest from having their interests at heart, their chances of living a basic, viable life. 'Our lives and our bodies', Viviane Namaste opens *Invisible Lives – The Erasure of Transsexual and Transgendered People*, 'are forged in details of everyday life [. . .] in the mundane and uneventful.'[17] After the annulment, Ashley fell back into penury, where she, like many transsexual women, has lived a large part of her life (her fortunes wildly fluctuate). Both Mark Rees and Juliet Jacques, author of a well-known *Guardian* online column on her transition and of the 2015 memoir *Trans*, fall in and out of the dole queue (the job-seeking line-up of the unemployed).[18] Even before the trial, Ashley's career as a successful model had been brought to an abrupt end when she was outed by the British press in 1961. Up to that point, like many transsexual people who aim to pass, she had lived in fear of 'detection and ruin' (in the words of Harold Garfinkel, in 1967, one of the first medical commentators to write sympathetically about transsexuality).[19]

As Susan Stryker and Aren Z. Aizura write in their introduction to the second of the two monumental *Transgender Studies Readers*, published in 2006 and 2013, contrary to today's obsession with the most glamorous cases, most transsexual lives 'are not fabulous'.[20] In 2013 the level of unemployment among trans people in the US was reported to be fourteen per cent, double that of the general population; forty-four per cent were underemployed, while fifteen per cent, compared to four per cent of the general population, had a household income of under $10,000.[21] Jacques gives statistics showing that twenty-six per cent of trans people in Brighton and Hove were unemployed in 2015, with another sixty per cent earning under £10,000 a year. This is also why so many, especially male-to-female transsexuals, take to the streets (to survive materially but also to raise the money for surgery). 'Suddenly,' Jacques writes, 'I understood why, historically, so many trans people had done sex work [. . .] I started to wonder if sex work might be the only place where people like me were actually *wanted*.'[22]

o   o   o

Transsexual people are brilliant at telling their stories. Doing so has been a central part of their increasingly successful struggle for acceptance. But it is one of the ironies of their position that attention sought and gained is not always in their best interests, since the most engaged, enthusiastic audience might be in pursuit of a prurient, or brutal, agenda of its own. Being seen is, however, key. At whatever stage of the transsexual journey or form of transition, the crux is whether you will be recognised as the other sex which, contrary to your birth assignment, you wish and believe yourself to be. Something has to be acknowledged by the watching world, even if, as can also be the case, transition does not mean so much crossing from one side to the other as hovering in the space in between (in the United States, only about a quarter of transgender women have had genital surgery[23]). Despite much progress, transsexuality, or transsexualism as the preferred term, is still treated today as anomaly or exception. However normalised, it unsettles the way most people prefer to think of themselves and pretty much everyone else. In fact, no human can exist without recognition. To survive, we all have to be seen. A transsexual person merely brings that fact to the surface of our lives, exposing the latent violence that lurks behind the banal truth of our dependency on other people. After all, if I cannot exist without you, then, among other things, you have the power to kill me.

While their material condition is lower, the rate of physical assault and murder of transsexual people is higher than for the general population. A 1992 London survey reported that fifty-two per cent of male-to-female and forty-three per cent of female-to-male transsexuals had been physically assaulted in that year.[24] A 1997 survey by GenderPAC found that sixty per cent of transgender-identified people had experienced some kind of harassment or physical abuse (GenderPAC is a lobbying group founded in 1996 by trans activist Riki Anne Wilchins with the aim of promoting 'gender, affectional and racial equality').[25] Several of David Valentine's study participants in *Imagining Transgender* (2007) were murdered in the course of his writing the book.[26]

Over the past decade, this violence has seemed to be steadily on the rise. In the first seven weeks of 2015, seven trans women were killed in the US (compared with thirteen over the whole of the previous year).[27] In July 2015 in California, two trans women were reported killed in one week.[28] In June 2019, the American Medical Association described violence against transgender people as an epidemic.[29] In the US only twenty-two states have laws to protect transgender workers, and only in 2014 did the Justice Department start taking the position that discrimination on the basis of gender identity, including transgender, constitutes discrimination under the Civil Rights Act.[30] The 2016 UK *Transgender Equality* report noted the serious results of the high levels of prejudice experienced by trans people on a daily basis, including in the provision of public services. Half of young trans and a third of adult trans people attempt suicide. The report singled out the deaths in custody of two trans women, Vicky Thompson and Joanne Latham, and the case of Tara Hudson, a trans woman who was placed in a men's prison, as 'particularly stark illustrations' (after public pressure, Hudson was moved to a women's jail). Stephen Whittle, co-editor of the first *Transgender Studies Reader*, was special adviser to this committee. At the end of *First Lady* Ashley also credits him for recent changes to the law.

'The intellectual work' of transgender studies, Stryker writes in her introduction to the *Reader*, 'is intimately connected to, and deeply motivated by, socio-political efforts to stem the tide of anti-transgender violence, and to save transgender lives'.[31] 'I saw', Jacques writes in *Trans*, 'that for many people around the world, expressing themselves as they wished meant risking death.'[32] The dedication of Namaste's book reads: 'For the transsexuals who have not survived.' In the present moment, the range and insistence of these voices matters more and more. In the US, violence against transgender people was of course bound to intensify under Trump, who has consistently made trans men and women the targets of hatred. One of his first moves was to ban them from the military (having seen off a legal challenge, the policy commenced in June 2019).[33] He has revoked protections for transgender people in public schools, which means they can now be obliged to use the toilet facilities that correspond to the gender they were assigned at birth.[34] He has proposed to define gender legally as either male or female and determined at birth, which effectively defines anyone who is transgender out of existence. The plan is to insert these strictures into Title IX, the federal civil rights law that prevents discrimination in education, which would make it impossible to use the law to fight discrimination against transgender people (as we saw in the previous chapter, Title IX has played a central role in the fight against sexual harassment).[35]

In 2007, Kellie Telesford, a trans woman from Trinidad, was killed in Thornton Heath in South London. Eighteen-year-old Shanniel Hyatt was acquitted of her murder on the grounds that she may have died as a result of a consensual sex game that went wrong or inflicted the fatal injuries herself (since she was strangled with a scarf, how she would have managed this is unclear). As Jacques points out in *Trans*, the *Sun* headline, 'Trannie killed in sex mix-up', anticipates the 'transsexual panic' defence, which argues that if a trans person fails to disclose before the sexual encounter, then they are accountable for whatever happens next (the shock of such a discovery is famously the pivot on which the 1986 film *Mona Lisa* turns).[36] Murder, this suggests, is the logical response to an unexpected transsexual revelation. 'Those moments', writes Jacques, 'when men are attracted to us when we "pass" and then repulsed when we don't are the most terrifying [. . .] all bets are off.'[37] 'She had hoped to avoid the worst possibilities of her new life,' the narrator of Roz Kaveney's novel *Tiny Pieces of Skull* observes after one particularly ugly encounter between the main transsexual character, Annabelle, and a policeman with a knife.[38] (The novel, written in the 1980s but only published in 2015, is based on Kaveney's post-transition life in Chicago in the 1970s.) In fact, whatever may have been said in court, we have no way of knowing whether Telesford's killer was aware that she was trans, whether her identity might have been ambiguous, whether – as with Corbett – this may indeed have been the lure. Either way, 'transsexual panic' suggests that confrontation with a trans woman is something that the average man on the street cannot be expected to survive. Damage to him outweighs, nullifies, their death. Not to speak of the unspoken assumption that thwarting an aroused man for whatever reason – stopping his body dead in its tracks – is a mortal offence.

That Telesford was a woman of colour is also crucial. If transsexual persons are disproportionately the targets of murder, transsexuals of colour comprise by far the largest number of victims – the seven trans women murdered in the US in the first seven weeks of 2015 were all trans women of colour.[39] When the American Medical Association adopted a plan at their 2019 Annual Meeting to increase awareness of violence against transgender people, they drew special attention to the increased physical dangers faced by transgender people of colour.[40] Today, those fighting for transsexual freedom are increasingly keen to address this racial factor (like the feminists before them who also ignored racial discrimination at first) – in the name of social justice and equality, but also in order to challenge the assumption that transsexuality is an isolated, freak phenomenon, beyond human endurance in and of itself. It is a paradox of the transsexual bid for emancipation that the more visible they become, the more they seem to excite, as much as greater acceptance, a peculiarly murderous hatred. 'I know people have to learn about other people's lives in order to become more tolerant,' writes Jayne County in her 1995 *Man Enough to Be a Woman* (one of the main inspirations for Jacques), but 'sometimes that makes bigotry worse. The more straight people know about us, the more they have to hate.'[41]

Feminists have always had to confront the violence they expose, and – in exposing – provoke, but in the case of the transsexual person, there seems to be an even shorter fuse between the progressive moment and the virulent, crushing payback. It is a myth, albeit one of liberalism's most potent, that knowing – finding oneself face to face with something or someone outside one's usual frame of reference – is the first step on the path to understanding. What distinguishes the transsexual woman or man, writes psychoanalyst Patricia Gherovici in *Please Select Your Gender*, her study of transsexual patients, is 'that the almost infinite distance between one face and the other will be crossed by a single person' (a space of acknowledged difference and otherness which is normally sacrosanct however close two people might get).[42] Perhaps this is the real scandal. Not crossing the line of gender – although that is scandal enough – but blurring psychic and physical boundaries, placing in such intimate proximity parts of the mind and different forms of human embodiment, which non-trans people have the luxury of believing they can safely keep asunder.

o   o   o

Trans is not one thing. If crossing over is the version most familiar in the public mind – the Caitlyn Jenner option, as we might say – there are as many transsexuals who do not choose this path.

In addition to transition ('A to B') and transitional ('between A and B'), trans can also mean 'A as well as B' or 'neither A nor B', i.e. 'transcending', as in above, or in a different realm from, both. Thus Jan Morris in *Conundrum* in 1974: 'There is neither man nor woman [. . .] I shall transcend both.'[43] Even that is not all. Once transsexuality is subsumed by the broader category of transgender – as it is for example in the *Transgender Studies Readers* – then there seems to be no limit. As if one of the greatest pleasures of falling outside the norm is the freedom to pile category upon category, like Borges's fantastic taxonomy of animals with which Michel Foucault opens *The Order of Things* (no order to speak of), or the catechisms of James Joyce's 'Ithaca' in *Ulysses*, whose interminable lists doggedly outstrip the mind's capacity to hold anything in its proper place. At a 'Binary Defiance' workshop held at the 2015 True Colors Conference, an annual event for gay and transgender youth at the University of Connecticut, the following were listed on the blackboard: non-binary, genderqueer, bigender, trigender, agender, intergender, pangender, neutrois, third gender, androgyne, two-spirit, self-coined, genderfluid (the variants have increased exponentially since then).[44] In 2011, the New York-based journal *Psychoanalytic Dialogues* brought out a special issue on transgender subjectivities. 'In these pages,' psychoanalyst Virginia Goldner wrote in her editor's note, 'you will meet persons who would be characterized, and would recognize themselves, as one – or some – of the following: A girl *and* a boy, a boy *in* a boy, a boy who is a girl, a girl who is a boy dressed as a girl, a girl who has to be a boy to be a girl.'[45] 'We are dealing', Stryker explains, with 'a heteroglossic outpouring of gender positions from which to speak'.[46]

These are not, however, the versions of trans that make the news. At the end of her photo session with Annie Leibovitz,

Caitlyn Jenner looked at the gold medal she had won as Bruce Jenner for the 1976 Olympic decathlon, and commented, as 'her eyes rimmed red and her voice grew soft': 'That was a good day. But the last couple of days were better.'[47] It's as if – even allowing for the additional pathos injected by Buzz Bissinger, who wrote the famous piece on Jenner for *Vanity Fair* – the photographic session, rather than hormones or surgery, was the culmination of the process (though Leibovitz herself insists the photos were secondary to the project of helping Caitlyn to 'emerge'[48]). What happens, as Jacques asks in relation to the whole genre of 'before' and 'after' transsexual photography, 'once the camera goes away?'[49] Not for the first time, the perfect, still visual image – unlike the rolling camera of the endless Kardashian TV saga – finds itself under instruction to halt the world and, if only for a split second, make it seem safe (like the answer to a prayer). The non-transsexual viewer can then bask in the power to confer recognition on the newly claimed gender identity, or not. The power is real: plaudits laced with cruelty. It is the premise – you are male or female – which is at fault. There has been much criticism of Jenner, often snide, for decking herself in the most clichéd, extravagant trappings of femininity. But her desire would be meaningless were it not reciprocated by a whole feverish world out there racing to classify humans according to how neatly they can be pigeon-holed into their gendered place. This is the coercive violence of gendering which, Stryker is not alone in pointing out, is the founding condition of human subjectivity.[50] A form of knowledge which, as Garfinkel already described it in the 1960s, makes its way into the unconscious cultural lexicon 'without even being noticed' as 'a matter of objective, institutionalised ie moral facts'.[51] In the twenty-first century this view has proved to be as pervasive as ever. Writing in the *Evening Standard* in 2015, Melanie McDonagh lamented the relative ease of 'sex-change' which she saw around her: 'The boy-girl identity is what shapes us most [. . .] the most fundamental [. . .] the most basic aspect of our personhood.'[52] Her article was entitled 'Changing Sex Is Not to Be Done Just on a Whim'. A whim? She had obviously not spoken to any transsexual people or read a word they have written. Likewise, Ian McEwan commented derisively on the decision to transition: 'The self, like a consumer desirable, may be plucked from the shelves of a personal identity supermarket, a ready-to-wear little black number', for which he was roundly and rightly slated (he later apologised).[53]

In her TV series *I Am Cait*, Jenner has been keen to extend a hand to transsexual women and men who do not enjoy her material privileges. She has made a point of giving space to minority transsexuals such as Zeam Porter who face double discrimination as black and trans – although it is Laverne Cox, in *Orange Is the New Black*, who has truly taken on the mantle of presenting to the world what it means to be a black, incarcerated, transsexual woman. Cox also insisted that, even now she had the money, she would not undergo surgery to feminise her face – Jenner's facial surgery lasted ten hours and led to her one panic attack: 'What did I just do? What did I just do to myself?'[54] But when faced with Kate Bornstein exhorting her to 'accept the freakdom', Jenner seems nonplussed (as one commentator pointed out, Bornstein used the word 'freak' six times in a three-minute interview). This was not a true meeting of minds. Like Stryker, Bornstein believes that it is the strangeness of being transsexual, the threat posed to those watching with or without sympathy, which is the whole point. Compare the impeccable, Hollywood 'moodboarded' images of Jenner broadcast across the world – 'moodboarded', the word used by the stylist on the shoot, refers to a collage of images used in production to get the right feel or flow[55] – with this image of Stryker in 1994, in perhaps her most renowned testament or performance, welcoming monstrosity via the analogy between herself and Frankenstein's creature: 'The transsexual body is an unnatural body. It is the product of medical science. It is a technological construction. It is flesh torn apart and sewn together again in a shape other than that in which it was born.' Stryker stood at the podium wearing what she calls 'gender-fuck drag':

> combat boots, threadbare Levi 501s over a black lace body suit, a shredded Transgender Nation T-shirt with the neck and sleeves cut out, a pink triangle, quartz crystal pendant, grunge metal jewellery, and a six inch long marlin hook dangling around my neck on a length of heavy stainless steel chain. I decorated the set by draping my black leather biker jacket over my chair at the panellists' table. The jacket had handcuffs on the left shoulder, rainbow freedom rings on the right side lacings, and Queer Nation-style stickers reading SEX CHANGE, DYKE, and FUCK YOUR TRANSPHOBIA plastered on the back.[56]

She was – is – wholly serious. It is the myth of the natural, for all of us, which she has in her sights. This is her justly renowned, exhortatory moment, unsurpassed in anything else I have read:

> Hearken unto me, fellow creatures. I who have dwelt in a form unmatched with my desire, I whose flesh has become an assemblage of incongruous anatomical parts, I who achieve the similitude of a natural body only through an unnatural process,

I offer you this warning: the Nature you bedevil me with is a lie. Do not trust it to protect you from what I represent, for it is a fabrication that cloaks the groundlessness of the privilege you seek to maintain for yourself at my expense. You are as constructed as me; the same anarchic Womb has birthed us both. I call upon you to investigate your nature as I have been compelled to confront mine. I challenge you to risk abjection and flourish as well as have I. Heed my words, and you may well discover the seams and sutures in yourself.[57]

For many post-operative transsexual people, the charge of bodily mutilation is a slur arising from pure prejudice. It is true that without medical technology none of this would have been possible. It is also true that the need for, the extent and pain of medical intervention put a strain on the argument that the transsexual woman or man is simply returning to her or his naturally ordained place – with the surgeon as nature's agent who restores what nature meant to be there in the first place.[58] Roz Kaveney's medical transition, for example, lasted two years, involving twenty-five general anaesthetics, a ten-stone weight gain, thromboses, more than one major haemorrhage, fistula and infections. She barely survived, though none of this has stopped her from going on to lead one of the most effective campaigning lives as a transsexual woman.[59]

In 1931, Lili Elbe – a successful Danish painter under her former name of Einar Magnus Andreas Wegener – died after a failed uterus transplant (the film *The Danish Girl* sentimentally changes this to the prior operation to create a vagina, so that she dies having fulfilled her dream). When I met April Ashley in Oxford in the early 1970s – she was in the midst of the legal hearing and Oxford was a kind of retreat – she expressed her sorrow that she would never be a mother. On this, female-to-male transsexuals have gone further. In 2007, Thomas Beatie, having retained his female reproductive organs on transition, became pregnant with triplets through artificial insemination. He lost the pregnancy after life-threatening complications but has since given birth to three children. In 2018, having halted testosterone treatment, Freddy McConnell gave birth after conceiving with donor sperm. A year later he lost his appeal to the Family and Administrative Division of the UK High Court to be registered as the baby's father. In the first legal definition of a mother in English common law, Sir Andrew McFarlane judged that maternal status, unlike gender identity, derives from the biological and physical process of giving birth and that, regardless of potential harm to the individual and any violation of his right to privacy, McConnell had to be registered as the baby's mother. (The term 'parent' was not an option as it is used in law to refer to the female partner of a biological mother.) McFarlane had reduced motherhood to biology and made it the limit case of trans experience:

The principal conclusion at the centre of this extensive judgment can be shortly stated. It is that there is a material difference between a person's gender and their status as a parent. Being a 'mother', whilst hitherto always associated with being female, is the status afforded to a person who undergoes the physical and biological process of carrying a pregnancy and giving birth. It is now medically and legally possible for an individual, whose gender is recognised in law as male, to become pregnant and give birth to their child. Whilst that person's gender is 'male', their parental status is that of 'mother'.[60]

A previous judgement, cited earlier in the report by McFarlane, had stated that 'the public interest in having coherent administrative systems was an important consideration.'[61] At the other end of the spectrum, the court overturned the decision to refuse a transgender woman any contact with the children she had fathered while living as a man on the grounds that it would cause them to be ostracised by the orthodox Jewish community in which they lived.[62]

For Stryker, any such attempt to align the trans body with the law would make little sense (I cannot imagine her anywhere near a court of law on these matters). In her vision, mutilation is at once a badge of honour and a counter to the myth of nature in a pure state. There is no body without debilitation and pain. We are all made up of endlessly permuting bits and pieces which sometimes do, mostly do not, align with each other. We are all always adjusting, manipulating, perfecting, sometimes damaging (sometimes perfecting *and* damaging) ourselves. Today non-trans women, at the mercy of the cosmetic industry, increasingly submit to surgical intervention to make them look like the woman they believe they were meant to be, an image without which they feel worthless (since nature is equated with youth, this also turns the natural process of ageing into some kind of aberration). 'I've seen women *mutilate* themselves to try to meet that norm,' says Melissa, mother of Skylar, a sixteen-year-old from New Haven whose story was told by Margaret Talbot for *Vanity Fair* in 2015. Skylar had 'top surgery' (mastectomy) with his parents' permission at the age of sixteen.[63] Shakespeare described man as a thing of 'shreds and patches' (the king in *Hamlet*), Freud as a 'prosthetic God', Donna Haraway for our times as a cyborg (Haraway is included in the first *Transgender*

Reader). Rebarbative as it may at first seem, Stryker's is in fact the most inclusive of visions. Enter my world: 'I challenge you to risk abjection and flourish as well as have I.' What you would most violently repudiate is an inherent and potentially creative part of the self.

o   o   o

The image of the transsexual world as a type of open church which includes all comers, all variants on the possibilities of sex, is therefore misleading. There are strong disagreements between those who see transition as a means, the only means, to true embodiment and those who see transsexuality as upending all sexual categories. For the first, the aim is a bodily and psychic integrity which has been thwarted since birth: 'Lili Elbe's story', writes Niels Hoyer, 'is above all a human story and each faltering step she takes is an awakening of her true self . . . [she] was willing to make the ultimate sacrifice to become the person within.' (Hoyer is the editor of Elbe's own notes and diaries, not to be confused with the ghastly novel by David Ebershoff on which the recent film is based.)[64] Jan Morris defines her transition as a journey to identity: 'I had reached identity'; Ashley speaks of her desire 'to be whole' and of her 'great sense of purpose to make things right, make everything correct'[65]; Chelsea Manning writes of 'physically transitioning to the woman I have always been'.[66] Such accounts seem to be the ones that most easily make it into the public eye, as if a shocked world can breathe out and heave something like a collective sigh of relief ('at least that much is clear, then').

For those who, on the other hand, see trans as a challenge to any such clarity, the last thing transsexuality should do is claim to be the answer to its own question, or pretend that the world has been, could ever be, put to rights. This is simply a normative delusion hugely exacerbated by a neoliberal order which now more or less covers the earth – rather like Scientology, of which Kate Bornstein was a fully paid-up member in what we might call her formative years. Scientology, Bornstein tells us, 'is supposed to erase all the pain and suffering you've ever felt in this and every other lifetime'.[67] It is also a type of surveillance state aimed at world domination which enjoins complete lack of secrecy or privacy on all its members (unflinching eye-to-eye contact obligatory during any conversation), and which of course cast Bornstein into the wilderness as a 'suppressive person' as soon as her ambiguous sexuality was revealed. This despite the fact that, according to Scientology, each human contains a thetan – the spirit of the person, which is not separate from the body, as in, say, Christianity, but embedded within it. Crucially, thetans have no gender. Bornstein's transsexuality is, therefore, as indebted to the Scientologists (something she indeed acknowledges) as it is her escape.

For Bornstein, as for Stryker, transsexuality is an infinite confusion of tongues. Neither of them is arriving anywhere. For Jay Prosser, on the other hand, the transsexual man or woman is enfolded in their new body like a second skin (his 1998 book, one of the most widely circulated and debated on the topic, has the title *Second Skins – The Body Narratives of Transsexuality*). As he describes on the first page, two weeks after completing a course of massive testosterone treatment, he began living full-time as a man, 'documents all changed to reflect a new, unambivalent status'. In fact, Prosser is more than attuned to the ambiguities of sexual identity. He knows that transition, however real, is grafted by means of fiction, that it is through the craft of story-making that transsexual people drive towards the resolution they seek (hence the 'body narratives' of the title, narratives which in his analysis track nothing if not the complexities of sexual being carried and enacted by the genre). Partly because he is so immersed in psychoanalytic thinking, he grasps how far sexual being – on the skin and in the bloodstream – plunges into the roots of who we are. Transition is testament to the at once alterable and non-negotiable fact of sexual difference: 'In transsexual accounts,' he writes, 'transition does not shift the subject away from the embodiment of sexual difference but more fully into it.'[68] This is why, for some, transsexuality, or rather this version of transsexuality, is conservative, reinforcing the binary from which we all – trans and non-trans – suffer. Freud, for example, described the long and circuitous path to so-called normal femininity for the girl – originally bisexual, wildly energised by being all over the place – as nothing short of a catastrophe (admittedly, this is not the version of female sexuality for which he is best known).

Yet for Prosser, to move from A to B is a form of definitive, and conclusive, self-fashioning or it is nothing. In the special issue of *Psychoanalytic Dialogues* on transsexual subjectivities, Melanie Suchet draws on Prosser in her analysis of Raphael, a female-to-male transsexual who explains: 'Boy has to be written on the body', an idea she struggles to accept. She has to move from her original stance that sexual ambiguity should be sustainable without any need for bodily change ('Crossing Over', the title of her essay, refers as much to her journey as it does to his).[69] Prosser talks of 'restoration' of the body.[70] Note how 'restoration' chimes with the 'born in the wrong body' mantra which, while deeply felt by many transsexual people, is also partly the child of a medical profession which for a long time would accept nothing less as the basis for hormonal or surgical intervention. In the 1960s, the profiles of candidates for medical transition were found to be strangely in harmony with Harry Benjamin's then definitive textbook on the subject – strangely, that is, until it was realised that they had all been reading it and brushing up their lines.[71]

But if the longing is for restoration, arrival, the end of ambivalence, then the infinite variables of transgender identity – which the UK report *Transgender Equality* admitted it could not keep up with – are a bit of a scam, or at least a smoke-screen covering over the materiality of a body in the throes of transition. A year after his book was published, Prosser wrote a palinode criticising his own equation of body, referent and real, and allowing much more space to the irreducible, even unspeakable, agony of transition. But the living flesh of the argument remains, albeit now traumatised and scarred.[72] In a move whose rhetorical violence he was more than ready to acknowledge, Prosser suggested in *Second Skins* that endorsing the performativity of trans, or rather trans *as* performativity (that is trans as something that exposes gender as a masquer-ade for everyone), verges on 'critical perversity'. Judith Butler was the main target, accused of celebrating as transgressive the hovering, unsettled condition which, as Telesford, Jacques and Kaveney testify, places the lives of transsexual people at risk.[73] There is another distinction at work here, a type of emotional division of labour between exhilaration and pain, brashness and dread, pleasure or danger (although these last two were com-bined, i.e. *Pleasure* and *Danger*, in the 1984 feminist anthology which made the case for a non-censorious feminist engagement with sex[74]). Or to put it another way, according to this logic, 'queers can't die and transsexuals can't laugh' – a formula lifted from a commentary on the work of transgender cabaret artist Nina Arsenault, who, while modelling herself on a Barbie doll, manages to cover all the options by performing herself as both real and fake.[75] There are no lengths to which Arsenault has not gone, no procedures she has not suffered, to craft herself as a woman, but she has done this not so much to embody femininity as to expose it, to push it right over the edge. Hence her parody of Pamela Anderson (who is of course already a parody of herself): an 'imitation of an imitation of an idea of a woman. An image which has never existed in nature.'[76]

o o o

The question of embodiment therefore brings with it another. Does the transsexual woman or man, in her or his new identity, count as real? I am genuinely baffled as to how anyone can believe themselves qualified to legislate on the reality, or not, of anyone else, without claiming divine authority (or worse). 'Once you decide that some people's lives are not real,' Jacques cites Kaveney, 'it becomes okay to abuse them.'[77] Placing 'real' women and men above trans 'fakers' is an invitation to violence. In her 2020 article on the gendered politics of pronouns, Amia Srinivasan cites philosopher Talia Mae Bettcher on the 'reality enforcement' that can follow: humiliating outings of the 'true', natal sex, or strip searches and rape.[78] In 1979 Janice Raymond pronounced in *The Transsexual Empire – The Making of the She-Male* that male-to-female transsexuals are frauds (on this issue, female-to-male seem to pose less of a problem even though surgical transition is much harder in their case). They should therefore be outlawed from women-only spaces, since these are spaces which feminists have struggled, after centuries of male oppression, to create for themselves. In today's parlance, Raymond was the first TERF or 'trans-exclusionary radical feminist' (the term used by some transsexual people and by those feminists who oppose her position). For Raymond, male-to-female transsexuals are patriarchy writ large, the worst embodiments of a phallic power willing to resort to just about anything to fulfil itself – hence 'transsexual *empire*'. Although I am sure this was not the intention, I have always found this argument extremely helpful in explaining to students the difference, indeed gulf, between phallus and penis since, according to this logic, the authority and stature of the former would seem to require the surgical removal of the latter. Or, in the words of Jacques, 'The simultaneous characterisation of trans women as unthinking supporters of male roles *and* politically aware enough to convince hardened feminists to admit them is a theoretical clusterfuck, and every critical thinker who let it past them – and plenty did – should be utterly ashamed of themselves.'[79]

Raymond was not without influence. In 1980 she was commissioned by the US National Center for Health Care Technology to write a paper on the social and ethical aspects of transsexual surgery, which was followed by the elimination of federal and state aid for indigent and imprisoned transsexual women and men (Raymond has denied her paper played any part in that decision).[80] A year later, Medicare stopped its coverage for sex reassignment, a rule only overturned in May 2014. That didn't stop the South Dakota State Senate from passing their bill in February 2016 requiring transgender students to use locker rooms and toilets that correspond to their birth-assigned gender, on the grounds that male-to-female transsexuals sneaking into women's toilets were a danger to women. This completely ignores the fact that it is the trans woman forced to use men's toilets and locker rooms who is likely to be subject to sexual assault. Similar legislation – known as the 'Bathroom Bill' – has been proposed in Arizona, Illinois, Kansas, Kentucky, Massachusetts, Minnesota, Mississippi, Missouri, South Carolina, Tennessee and Texas. In a partial victory against the trend, North Carolina reached a settlement in which transgender people could not be prevented from using facilities that corresponded to their gender.

In the UK, Germaine Greer has been perhaps the best-known advocate of this position, or a version of it. She notoriously described male-to-female transsexuals as 'pantomime dames', had to resign from Newnham College, Cambridge, more or less as a consequence (after opposing the appointment of transgender Rachael Padman to a fellowship at the all-women college) and is now the object of a no-platforming campaign.[81] 'What they are saying', Greer responded when the issue arose again in November 2015, 'is that because I don't think surgery will turn a man into a woman I should not be allowed to speak anywhere.'[82] She is being disingenuous. This is Greer in 1989, the quotation courtesy of Paris Lees, one of the most vocal trans activists in the UK today:

On the day that *The Female Eunuch* was issued in America, a person in flapping draperies rushed up to me and grabbed my hand. 'Thank you so much for all you've done for us girls!' I smirked and nodded and stepped backwards, trying to extricate my hand from the enormous, knuckly, hairy, be-ringed paw that

clutched it [. . .] I should have said, 'You're a man. *The Female Eunuch* has done less than nothing for you. Piss off.'
The transvestite [*sic*] held me in a rapist's grip.[83]

'All transsexuals', Raymond stated, 'rape women's bodies by reducing the real female form to an artefact.'[84] With the exception of incitement, of which this could be read as an instance, I tend to be opposed to no-platforming: better to have the worst that can be said out in the open in order to take it down. I also owe Greer a personal debt. Hearing her as an undergraduate in Oxford in 1970 was a key moment in setting me on the path of feminism. But reading this, I am pretty sure that, were I transsexual, I wouldn't want Greer on any platform of mine.[85]

Apart from being hateful, Raymond, Greer and their ilk show the scantest disregard for what many transsexual people have had to say on this very topic. However fervently desired, however much the fulfilment of a hitherto thwarted destiny, transition rarely seems to give to the transsexual woman or man an unassailable confidence in who they are (and not just because of the risk of 'detection and ruin'). Rather it would seem from their own comments that the process opens up a question about sexual being to which it is more often than not impossible to offer a definitive reply. This is of course true for all human subjects. The bar of sexual difference is ruthless but that does not mean that those who believe they subscribe to its law have the slightest idea of what is going on beneath the surface, any more than the one who submits less willingly. For psycho-analysis, it is axiomatic, however clear you may be in your own mind that you are a man or a woman, that the unconscious knows better. 'To the extent that someone insists at the level of their consciousness that they are heterosexual,' stated French-Egyptian psychoanalyst Moustapha Safouan, 'you can be sure that the absolute opposite is being asserted in the unconscious' (hence the 2007 case of Republican senator Larry Craig, who went from endorsing anti-gay legislation to being arrested for cruising in an airport).[86] Freud once stated that, given a primary universal bisexuality, sex is an act involving at least four people. The 'cis' – i.e. non-trans – woman or man is a decoy, the outcome of multiple repressions whose unlived stories surface nightly in our dreams. From the Latin root meaning 'on this side of', as opposed to 'across from', cis is generally conflated with normativity, implying 'comfortable in your skin', as if that were the beginning and end of the matter.[87]

'If transsexuality marks a response to the dream of changing sex,' writes psychoanalyst Catherine Millot in her 1983 *Horsexe – Essai sur le transsexualisme*, 'it is clearly the object of dream-making, and phantasizing in non-transsexuals' (remember Arthur Corbett). Millot has been criticised for pathologising transsexuality, reading it as a doomed attempt to thwart the fact of sexual difference (Bornstein cites her alongside Raymond as one of the worst offenders). Certainly, as a Lacanian psychoanalyst, she believes that it is the role of the phallus to bring the world sexually to heel. But she also knows that it cannot possibly succeed. This patriarchal dispensation is delusional: 'At another level, the phallus is the symbol of the non-sense of desire [. . .] The fundamental reason for the unreason, the derangement, of desire' (although these lines tend not to be quoted).[88] Desire is aberrant, by definition, and heterosexuality is never what it seems to be. If the phallus rules the world, it is also, without knowing it, a bit of a clown (like the emperor with no clothes).

Who, exactly, we might therefore ask – trans or non-trans – is fooling whom? Who do you think you are? – the question anyone hostile to transsexual people should surely be asking of themselves. This is not the same as saying that gender is always a performance since – as anyone will know who has read Judith Butler on abjection and melancholia, that is, post *Gender Trouble* – we are talking about a far more agonising and radical self-deceit. 'The endorsement of heterosexuality', writes Juliet Mitchell, 'can hide the dangers in some of its practices.' So-called normality can be the cover for a multitude of 'sins'. She is recounting the famous psychoanalytic case of the 'vagina man', the subject of an earlier case study by psychoanalyst Adam Limentani, who during intercourse fantasised that he was himself being penetrated, which meant that to have sex was to be unfaithful to himself (he was fucking another woman), and that he could never, psychically, be father to his own child (whose child would it be?). Women can share the same syndrome – a fantasy that their vagina is not really their own but belongs to somebody else – although since they appear to be 'normal', to be fulfilling their biological and lawful destiny, no one would ever guess.[89] Even with the apparently straightest man or woman, there is no telling.

This is a selection of quotes from transsexual narratives, suggesting that as often as not the writers both know and don't know who they are, or even – in some cases – who precisely they want to be:

Some transsexuals are no happier after surgery, and there are many suicides. Their dream is to become a normal man or woman. This is not possible, can never be possible, through surgery. Transsexuals should not delude themselves on this score.

If they do, they are setting themselves up for a big, probably lethal, disappointment. It is important that they learn to understand themselves as transsexuals.

April Ashley, *First Lady*[90]

The '*trans*' prefix implies that one moves *across* from one sex to another. That is impossible [. . .] I was not reared as a boy or as a young man. My experience can include neither normal heterosexual relations with a woman nor fatherhood. I have not shared the psychological experience of being a woman or the physical one of being a man.

Mark Rees, *Dear Sir or Madam*[91]

'I live as a woman every day.'

'Do you consider yourself to be a woman?'

'I consider . . . Yes, yes, but *I know what I – I know what I am* . . . I do everything like a woman. I act like a woman, I move like a woman . . . I know I'm gay and I know I'm a man.'

Anita, Puerto Rican transgender sex worker
interviewed by David Valentine[92]

My body can't do that [give birth]; I can't even bleed without a wound, and yet I claim to be a woman [. . .] I can never be a woman like other women, but I could never be a man.

Susan Stryker, 'My Words to Victor Frankenstein'[93]

I certainly wouldn't be happy with the idea of being a man, and I don't consider myself a man, but I'm not going to try and convince anyone that I'm really a woman.

Jayne County, *Man Enough to Be a Woman*[94]

It had been such a relief for me when I could stop pretending to be a man. Well it was a similar relief not to have to pretend that I was a woman [. . .] I was now a lesbian with a boyfriend, but I wasn't a real lesbian and he wasn't a real boy [. . .] no matter what I bought – I'd look in the mirror and see myself as a man in a dress. Sure, I knew I wasn't a man. But I also knew I wasn't a woman.

Kate Bornstein, *A Queer and Pleasant Danger*[95]

I have a male and female side [. . .] I don't know how they relate [. . .] I had to ask myself: *how trans did I want to be?*

Juliet Jacques, *Trans*[96]

As the oestrogen started to change her body, Jacques felt for the first time 'unburdened by that disconnect between body and mind'. She even wondered whether one day the original disconnect might be 'hard to recall'. But this did not stop her from asking in the same moment: '*What* kind *of woman have I become?*'[97] Soft-spoken and deep-voiced, understated and urgent, Jacques comes across as a woman carrying an ambiguity she does not seem to want, or feel able fully to shed. She is also as keen to talk about Norwich City and the underground music and counterculture scene as she is to tell her tale of transition –

why indeed is it assumed that transition is all transsexual people ever have to talk about? No performance (except to the extent that anyone appearing in public is of necessity performing); no exhilaration (she is one of the few transsexual people I have read or heard willing to explore their own depression); no definitive arrival anywhere. Affirmed and subdued by her own experience, she confounds the distinction, not just between male and female, but also between the emotional atmospheres which the various transsexual identities are meant – instructed might be the right word – to personify. On this matter, the argument, the insistence on playing it one way or another, can be virulent.

The statements I quote are not therefore uncontroversial. Bornstein has been labelled 'transphobic' and picketed by some in the transgender community for refusing to claim male or female gender and for her stance on the issue of women-only spaces: 'I thought every private space has the right to admit whomever they want – I told them it was their responsibility to define the word *woman*. And I told the transwomen to stop acting like men with a sense of entitlement.' 'I give great sound bites on sex,' she apologises to a furious Riki Ann Wilchins, who had invited her to speak, 'but I always fuck up politics.'[98] In a wondrous twist, Paris Lees credits Germaine Greer for guiding her to insight on this matter:

> Greer caused me to question my identity, and form a more complex one. She was right: I am not a woman in the way my mother is; I haven't experienced female childhood; I don't menstruate. I won't give birth. Yes, I have no idea what it feels like to be another woman – but nor do I know what it feels like to be another man. How can anyone know what it feels like to be anyone but themselves?[99]

Not all transsexual people take this position. At the feminist conference 'In Conversation with the Women's Liberation Movement', held in London in September 2013, I sat behind two trans women who objected when the historian Sue O'Sullivan described how 1970s feminism had allowed young women for the first time to explore, to claim as intimate companion, their own vagina. Her account was seen by them as transphobic for excluding trans women, who most likely will not have had that experience in their youth but who are 'no less women' for that. There are trans women for whom, on similar grounds, the words 'vagina' and 'vulva' should not even be used. Trans women have also objected to lines of intellectual enquiry which, they feel, unjustly put their lives under the microscope (in October 2018, fifty academics wrote to the *Guardian* describing how they felt obstructed in their research by transgender activists).[100] But this is not the whole story – nor even half of it. I have become weary of those feminists who leap at such moments to discredit the voices of trans women, without so much as a nod to the historic prejudice and violence against them. That trans people might feel defensive about available vocabularies and what is said about them needs to be understood in context. As Susan Stryker has pointed out, things are said about trans people which, if said about many other minorities, would see print only in the most hate-riddled, white supremacist, Christian fascist rags.[101]

In fact, I would say it is because trans women prise apart the question 'Who is a real woman?' with such pain, because they have been on their very particular journey, that they should be listened to. And not just because it is so manifestly self-defeating for feminism and transgender, two movements fighting oppression, not to talk to each other. For me, trans women have earned their place at the banquet of feminism. They should be welcome at the Ladies' Pond on London's Hampstead Heath, where the decision to allow them entry in May 2019 – after a consultation involving twenty-one thousand people – was met with intense opposition. With strong echoes of Janice Raymond, those who objected repeated the language of violation, characterising trans women as men enacting a charade – pretending to be women, to put it at its most simple – in order to invade women's space.[102] Why, we might ask, are the rare instances when this might occur seized on, as if representative, as if the only story to be told? Excluding transgender women from women-only spaces merely adds to the world's quotient of hatred, which is surely rife enough. Today, the atmosphere surrounding these debates can fairly be described as toxic, as the fundamental aim, which must surely be to see acceptance of trans people, women and men, as an issue of basic rights and freedom, blurs almost beyond recognition. This is writer So Mayer, who remembers visits to the Pond as a little girl, at a time when the shame, pain and complications of her body made her uneasy at being assigned female:

It feels, these days, that even the mallards and moorhens seem to police gender with the beady gaze of their Jesuitical authority. External protestors disrupting a recent Kenwood Ladies' Pond Association meeting about allowing transwomen swimmers to continue using the Ladies' Pond (as they long have) wore the WOMEN ONLY sign from the pond gate around their necks, a gross invocation of slave auctions [. . .] It gives me reservations about the pond as a community; it gives me, literally, a sinking feeling, heavy as lead.[103]

o o o

Another reason why trans and feminism should be natural bedfellows is that male-to-female transsexuals expose, and then reject, masculinity in its darkest guise. This side of the argument is missed by Greer et al., who tend to overlook the fact that if you want more than anything in the world to become a woman, then chances are there is somewhere a man who, just as passionately, you do not want to be. 'I stopped my life living as a man,' Bornstein writes of her father in the prologue to *A Queer and Pleasant Danger*, 'in large part because I never wanted to be a man like him' (coming to terms with his ghost is one of her motives in writing the memoir).[104] One of Nina Arsenault's earliest memories is of boys knifing magazine images of women. 'I know this is exactly what I will be when I grow up.'[105]

In the first half of *Conundrum*, Morris offers the reader a paean to maleness: the feeling of being a man 'springs specifically from the body', a body which, 'when it is working properly', she recalls, is 'a marvellous thing to inhabit [. . .] Nothing sags in him' (never?). But this self-same masculinity, epitomised by an assault on Everest timed to coincide with the Queen's coronation, is 'snatching at air', a 'nothingness', which leaves Morris dissatisfied 'as I think', she concludes, 'it would leave most women'. 'Even now I dislike that emptiness at its climax, that perfect uselessness' (as good a diagnosis of the vacuity of phallic power as you might hope to find). If you are a man, you can spend a lifetime striving for this version of masculinity, never to discover the emptiness and fraudulence at its core. Despite a relatively lowly upbringing in the Welsh countryside, somewhere Morris is, or rather was, an upper-class English gent imbued with the values of his sex and class – the family on the mother's side descends from 'modest English squires'. When Morris sheds maleness, it is therefore a patriotic, militarist identity, with its accompanying imperial prejudice, that she leaves, at least partly, behind: 'I still would not want to be ruled by Africans, but then they did not want to rule me' (though even this does not quite make it to the question of who Africans might want, and not want, to be ruled by). This legacy is hard to relinquish. Released from her 'last remnants of maleness', she returns from Morocco, where she underwent her transition, 'like a princess emancipated from her degrading disguise, or something new out of Africa.'[106] Morris was operated on by Dr Georges Burou, the same surgeon who had carried out the surgery on Ashley in 1960 and one of the first to undertake the procedure. By 1972, the operation was available in the UK, but Morris chose to go abroad when it was made a legal condition that she first divorce her wife, with whom she had fathered five children.

The issue of masculinity is in some ways more present for female-to-male transsexuals. After Brandon Teena was murdered in Nebraska in 1993 along with Lisa Lambert, in whose house Teena was living, and Phillip DeVine, a disabled African American (the basis for the 1999 award-winning film *Boys Don't Cry*), it became a topic for debate whether Teena should be seen as a female-to-male transsexual without access to sex reassignment surgery or a transgender butch who had chosen not to transition.[107] We will never know. What we do know is that he was raped shortly before he was murdered by the same young local boys who, intent on returning him to the body which in their eyes he denied, were also enraged at the success he was having with local girls. 'This case itself hinges on the production of a "counterfeit" masculinity,' Jack Halberstam writes in his in-depth reading of Teena's murder in *In a Queer Time and Place*, 'that even though it depends on deceit and illegality, turns out to be more compelling, seductive, and convincing than so-called real masculinities with which it competes.' For this reason, he continues, 'the contradiction of his body signified no obstacle at all as far as Brandon's girlfriends were concerned.'[108] Indeed it might have been the draw. In the small-town rural America where Teena lived, male crime passed effortlessly down the generations. 'You keep seeing the same faces,' Judge Robert Finn observed to the journalist John Gregory Dunne. 'I'm into third-generation domestic abuse and restraining orders.'[109] He was talking about husbands and lovers whose fathers and grandfathers had appeared before him on the same charges during his sixteen years on the bench. Teena offered the girls 'sex without pregnancy or fisticuffs'.[110] Skylar, the teenager profiled in *Vanity Fair* in 2015, decided not to go for genital reconstruction, not feeling the need to be, in his words, a 'macho bro'.[111] In her attempt to be the man she was born as, Ann Black had served in the Black Watch Regiment for twelve years in Berlin: 'If I didn't join the army, I probably would have gone down the road that would have seen me in jail.' (Black was speaking on the 2015 BBC documentary *Transsexual Stories*.)[112]

What are you letting yourself in for if you choose to become a man? What is the deal? At a key stage of his transition, Raphael says to his analyst Melanie Suchet, 'If I want them to treat me like a guy, I have to be a guy.' 'He is quiet. We are both quiet,' Suchet observes. 'There is a growing sense of unease in the space between us. I sense my body tensing up. Who am I going to end up sitting in the room with?' 'You really think you have to be a misogynist to be recognized as a guy?' she asks him. 'I am afraid that I am going to become a complete asshole,' Raphael replies. 'What if I am this sexist bastard?'[113]

In fact, it turns out that it is only as a man that Raphael can allow himself a form of passivity and surrender which was too dangerous for him as a girl. Slowly over the years the analysis uncovers that as a female child he had been the receptacle of vicious maternal projections and may have been abused by his mother. Becoming a man therefore, amongst other things, allows him to become the girl which, as long as he was lodged in a female body, he could never dare to be. 'I want my body to say, "Here this is Raphael. He's a guy, but he's not only a guy. He's a female guy, who sometimes wants to be able to be a girl."'[114] (Raphael is the patient Virginia Goldner describes as 'the girl who has to be a boy to be a girl'.[115])

o   o   o

Raphael does not welcome the link Suchet proposes between being a transsexual and his childhood abuse, and complains that she is delegitimising and invalidating his experience by analysing it as the disturbed outcome of a traumatic past (although, as should not need stating, trauma is not pathology but history). He is not alone in making this case. Although it is recognised that the incidence of mental disturbance among transsexual people is no greater than among the population at large, transsexual people have to fight the stigma of psychopathology, not least because any sign of it during medical consultation is likely to disqualify them from surgery, where the only narrative that passes is the one that confidently asserts that they have always known who they really are.[116] In 1980, transsexualism (in adolescents and adults) and

Gender Identity Disorder (in children) entered the American Psychiatric Association's *Diagnostic and Statistical Manual of Mental Disorders* (DSM III) – homosexuality had been officially removed from the registry in 1973. The struggle to have these categories dropped in turn, precisely as delegitimising, then runs up against the problem of seeming to imply that all other disorders in the manual legitimately belong there.[117] Gender Identity Disorder was subsequently replaced with Gender Dysphoria, intended to be less pathologising. (Being included in the manual has the 'advantage' of allowing some insurance companies to cover the transition process.)

In *Imagining Transgender*, one of David Valentine's key informants, Cindy, suffers from depression. 'Her history', he comments, '– of child abuse, rape, drug addiction, alcoholism, suppression of feelings – is one that is all too common among transgender-identified people.'[118] And, of course, among many non-transsexual people (the class issue here is glaring). It is the link, balance or causal relation between inner distress and the world's cruelty that is so hard, if not impossible, to gauge. 'How', Goldner asks in her introduction to *Transsexual Subjectivities*, 'are we to distinguish "psychodynamic" suffering from the trans-phobic "cultural suffering" caused by stigma, fear, hatred?'[119] 'I know', writes Jacques, 'there will be difficulties both with things inside my head, and with intolerant people in the outside world.'[120] In response to this ambiguity, and to the misuse of intimate, personal history to run the transsexual person to ground, like the homosexual before, some argue that aetiology or the search for causes should simply be dropped. '[When] it comes to the origin of sexual identity,' New York psychoanalyst Ken Corbett (no relation to Arthur) wrote in 1997, 'I am willing to live with not knowing. Indeed, I believe in not knowing . . . [I am not interested in] the ill-conceived etiological question of "*Why*", I am interested in *how* someone is homosexual.'[121] For me, however, this is a false alternative. Why, in an ideal world – which of course none of us are living in – should the ethical question of how we live be severed from knowledge of how we have come to be who we are? What, we might ask instead, is the psychic repertoire, the available registers of admissible feelings, for the oppressed and ostracised? It is a paradox of political emancipation, which the struggle for transsexual freedom brings starkly into focus, that oppression must be met with self-affirmation and nothing less, as in: 'I have dignity. You will not overlook me.' To vacillate is political death. No second thoughts. There is no room for doubt or the day-to-day aberrations of being human. Jacques describes the intense pressure she felt herself under 'to depict my life as blissful'.[122] At moments I felt I have been watching the range of permitted utterances for the transsexual person narrow into a stranglehold: 'I am discriminated against.' 'I suffer.' 'I am perfectly fine.' 'There is nothing wrong with me.'

I think this might be why, reading transsexual narratives, I often get the sense of a psychic beat missed, of there being parts of the story which do, and do not, want to be told, moments which reach the surface, only to be forgotten or brushed aside in the forward march of narrative time. As though the personal could be a front for the personal, covering over what it ostensibly, even generously, displays (or as Jacques puts it in relation to 'before' and 'after' photographs, having 'the strange effect of masking the process of change as they seem to reveal it').[123] For example, Mark Rees, registered as a girl at birth, was one of twins; his twin sister died at five days old. His parents tried to hide their disappointment when three years later another girl was born – they had wanted a boy – who then turned out, compared with Mark, to be the 'perfect' female child. A male-to-female transsexual who prefers not to be named was identified as dyspraxic as a young male child, born to a mother who had earlier suffered an ectopic pregnancy and who subsequently gave birth to a daughter with no trace of disability who at last fulfilled the parents' dreams. There can be no 'wild' analysis of these histories, but it is hard not to see the shadow of death and an intolerable burden of idealisation fall, along the rigid, relentless axis of sexual difference, across these young bodies and minds. These moments are coercive, but once given their due place, they also increase the options for understanding. They show transsexuality, like all psychic identities, as an exit strategy as much as a journey home.

There is a rage against the original body in many of these stories, especially in the male-to-female narratives I have read. April Ashley, Mark Rees, Juliet Jacques all write of the hatred, revulsion, abhorrence (their words) with which they view their male genitals before surgery – Jacques: 'I just want this fucking thing off my body right now.' After her surgery, she wakes up to the 'horrific realisation': '*It's still there!*' before remembering that another transsexual woman who underwent surgery before her had warned her that this is *the* dream.[124] 'Other forces', writes Lili Elbe in her memoir, 'began to stir in my brain and to choke whatever remnant of Andreas still remained there [. . .] Andreas has been obliterated in me – is dead.'[125] The pre-surgical body is, it seems, ungrievable (Judith Butler writes of 'ungrievable lives', referring to the dead bodies of the enemy in wartime that do not count or matter).[126] Faced with which, New York-based psychoanalyst Avgi Saketopoulou has made it a core part of her clinical engagement with transsexual patients for them to find a way to recognise and mourn the body they are leaving behind (the only basis, she suggests, for a successful surgical transition): 'The body one has needs to be known to the patient, *so that, when necessary, it may eventually be given up.*' For psychoanalysis this is a radical move in itself: 'We have to accept', writes Saketopoulou, 'that when it comes to trans experience it's often the body – and our old theories – that have to cave.'[127] But without some respect for how deep the stakes are, how driven the impulse, the story becomes harder to fathom. It then risks being delivered straight into the arms of the crazy narrative, beyond all human understanding, with consummate and unforgiving ease. Nor do such insights have to undermine the more straightforward tale of a mistake being at last redressed. They are rarely to be found in each other's company, but no one gains from the belief that the two forms of understanding cannot tolerate each other.

In saying this, I realise I am repeating, in psychoanalytic terms, the call made by Sandy Stone as early as 1987, in her famous reply to Janice Raymond, 'The Empire Strikes Back – A Posttransexual Manifesto', in which she writes about having been personally attacked for working at an all-woman music collective. The process of '*constructing a plausible history*', in other words 'learning to lie effectively about one's past', Stone wrote, was blocking the ability of trans people to represent the full 'complexities and ambiguities of lived experience'.[128] The one thing Dean Spade, legal activist and theorist, learns from counselling sessions is that 'in order to be deemed real, I need to want to pass as male all the time, and not feel ambivalent about this.'[129] 'We have', Stone warned, 'foreclosed the possibility of analysing desire and motivational complexity in a manner which adequately describes the multiple contradictions of individual lived experience.'[130] 'Plausible' is the problem. It obliges the trans person, whatever the complexity of experience, to hold fast to the rails of identity. It turns the demand to take control of one's own life, which is and has to be politically non-negotiable, into a vision of the mind as subordinate to the human will (the opposite of what the psychic life of the mind can ever be). And it leaves no room for sexuality as the disruptive, excessive reality and experience it mostly is. I have been struck by how little space for sex so many of these accounts, before and after, seem to offer. Kate Bornstein is one exception (she always pushes the boat out). In discussion with Paris Lees in London in February 2016, her refrain, first spoken loud and clear and then muttered more or less throughout the exchange, was 'sex, sex, sex'. In *A Queer and Pleasant Danger*, she invites her readers, should they be so inclined, to skip several pages near the end of the book where she recounts an intense, in the end personally self-defeating, sado-masochistic interlude. Bornstein herself makes the link back to the operating table. In the prologue, she describes cutting a valentine's heart above her heart as one way of dealing with searing pain. Once one barrier falls, then, if you choose not to keep the lid on, so, potentially at least, do all the rest.

o   o   o

From the middle of this past decade, trans has been everywhere, hitting the newsstands in the US and UK on a more or less daily basis. Not just the most photogenic instances such as Caitlyn Jenner and Laverne Cox, or *The Danish Girl*, or the August 2015 special issue of *Vanity Fair* on *Trans America* (co-edited by *GQ*, the *New Yorker*, *Vogue* and *Glamour*), from which a number of my stories are taken; or Estrella Vázquez, the first muxe (indigenous Mexican transgender) woman to appear on a *Vogue* cover, in November 2019; but also, for instance, the somewhat unlikely sympathetic front-page spread of the *Sun* in January 2014 on the British army's only transgender officer ('An officer and a gentlewoman'); plus the Netflix series *Transparent*; Bethany Black, *Dr Who*'s first trans actress; *EastEnders*' Riley Carter Millington, the first trans actor to play a regular transgender character in a mainstream UK soap opera; and Rebecca Root of *Boy Meets Girl*, the first transgender star of a British television show; or again reports of the first trans adopters and foster carers; or the surge in children seeking gender change, as reported by the London Tavistock Clinic which, together with the Portman NHS Trust's Gender Identity Service, provides the sole gender identity referral programme in the UK. Referrals had risen from 97 in 2009 to 697 in 2014–15. In 2015–16 the number of referrals rose to 2,016, and to 2,519 the following year (although the year-on-year rate of increase had declined during this period).[131]

In relation to this increase, we can watch being rehearsed all the questions I have tried to outline here, now etched over the body of the child. Transgender children in the UK today have the option of delaying puberty by taking hormone blockers, can take cross-sex hormones from sixteen and opt for sex reassignment surgery from the age of eighteen. Cassie Wilson's daughter Melanie announced he was Tom at the age of two and a half (at five he commenced annual appointments at the Tavistock); as soon as Callum King could talk, she said she was a girl, and from two or three years old, she refused to reply if anyone addressed her by her birthname. In 2004, the mental health charity Pace surveyed two thousand young people who were questioning their gender: forty-eight per cent had attempted suicide and fifty-eight per cent self-harmed. 'They kill themselves,' comments Julia's mother. 'I want a happy daughter, not a dead son.' According to a 2016 report, children whose desire to transition is supported by their parents experience developmentally normal levels of depression and only minimal elevation of anxiety.[132] Neuroendocrinologist and psychologist Vickie Pasterski has spoken of the 'improved mental health and well-being of children' who are 'clearly and consistently' supported in their wish to be the other gender (in her TED talk of 2019, Pasterski also described gender as a 'kaleidoscope').[133] Critics of this viewpoint have seized on research studies suggesting that eighty per cent of children presenting with gender dysphoria will not persist with their cross-gender identification as they get older, but the figures are misleading. They are based on a pre-2014 diagnostic criteria of gender variance which did not require children to state that they wanted to be the other gender.[134] Julia could in fact be seen as an example. She likes to ask her female friends at school if they would like to be a boy for a day just to see what it would feel like, and whatever they answer, she retorts, 'I don't have to because I'm both.'[135]

Although many transgender children feel unable to talk to their parents, in some cases the desire for transition seems to come at least as much from the parents and other adults as from the child. One mother in San Francisco was told by the school principal that her son should choose one gender or the other because he was being harassed at school. He could either jettison his pink Crocs and cut his long blond hair, or socially transition and come to school as a girl (he himself, having abandoned the dresses he used to like wearing, had never had any trouble calling himself a boy). She was wary: 'It can be difficult for people to accept a child who is in a place of ambiguity.'[136] At a conference in Philadelphia, attended by Margaret Talbot, the journalist writing about Skylar, one woman admitted that she was the one who needed certainty: 'We want to know – are you trans or not?' 'Very little information in the public domain', comments Walter Meyer, Texas-based child psychologist and endocrinologist, 'talks about the normality of gender questioning and gender role exploration . . . It may be hard to live with the ambiguity but just watch and wait.'[137] 'How', asks Polly Carmichael at the Tavistock, 'do we keep in mind a diversity of outcomes?'[138] What desire is being laid on a child who is expected to resolve the question of transition? On whose behalf? Better transition over and done with, it seems, than adults having to acknowledge, remember, relive, the sexual uncertainty of who we all are.

In February 2019, the difficulty of these questions came to a head at the London Tavistock and Portman Clinic when David Bell, staff governor at the time, wrote a highly critical report suggesting that irreversible blockers and cross-sex hormones were being given far too readily to adolescents without proper assessment of what might be the psychic factors at play; it also reported staff feeling intimidated for raising any such concerns (in February 2020, a review of such treatments was announced by NHS England).[139] The Tavistock rejected the claims as unsubstantiated. Within the available and diminishing resources, the clinic insisted that it was taking due time and care (in turn one governor and five clinicians resigned). *The Times*'s headline described what was going on as an 'experiment on children'; others spoke of children in 'danger', terms surely fuelled by a sexually charged backlash against transgenderism, though this seems to have received no commentary.[140] Some of those interviewed attributed the problem to lobbying by trans pressure groups – Mermaids, Gendered Intelligence and the Gender Identity Research and Education Society – a claim which each of these groups denied (it is not clear why a pressure group that lobbies, as opposed to just protesting, is somehow seen as disqualifying its own claim). It was also suggested that homophobia at school was playing a key part in the desire to transition. Better to be a boy than a lesbian girl who will be the object of bullying and derision. The idea that young people were making such a momentous decision on the basis of a rational calculation of the relative social losses and gains seems somewhat at odds with the idea of them as complex, unconsciously driven and conflicted psychic subjects.[141] Yet again we see the tension between a respect for the inner life and the struggle for freedom. How to keep the former in view while affirming the right to transition in a still mostly hostile world? In this context, being 'trans affirmative', a phrase used with reference to doctors and patients responding to a trans child, appears to be seen as a bad thing. Although it is also true that psychoanalysis affirms nothing, its sole aim being to bring to light, without judgement of any kind, whatever resists passing over the threshold into human consciousness.

The increase in trans children may be amongst the most striking, and for some shocking, new developments. But transgenderism is not new. Far from being a modern-day invention, we might instead see it more like a return of the repressed, as humans slowly make their way back, after a long and cruel detour, to where they were meant to be. One of my friends, when she heard I was writing on the topic, said we should all hang on in there as the ageing body leads everyone to trans in any case (I told her she had somewhat missed the point). The Talmud, for example, lists six genders (though Deuteronomy 2:5 thunders against cross-dressing). 'Strange country this,' Leslie

Feinberg cites a white man arriving in the New World in 1850, 'where males assume the dress and duties of females, while women turn men and mate with their own sex.'[142] Colonialists referred to these men and women as *berdache*, setting wild dogs on them, torturing and burning them. In pre-capitalist societies, before conquest and exploitation, Feinberg argues, transgender people were honoured and revered. Feinberg's essay, 'Transgender Liberation – A Movement Whose Time Has Come', first published in 1992, called for a pan-gender umbrella to cover all sexual minorities. It was the beginning of a movement. The first *Transgender Reader* stretched back into the medical archive and then forward into the 1990s: the activism of that decade was the ground and precondition for the engagement, defiance and manifestos which, in the face of a blind and/or hostile world, the *Reader* offered. These volumes are vast, they contain multitudes, as if to state: 'Look how many we are and how much we have to say.' We need to remember that these bold and unprecedented interventions predated by more than two decades the phenomenon known as 'trans' in popular culture today.

At the end of his foreword to the first *Transgender Studies Reader*, Stephen Whittle lists as one of the new possibilities for trans experience opened up by critical thought the right to claim a 'unique position of suffering'.[143] But, as with all political movements, certainly any grounded in identity politics, there is always the danger that suffering will start to become competitive, a prize possession and goal in itself. The example of the *berdache*, or of Brandon Teena caught in a cycle of deprivation, shows, however, that trans experience can never be – without travestying itself and the world – its own sole reference point. However distinct a form of being and belonging, it has affiliations which stretch back in time and across the globe. I have mainly focused on stories from the US and UK but transgender is as much an issue in Tehran, where trans people have had to fight against being co-opted into an anti-Islam agenda that makes sexual progressivism an exclusive property of the West (in fact sex reassignment was legalised following a personal diktat from the Ayatollah Khomeini); and in India, where the *hijras* (men who wear female clothing and who renounce sexual desire by undergoing sacrificial emasculation) are recognised and esteemed as a third sex.[144]

Like the tales of anybody's life, all the accounts I have discussed are caught in histories not of their own choosing. These stories also need to be told. Ashley, for example, a child of the Second World War, finds herself in a circle that includes Joseph Goebbels's sister-in-law, who inherited his wealth and property after he and his wife murdered their six children and then killed themselves. 'I was to find', Ashley writes of their growing friendship, 'that most people had secrets – some in their own way, as delicate as mine.'[145] The link between them goes deeper than she might have realised. Magnus Hirschfeld, sexologist, founder of the first gay rights organisation and an early advocate for transgender people, was described by Hitler as the 'most dangerous man in Germany' – the Nazis destroyed his institute and burned his research collection (a chapter from his book on transvestites is included in the first *Transgender Reader*).[146] The war is her story. Ashley's mother, who hated her and would regularly pick her up by her ankles and bang her head on the floor, worked at the Fazakerly bomb factory, losing much of her hair and all her teeth from being around TNT (one of her friends burned up from the exposure and died). 'As a child growing up during the Second World War,' Ashley begins her memoir, 'I was generally badly treated by everybody.' She was also abused as a child by the husband of a couple the family were very close to.[147]

In 2016, Caitlyn Jenner voted for Donald Trump, despite his party's dire record on LGBT issues, although she has now revoked her support and says that it was a mistake.[148] She was, however, being consistent with her own past. As the world-renowned athlete Bruce Jenner, Bissinger recalls, she had once been a weapon in the Cold War: 'Mom and Apple pie with a daub of vanilla ice cream for deliciousness in a country desperate for such an image.' 'He had beaten the Commie bastards. He was America.' In an article in the *New York Times* in 1977, Tony Kornheiser described Jenner as 'twirling the nation like a baton; he and his wife, Chrystie, are so high up on the pedestal of American heroism that it would take a crane to get them down.'[149] Who is to say that something of that dubious political aura has not made its way, like a lingering scent, into the phenomenon that is Caitlyn Jenner today?

For Jayne County, by contrast, being a trans person was her ticket to the other side, what she calls the 'flaming side of gay life'. One of the most successful plays she wrote and performed, *World – Birth of a Nation*, included a scene of John Wayne giving birth to a baby out of his anus (not how most people like to think of the birth of a nation, or indeed John Wayne). The *Village Voice* gave it a rave review. County was brought up in a right-wing rural America of Biblical prophecy where the Beast took the shape of a United Europe with Germany at its head (Germans would apparently unite with the Arab nations against the Jews). She credits Bill Clinton with fostering an atmosphere in the 1990s where the US was 'wide open for people of all variations of sexuality, including trannies of every shape, size and colour'. But already by the

middle of the decade when she returns from the Berlin underground, the conservative right were beginning to take power,
and the Democrats, with their liberal stand on abortion, gay
rights and prayer in school, were seen as disciples of Satan 'by
Baptist bastards, Republican retards and right wing Christians'
(no change there then). 'This', she asserts, 'just makes me more
defiant than ever. I'll get more and more outrageous just to
freak them out.'[150] These are the last lines of her book (she had
previously been planning to retire to her home community,
dress in more subdued fashion and settle down). We do transsexuality no favours if we ignore these contexts, throwing the
transsexual person onto the sidewalk of history. As if, after all,
trans reality is merely a tale which transsexual people are telling
themselves, cut off in an isolation ward, leading a strange life
all of their own (which must surely increase the voyeurism, the
over-intense focus from which they suffer).

o   o   o

In 1998, the Remembering Our Dead project was founded in
the US in response to the killing of Rita Hester, an African-
American trans woman who was found murdered in her
Massachusetts apartment. By 2007, 378 individuals had been
registered and the numbers are climbing today. Such com-
memoration is crucial but also risky. There is a danger, Sarah
Lamble writes in the second *Transgender Studies Reader*, that
'the very existence of transgender people is verified by their
death': that transsexual people come to define themselves as
objects of violence over and above everything else (the violence
which afflicts them usurping the identity they seek). 'In this
model,' Lamble continues, 'justice claims rest on proof that

one group is not only most oppressed but also most innocent', which implies transsexual people could never be implicated in the oppression of others.[151] Apparently, the list of victims in the archives gives no information about age, race, class or circumstances, although the activists are mostly white, the victims, as already noted, almost invariably people of colour, so when the images are juxtaposed, they reproduce one of the worst tropes of colonialism: whites as redeemers of the black dead. At the core of the remembrance ceremony, individuals step forth to speak in the name of the dead. What is going on here? What fetishisation – Lamble's word – of death? What is left of these complex lives which, in failing fully to be told, fail fully to be honoured?

We are witnessing a sea-change, although this does not make the news. Now the call has gone out not only for the necessary cataloguing of violence against transsexual people and its recognition as oppression, but for this also to become part of a wider, more politically expansive vision. We are witnessing, I would tentatively suggest, the first inkling that the category of the transsexual might one day, as the ultimate act of emancipation, abolish itself. In one of her best-known essays, 'Women's Time' (1981), psychoanalytic and literary theorist Julia Kristeva argued that feminism, and indeed the whole world, would enter a third stage in relation to sexual difference: after the demand for equal rights and then the celebration of femininity as other to the norm, there will come a time where the distinction will finally disappear as a metaphysical relic of a bygone age. In *Transgender Studies Reader 2*, Morgan Bassichis, Alexander Lee and Dean Spade call for a trans and queer movement which would set its sights above all on the neoliberal agenda which exacerbates inequality, consolidates state authority and increases the numbers of incarcerated across the globe. So far the official US response to the regular and fatal violence meted out to trans and queer people has mostly been hate crime legislation, tacked onto defence bills, which increases prison sentences and strengthens local and federal law. In 2007, the Employment Non-Discrimination Bill was gutted of gender identity protection. Bill Clinton – *pace* Jayne County – may have liberalised the sexual life of the nation, but on his watch, the 1996 Personal Responsibility and Work Opportunity Reconciliation Act limited aid and increased penalties for welfare recipients. Viewed in this light, Clinton becomes, like former UK Prime Minister David Cameron, a leader whose social liberalism, including on sexual matters, is what allowed him to drive through brutally unjust economic policies with such baffling ease (Cameron will now go down in history as the leader who precipitated the disastrous Brexit referendum of 2016).

'Critical trans resistance to unjust state power', the editors of the *Reader* introduce their essay, 'must tackle such problems as poverty, racism and incarceration if it is to do more than con-solidate the legitimate citizenship of the most privileged seg-ments of trans populations.' Once you talk about privilege, then everything looks different. Bassichis, Lee and Spade are calling for transsexuality and queer to become part of a movement, no longer geared only to sexual minorities, but embracing the wider, and now seen as more radical, aim of abolishing prisons in the US. 'We can no longer', they state, 'allow our deaths to be the justification of so many other people's deaths through policing, imprisonment and detention.'[152] There is also a link here to the issue of sexual assault and the legal fightback against it which was the topic of Chapter One – amongst those accused of such crimes, the number of men of colour is, in the words of Harvard Law School professor Janet Halley, 'creepily high'.[153] No struggle for emancipation can afford to be co-opted by discriminatory and death-dealing state power. The regular and casual police killings of black men on the streets of America come most immediately to mind as part of this larger frame in which, Bassichis et al. are insisting, all progressive politics should be set. A reality and demand given renewed urgency by the May 2020 police murder of George Floyd in Minneapolis in the midst of the pandemic, to which we must add Breonna Taylor from Louisville, Kentucky, the mother of an eight-year-old, killed in March while sleeping in her home. In the *Transgender Reader*, Bassichis and fellow editors are given the last word (theirs is the final essay in the book).

Death must not be an excuse for more death. Obviously it is not for me to make this call on behalf of transsexual people. I have written here from the position of a so-called cis woman, a category which I believe, as I hope is by this point clear, to be vulnerable to exposure and undoing, to say the least. Today, transsexuals – men, women, neither, both – are taking the public stage more than ever before. In the words of the *Time* cover story in May 2014, trans is 'America's next civil rights frontier'.[154] Since then, the world has moved back and forward, sometimes, it seems, almost in a single step. On 12 June 2020, Trump added to his vicious anti-trans agenda the removal of transgender civil rights in relation to health care.[155] Three days later, in a surprise victory, widely welcomed as a partial riposte to Trump, the US Supreme Court invoked the civil rights law of 1964 to guarantee trans, gay and lesbian people full protection at work.[156] Healthcare, work protection, civil rights, incarceration – each one resonates in the fight for trans freedom. Perhaps, even though it does not always look this way on the ground, trans activists might – just – be in a position to advance what so often seems impossible: a political movement that tells it how it uniquely is, but without exclusivity, without, in a world of rampant injustice, separating one struggle for equality and human dignity from all the rest.

3

TRANS AND SEXUAL HARASSMENT

The Back-story

In the mid-1890s, at the very beginnings of psychoanalysis, Sigmund Freud encountered a young girl up a mountain in the Hohe Tauern, one of the highest ranges of the eastern Alps. From her dress he decided she was not a servant girl, though she had served Freud dinner in the inn where he was staying; more likely, he surmises, the landlady's daughter. Still, she is the only woman among five in his early work, *Studies on Hysteria,* endowed with no title – 'Fräulein', 'Frau' or 'Miss' – but simply named as 'Katharina' (though Freud cites himself addressing her as Fräulein twice during his account). Slowly but surely, he unravels a tale of sexual abuse by her father, corrected by Freud in a final footnote from the 'uncle' who had been referred to throughout: 'The girl fell ill as the result of sexual attempts on the part of her own father' (the German *'den sexuellen Versuchungen'*, meaning 'sexual temptations' but translated somewhat flatly by Strachey as 'sexual attempts', suggests seduction, but no less abuse).[1] It is the shortest, simplest case in the book, perhaps in all of his work. At the very least it seems fair to believe, as Freud himself observes, that he could only fully hear Katharina because, in terms of geography and class, he had got away from it all. One analyst working today has suggested Freud made a fatal error in coming down from the mountain, literally and metaphorically, where his thoughts, the encounter between 'physician' and 'patient', were so free-wheeling, fluent and clear.[2]

Mostly, however, analysts have tended to agree that it is only when Freud moves from this moment – the violation it narrates – into the more complex realm of unconscious fantasy that psychoanalysis proper will begin. And yet the tale of traumatic violence and its memory shadows the rest of Freud's writing, and if anything widens its reach. It is at the heart of his final great work, *Moses and Monotheism*, as the founding trauma of a people, his own, who have buried the memory of the violence that constituted them as a people (by suggesting there were two men named Moses, the first one murdered by his own followers, Freud places an act of violence at the origins of the social tie).[3] It is at the heart of the second topography, or scheme of the mind, where the concept of the death drive erupts from the traumatic entrails of the First World War.[4] And it is, I suggest, no less present in Freud's late account of female sexuality, which tracks the ruinous path into normality for the wild, active little girl, for whom all the options of the world were originally and gloriously open. She must subdue her nature in the service of the species, a path he describes in the 1931 paper on the topic as – his words – 'damage' or 'catastrophe'. (The German *Umsturz* has the military connotation of a putsch or coup d'état to which her active drives fall 'victim': *geschädigt*).[5] This makes 'normality' a distortion and/or sacrifice. As I say to my students, contrary to one influential critique, psychoanalysis never states: It is not true that you were abused, or: Whether you were abused does not matter. Rather that the ills of the human condition are generic: Even if you were not abused, *it still matters*.

'The requirement [. . .] that there shall be a single kind of sexual life for everyone', Freud writes in *Civilisation and Its Discontents*, is 'the source of serious injustice' ('*Ungerechtigkeit*').[6] For a woman, Freud comes close to saying, normality in and of itself is an injury from which no girl will fully recover. The news that she is a girl will arrive, not as biological revelation from inside her body as the traditionalists insist against Freud, but more as a form of psychic puzzlement, when the outside world inflicts its demand that she crunch her sexuality into shape. It is a type of invasion. In her 1930 paper on masochism in the mental life of women, deemed by feminist critics to be one of her most offensive, psychoanalyst Helene Deutsch makes the remarkable observation that it is through masochism – fantasies of castration or rape at the hands of the father – that a woman enters her sexual role (in another paper she talks of the 'primary traumata' of the little girl's early sexual life). She is not, as I see it, licensing misogyny and assault but making the far more startling suggestion that violence against women is psychically inscribed at the heart of a woman's journey into her sexual 'destiny'.[7] As if on cue, nearly a century later, Melanie Suchet's trans patient Raphael, discussed in Chapter Two, will explain that only if 'boy' is written on his body will he be able to avoid this threatening internal scenario and allow himself to be penetrated without dread. 'To be vulnerable from the position of a girl', Suchet comments, 'is too dangerous.'[8]

One of the boldest images from Freud's early work is his description of the hysterical patient to whom he briefly alludes in his 1908 paper 'Hysterical Phantasies and their Relation to Bisexuality', who pressed her dress up against her body with one hand (as a woman) while trying to tear it off with the other (as a man), which he reads as a scenario of rape.[9] And shorn of its chauvinistic underpinnings – something I always recommend wherever possible in relation to Freud – the concept of castration is best read, surely, as indicating the brute reality of sexual difference, the axe that must fall for both boy and girl to be frogmarched into their allotted sexual place. We might call it the savagery of sexual difference in a so-called civilised world.

So, psychoanalysis begins with the abuse of the landlady's daughter by her father, a coercion that then spreads into the very heart of the norm – of what is being asked *of* women by asking them to *be* women – and from there across the warring land-scape of nations. As trauma widens its remit, one of its hardest and most persistent calls, it turns out, is that girls should be girls, and one of psychoanalysis's most radical propositions, for me to this day, is that no girl or woman ever simply is. Sexual abuse, we might then speculate, has as one of its aims to mark the woman's body, to destroy any ambiguity on the matter. (The 'corrective' rape of lesbians reported in post-apartheid South Africa would just be one expression of what is somewhere always at stake.) And it goes without saying, if sexual abuse is designed to remind the girl or woman of what she is, it is also intended to confer on the mostly male agents who carry it out a similarly fraudulent authority about a masculinity no less unsteady and unconvinced by itself. Abuse could be described as male per-formativity in its degenerate mode: 'I am a man.' It is a form of policing. 'Pain', writes Sara Ahmed, 'involves the violation or transgression of the border between inside and outside, and it is through this transgression that I feel the border in the first place.'[10] Ahmed is the feminist philosopher who resigned from Goldsmiths University in London in 2016 over its failure to deal adequately with issues of sexual harassment. Abuse, I read her as saying, lays down its fraudulent law, violating the border and enforcing it in one and the same breath.

Behind the issue of sexual harassment, therefore, lies, barely concealed, the vexed question of sexual difference. Blood

brothers, as one might say. And the question of sexual difference, which Freud acknowledges as 'interminable' in his late
work, brings us back to the voices of trans people. 'Everyone',
writes Kate Bornstein, 'has to work at being a man or a
woman' but 'transgender people are probably more aware of
doing the work.'[11] Despite the recent attention to trans experience and the real shift in public consciousness, such an idea
remains anathema to many (no surprise for psychoanalysis,
which knows that change at the level of conscious life is never
enough). Or even an abomination, an 'impossible breach in
the normality of life, like a sudden vicious murder' – words
used by Esi Edugyan in *Washington Black*, one of the novels
shortlisted for the 2018 Booker Prize, to describe two porpoises
joined in utero, foetuses sharing a single body: miracle and
monstrosity, both.[12] Indeed, for such a way of thinking, the
very idea of 'work' in relation not only to trans but also non-
trans identity – Bornstein is nothing if not inclusive – would
be as abhorrent as it is senseless. 'If you want a country with
sixty-three genders, vote Clinton,' read one tweet on the night
of the 2016 US election. 'If you want a country where a man is
a man and a woman is a woman, vote Trump.'[13]

To which we might add, 'If you want a harasser in the White
House, vote Trump' – which is of course exactly what happened, as it turns out not only in the White House but also
on the Supreme Court, both of them with bluster and without
apology. When Brett Kavanaugh, then nominee to the Court,
testified in his defence against the allegation of sexual assault
by Christine Blasey Ford – an assault she experienced as life-
threatening at the time – I know I was not alone in hearing
his words as one of the most brazen and panicked displays of
male entitlement on record, with no awareness, or at least not

at the time, that it was this self-same version of masculinity that inculpated him and makes him unfit for office.[14] Trump's statement that now everyone could see why he had nominated Kavanaugh had an irony of which he too was manifestly unaware. At the height of the 2016 election campaign, Rudy Giuliani agreed on CNN that Trump's 'pussy grabbing' remarks had delivered a picture of sexual assault that was 'really offensive on a basic human level' (although it did not stop him a few years later from wading in on the side of Kavanaugh). Trump is reported as responding to his 'treachery': 'Rudy, you're a baby! They took your diaper off right there [. . .] When are you going to be a man?' (The title of Bob Woodward's book from which that quote is taken is *Fear*).[15]

Of course feminists have been calling out this fraudulent, dangerous version of masculinity for ever. As I was first writing this chapter, I came home one evening to an email from a complete stranger from Pennsylvania reminding me and thanking me, with reference to the drama unfolding in the Supreme Court, for these words I had written decades ago about Virginia Woolf: 'What interested Woolf was patriarchy not as untrammelled authority, but as a form of raging – authority gone frantic because it is losing its grip.' To cite Hannah Arendt once more, it is illegitimate and/or waning power that turns most readily to violence. 'The ego' of the narcissistic patient, writes analyst Benjamin Margolis, 'is unstable, shifting in outline, unsure of its functions, and insecure in relation to the external world.'[16] He was writing in 1983, but he could just as well have been describing the beyond-crass masculinity of Donald Trump. We could say that both trans experience and abuse are in touch with the injustice of sexual difference, to which the first responds with a cry for freedom, the second with unmitigated terror.

From abuse to the myth of masculinity and femininity in a pure unadulterated state – psychoanalysis, I suggest, was the first to make the connection, which trails from one end of Freud's work to the other. Psychoanalysis is, therefore, one of the places we need to go to understand the fraught and potentially generative line that runs back and forth between sexual harassment and trans experience. My basic proposition is that, psychoanalytically speaking, they are the flip sides of the same coin, or even, in the domain of the unconscious, one and the same thing. Or to put it another way, for a culture not unduly sympathetic to psychoanalysis – and some would say the hostility is getting worse in an increasingly commodified world – the fact of abuse and the increasing visibility of trans experience, as they clamour more loudly for our attention, together constitute the return of the psychoanalytic repressed. Returning here to the voices and stories from which I have learnt most, my aim is to open up the dialogue, to get them to talk to each other.

o o o

The real name of Katharina in the Alps was Aurelia Öhm-Kronich. In fact, this case, contrary to Freud's own suggestion, is not simple at all, and its complexity still resonates today. Katharina was suffering from attacks of suffocation, from dizziness, from the feeling of a weight crushing her chest. 'I always think I am going to die.' She is hallucinating a face which, it will emerge, is the face of her abusive father, a face whose terrifying contortions are due not solely to lust, but also to rage: 'He kept threatening he would do something to me; and if he caught sight of me at a distance, his face would get distorted with rage and he would make for me with his hand raised.

The face I always see now is his face when he was in a rage.'[17] This face condenses sexual power and vengeance; the suffocation experienced by Katharina shows her as the quarry of both. In fact the revelation of abuse comes late – or late-ish since the whole story emerges, somewhat unbelievably, in the course of one brief afternoon stroll. And, when it does, it is a cause of 'astonishment' to Freud. What Freud starts by looking for and first elicits from Katharina – though he also admits this is pure guesswork – is a more recent memory when she caught her father with her cousin, Franziska, and then told her mother. It is this that precipitated the break-up of her family and her father's wrath. Wrongly, Freud believes this later memory to be the source of all her troubles because it confronts her with the full truth of what she had experienced at the hands of her father, but barely understood, those several years before. 'I had found often enough', he states, 'that in girls [hysterical] anxiety was a consequence of the horror by which a virginal mind is overcome when it is faced for the first time with the world of sexuality.'[18] On 30 May 1893, the year of *Studies*, Freud wrote to Wilhelm Fliess: 'I see quite a possibility of filling another gap in the sexual aetiology of the neuroses. I believe I understand the anxiety neuroses of young people who must be regarded as virgins with no history of sexual abuse.' Sexuality, he wrote, was 'coming closer and closer', a background of things 'seen or heard and only half-understood'. This letter, the editors comment, is the first hint of sexual seduction in Freud's thought.[19] Katharina's story comes part way, but only part way, in support. She is indeed horrified, she can barely catch breath, but whether this is the outcome of the early abuse, of her later-dawning, fuller understanding of sexuality, or of her father's vicious rage is unclear – most likely all three.

For me this case contains all the traces of the drama that will erupt in the form of abuse in our times, indicating at one level that not much has changed. A father abusing his daughter, making her feel her life is at risk, both in the act – think Christine Blasey Ford – and in the repercussions when she dares to speak. 'We'll keep that in reserve,' Katharina's mother responds to the revelations of abuse by her daughter. 'If he causes trouble in the Court, we'll say that too' (we can only hope that they would get a better hearing than likely today).[20] At the same time, in his somewhat gauche attempts to theorise this moment, Freud introduces concepts which will progressively take up their central place in the account of human sexuality to come – deferred action or 'afterwardness', in which the mind takes time to fully register what confronts it, and the primal scene through which the child mentally stages a sexual act which remains beyond their full knowledge. For psychoanalysis, sexuality is bound to the time of the unconscious, and is first registered by the psyche as a staged drama before anything else. (Already we can see in outline Judith Butler's idea of the performative dimension of human sexuality, the idea that the sexual identities we assume only work if, like puppets, they are made to enact themselves.[21])

The question becomes – what does the discovery of human sexuality, as pleasure and/or danger, do to the human mind? Freud will progressively downplay the fact and extent of abuse, as he will relinquish the idea of the sexual innocence of young girls, but in this earliest of his cases, another insight seems to me to be struggling to be born. Sexuality is anguish. It first erupts in another place – *ein anderer Schauplatz* (Freud's term for the unconscious). There is something in sexuality that evades our mental grasp. Acknowledging that much might, however, be a first step in avoiding its worst outcomes – a sexual identity which brooks no argument and subjects the other to unremitting power: whether in the shape of fathers who abuse their daughters, or anyone who asserts, in the teeth of all the evidence, that there is no problem, that as far as human sexuality is concerned, the world is exactly as it should and always will be; above all, that in the realm of sexual matters, we all know exactly who we think we are. Trans experience of course tells the other story. Which is why I see it as no coincidence that the two realities – sexual abuse and trans – have erupted into public consciousness at more or less exactly the same time.

It is worth recalling the disturbance that these early ideas provoked. Freud had thrown a spanner into a version of sexuality, as graced and enforced by God and his servants, that persists, in all its numbing coerciveness, to this day. He had added an unnameable dimension. Track this a little further, and we then find that the issue of harassment rears its head once more in the earliest days of psychoanalysis. Dr T. D. Savill was a London-based physician and pathologist, working at the start of the new century when Freud's ideas had just begun to circulate (like Freud, he had also translated the *Clinical Lectures* of the eminent neurologist Charcot at the Salpêtrière Hospital in Paris, where Freud first encountered hysteria as a young doctor). Savill was one of the three members of the Medical Committee set up in 1908 at the London West End Hospital for Diseases of the Nervous System, Paralysis and Epilepsy, to adjudicate the charges brought against Ernest Jones – a key figure in the history of psychoanalysis who was Freud's close colleague and would become his first biographer – in response to allegations of sexually inappropriate behaviour towards one of the young female patients in the hospital's care. The girl complained that Jones raised sexual matters during their conversation; Jones responded that he had been encouraged to do so, more or less to test out Freud's hypothesis, by one of the physicians on the case. He resigned from the hospital and left the UK for Canada under a cloud the following year.[22]

At this stage in his career Jones was known in psychoanalytic circles for his minimal grasp of Freud's views on the place of sexuality in the aetiology of the neuroses (if anything he seems to have alluded to these views to get himself off the hook). Savill, on the other hand, was up to speed and rejected them completely. For Savill, writing in *The Lancet* in 1909, hysterical disorder was precipitated by physiological alterations in the brain, by vasomotor or vascular change. Refusing to acknowledge this reality, he argued, psychoanalysis was needlessly and destructively calling 'into activity [. . .] the dead memories of a sexual past', reviving emotional 'shocks' related 'directly or indirectly to sexual matters' and thereby placing the patient and the physician at risk: 'there is a good deal of danger', he writes, 'both to the patient and to the physician in undertaking such investigations and such a line of treatment.'[23]

What is being said here, if not that a therapy which invokes past trauma is no better, in some ways worse, than the original trauma itself? ('Hazardous', 'harmful', 'wholly unjustifiable'.) 'Shock' is eloquent, a concept first borrowed by Freud from Charcot, who used it to describe the shocks to the nervous system which he saw as the cause of hysteria. Walter Benjamin, the German Jewish philosopher, gives the concept an added political dimension when he lifts it straight from Freud to describe the mind stunned by the crushing modernity of the city streets: sexuality and rampant capitalism both rendering the psyche defenceless. Savill's vocabulary is telling: it is the medical establishment itself which becomes the 'virginal mind' overcome with 'horror' in the face of sexuality. As if psycho-analysis were a form of assault – playing fast and loose with the bodies and minds it is meant to cure.

As is now known, the case of Jones is not aberrant or exceptional. Abuse will track the profession in ways surely unanticipated by Freud, even though, for some, his analysis of his own daughter, Anna, is felt to have been inappropriate and left a legacy of misjudgement in its train. In her powerful book *Mortal Gifts – Death and Fallibility in the Psychoanalytic Encounter*, Boston-based psychoanalyst Ellen Pinsky has recently argued that sexual misconduct is more or less endemic to psychoanalysis. At the very least, it is latent to the 'Olympian delusion' of mastery which nestles inside the psychoanalytic scene. Against any such delusion, the task of the analyst, she suggests, is to allow fallibility and death, including the mortality of the analyst, into the consulting room, as the sole true way to abrogate her or his own powers. Nor does a recourse to selflessness, or putting the interests of the patient first, guarantee the avoidance of harm: 'The more the therapist believes in an heroic capacity for selfless service to the patient,' writes Pinsky, 'the more he's conceptualised as above being a subject himself, the greater the danger of erasing the line that keeps the patient safe.'[24]

Self-effacement is, then, the other face of tyranny: even, she elaborates, 'a visitation as bull or swan or eagle'.[25] I was struck by that bull, swan, eagle, harsh visitants from the fields, waters and skies (each one drawn from the ravages of Zeus, also the perfect evocation of abuse). Perhaps those early physicians had a point. Calling up the shock of human sexuality places us all in mortal danger. As well as everything else it is capable of doing, sexuality threatens. Provided we add that the greatest threat of all stems from the belief that sexuality is your possession, that brandishing sexuality – 'pussy grabbing', as one might say – exempts you from human failing, as opposed to exemplifying it in its worst guise. An abuser in the White House is as predictable as it is frightening, because it brings to life the fantasy of sexuality as unqualified power. 'Fantasy' is key. For Juliet Mitchell, such men would fall under the category of 'male hysteric', another figure from early psychoanalysis which, she suggests, has been lost, though never more in need of recognition than today.[26] ('I might have been too emotional,' Kavanaugh said later about his own testimony, as if he himself, without explicitly acknowledging it, was trying to head off the slur.) As I understand it, to such a fantasy of power without limit everything creative in psychoanalysis is opposed. We need, then, to hold on to two insights, even if in today's calling out of harassment they appear at times to be at odds with each other. First, most obviously: sexual abuse is real, whether from fathers, therapists, academics, presidents, Supreme Court judges. The claimant must be heard – the clarion call of #MeToo. Trump's public mockery of Blasey Ford's testimony, to the jeering approval of his Mississippi audience – they chanted 'Lock her up!' – plus his later dismissal of the charges as a hoax tells us how far on this basic premise we still have to go (needless to say, additional accusations brought against Kavanaugh from his student days made no difference).[27] And then: sexuality is aberrant. It is no man's servant.

o o o

In one sense that election-night tweet – 'If you want a country with sixty-three genders, vote Clinton. If you want a country where a man is a man and a woman is a woman, vote Trump' –

was right. Sexual difference, in its accredited version, and trans experience belong in different worlds (a hardening of the arteries versus an opening of the pores). And yet, it is not of course true that for a transsexual person, sexuality falls outside the remit of the law. Indeed, this issue has moved centre stage in debates, at times virulent, on transgender issues in the UK. In January 2016, the House of Commons report *Transgender Equality* found that the medical certificate required for legal registration of a new gender pathologised transsexuality and was 'contrary to the dignity and personal autonomy of transsexuals'.[28] In response, a consultation on reform of the 2004 Gender Recognition Act was commissioned and published in July 2018. The proposed new Act would make legal recognition of a transgender person no longer dependent on medical sanction but on self-declaration by the person concerned. In June 2020, Boris Johnson shelved the changes indefinitely via a press announcement, doubtless thinking he could avoid controversy by slipping the issue under the wire of the pandemic.

This idea of self-declaration has uncanny, and no doubt unintended, resonances with French psychoanalyst Jacques Lacan's formula for psychoanalytic training – '*l'analyste ne s'autorise que de lui-même*' – almost untranslatable but which roughly means: 'the analyst takes his or her authority from her or himself alone', or 'only the analyst can authorise her or himself as analyst' – a progressive and ultimately failed experiment that came in response to a psychoanalytic training virtually unaltered since 1923.[29] In relation to transgender, what is striking about the proposed legal move is that, as with Lacan's experiment, the law is more or less proposing to do away with itself. On this matter, the UK could not be further from the US, where, as we saw in Chapter Two, the Trump administration has proposed to define transgender subjects legally out of existence.

The proposed change in UK law was by no means received by the trans community as an unequivocal blow for freedom. Medical certification may well be an affront to a trans person's dignity and autonomy, but it also can be the sole basis, in the US for example, on which medical insurance for the transition process can be secured. But the divisions also go much deeper. Out of the many objections to the legal proposal in the UK, one, from inside the trans community, stood out for me. In a letter to the *Guardian* in May 2018, a group of trans signatories argued that a line can and must be drawn between a trans person who has undergone surgery and one who has not. The proposal, they write, 'blurs the distinction between us and transgender people who remain physically intact'.[30] For the signatories, the risk is that 'male-bodied people', including sexual fetishists, will use the Act to demand access to women-only spaces. Clearly they do not consider such women to be 'real' women – 'male-bodied' is the giveaway. They do not, however, reproduce the worst version of this argument: that, by invading women's spaces, male-to-female transsexuals are the worst embodiments of phallic power (they themselves would not be immune from such a charge).

Their fear is not groundless. In September 2018, male-to-female transgender inmate Karen White, a paedophile with a history of grievous bodily harm and multiple rapes, sexually assaulted fellow prisoners after she had been transferred to New Hall, a women's prison in Wakefield, West Yorkshire (she was subsequently sentenced to life imprisonment). The Ministry of Justice issued a statement that, before any such transfer, past history of this kind will henceforth be taken into account.[31]

We need, however, to be wary of the publicity afforded by such examples. Examples such as White's, stated Jenny-Anne Bishop from the transgender rights group Transforum, are rare.[32] Most often the violence flows the other way. Trans subjects, we know, are regularly the objects of sexual violence (a fact which those objecting to the Gender Recognition Act barely, if ever, mention). Trans women are routinely targeted in male jails, as they are when forced to use men's toilets. Instead, the argument that trans women in women's facilities are a threat to other women has the upper hand. As we have already seen, it has been inscribed with renewed venom into legislation across the US under Trump which, flouting – indeed courting – the danger faced by trans women in men's facilities, insists that trans people must use the toilets corresponding to the gender in which they were born.

What struck me about that *Guardian* letter's phrasing – that the proposal 'blurs the distinction between us and transgender people who remain physically intact' – are those words 'physically intact'. Genuine transition, it suggests, relies on the insignia of mutilation or bodily harm. Only a body inscribed with the mark of sexual difference is real. Trans identity must be based on a wound. The law seeks to suspend itself in the domain of sexual life. The response is to summon a version of sexual difference grounded in pain. Nor is this logic wholly absent from another, no less eloquent, side of this debate. Kate Bornstein is one of the trans activists from whom I have learnt most about the idea of a trans life, not as crossover, but as a seemingly endless plethora of sexual behaviours and forms. Rather than bringing her journey to an end, undergoing male-to-female surgery opened the path to sexual infinity. Her memoir, as we saw, begins with her cutting a valentine's heart into her chest

above her own, an act she herself links to her gender reassignment surgery.[33] But for Bornstein, the wound grounds nothing
in terms of sexual difference. Instead it – sometimes painfully –
intensifies the sexual possibilities on offer (the pages on
sadomasochism which she advises her reader to skip if they so
choose). And as we saw in Chapter Two, Bornstein has also
stated publicly – to the anger of others in the trans community –
that people should be free to invite who they want into their
private spaces, and that trans women who object should 'stop
behaving like men with a sense of entitlement'.

I know that the idea of a self-inflicted or freely chosen
wound is one of the main causes of revulsion towards trans
people in the so-called straight or 'cis' world ('How can they?'
is the refrain; 'How can we not?' the reply). This too has been
a challenge to psychoanalysis. For Melanie Suchet and Sandra
Silverman, in their complex, open-minded and profound rendering of working with trans patients, the prospect of their
patients undergoing full surgical transition represents a crossing point, one which they both, as analysts, felt, at least to
begin with, unable fully to countenance.[34] Although in the last
chapter, we also encountered analyst Avgi Saketopoulou, who
sees her primary clinical task with patients undergoing surgical
transition as being to help them find a way to acknowledge and
mourn the reality of the body they are leaving behind.[35] But disquieting as this prospect undoubtedly seems to many, might it
be that these acts simply bring to the surface of consciousness,
or enact in Technicolor, a violence latent for all of us, as Helene
Deutsch describes it, in the way that sexuality unconsciously
organises itself? 'The word sex', writes André Green in his 1973
essay on the neutral gender, 'is thought to come from *secare*:
to cut, separate.' Once united, the two sexes had to be split

asunder: 'Where there is a difference,' Green continues, 'there is a cut, a caesura.'[36]

Barely a century ago, the idea that we all harboured in our unconscious the residues of a bisexual polymorphous perversity was unassimilable to most (another reason why Freud's move from abuse to unconscious fantasy can hardly be read as him playing safe or trying to restore his credibility with the establishment). After all, it is surely fundamental to psychoanalysis that the most troubling components of sexual life are something we all would be better off recognising hidden inside ourselves. To put it at its most simple, psychoanalysis, as I see it, presents us – presents the world – with two unassailable propositions: things are harder than we would wish, and we are all weirder than we like to think we are. Both of course carve through the pretensions and iniquities of our present neoliberal world, which pretends that, if you only try and buy hard enough, perfection is on offer for all. In the words of Moustapha Safouan in his book on post-Oedipal civilisation, 'there is nothing as remote from sexuality as capital.'[37]

Granted, the cut is not a wish shared by many. Unless perhaps in some of our dreams. To recall one of the striking moments encountered by Vanessa Grigoriadis while researching US campus sexual harassment: the student who explained how he had come to understand that women's so-called rape fantasies are not real because 'men don't want their penises cut off but dream about it anyway' (somewhat unbelievably, he was one of the most sympathetic male students whom she met in the course of her investigation).[38] Lacan once stated that, in the case of the hysteric, the membrane between ego and unconscious is wafer thin, thereby allowing us to glimpse what usually remains invisible. Perhaps, then, by placing the *agon* of sexual difference in full light, the trans world is speaking a truth on behalf of everyone. At the very least, trans discourse brings to the surface of consciousness the damage and injustice at the heart of the norm, something which the trans community experiences perhaps more acutely than most. In the words of Susan Stryker:

> A gendering violence is the founding condition of human subjectivity; having gender is the tribal tattoo that makes one's personhood cognizable. I stood for a moment between the two violations, the mark of gender and the unlivability of its absence. Could I say which one was worse? Or could I only say which one I felt could best be survived?[39]

We know that trans existence is a life-or-death matter: the murder rate of transsexual people is significantly higher than among the non-trans population and is on the rise, as is the rate of suicide and attempted suicide. 'Everyone needs to vote on November 6 as if lives depend on it,' LGBT activist Diego Sanchez of PFlag National stated just before the 2018 US midterm elections, in response to Trump's proposal to abolish the legal existence of transgender people, 'because they do.'[40] In his essay in the first *Transgender Reader*, Dean Spade cites a male-to-female transsexual addressing the therapeutic profession at a time when clinical screenings were obligatory: 'What right do you have to determine whether I live or die?' (The article is called 'Mutilating Gender'.)[41] 'We have been raised', Audre Lorde wrote in her 1981 paper 'The Uses of Anger', 'to view any difference other than sex as a reason for destruction.'[42] She was of course referring to differences of age, class and race – above all of race. We seem, in the worst sense, to have come a long way since then. Today violent racism is still with us, while sexuality has become one of the most violently contested realities of the modern world.

At opposite poles of the political spectrum, abuse and transgender confront us with the most disturbing dimensions of human sexuality (a bit of a stand-off, it would seem). On condition that we recognise, as Freud began to in the Alps, that these aspects of sexuality are not supplements to human sexuality but reside at its very core. In their starkly different ways, abuse and transgender both alert us that our sexual arrangements are not innocent. To believe otherwise is truly to return to the era before Freud. Sexuality is tarred with the brush of violence, the phantom limb of the normality we are all so blithely and deceptively meant to share.

In the course of his life, not least faced with the darkness descending over Europe throughout the 1930s, this was an issue by which Freud became increasingly preoccupied, scrambling his best attempts at lucidity. In his second attempt to map the human mind, he divided psychic life between Eros and destructiveness, as if they were opposites or poles apart from each other. This dualism came close on the heels of the binaries of his first mental schema – reality versus the pleasure principle, or ego- versus object-drives – but like all great binaries, this one too will fail. 'The satisfaction of [the] destructive impulses', he concedes in his renowned exchange with Einstein on war, 'is of course facilitated by their admixture with others of an erotic and idealistic kind.'[43] Far from subduing the worst of the human heart, Eros can fuel its cruelty. Freud has come a long way from his 1914 essays on war where he had more confidently proposed that the erotic impulses were best suited to keeping the destructiveness of the ego at bay. But it is now 1932. Freud is struggling to preserve Eros as unequivocal force for the good in an increasingly perilous world.[44] Hitler will be elected to the chancellery the following year.

I do not wish to run the line from Trump to Hitler – as Michael Moore does in *Fahrenheit 11/9*, which at one point grafts Trump's voice onto footage of Hitler addressing a Nazi rally. I do not think today we are (yet) dealing with fascism, though Brazil, Hungary, Turkey, India are getting close. But the two leaders surely have in common their ability to mobilise and license as sheer pleasure the closely guarded obscenity of the unconscious. Think of the boost given to the Republican voting base in the immediate aftermath of the Kavanaugh affair: the 'virtual mob that has assaulted all of us in the course of this process', observed Republican majority leader Senator Mitch McConnell after the confirmation, 'has turned our base on fire'.[45] Only brute sex was rousing enough, whereas tax cuts and a 'booming' economy up to that point had provoked indifference. More simply, I would suggest that if we do not recognise Eros as fuelling the present danger, we will be ever more powerless to halt it. We might of course be powerless anyway.

o o o

So where's the hope? At moments, surely, it is to be found in the consulting room where the most angular defences, the walls that obstruct a life lived, fully and painfully, can at moments, for both patient and analyst, fall away. Although even in the consulting room, the powers of resistance to the inner world know no bounds (another mournful discovery of Freud's later working life). Still, for many years, as a kind of opening gambit, I would ask students who were sometimes hostile to psychoanalysis to identify the places in the wider culture where a woman could freely state that she is not a woman, or a man that he is not a man, with no danger of being mocked or carted away. One of my favourite moments in the whole of Freud's work is a 1915 footnote to *Three Essays on the Theory of Sexuality*: 'Thus, from the point of view of psychoanalysis the exclusive sexual interest felt by men for women is also a problem that needs elucidating ['*ein der Aufklärung bedürftiges Problem*'] and is not a self-evident fact that is ultimately of a chemical nature.'[46] '*A problem* that needs elucidating' – imagine for a second going to your doctor to say you had a problem, that you were only attracted to members of the opposite sex (come to think of it, this might be no bad thing).

The answer to my question, I suggested, was therefore first psychoanalysis, then, and no less, literary writing – where as a matter of course a woman author is licensed to enter without inhibition the bodies and minds of her male characters, and the reverse. Like the speech of the analytic patient, literature is also best registered with the free-floating attention of what Freud once described as the 'third' ear. So my final turn in this chapter will be to literary fiction, a constant companion throughout this book. Not least because, with renewed conviction after reading the 171 submissions to the Man Booker Prize in 2018, literature remains for me the place where, as part of the ever more urgent bid to change the world, the unthinkable can still be written and heard: 'unspeakable things unspoken', in Toni Morrison's words. At the very beginning of psychoanalysis, in *The Interpretation of Dreams*, Freud insisted that the poets and writers, to whom he so often appealed, had got there before him, that they were the only ones who really knew what he was talking about. Along similar lines, Lacan once stated that only students and literary enthusiasts could possibly grasp the concept of the unconscious because, unlike scientific and historical positivists, they were not fazed by the idea that one word, one sign, one gesture, one fragment of a dream – in a potentially infinite trail of significations – could, in the very same moment, mean more than one thing (like sexual identity, one might say).

Two novels from that 2018 prize shortlist push trans and abuse in the reader's face, as incontrovertible truths of our world. Each of them does so in a way that talks back to, while also going beyond, what I have been trying to explore in this chapter. So first, what if Oedipus were trans? What if Tiresias entered the body of Oedipus, usurped his skin? This is the wager of *Everything Under* by Daisy Johnson, who tried to write this novel three times and destroyed each version before lighting on this final tale.[47] *Everything Under* mainly takes place on the waterways of England, on canals and barges, a life that dips beneath the solid surfaces of the world. It describes the anguished search of a young woman, Gretel, for her mother who, after they had first lived together on the rivers, disappeared from her life when Gretel was thirteen. This it turns out is a pattern. The mother had abandoned her first baby, also originally named Gretel, who the narrator manages to trace to her adoptive family, where she was renamed Margot. They have not seen her since she left, suddenly and with no explanation, as a young teen. Slowly we discover that the family's next-door neighbour, a male-to-female trans soothsayer who was the only person Margot had ever trusted as a friend, had told her to leave after warning her of a threatening Oedipal fate. In flight from her destiny, Margot begins her own transition and becomes Marcus, shedding all the insignia of the sexual identity she has been made to fear (an added twist to Oedipus's no less failed attempt to spare himself).

What happens next is of course predictable. Lighting on the river, Marcus is taken in by an old man who, unbeknownst to him, is his father (still mourning the disappearance of his baby and her mother years ago) and whom Marcus accidentally kills. Appalled at his deed, he moves downriver, where he finds the second Gretel and her mother, with of course no awareness of the affinity between them. He and his mother become lovers. Somewhere the mother knows, as she was bound to discover, that he had once been a girl, and also – perhaps – that this is her own first, long-lost child. Since Marcus has to this point been portrayed as a young teen, the novel at least raises the question as to whether the mother, knowingly or unknowingly, has sexually abused her own daughter (an idea that had not occurred to any of us on the Booker jury till the chair shockingly raised it at our final meeting).

Believe it or not, *Everything Under* is an easy, often pleasurable read, in which every step of this tortured and tortuously complicated plot, like the waters on which it is set, beautifully and effortlessly flows. This is a retelling of Oedipus for our time. It lifts the figure of Tiresias – the man-woman, struck blind for telling the truth of women's sexual pleasure – from the fringes of the classic tale and into the heart of the story, where the sexual positions of male and female are muddled beyond recognition or repair. In doing so, the novel scuppers once and for all any normativity which, in the psychoanalytic reading, this mythical tale – despite the catastrophe to which it unfailingly attests – is somehow intended to embody as a lesson for us all. It is a kind of imaginative gambit: if Oedipus were trans? What does this do to the story in which we, as Western subjects, have been asked to recognise ourselves? 'All we ever deal with in analysis, whether therapeutic or so-called training analysis,' writes Safouan, 'is with Oedipal dramas that have failed' ('*des Oedipes échoués*' – the French plural is impossible to translate).[48] Whatever our sexual affinities and identities, this novel suggests, there is no comfortable place to be sexually in the modern world. It sets this wager in the disconsolate and yet also magic society of misfits, fringe beings whose marginal existence is intensified by, but by no means reducible to, the theme of trans experience which runs so unerringly through the book (the novel offers a cautionary tale which is as fully social as it is sexual).

Everything Under is agonising. In the end, Marcus drowns, the mother hangs herself. Johnson thus sees off the common charge that trans people are living lives of commodified delusion which pit the idea of free choice in the realm of sexual identity against psychic history and unconscious pain. Trans experience is another way of being, but – as it appears in pretty much all the trans narratives I have discussed so far – like Oedipus, it is in no way a happy solution to everything. To imply as much would align trans subjects with the false perfectibility of a consumer culture in denial of itself, laying on them a no less unjust burden of happiness.[49] As if anyone, trans or non-trans, fully resolves their unconscious sexual lives, a tempting prospect to which Freud himself was by no means immune. In his 1924 paper 'The Dissolution of the Oedipus Complex', he suggests that masculinity emerges when Oedipal desire in the male child is dashed to ruins and all traces obliterated. As more than one commentator has pointed out, he is not only offering a false image of masculinity shorn of conflict (heaven help us), but, since nothing ever perishes in the unconscious, he is also going against every fundamental insight of psychoanalysis itself. I read Johnson's novel as setting us two tasks – allow for the fluidity of the world, trans freedom as we might call it. But recognise that we are not masters of our destiny. Keep the difficulty of the psyche in sight.

o o o

To end, then, with the 2018 winning novel, Anna Burns's *Milkman*, whose acclaim and notoriety have been boundless. Readers have been stunned by its prescience in relation both to #MeToo and to the question of the Irish border which has been so central to the fight over Brexit in the UK, more than once bringing the negotiations to a complete standstill. In fact Burns finished her novel in 2014, before either of these hit the news, and then took four years to find a publisher. *Milkman* has been heralded as *the* novel of the #MeToo generation. It is a story of 'encroachment', a term which I would like to see pass into the common lexicon. 'Encroachment' is visited by a paramilitary in his forties on the eighteen-year-old narrator whose unbroken voice tells the tale. He is sinister, invasive, threatening, and even without physical contact, he undermines her body and soul. The novel therefore offers the definitive riposte to those who try to take down the #MeToo movement by arguing that anything other than a violent sexual assault, for which the plaintiff must scour the whole world and her own body for forensic evidence, does not count (Evangelist Franklin Graham and various Republicans have claimed that because Kavanaugh did not actually rape Blasey Ford, but merely assaulted her and then stopped, his 'honourable' character was untouched).[50] In fact, violent assault against women is also present from the first page of this novel, which opens: 'The day Somebody McSomebody put a gun to my breast . . .'[51] In *Milkman* there are no proper names. The voice that tells the tale is 'middle sister', the encroacher is simply Milkman, which in fact he is not. The novel thereby becomes generic for any sectarian world, even as its place and time are unmistakeably 1970s Belfast in the midst of what has come to be known as 'The Troubles'. For those who thought the Troubles ended with the Good Friday Agreement of 1998, the question the novel raises, the question Brexit has raised with its threat of a new hard border between the North and the South, is whether indeed the Troubles ever truly went away (one of the worst potential disasters of Brexit is what it will reignite in Ireland).

Milkman uses the ambient violence of the city to press his case. He follows her, haunts her, shows up out of the blue in places he should not even know she might be, threatens to have her 'maybe-boyfriend' killed. He first pulls up alongside her in a van, when she is walking and reading, an activity she cherishes as her bid for freedom in the midst of a violence-riddled world. As Christopher Bollas argues in his paper on incest, what abuse destroys above all is the victim's capacity for reverie.[52] Until Milkman appeared on the scene, this young girl thrived on her ability to time-travel in her mind (she reads mainly nineteenth-century books because, for good reason, she does not like the twentieth century). Milkman does away with it all. 'My inner world', she says in the middle of the story, 'had gone away.' He inflicts her with 'numbance', another word which needs to pass into the general lexicon. 'He'd infiltrated my psyche [. . .] This felt an injustice.'[53]

In fact her love of reading while walking has always been taken as the sign of a risky independence of spirit. She is branded crazy or 'beyond the pale' by the surrounding community, which now begins, on the basis of the odd sighting –

i.e. no evidence whatsoever – to churn the rumours that she is Milkman's mistress. Any respect she had once enjoyed starts to wither as she is hemmed more and more tightly into a suffocating psychic and social world. 'I came to understand', she comments, 'how much I'd been closed down, how much I'd been thwarted into a carefully constructed nothingness by that man.' Any sexual pleasure she took in her young life is destroyed. Her 'maybe-boyfriend's' physical attentions, which she had craved (no 'maybe' about it), she starts to find 'repulsive'.[54] Every attempt she makes to describe what is happening to her to anyone else, including her mother, meets with disbelief and a ratcheting up of the sexual slurs against her. Only her own voice telling her tale, its extravagant resilience and humour in the face of all odds, saves her. This is interior monologue as talking cure. It is also a tribute to the power of writing to foster resistance and to create a fairer world.

To circle back to where this chapter began: this is a young girl who is roughly the age of Katharina when she met Freud in the Alps at the turn of another century. We might, therefore, be tempted to lament how little has changed from then to now in terms of the abuse of young women. And yet, *Milkman* also allows us to marvel at the resourcefulness which such women, in their struggle to be heard, are claiming for themselves today. In one key scene she is confronted by a cohort of paramilitary groupies who abhor the 'secure, safe bubble, the nine-to-five, decent bubble' in which women are meant to want to exist, and who relish the potentially fatal dramas of their own freely chosen lives (Eros and Thanatos together). At the same time, finding herself cornered, she begins to feel she is being inducted into a shocking form of sexual knowledge which has come too soon (remember Freud on Katharina). 'These women', she laments, 'were threatening to present sex to me as something unstructured, something uncontrollable, but could I not be older than eighteen before the realisation of the confusion of the massive subtext and the contraries of sex should come upon me and uncertain me?'[55] Alongside 'encroachment' and 'numbance', the book surely takes the prize for the use of 'uncertain' as a verb: 'should come upon me and *uncertain me*'.

As with Katharina we are faced with the question of what the shock of sexuality does to the unprepared mind; we are also faced with the possibility – which, I have suggested, becomes no less central to psychoanalysis – that sexuality is the one thing for which the mind will never be fully prepared. In *Milkman*, the violent reality of abuse and the 'uncontrollable' 'contraries' of sex subsist side by side on the page: 'my irreconcilables', 'those uncontrollable irrationalities', 'the ambivalences in life', or 'the weird something of the psyche', to pluck another of my favourite phrases from the book.[56] As we have already seen, it is surely one of the biggest challenges of our time to call out the first without feeling one has to silence or sacrifice the complex, uncertain truth of the second. How to fight for the rights of women, the dispossessed and powerless, or anyone who is discriminated against and, at the same time, demand a more psychoanalytically understanding world.

Milkman is not about trans experience, but, sure as hell, it is about borders. Everyone in the novel is living on the border, a border policed by bombs, blasts, killings and atrocities which seem to be as indiscriminate as they are precise in their aim. No one escapes. As I watched this border reap its deadly effects for the duration of the novel, it was impossible not to think of that other border, that of gender, which is today manned no less fiercely and with no less lethal effect. So, to repeat that earlier question, where's the hope? How to think differently? Or in the words of our narrator, 'how to live otherwise?' In her self-blinding world, just having such a thought is enough to drive anyone mad. But 'This was not schizophrenia,' she insists. 'This was living otherwise. This was underneath the trauma and darkness a normality trying to happen.'[57] ('Normality' is one of my least favourite words but in this case I welcome it.)

Which brings us, finally, to the 'wee sisters'. I challenge any reader of this novel not to fall in love with the wee sisters, who, in their wildly funny embodiment and spirit, allow us to wend our way back to the idea of trans. Philosophers, lexicographers, classicists, multi-linguists, political thinkers and satirists way before their time, there is no limit to their zany, precocious 'thirst for knowledge and for intellectual adventure' (they are seven, eight and nine). To call them genius is not going too far. They are for me the heroines of *Milkman*. Near the end of the novel, they announce to middle sister that any cuts and contusions she might see on their bodies are the result of them dressing up in the clothes of a grown-up couple – renowned for having abandoned their four teenage sons in Belfast to take up an international dancing career – and prancing around in the streets. And 'not just in our street but in every street of the area – even across the interface road in defender areas, for I'd had a peek in and noticed them one day as I was walking and reading my way into town.'[58]

The wee sisters have quite simply flouted the borders, flying in the face of the world's worst defences. Like transgender subjects, they have transformed the border into something halfway between a joke and a screaming question about itself. 'They had achieved that outstanding status of straddling the sectarian divide,' middle sister pronounces, brimming with admiration, 'a feat probably meaning nothing outside the sectarian areas in question, but which inside equated with the most rare and hopeful occurrence in the world.'[59] This is of course 'play', which British psychoanalyst D. W. Winnicott famously ascribed to the transitional spaces of the human mind as the source of all creativity (transitional to trans would be a whole other topic).[60] When we find these spaces – in the session, on the page, in the streets – they surely deserve to be ranked among 'the most hopeful occurrences in the world'. Even if they have never felt more hard to achieve and so urgently needed than in the abusive times in which we are living.

4

FEMINISM AND THE
ABOMINATION OF VIOLENCE

When I was working on Sylvia Plath more than twenty years
ago, I discovered that, almost simultaneously, the distinguished
critic and biographer Diane Middlebrook was working on
Anne Sexton. On completion of our books – we shared at least
one train ride on our way to readings across England – we were
both in a state not only of exhilaration, but also shock. Both
poets had required us – a requirement each of us experienced as
an exclusive, personal invitation – to immerse ourselves in what
it meant to suffer as a woman in the 1950s and early 1960s. But
they did so with such vigour and riotousness as to deprive us
of, or at least exceed, the most obvious narrative of subordination which you might expect such suffering to evoke. Sexton
and Plath were angry – they had a lot to be angry about. But
in both cases, the anger did not block, as it so easily can, the
complex internal reckoning which as women they conducted
with themselves.[1]

If this central reality united our projects and fuelled our
respect and love for the two poets, it also overrode what was the
most striking discrepancy between our experiences in writing our
books. At every turn, I – like so many Plath scholars – had been
obstructed by the Plath estate, Olwyn and then Ted Hughes,
who hated my book and insisted it was a biography, which it
wasn't.[2] They felt I had transgressed the boundary between literary criticism and life story, a life story whose true version they

knew themselves, without reserve, to be in sole possession of. Diane's problem was the opposite. If anything the Sexton estate had been too co-operative, flooding her with what today we call 'too much information', whether in the form of the release by Sexton's analyst of the tapes she made after her sessions, at his instruction, to prevent her obliterating them from her mind, or in the revelations by Sexton's daughter, pressed upon Diane, of being intimately invaded by her mother.

If that moment has stayed with me, it is because of the ethical dilemma we both faced. Neither Sexton nor Plath lived to see the birth of second-wave feminism. It is tempting, and not wholly inappropriate, to think that if they had enjoyed the advantage of feminist insight and solidarity they might both have been alive today. Certainly, their anguish as women was rooted in the perils of domesticity and child-rearing, which would become the target of that wave of feminism's opening and loudest complaint, and for which they were amongst the first to craft the poetic language, to give it voice. But that was not all. Sexton was an emotional hurricane. At the centre of that hurricane there is a tale of domestic abuse – by her father, possibly by her beloved aunt, later of her own daughter. As this story migrates across genders and generations, there is no neat version to be told. It swallows up too many people, regurgitates through Sexton's life and writing (such regurgitation is of course recognised today as the hallmark of abuse). Plath, for her part, felt herself trapped by a desire which drowned her in its intensity and left her stranded on the far shore of a domestic ideal which was a travesty of her own fierce and expansive imaginative reach.

What we shared was our respect for the psychic risks that being a poet allowed both these women to take, together with the conviction that the energy with which they both did so is more important than the fact of their deaths. 'What I most want to know about women in the past' is not, therefore, as legal theorist and feminist Catharine MacKinnon put it in an article of 2006, 'how did she die?' My question is rather: 'how did she live?'[3] And I also want that question to be able to gather whatever it may find, however messy and unexpected, on its path. It is a central proposition of this book that feminism has nothing to gain by seeing women solely or predominantly as the victims of their histories.

If I quote MacKinnon it is not just because she represents a viewpoint from which I dissent, nor because I know there are many feminist scholars who draw productively from her work. It is also because, as she has most loudly and consistently alerted us, the times we live in oblige any feminist to reckon with the increasing, or certainly increasingly visible, violence against women that we are witnessing today. In March 2014, Gayatri Spivak gave the Juliet Mitchell lecture in Cambridge on rape both as a – if not *the* – crime of identity and as the 'indestructible unconditionality' of the human: 'We are – male and female – raped into humanity,' she stated. 'This is the human condition.'[4] This did not of course stop her from naming rape as the crime against women which it mostly is. In 2018, Congolese doctor Denis Mukwege was awarded the Nobel Peace Prize alongside Nadia Murad, a young Yazidi woman who had been captured by Isis as a sex slave. At the Panzi hospital in Bukavu in the eastern DRC, where he worked, fifty thousand or more rape victims had been treated over the past twenty years.[5] Feminism today cannot *not* talk about such crimes, whether rape as a war crime, female genital mutilation, or domestic abuse. To select just some out of a steadily increasing barrage of statistics and reports from the past decade: A survey of forty-two thousand women across the twenty-eight EU member states, released in March 2014, found violence against women to be an extensive human rights abuse throughout Europe, with one in three women reporting some form of physical or sexual abuse since the age of fifteen. The UK had the joint fifth-highest incidence of physical and sexual violence.[6] In April 2019, a World Bank special report, *Gender-Based Violence (Violence Against Women and Girls)*, described such violence as a 'global pandemic'.[7]

According to women's rights activists in the UK, rape has effectively become 'decriminalised'.[8] The UK Crown Prosecution Service's 2019 Annual Report on violence against women and girls reported slumping prosecutions for the crime, which fell by thirty-two per cent in the previous year to a ten-year low, despite the number of reports of rape doubling over six years to almost six hundred thousand.[9] It has since emerged that tens of thousands of cases may have been dropped because of secret targets implemented by the Home Office, which encouraged prosecutors to take 'weak cases' out of the system. In a statement to the *Law Society Gazette*, the Crown Prosecution Service admitted that such targets were inappropriate and may have acted as a 'perverse disincentive' in relation to cases that were not 'straightforward' (a term that could be applied to almost all rape cases given the problem of witnessing, as we saw in Chapter One).[10] In September 2019, the action group End Violence Against Women launched a legal challenge against the CPS over its failure to pursue rape cases due to a covert change in policy.[11] In August 2020, in the face of incontrovertible evidence of a fall in prosecutions to their lowest-ever level, Boris Johnson announced new conviction targets for rape cases – blundering in as usual, as if setting a target in this domain will solve the problem (a bit like past commitments, which have proved useless, to reduce waiting lists for the NHS).[12] Again the problem is by no means exclusive to the UK. In the US, an October 2018 report announced that less than one per cent of rapes and attempted rapes end up with a felony conviction.[13]

Most of the violence against women is carried out by a current or former partner, with nearly one in four women in relationships reporting partner abuse in the EU survey. In 2019, domestic killings of adults in the UK reached a five-year high, with three quarters of the victims being women (ninety-four per cent of all women killed by men in 2018 knew their assailant).[14] In February 2020, it was reported that the number of women killed by a current or former partner had surged by a third to a fourteen-year high.[15] A report in October 2018 concluded that more than forty per cent of all homicides in fifteen US states involved women murdered by intimate partners. The gender 'balance' is glaring. Between 2003 and 2012, sixty-five per cent of women victims of violent crime in the US knew their assailants, as compared with thirty-four per cent of men: 'A staggering portion of violence against women is fatal,' the Center for American Progress reported in 2014, 'and a key driver of these homicides is access to guns' (the article was entitled 'Women Under the Gun').[16]

Disturbingly, the incidence of abuse against women does not seem to decline with a rise in equality. Violence against women in Denmark, Finland and Sweden, each praised for their gender equality, outstrips the UK rate. Central to the problem is that domestic abuse is one of the least reported crimes.[17] As we saw in the chapter on sexual harassment, refuges are full of women who have, until a final breaking point, found it impossible to tell their stories or to leave a violent home. The statistics are therefore, as always, misleading, perhaps in the case of such abuse even more so than usual. We rarely hear of the obstacles that litter the path between sexual violation and language (where it is not just a matter of finding the courage to speak) – compounded of course by the institutionalised refusal of those in positions of authority to listen. All of this was massively aggravated during the pandemic, when lockdown trapped women with abusive partners in their homes (a global phenomenon which stretched from the UK and US to China and Spain). Though emergency funds were eventually released by the UK government, the crisis should also be seen as one of their own making, since it was government cuts that had reduced the number of refuges and safe havens in the first place. Even today, the effect of those cuts is still being felt, as refuges with free places are turning away migrant women who do not speak English because they no longer have the funds for translators.[18]

These statistics are chilling. But I do not want to carry on listing all the forms of global violence against women, as it is one feminist tactic to do. Feminism is not served by turning violence into a litany, as if the only way to make us think about such violence is by verbally driving it home. When we look at the picture of a woman who died on 9/11, the first and only feminist question should not be, to my mind – MacKinnon again – 'who hurt her before?'; nor, when we look at the bones of a woman from an ancient civilisation, do I want us to see her, and them, as, inevitably, broken.[19] Such a strategy does not help us to think. It is a central argument of this book that violence against women is a crime of the deepest thoughtlessness. It is a sign that the mind has brutally blocked itself. The best way for feminism to counter violence against women, I argue throughout these pages, is to speak of, to stay and reckon with, the extraordinary, often painful and mostly overlooked range of what the human mind is capable of. The title of this chapter is 'Feminism and the Abomination of Violence'. Violence for me is part of the psyche. A crime to be detested and cast off, but also something which one feminism, in the very force of that gesture – however necessary, however right at one level – then itself repudiates, renders unthinkable, shuns beyond the remit of the human (precisely abominates). At that moment, feminism finds itself replicating that part of the mind which cannot tolerate its own complexity. It thereby becomes complicit with the psychic processes which lead to the enactment of violence itself. For me it then becomes crushing – or to put it more crassly, cuts off its nose to spite its face.

o   o   o

I take my idea of thoughtlessness from Hannah Arendt, to whom – along with Melanie Klein – I appeal here as offering a new way of thinking about violence against women in our time. Following and anticipating Sexton and Plath, both Arendt and Klein suggest that there is something about the process of human thought that is often insufferable, not least because thinking acts as a brake on the fantasy that the world is there to be mastered, and thereby prevents that dangerous fantasy from doing untold damage by running amuck or away with itself. For Arendt, violence is a form of radical self-deceit – or 'the impotence of bigness', to recall her evocative phrase – which punishes the world, punishes women, we can say, for the limitations of human power (the gender implications of her phrase 'impotence of bigness' are surely glaring even if she does not fully draw them out herself).[20] To quote again what is for me one of her key statements: 'What I propose, therefore, is very simple,' she writes at the beginning of *The Human Condition*, her meditation on the conditions of human existence in the modern world; 'it is nothing more than to think about what we are doing.' As often with Arendt, such simplicity is deceptive. Thinking as process has to be fought for. It is threatened from all sides, by modern pseudo-knowledge which leaves us at the mercy of every gadget which is technically possible, 'however murderous it is', and by the muteness of sheer violence: 'Only sheer violence', she writes, 'is mute' (in the realm of politics, all other forms of behaviour are transacted in words).[21] For Arendt, therefore, the mind is under siege, and thinking is the only restraint against murderous know-how and the cruel silence of sheer violence which mutes both itself and its victims.

Arendt wrote *The Human Condition* in the 1950s (it was published in 1958) – the moment of course of Sexton and Plath – when the power of death-dealing technology had reached new heights: from industrial genocide to the atom bomb. 'The technical development of the implements of violence', she writes in her later 1970 study *On Violence*, 'has now reached a point where no political goal could conceivably correspond to their destructive potential or justify their actual use in armed conflict.' The 'suicidal' development of modern weapons involves 'a massive intrusion of criminal violence into politics'.[22] Behind this analysis is her indictment of the myth of progress which the United States, where she arrived as a refugee from Nazism in the 1930s, believed itself to embody beyond any other nation. For Arendt, 'Progress' is a ruthless illusion, a self-fulfilling prophecy, which leaves itself no escape clause other than the increasingly violent enactment of itself. In other words, so-called progress leads directly to the burnt bodies of Vietnam.

Arendt is not, to put it mildly, most famous for her contribution to feminism, any more indeed than Melanie Klein, on which more later, although the case for Arendt's contribution to feminism has been made strongly by scholars such as Seyla Benhabib and Mary Dietz, whose readings are the starting points for mine.[23] But there is an important gender dimension to her work (and, I will be arguing, to Klein's). It is there in that 'impotence of bigness' – a phrase at the heart of this chapter. But, almost despite herself, Arendt can be seen as the forerunner of one feminist analysis which traces women's subordination, and the violence which is so often its consequence, first and foremost to the division of labour in – or rather consignment of women *to* – the home. Arendt's political ideal is the Greek space of the *polis* or city-state. Indeed, so invested is she in the Athenian model of democracy that she has often been accused of overlooking, or, worse, reinforcing, the status of women and slaves on whose bodies and backs it built itself. But Arendt makes it clear that if the home and family life are pre-political, it is because they are the place 'where the household head ruled with uncontested despotic powers'. It is because the paterfamilias rules with such absolute power in the household that it remains outside the domain of politics: 'Even the power of the tyrant was less great, less "perfect" than the power with which the *paterfamilias*, the *dominus*, ruled over the household of slaves and family.'[24]

The consequence is violence in the home. Freedom belonged exclusively in the political realm, whereas the household was the place of necessity – read the base and messy environment of creaturely life (or housework, as we call it today). It is this domain which must be mastered for man to be free. Out of this forced discrimination, violence surely follows. Because, in Greek thought, 'all human beings are subject to necessity,' Arendt explains, 'they are entitled to violence towards others.' Violence then becomes the 'pre-political act of liberating oneself from the necessity of life for the freedom of the world'. That is why to be a slave means not just loss of freedom, but being subject to man-made violence. And this is also why there is no real sexual division of labour – nothing one could even grace with the epithet of 'separate spheres' – since such a notion relies on an at least formal assumption of equality between man and women, whereas no such assumption existed. Women and slaves – Arendt is surely hardly condoning the equation – stand in, and for, the place where the necessity of the world is subject to brute mastery. While the ancient household head might of course exert a milder or harsher rule, he knows 'neither law nor justice'.[25] Or to put it another way, it is because women and slaves are called upon to redeem the frailty of human, bodily life – what Judith Butler would call 'precarious life' – that they are the objects, in fact they *must be* the objects, of violence.[26]

The key word is 'mastery'. It is for Arendt, in the world and in the heart, a delusion. Thus when she goes on to make her famous distinction between violence and power which is at the centre of *On Violence*, what matters is that a government will have recourse to violence in direct proportion to a decline in its authority and power, a decline which such violence is desperate to redress (violence is always desperate). 'Rule by sheer violence', she writes, 'comes about when power is being lost.'[27] State violence, we could say, is the last resort of the criminal (as we saw so cruelly in the crackdown on the streets of Egypt, in the government response to Tahrir Square in 2012, and throughout the world since then). When a state 'starts to devour its own children', Arendt observes, 'power has disappeared completely' (think Syria). 'We know or should know', she insists, 'that every decrease in power is an open invitation to violence – if only because those who hold power and feel it slipping from their hands [. . .] have always found it difficult to resist the temptation to substitute violence for it.' And she observes: 'Impotence breeds violence and psychologically this is quite true.'[28]

Arendt's distinction between violence and power is important in relation to a feminism that wishes to align violence with male power of which it then becomes the inevitable expression (which makes female power, as MacKinnon once famously put it, 'a contradiction in terms'[29]). Instead, Arendt allows us to see such an equation as the lie that violence *perpetuates about itself*, since it will do anything – destroy women and the world – rather than admit that its power is uncertain. Women become the scapegoats for man's unconscious knowledge of his own human, which means shared – that is, *shared with women* – frailty ('The Frailty of Human Affairs' is the title of one section of *The Human Condition*). Such frailty takes us to the darkest corridors of life and of the mind, to 'the realm of birth and death' which must be excluded from the public realm because 'it harbors the things hidden from human eyes and impenetrable to human knowledge. Impenetrable because man does not know where he comes from when he is born and where he goes when he dies.'[30] Violence, then, is man's response to the fraudulence of his power and the limits of his knowledge. 'Impotent bigness' indeed.

In her constant return to what cannot be mastered or fully known by the mind, Arendt, as I read her, is – perilously or brilliantly, depending on your viewpoint – skirting the domain of psychoanalysis, for which her stated antipathy is well known. But it is very hard not to read her account of things impenetrable to the human mind as having much in common with the Freudian concept of the unconscious which signals – over and above the sexual debris of its contents – the limits of man's cognisance of the world and of himself. In Arendt's account such limits strike the body politic as much as they do the human heart. This is her vocabulary for both these realms: 'boundlessness', 'unpredictability' and 'the darkness of the human heart'. We live, she states, in an 'ocean of uncertainty', against which there is no redress. It is the human condition. Men are fundamentally unreliable since they 'can never guarantee who they will be tomorrow'. And how, she asks, can you see or foretell the consequences of an act 'within a community of equals where everybody has the same capacity to act?' To be part of the body politic means relinquishing your control over the future – yours and that of the other who is your equal, *because* they are your equal. Man's 'inability to rely upon himself or have complete faith in himself', which, she insists, 'is the same thing', is 'the price human beings pay for freedom'. At the same time, 'the impossibility of remaining unique master of what they do' – read subordinating another to your power – 'is the price they pay for plurality and reality'.[31] If Arendt describes such open, equal participation in the unpredictable reality of the world as a 'joy' (her word), she has also laid out with stunning clarity the unwelcome nature of her own insight and, hence, the lengths men will go to to deny that insight and subordinate the world, in which I include women, to their purpose.

In *The Life of the Mind*, which was Arendt's last work, she takes this further. Now thinking appears even more clearly as the other side of false mastery and knowledge. This is why, for example, she insists that the correct translation of the philosopher Immanuel Kant's *Verstand* is not 'understanding' but 'intellect' or 'cognition' because it represents the 'desire to know', as distinct from *Vernunft*, which arises from the 'urgent need to think'. 'To expect truth to come from thinking', she writes, 'signifies that we mistake the need to think with the urge to know', a need 'that can never be assuaged'. Both are anguished but one in the service of hammering the world into place, the other by its own interminable process, which has no end on which it can brand its name. Only intellect or cognition believes it can answer the unanswerable questions; that it can seize the world in its mental coil. Philosophers of this persuasion, she tells us, are 'like children trying to catch smoke by closing their hands'.[32]

Against this false and futile knowing, Arendt places, even more strikingly in this last meditation, a thinking ego which moves among 'invisible' essences, that is strictly speaking 'nowhere', 'homeless in an emphatic sense', which led, she suggests, to the early rise of 'cosmpolitanism' amongst philosophers.[33] Way ahead of her time, Arendt calls up her answer to the violence of the times in the terms – homeless, nowhere, cosmopolitan – which will be so central to the literary and cultural theory that will follow, although rarely acknowledge, her. To which we can add today the indeterminate, flux-ridden, migratory nature of our world to which modern states react with such merciless violence. Arendt seizes her terms from the history of the refugee and the exile, the stateless, whose predicament had been her own and which she did so much to articulate and dignify.[34] True thought, then, is a form of memory which exerts no dominion, ousts no one from their own space, because it remembers that it is or once was radically homeless. We could not be further from the despotic ruler of the Athenian household who dispenses violence to his women and slaves because it is in the remit of his own power, or rather because it is the only way he can struggle to exert control over the debasing, corporal necessities of life. Nor from the modern-day state that turns to violence in order to shore up a power that has lost all legitimacy. Arendt's life of the mind does not, then, point to some realm of abstract contemplation – her plea for thought is the child of its time.

Perhaps then we should not be surprised, although I admit that I was, to find Arendt slowly inching her way to the world of the dream – the 'royal road to the unconscious', as Freud called it (till the end of his life, he saw *The Interpretation of Dreams* as his most important work). Whatever the achievements of the thinking ego, it will, Arendt writes, never be able to 'convince itself that anything actually exists and that life, human life, is more than a dream'.[35] To illustrate this suspicion – among the most characteristic of Asian philosophy – she then selects the Taoist story of Chuang Tzu, who dreamt he was a butterfly only to wake not to the unerring sureness of who he really was, but to the realisation that perhaps he was a butterfly dreaming he was Chuang Tzu (the same example is used by Jacques Lacan to evoke the vanishing of the human subject in relation to the unconscious).[36] But Arendt being Arendt does not of course leave it there. The dream returns – in the conclusion to *The Life of the Mind* – as the great equaliser in the shape of the king who dreams he is an artisan (since his quotient of life in that moment is no different from the poor artisan who dreams he is king). Moreover, she writes, 'since "one frequently dreams that he is dreaming,"' (she is citing Pascal's critique of Descartes), 'nothing can guarantee that what we call our life is not wholly a dream from which we shall awaken in death.'[37] The personal resonance of such moments in this, her last, uncompleted, book are surely striking. Arendt is exploring and relinquishing her own powers.

Something is creeping back into Arendt's writing. Remember the Greek citizen who mingled freely in the polis on condition of ruling with a rod of iron in his home. Remember too that, if women had to be subdued, it was because women were required to subdue in turn, and on his behalf, the messy, bodily frailties of life, the realm of birth and death that 'harbors the things hidden from human eyes and impenetrable to human knowledge'. What seems, therefore, to be happening here is that this banished, hidden, despised domain of the Graeco-Roman dispensation is, in this final work, taking vengeance on the murderous technocratic know-how of the modern world, as slowly but surely it beats a path back into modernity as its only hope. I think we are talking about the return of the re-pressed. The options are stark. Violence or the dark, shadowy innermost recesses of the hearth and heart where all knowing comes to grief. Violence or the world of the dream.

Cue Melanie Klein. But before leaving Arendt for Klein, there is a crucial link to be made to Rosa Luxemburg, for whom Arendt's enthusiasm knew no limits. There is the deepest and fully acknowledged debt. In all the works by Arendt discussed so far, spontaneity – Luxemburg's central concept and another humble reminder of the unpredictable reality of the world – is a refrain.[38] But there is one moment when Arendt calls on Luxemburg which is of particular value for what I am trying to evoke here. She is talking about love. In its highest manifestation, Arendt writes, when the willing ego pronounces '*Amo: Volo ut sis*', what it means is 'I love you; I want you to be.' Not, she goes on, 'I want to have you', or 'I want to rule you.'[39] Love without tyranny. Compare this free-wheeling, uncontrolling version of love with Rosa Luxemburg. 'Blessed are those without passion,' she wrote to her last lover, Hans Diefenbach – a relationship conducted by correspondence from prison – 'if that means they would never claw like a panther at the happiness and freedom of others.' Then she qualifies: 'That has nothing to do with passion [. . .] I possess enough of it to set a prairie on fire, and still hold sacred the freedom and the simple wishes of other people.'[40] True passion stakes no claim. Like democracy, it does not own, control or master the other. It lets the other be. The line from the personal to the political – famous feminist mantra – could not be more clear, provided we recognise that it can be crossed in both directions. With Luxemburg, you barely have to scratch the surface. We are talking about sexual politics.

o o o

Whenever I address the topic of violence against women, I am always asked about boys. If so many of them, as men, turn out to be so ghastly, where does it all begin? Psychoanalysis, notably in the writings of pioneering psychoanalyst Melanie Klein, might, I suggest, cast some light on this question. In the middle of the Second World War, Klein finds herself with an unexpected opportunity: to analyse a ten-year-old boy known as Richard over what they both know in advance will be the restricted time-frame of four months. She takes notes after every session – several verbatim – and then collects them into one of the first full-length accounts of what her editor Elliott Jaques describes in his foreword to the published volume as a 'total analysis'.[41] The fact that this is only made possible by the conditions of the war – evacuation from London – a war which will colour the analysis at every turn, is seen not as obstacle, but as the core of the process. Richard's distress is multi-layered and over-determined. This in itself demonstrates the futility of trying to locate childhood anxiety either inside the mind or outside in the world (as if one precluded the other). He is an avid follower of the war – reads three newspapers a day, listens to all the news on the wireless, and threatens suicide at the fall of Crete if Britain should be defeated. But his fear of Hitler is overlaid – driven, perhaps, we do not have to decide which comes first – certainly matched, by his fear of his father. The two are inseparable. And what he fears most from his father is what he is doing, or capable of doing, to his mother.

'Just now he had spoken of the terrible things the Austrian Hitler did to the Austrians. By this he meant that Hitler was in a way ill-treating his own people, including Mrs K., just as the bad Daddy would ill-treat Mummy.' Or again: 'Mrs K. interpreted R's desire for peace and order in the family, his giving way to Daddy's and [his brother] Paul's authority, as a means of restraining his jealousy and hatred. This meant there would be no Hitler-Daddy, and Mummy would not be turned into the "pig-sty" Mummy, for she would not be injured and bombed by the bad father.' Hitler-Daddy. Klein's interpretations are famously blunt, some would say coercive. But this very bluntness, I suggest, has served to obscure something that is also staring us in the face. 'Ill-treat', 'injure', 'bomb'; Mummy as a 'pig-sty' for the garbage of the world and of the heart. Like Arendt, Klein is not best renowned as a feminist thinker. Nonetheless, when she looks into Richard's fantasy world, what she sees there – what she urges him to see – is a scene of domestic violence. At one point Richard asks obsessively and solicitously about the number of Klein's other, especially child, patients. Interpreting this as the rivalry and fear of displacement it clearly is, she then also suggests that perhaps he wishes her to have child patients in the same way as he wanted Mummy to have babies, because '*they were less dangerous than men.*'[42]

It is central to one radical feminist argument that the worlds of war and peace are no different. For MacKinnon, the 1990s assault on Bosnian women and their resistance to it challenges 'the lines between genocide and war and, ultimately, between war and peace'.[43] The significance of 9/11, which she describes as an 'exemplary day of male violence', is that the number of people killed in the twin towers and Pentagon on that day was almost identical to the number of women murdered by men, mostly their male partners, in the US over the average year. MacKinnon is rightly challenging the indifference of national and international law towards violence against women compared with the military response to the attacks of 9/11. Although when she asks, 'Do these women not count as casualties in some war? Will the Marines not land for them?'[44] I take my leave. To my mind the last thing feminists should be calling for is the US forces landing or striking anywhere in the world any more than they do, mostly disastrously, already.

But what is never discussed in this argument, which assumes a perfect fit or continuity between manhood and a violence of which it becomes the supreme and deadly fulfilment, is the terrain in which men, and before them boys, do psychic battle. Crucially, in Klein's account, that terrain is not free of violence. It is drenched in it. She is the arch-theorist of psychic violence, more specifically of matricide, as Julia Kristeva points out in her study of Klein.[45] In the case of Richard, the line between war and peace is indeed thin to the point of breaking. To differentiate them is his most urgent task. It is the work to be done. Richard's challenge, as

for many boys, is to resist the pull of the most deadly masculine identifications the world has on offer. Were that not an
available option for him, indeed for men more generally, then
feminism would surely be on a hiding to nothing; it would be
on a losing battle – for ever. If the child is father to the man,
then, Melanie Klein's life's work suggests, what that means is
always, urgently and painfully, up for grabs. There is always
still everything to play for.

If there is a profound link here for me to the ideas of Hannah
Arendt, it comes through the category of thought. Richard is a
boy who 'knows his blows', a slip of the tongue for 'blows his
nose' which he made early in the analysis and which is as fate-
ful as it is wondrous (it points the way to the reckoning with
violence which will be at its core). Goebbels and Ribbentrop
become especially intense objects of hatred when they dare to
say that Britain was the aggressor in the war. In this flagrant
act of projection, they are way behind Richard himself since
the whole of his analysis is an inner negotiation with the violence which he feels himself capable of. He knows his blows.
Remember that lying was the target of some of Arendt's fiercest
political critique ('Lying in Politics', which gave rise to her idea
of impotent bigness, was the title of her 1972 indictment of the
Vietnam war). Lying is, as we know, the collateral damage of
warfare, whose first casualty is truth. Klein is providing the psychic backdrop to Arendt's protest against the corruption and
deceptions of political life, which, certainly in the US and UK,
are if anything more flagrant today. In Richard's narrative, lying
is a form of self-harm, an act of blinding which then becomes
the trigger for increasing violence against the other. When
Klein suggests that Richard's moral outrage at Ribbentrop's lies
might be due to the fact that he too is capable of aggression, I

read her as saying that the one who deceives himself on such matters becomes his own – although by no means only his own – worst enemy. Lying drives aggression in deeper, leaving it no outlet finally other than the destruction of everything that litters its path (Hitler-Daddy assaulting pig-sty Mummy). When Klein offers this interpretation, Richard remains silent, 'obviously thinking over the interpretation and then smiled.' When she asks him why he smiled, 'he answered that it was because he liked thinking.' This does not mean that he mentally submits to her or lacks his own psychic freedom: 'How', he insists at one moment, 'can you really know what I think?'[46]

For psychoanalysis, thinking is not of course exactly thinking as it is most commonly understood. Returning to Arendt's insistence on the Kantian difference between the 'urge to know' and the 'need to think', we could say that psychoanalysis pitches its tent firmly on the side of the latter. Unconscious thinking does not know its own ends. Epistemophilia, as the strongest impulse of the infant, was a term introduced by Klein into the psychoanalytic lexicon. We yearn to know (*Sehnsucht* or yearning was Rosa Luxemburg's favourite word). Driven by sexual curiosity, the infant is pitched into a dark, shadowy world where she or he will struggle to find a place and which she or he cannot fully control, an 'ocean of uncertainty', as Arendt might say. Such control would be as murderous as it is phoney. It is the violent solution of the bad father who lashes out at the mother as a way of getting rid of what he cannot bear to countenance in himself.

In this sense, Melanie Klein can be seen as the silent psychoanalytic partner of Hannah Arendt, and both of them together as partners in the investigation of crime. Klein is exploring the underbelly, giving flesh and blood to the 'passions of the hearth' outlawed from the *polis* by the Greek city-state. And for Klein, as for Arendt, what is at issue is once again what we might call impotent bigness. 'Richard's love was genuine,' she comments, 'when his predominant attitude was to protect me against the bad father, or when he himself felt persecuted by the internal father and expected protection from me' – that is, when Richard refuses the invitation to identify with the violent father in his head. 'He became artificial and insincere,' she continues, *'when he felt he possessed the powerful penis with which he could ally himself in a hostile and dangerous way against me.'*[47] Only a boy who relinquishes the fantasy of the powerful penis will stop himself from attacking the mother. Ceding his omnipotence at the very moment he is most compelled by it is the only path to a viable masculinity – calling the bluff on impotent bigness, as we might say. Certainly it is the only way that this young boy, on the verge of puberty, can behave towards his woman analyst like a gentleman. Violence against women is the boy's deepest wish and worst fantasy. But if he knows this, can give it thought, then it becomes a fantasy he is less likely to act upon.

If Klein is key to my understanding of violence, it is because she is sentient of just how high the stakes are, how treacherous the ground on which she moves. She is dealing with psychotic anxiety, which is far more disturbing than neurosis, and in which she believes all human subjects have their share. The greatest anxiety that afflicts the infant, boy or girl, is that he or she has destroyed the object; a fear which she distinguishes crucially from the anxiety that she or he might do so (which at least leaves open the possibility that you and the world might survive). On such finely graded psychic distinctions the health of her patients relies. Hitler-Daddy goes on killing because he has nothing left to lose. For Klein, to sidestep or skirt this perilous domain in the analytic encounter would, therefore, be a sop to, or complicit with, a world in denial (the lies of Ribbentrop). The implications for her practice – what made her and still I think makes her so controversial and vital – resides in this. It was also at the heart of her famous dispute with Anna Freud, who wanted to pitch the analyst on the side of her patients' ego, of their most fervent wish to believe in their best self.[48] In an extended footnote to the twenty-first session with Richard, she explains why she goes so far and why she believes it makes her patients better:

> It is in fact striking that very painful interpretations – and I am particularly thinking of the interpretations referring to death and to dead internalised objects, which is a psychotic anxiety – could have the effect of reviving hope and making the patient feel more alive. My explanation for this would be that bringing a very deep anxiety nearer to consciousness, in itself produces relief. But I also believe that the very fact that the analysis gets into contact with deep-lying unconscious anxieties gives the patient a feeling of being understood and therefore revives hope. I have often met in adult patients the strong desire to have been analysed as a child. This was not only because of the obvious advantages of child analysis, but in retrospect the deep longing for having one's unconscious understood had come to the fore. Very understanding and sympathetic parents – and that can also apply to other people – are in contact with the child's unconscious, but there is still a difference between this and the understanding of the unconscious implied in psycho-analysis.[49]

In such moments, Klein is making a plea – one I would wish to endorse – for a more psychoanalytically attuned world.

So, in what, then, might the renewal of hope consist (which must be the only question)? At the end of a treatment whose long-term effects Klein is not in a position to predict, Richard begins to feel compassion for his enemies. We are on the last page: 'He no longer felt impelled to turn away from destroyed objects but could experience compassion for them [. . .] Richard, who so strongly hated the enemies threatening Britain's existence at that time, became capable of feeling compassion for the destroyed enemy.'[50] This too is a political as much as a psychic point. Before we dismiss it as unrealistic or sentimental (or both), we might remember that had the Allies felt sympathy for, and been less punitive towards, a defeated Germany after the First World War, we might not have witnessed the Second.

In an important essay on brotherhood and the law of war, Juliet Mitchell suggests there is an irreconcilable contradiction in how women are viewed in war.[51] They are both the defeated and protected – in double jeopardy. Rape as a war crime would then belong at the opposite psychic pole to what Richard arrives at here. No compassion. Probably no recognition of what you have done. Certainly no place for your own dead objects inside your head. Instead the enemy you have defeated has to be destroyed and degraded over and over again. On this, for me, Klein's bombed, damaged, pig-sty Mummy and Arendt's thoughtlessness belong together. Klein was no social commentator, but she has described a world which repeatedly condemns itself to violence, and where women pay the price for the drive, shared by so many men of our time, towards a self-blinding repudiation of the life of the mind.

o o o

To return, finally, to literary writing, which is where this chapter began. Not to Plath and Sexton but to two modern-day women writers who I think bring what women can do with words, disturbingly, into its next phase, into our time where violence against women seems to have been raised to a new pitch. First Temsula Ao. Then the Irish writer Eimear McBride. Ao is Naga. She comes from that part of India which received the brunt of the newly independent nation's drive to crush anything that might tar the image of national unity which it so needed to believe in and project to the outside world. In fact the Naga rebellion predated independence as the Naga National Council was formed in 1946. The violence in Nagaland is not widely known. Gandhi had stated that, after struggling for freedom, of course India would respect the desire for independence of any of its peoples. Perhaps it is because he promised what he could not deliver that the state then struck with such viciousness against the secessionist Nagas.[52]

Ao entitles her collection of short stories *These Hills Called Home – Stories from a War Zone.* She means it. She does not spare her reader. Neither of my two writers spare their readers – indeed not sparing the reader is the point, so this final turn to literature is not intended as a soft landing. As Ao states in her preface – 'Lest we forget' – her aim is to probe how the atrocities of that era have 'restructured or even "revolutionised" the Naga psyche'.[53] Government forces would enter the villages with the intention to degrade, humiliate and maim. In one story – 'The Last Song' – a young girl, Apenyo, who starts singing almost from birth and becomes the lead soprano of her school, renowned across the land, carries on singing as a government soldier yanks her off to the local church where he and his fellow soldiers rape both her and her distraught mother and then kill them. Apenyo's song then echoes through the village for years as 'one more Naga village weeps for her ravaged and ruined children'.[54]

The story I will briefly focus on here is 'An Old Man Remembers'. It is for me one of the most courageous stories of the collection, first for so boldly entering the life of a man's mind and secondly for what it finds there. Sashi is a man who has been part of the Naga resistance, although what he remembers is not a heroic struggle but a moment of violence which has haunted him ever since. The story is therefore a counter-myth. It is also a talking cure. His ageing body is wracked with pain at least partly, the story suggests, because he cannot bring himself to tell the grandson who so lovingly tends him the truth about the war. 'Grandfather, is it true,' the little boy asks him, 'that you and grandfather Imli killed many people when you were in the jungle?' He is completely thrown, has never spoken about his jungle days: 'It was as though that phase of his life was consigned to a dark place in his heart and would be buried with him when his time came. But now the question of a disturbed child stirred old spectres and left him speechless for a long time.' He has been hurled a question 'from the other side of history'. When Sashi starts speaking, it is 'like the massive gush of a waterfall which now threatened to drown both storyteller and listener'.[55]

What matters is not so much the main incident he remembers, which brutally conveys 'how youngsters like Imli and him were transformed into what they became in the jungle'. More crucial is the fact that the morning after the act, the young Sashi and Imli decide anxiously and hesitantly to go back to see what they had done in the night. They, and the reader, have to look at the one they have destroyed. Facing your own violence therefore provides the core of the story as well as its narrative frame. As the grandfather tells this story, he starts to weep. The young boy is baffled – 'after all, they were enemy soldiers, weren't they?' Why would you weep for your enemy? 'Once in a lifetime,' the grandfather says to the boy, 'one ought to face the truth.' To portray the Naga resistance as the agents rather than the victims of violence goes against the grain of how this community, with more than slight justification, views itself since they were after all the targets of the most violent barrage of state power. But for Temsula Ao, the future of her world depends on its doing so. 'And the earth continued to be' are the last words of the story.[56]

Finally Eimear McBride, who crashed onto the literary scene in 2013 with the publication of her first novel, *A Girl Is a Half-formed Thing*, which won the 2014 Bailey's Prize, formerly the Orange Prize for Women's Fiction. As has now become part of its mythical status, the novel languished unpublished for nine years until the independent Galley Beggar Press took the risk of publishing it. 'This was something', wrote the publisher Sam Jordison, 'for which we were prepared to go bankrupt.'[57] Commentaries have rightly focused on the form of the writing, above all on the shortness of the sentences and the absence of the comma – although that is not quite accurate. There are commas but they are used very sparingly and to dramatic effect. But the overall impression is of a voice starting and stopping, choking almost on its own breath, as in these now famous opening lines: 'For you. You'll soon. You'll give her name. In the stitches of her skin she'll wear your say. Mammy me? Yes you. Bounce the bed, I'd say. I'd say that's what you did. Then lay you down. They cut you round. Wait and hour and day.'[58]

The fact that we are, as we soon discover, inside the womb simply adds to the suffocating effect. This is a voice – the only and unnamed voice in McBride's novel – repeatedly halted in its tracks (a kind of breathlessness which places writing on the border between life and death). The break-up of language and the more-or-less dismemberment of the woman's body are inseparable (the language manages to be as unrestrained and free-wheeling as it is broken and clipped). It a story of sexual abuse – by the uncle, and then, as we are later told, of the mother by her own father: 'Lie across each other's beds we tell each other sorts of things. It makes us such close friends. No bits pieces left unsaid. And truth now tell the truth we say. Her father felt her up. It makes her red and cry. Daddy still loves her the best but he wouldn't want anyone else to try. That is love.'[59] Abuse passes down the generations. Think back through the grandfathers, as, perverting Virginia Woolf, one might say. She famously suggested that women writers feed their imaginations back through the generations of their foremothers: 'Who', Woolf asked, 'shall measure the heat and violence of the poet's heart when caught and tangled in a woman's body?'[60]

At the opposite pole from trauma as unspeakable, which is one fashionable account of trauma, *A Girl Is a Half-formed Thing* is traumatised speech with no exit. 'Out my mouth like a mad thing raving clawing out my eyes.' Once you start talking, you never stop (McBride might also be miming and sabotaging the Catholic confession). As a reader, you are given no cover. You have nowhere else to go other than the narrator's head. Her brother is dying – she has known this since before she was born (from inside the womb where the novel begins). As a child, she is slapped, rammed, bruised and bloodied by her mother, who she also describes as her 'close friend'.[61] Her uncle rapes her as a thirteen-year-old girl. She responds with a form of crazed promiscuity that allows men, including the uncle, repeatedly to tear her to pieces. This is modernism as slut walk, language as a type of syncopated abuse – the constant line breakage as the literary form for injury or self-harm (as Anne Enright put it in her review of the book, 'you can almost hear the blows in the rhythm of the words').[62] To take just one example – a rare sentence with commas: 'I met a man. I met a man. I let him throw me round the bed. And smoked, me, spliffs and choked my neck until I said I was dead.'[63] The fact that this can also be read as a nursery rhyme simply intensifies the violence.

At the end of the novel, when her brother has died, she walks out on the pious mourning party of the gathered relatives and heads for the woods where she knows – she seeks it out – she will meet with a violent sexual encounter, one of a trail that have run through the novel, but which, in terms of what it does to her, and to the language of the text, makes everything that has preceded it seem – almost – harmless. This passage, which is not the worst of it, comes after the encounter itself when, you could almost say, she is collecting herself. Whenever I have presented McBride in public, I have always projected this passage for the audience to read silently to themselves as I cannot bear to read it out loud:

> I lie thisright place for me with my fingers ripped onthebody
> Mine is Lie in the ground faceWhere I Right for meyes.
> Think about your face. Something. Shush now. Right now.
> FullofslimeThere better now. And I am. Done with this done.
> Fill the air up. Smear the blood up is there any no no t reeeeelly.
> My work is. I've done my I should do. I've done the this time
> really well. And best of. It was the best of. How. Ready now. I'm

screaming in the blackness. Scream until I'm done my body. Full of nothing. Full of dirt the. I am. My I can. There there breath that. Where is your face off somewhere. Where am I lay down this tool. I fall I felled. I banged my face head I think. Time for somewhere. Isgoing home.[64]

Hardly any of the first reviewers and critics of this novel dwelled on the sexual violence at its core.[65] Adam Mars-Jones, who wrote one of the earliest reviews in which he predicted its extraordinary success, told me he left it out for fear that readers would be put off. The moment will lead, more or less, to her drowning, which is how the novel ends. But note two things about this passage. First, the 'you' – as almost constantly throughout the text – is her brother (from before her own birth till after his own death): 'Think about your face.' The destruction of herself is therefore her loving return to him and a form of care: 'There there'. This, incidentally, is why to describe this text as all interior monologue is not quite right. She is nearly always somehow speaking to him. Secondly, the narrator goes out looking for the violent encounter and knows where to find it. As well as everything else it monstrously is, it is also her achievement: 'My work is. I've done my I should do. I've done the this time really well. And best of. It was the best of.' Crucially, therefore, she is her own agent. Violence is sought. As well as being viciously what men do to her, it is a component of her grief. None of this mitigates anything; the protest against violence is not lessened but intensified. For me, the genius of McBride's novel is that she can get all of this onto the same page or line or word, into the strangulated syntax of her prose.

If McBride plunges us into the worst – and I have not conveyed the half of it – she also, like Sexton, like Plath, gives us a voice that brilliantly orchestrates its own sorrow and rage. The fightback is in the words, in what a mind – the life of the mind no less – can do with its own history. Along with the necessary fight for public and legal recognition of violence against women, this continues to be, as I see it, one of women's best weapons against cruelty and injustice. As feminists, we do not have – should not be asked – to choose between the two, at least not in the world I want to live in.

5

WRITING VIOLENCE

From Modernism to Eimear McBride

What might be the relationship between experiment in language and the violence of the modern world, between a truncated sentence and a truncated life? What drives syntax askew, makes language stall completely or spill over its proper borders, mess with itself? We have become used to thinking of modernism as an early-twentieth-century European crisis of representation provoked by the collapse of empires and impending war, when the seemingly fixed barriers of class, gender and racial privilege started to implode. In fact, for one influential version of this account, the crisis begins earlier, in 1848, when revolutions across Europe shredded the belief of the bourgeoisie that they were the class of progress. Up to that point, it was possible to see language as immune to social and political contradictions, lord of all it surveyed, blind to the role it plays in shaping a world it claimed merely, and innocently, to reflect. Modernist writing, famously difficult, is the appropriate form for that crisis. Most simply, it brings to an end the illusion that either language or the world can be made safe.

In recent years, a revival of the discussion about the difficulty of modernism, and its relation to the world's violence, has taken two forms which might seem at first glance to be at odds with each other. In the first version, there is an intractable difficulty inside modernism, explored by its key writers and artists, which consists in a refusal to submit to the norms of representation.[1] If that refusal was historical, tied to the early decades of the twentieth century – 1910 and 1922 competing for the key slot – it was because it alerted us to a crisis of authority. A broken world snatched from the writer and artist their confidence that reality could be seized, or simply recorded, in the work. All the work could do, or any viable work could do – although that was a huge amount – was to register its awareness of the fragility of its own grasp on what it struggled to represent. That this should be accompanied, some would say precipitated, by a loss of belief in the cohesion of the artistic – of any – consciousness is central to the argument. The most important literary modernists – say Joyce, Woolf, Proust, Kafka – robbed us of a double illusion: that the world, that human subjectivity, could ever be fully known. The form of their writing, precisely its difficulty, was therefore the logical outcome of a dilemma, one which persists in our time, unless of course you think the world now hangs more or less perfectly together (the end-of-history argument which is now generally agreed to have fallen flat on its face). At the same time, and this is central to the recent version of this polemic, most writers today seem to carry on blissfully and naively as if none of this had ever happened.

The other case for the difficulty of modernism has been given one of its strongest articulations by the philosopher John Gray.[2] For Gray the modern is contaminated by an Enlightenment dream from which it never wholly emancipated itself. His story is the reverse of the one just described, or rather its subtext. According to Gray, the modern – as distinct from literary modernism – is heir to the Enlightenment belief in the perfectibility of the world, a belief that spawned Nazism, and which gives rise to revolutionary terror of the kind represented by 9/11. The aim, which according to Gray unites these two hideous moments, is to produce a new human being, an aim that is unequivocally modern (we cannot therefore see Al-Qaeda as some uncivilised throwback in time). What Gray wants is a way of thought which relinquishes that fantasy and allows the world to proliferate in all its unmanageable difference from itself. Crucially that desire is not Utopian. Utopia is on the wrong side of this argument. It is a type of perversion that aims to subordinate the world to its own will. It is here that, to my understanding, Gray rejoins the first argument. In both cases, what is yearned for is a world that has shed the myth of perfection, of unity, of harmonious self-possession which is seen to have licensed some of the worst atrocities of modern times. Better hesitancy than total belief of any kind, and better a world that falls apart under the pressure of its own already existing fault lines, than an apparently seamless capitalism, as resilient as it is cruelly unjust, sweeping without check or inhibition across the globe.

If these two arguments might appear to contradict each other, it is only in the sense that Gray is describing the persistence of the Enlightenment myth which modernism was meant to have broken. Shadowed behind this discussion is Adorno and Horkheimer's 'dialectic of enlightenment' – the title of their famous 1944 book – where, they insist, the fallen nature of man cannot be separated from social progress and the belief in the reason of the world that upholds it. They are referring to anti-Semitism, to the ease with which 'enlightened civilisation' reverts to 'barbarism', of which Nazism was providing such a glaring instance. 'Not merely the ideal', they write at the end of the introduction, 'but the practical tendency to self-destruction has always been characteristic of rationalism, and not only in the stage in which it appears undisguised.' In such a world, language is always in danger of becoming 'apology' or 'mechanised history', of losing its dissonance. 'There is', they claim, 'no longer any available form of linguistic expression which has not tended towards accommodation to dominant currents of thought; and what a devalued language does not do automatically is proficiently executed by societal mechanisms.'[3] For Adorno and Horkheimer, writing in the aftermath of Nazism, only a radical re-evaluation of the language we use will save us from the deadly plenitude of false, instrumental reason and the ravages of capitalism that accompany it.

If we want to grasp the interface between literary writing and the worst of the world, both in literary modernism and after, then, to my mind, these ideas go too far and not far enough. Too far in the suggestion that today there are barely any writers who remain true to the modernist vision, as if there were just a few select people, or writers, who were living disabused lives, only a handful aware of the ease with which language can become the handmaiden of a corrupt world. Toni Morrison, who I was dismayed to see summarily dismissed on these grounds by Gabriel Josipovici in his study of modernism, will be summoned as a vital counter-example in what follows, as one of several women writers discussed in these pages who take the link between violence and writing to its next stage.[4] In any case, these dismissals are sheer elitism, a charge regularly levied against modernism, but in this case even truer of its fervent defenders, for whom so few writers – so few women writers – make the cut. But these same ideas also do not go far enough. We need to pause at this idea of fragmentation, loss of cohesion, and ask where it might take us. What does it mean in terms of anguish for a mind to lose its way, relinquish its authority over itself? And, to which violent history or histories might it bear witness in that process?

To answer these questions, we need to enter the furthest recesses of the mind, first via Sigmund Freud, whose work was one of the most important starting points of these debates; then into the heart of literary modernism; and finally into more recent writing by women. It is in order to wrest language from the historical violence of slavery that Toni Morrison twists her language to purpose. And Eimear McBride, as we have already touched on, creates a new form of writing to match the violence of our times. She is, by her own account, the undutiful daughter of modernism, who tears language apart in the face of the sexual abuse of women and girls.

o   o   o

To start, then, with Freud. If 1922 is one of the key years of modernism – *Ulysses, The Waste Land* – Freud's *Beyond the Pleasure Principle* came barely two years before (it was first published in English in 1922). *Beyond the Pleasure Principle* is the text that marks the division between Freud's first and second topography or schema of the mind, ushering in the concept of the death drive which indicates the human tendency to destruction, the demonic principle in woman's and man's deepest relationship to others and to themselves. In this text, Freud introduces something radically unmasterable about human subjectivity which goes beyond the concept of the unconscious on which his previous work, indeed the very founding of psychoanalysis, had been based. These new ideas were precipitated by the traumatic aftermath of the First World War, which led to a run of papers on mourning and melancholia and on war and death, all of which were written during that war. As Eric Hobsbawm observed, the twentieth century which gave birth to modernism ushered in new forms of prosperity in the Western world, but also witnessed killing on a scale never seen before.[5]

Freud died weeks after the outbreak of the Second World War, so he did not live to see the worst. But, in one of his most poignant meditations, 'A Disturbance of Memory on the Acropolis', written in 1936 when the war was already on the horizon, it is almost as if he did. At the very least, this short work suggests some foreboding of the lengths the mind will go to in its efforts to master itself. Like the writing on the death drive, this text pushes the limits of the psyche beyond where he had previously taken them. It is a story about memory. Freud arrives at the Acropolis with his brother as a man of forty-eight and is struck with amazement at the reality of the monument he sees before his eyes: 'So all this really *does* exist, just as we were taught at school.' He did not believe it really existed, because, he now remembers, as a boy, weighed down by a father who had not roamed the earth, he never thought he himself would, or should, get there. At its simplest, therefore, this is a story of a son who cannot bear to outdo his father – a classic, if somewhat restrained and well-behaved version of the Oedipal drama – but who can only recognise the inner conflict to which this pain had subjected him as a young man when his own 'powers of production', as he puts it, 'are at an end'.[6] Freud is near the end of his life. He offers this memory – a memory of a disturbance of memory – to his friend Romain Rolland on Rolland's seventieth birthday, although it can equally be read as Freud's own double-edged eightieth birthday gift to himself.

What makes this text stand out for me is the effect of this set of strained recollections and moments of disenchanted recognition on Freud's mind. He calls it 'derealisation' ('*Ent-*

fremdungsgefühl'), a term he has hardly ever used before, to indicate that something is not just being repressed, but being blotted out – scotomised – as if it was never, had never been, could never be, there. These 'derealisations', he comments, are 'abnormal' mental structures, 'remarkable phenomena that are little understood'.[7] Way beyond the creative fantasy of the hysteric, the elaborate rituals of the obsessive, the artistic night-stalking of the dreamer, he is therefore talking about what the mind will do to avoid what it cannot bear to know about itself. The world fades and goes blank, wipes itself off the page. There is a violence in this story. Better the world or this bit of the world cease to exist, rather than be confronted with what I, as a flawed, divided human subject, cannot bear to contemplate.

If I see this late work as brushed by the war on the horizon, it is because this wipe-out, this ruthless, world-destroying ego will go to any lengths to ward off any challenge to its own deluded comfort. In this, it surely bears a resemblance to John Gray's account of the false unity of the post-Enlightenment world, and the potential for terror it contains – by which I mean the terror of totalitarianism and state violence, being unleashed at the time Freud was writing, as much as terror in the sense in which it is most commonly used, and misused, as a term today. It is one of those moments in Freud's thinking when the borderline between history and psyche is paper thin. Freud knows that his attempt to read this moment in terms of guilt towards the father is too neat. He knows that this is a case where the law of the father does not quite do the trick (even if he offers it as the key to the mystery). Instead, hovering on the edge of that too predictable Oedipal interpretation is a world that disappears, carrying off the supreme symbol of

Greek civilisation with it, all because of something which an over-defensive mind simply cannot tolerate.

This suggests a very specific way in which the question of modernism and that of memory are inextricably linked. Modernism is not a set of formulae about the modes of writing that best match the disenchantment of the world. It is not just a way of registering that world in the form of its disenchantment, a kind of laying down of arms before the world's unwillingness to be subdued to thought. More than that, it is a way of recording – although that is not quite the right word – a failure of historical memory in the formation of memory itself. That, as I see it, is what Freud's paper is touching on. To put it another way, a key driving question for modernism is: how can the mind take the measure of history, when history will submit neither to the reason of the world nor to the mind that confronts it?

To take another moment, this time from the very heart of the modernist canon, when the reference to the Second World War is explicit. Virginia Woolf's last novel, *Between the Acts*, recounts the staging of a pageant in an English country house in the summer before the war. The programme for Miss La Trobe's performance announces: 'The Present Time. Ourselves.' The narrator then questions: '"Ourselves . . ." But what could she know about ourselves? The Elizabethans yes; the Victorians perhaps; but ourselves; sitting here on a June day in 1939 – it was ridiculous. "Myself" – it was impossible.'[8] The novel was mostly written, in the words of Frank Kermode in his introduction to the Oxford World's Classics edition of 1992, at a 'desperate time, when France had fallen and Britain was under heavy attack from the air'. But as he also suggests, the summer of 1939 where it was set was perhaps the real moment of crisis, the moment when war became inevitable: Barcelona fallen to

Franco, Austria and Czechoslovakia swallowed by Hitler, and Poland under threat – 'unmistakeably', Kermode writes, 'the last moments of the old world'. So Woolf situates her novel not in the midst of the war, the moment of writing, but on the threshold 'between a known past and an unknown but probably appalling future'.[9] Pushing this slightly, we could say then that she makes the tense of the novel the future perfect as defined by Lacan. Not what I was in what I still am (repetition), nor what I once was but am no more (repression), *but what I will have been in the process of what I am becoming*.[10] For Lacan this is analytic time. If it is the tense of hope, it is also ghostly: the future shadowed by a past still struggling fully to be born. In *Between the Acts*, Woolf brings out its gothic potential, appropriately enough at a historical moment when it is unclear whether what one was 'in the process of becoming' is something she or anyone else could, or would, survive.

The violence of that moment to come, or intimations of it, are also to be found inside the narrative of Woolf's novel. In the middle of this story of English lawns and pageantry, blood stains the page. A newspaper report tells of a girl raped by a soldier; a snake suffocating with a toad in its mouth is stamped on by one of the garden party, who then strides to the barn with blood on his shoes: 'Action', we are told, 'relieved him.'[11] Thus Woolf reminds us that the violence of the coming war is not alien to the country that will have right on its side but has its place too at the heart of England (Woolf's scandalous argument in *Three Guineas*, her essay on women and war, written two years before).[12] Virginia Woolf is not the only woman writer to tread this path. There are echoes here of Rosa Luxemburg writing on the ethics of violence: 'a man who hastens to perform an important deed and unthinkingly treads on a worm on his way is committing a crime.'[13] In the hands of Woolf, the world crumbles and precariously restores itself, in response to a history to which she could not possibly know if literature would any longer be equal (even asking the question does not wholly make sense). History is not backdrop. More like an unwelcome visitor, grinding all certainties into the dust; or a snake suffocating on its own prey. That image might do as a less lyrical, profane version of Walter Benjamin's 'Angel of History' with his face turned to the past as the wreckage of history piles up at his feet.[14] In Woolf's hands, the historical crisis and the collapse of belief in the integrity of the self are inseparable: '"Myself" – it was impossible.' This is a late work by Woolf, but it casts its shadow back across the century. What it suggests is that the famous loss of authority, proclaimed by modernism, is visceral, neither measured nor polite, and inseparable from forms of historical violence for which we are accountable, but which the mind finds almost impossible to get the measure of or fully to countenance (the two points are the reverse sides of the same coin).

A striking instance of what I am trying to convey occurs in Josipovici's *What Ever Happened to Modernism*, in which he laments its passing. He is commenting on Rosalind Krauss's reading of Picasso's 1912 collages, in which drawings of a violin are intercut with pieces of newspaper. The fragments are replete with the horrors of the Balkan war which had started that year. After Krauss, Josipovici concludes that we cannot read them either as a statement of Picasso's pacifism nor even, as some critics have suggested, as conversation pieces with left-leaning friends who shared his antipathy to war. 'Both', Josipovici asserts with dismaying authority, 'are false conclusions, both deny the radical multivoicedness of Picasso's collage.'[15] But if you go back to Krauss's *Picasso Papers*, the break-up of the visual space and the Balkan atrocity are more deeply connected than this might suggest. This is Krauss: 'Another depth speaks as well from the very surface of the newsprint fragment [. . .] This is the "depth" – historical, imaginative, political – of a place to which the word *Tchataldja* [which stands out on the page] refers, the name of the battle site in the Balkans from which this dispatch was sent.'[16]

At the moment of the collages, André Tudesq, editor of the avant-garde magazine *Les Soirées de Paris*, one of Picasso's friends, was reporting on the wars. In one of his dispatches, he tells the story of a battle in which the Turks were routed. 'A pursuing Serb,' Krauss continues, 'obeying the rules of combat, asks a wounded soldier: "Christian or Muslim?" Receiving no answer he lops off the soldier's head.'[17] Krauss is indeed impatient of those who, drawing on the history she has herself so meticulously documented, would conclude that what we are listening to is Picasso's beliefs – including, presumably, his hatred of war. These paintings are not statements. But what seems to be missed in this discussion is the possibility that there might be the most intimate relationship between, on the one hand, the disintegrating form and, on the other, the history, dense to the point of illegibility, which is being offered, but also torn to pieces, on the page. Picasso is multi-voiced. Of course. But how and why? A soldier either will not answer a death-dealing question or is unable momentarily to find the strength and voice of his own faith. What does lopping off his head – crushing snakes – have to do with the difficulty of modernism? Everything, I would suggest. Freud's moment on the Acropolis, Woolf's snake in the garden, are telling us that the effort to get our minds around history comes at a potentially deadly cost. Which is why describing modernism in terms of the loss of literary authority, or as an inability to subdue history to the word, strikes me as insufficient. What I have been describing is more delirious than that. If we resist knowledge of the violence of history, then what does such violence, when it makes its way onto the page, do to literary writing? We can hardly expect it to remain demurely in place.

From inside another suppressed history, Toni Morrison's 1996 Pulitzer Prize-winning novel, *Beloved*, makes this delirium palpable. This should be enough to secure her place in any pageant of troubled writing, as she bears witness to our inability to confront one of the worst chapters of Western history. Morrison is enjoining America to remember slavery. In interviews she has explicitly stated that this was her intention. She then gives us that history, not as document or in the form of realist narrative, but as a hallucinogenic trans-generational haunting over which the story, the reader, the characters, can get absolutely no grip. 'Nights are becoming sleepless,' she writes of the novel. She is bringing racial trauma out of the dark, since 'race', she suggests, is still 'a virtually unspeakable thing'.[18] The book tells the story of Sethe, who murdered her baby rather than allow her to be taken back into slavery and who is then visited by that child as a young woman ghost. Already we are in a world which defies comprehension and whose story can barely be told. The book begins: '124 was spiteful. Full of a baby's venom.'[19] In a brilliant article on her own writing, Morrison comments on why she chose to open her novel with numbers rather than words: 'numbers have no adjectives, no posture of coziness or grandeur or the haughty yearning of arrivistes and estate builders for the parallel beautification of the nation they left behind, laying claim to instant history and legend.'[20] No beautification, no instant history, nothing cosy or grand. If you are going to tell this history, it cannot be in the old forms. This is the modernist question deflected through the annals of race. In those first words – '124 was spiteful' – she took the risk, as she puts it, of confronting the reader 'with what must be immediately incomprehensible'. That 'must' is wonderfully ambiguous: 'should' or 'cannot help but be'. As if to say: This you cannot, should not, try to understand, but I will none-theless take you there.

At one point in the novel, Sethe is talking to her other, liv-ing daughter Denver. Denver has hallucinated another young woman, Amy, who once long ago rescued Sethe. With no fore-knowledge of who this woman is, or of the event lost in her mother's past, Denver sees her, in a white dress, wrapping her arms around her mother, massaging her swollen legs and feet. How can this be? How can you see what is not there? On the other side of repressed memory. *Beloved* presents us with mem-ory in your face. Not too little memory, but too much. Memory which, like the murdered baby, has insanely become flesh. How can you, can anyone, get their mind around this? Far from being dropped from contemporary writing, this fundamental question of modernism, under pressure of an unspeakable his-tory of violence, has been raised by Toni Morrison to a new pitch. Sethe is talking:

> What I remember is a picture floating around out there outside my head. I mean, even if I don't think it, even if I die, the picture of what I did, or knew, or saw is still out there . . . And you think it is you thinking it up . . . But no. It's when you bump into a rememory that belongs to somebody else . . . if you go there – you who was never there – if you go there and stand in the place where it was, it will happen again; it will be there for

you, waiting for you. So, Denver, you can't never go there. Never. Because even though it's all over – over and done with – it's going to always be there waiting for you.[21]

Morrison's writing stitches the question of what can be verbally transmitted through the generations into the fabric of the words. Today we know that this legacy of slavery is still with us given the return of slave labour, whether in the form of Thai fishermen, subjected to inhumanly degrading treatment, whose catch feeds the prawns which land on the dining tables of the West; or the migrant women workers, lured to Great Britain with the promise of freedom and wages, who find themselves locked into the basements of Knightsbridge and Kensington homes – in one report, round the corner from where Virginia Woolf once lived.[22] In 2016, University College London launched the Legacies of British Slave-ownership project, directed by the feminist historian Catherine Hall, which has tracked the material, financial legacy of slavery in Great Britain. It was met with a chorus of denials ('not in the UK, surely not, this was surely America's problem') at the same time as getting over two million hits in the days it went live.[23] After the police killing of George Floyd in Minneapolis in the midst of the pandemic, and the renewed confrontation with slavery it has provoked, the organisers found themselves bombarded with media requests, as the site acquired new, urgent relevance.

o   o   o

As we encountered her first in the previous chapter, Eimear McBride is today's writer of sexual abuse. She has picked up the trail of literary modernism and shoved it, screaming and kicking, into a new eviscerating phase. When she made her first appearance in 2013 with *A Girl Is a Half-formed Thing*, she proudly trailed James Joyce in her wake, stating her allegiance to European modernism. In this alone, she sees off the argument that modernism has been betrayed by most of today's fiction (as if, with reference to the UK, literature had prematurely taken the path of Brexit). McBride has stated firmly that she wishes to be considered as a European writer: 'I'd like to set up my stall as a European writer [. . .] I probably belong in the diaspora set because I only have clarity from a distance.'[24] Her greatest debt is to *Ulysses*. It overturned her universe, changing everything she had ever understood about what language could do. As a woman in her twenties, already intent on being a writer, she opened its first page on a bus in Tottenham, North London, and, when she got off at Liverpool Street, 'I don't think it is an exaggeration to say the entire course of my life had changed.'[25] In the hands of McBride, modernism is alive and well (although being alive and well is precisely what *A Girl Is a Half-formed Thing* throws into the deepest question).

One reviewer even went so far as to take a passage from Molly Bloom's monologue and rewrite it with full stops throughout as a way of conveying how alienation works in the two registers: unending flow on which nothing can get a grip (Molly), and a voice that constantly shudders and halts. This is Molly Bloom stripped of any lyric remnant. It also, for me, evokes other great woman modernists, such as Elizabeth Bowen, from whom McBride seems to borrow, whether consciously or unconsciously, the disconcerting habit of placing prepositions at the end of her sentences, leaving the reader in a type of frantic, and vulnerable, suspense. It is one of the best ways of *not* ending a sentence: 'That clouds and wind skiteing sand spray floats of it up'; or 'Coffee quiet new beginning is the boiling kettle bowl of'; or 'Wave and wave of it hormone over'; or 'Stinking smothered by life by.'[26] As is clear from those last two, McBride raises the temperature of this syntactic move (as if a sexual body were left dangling over its own edge, which would be one definition of sex). Another link would be May Sinclair, whose *Life and Death of Harriett Frean* turns on what happens, or might have happened, to Harriett Frean as a child in the lane at the back of her house where she has been forbidden to go. In Sinclair's novel, you cannot ever answer the question of what actually took place or its consequences. 'The man came out and went to the gate and stood there. *He* was the frightening thing.'[27] That '*He* was the frightening thing' can be read as much as the baffled, over-coerced Victorian child trying to figure out what the danger might be, as seeing it for what it brutally is. You never know. The uncertainty does not, however, stop this moment from spreading across the whole text, like the campion flowers in the lane that merge with her mother's mouth, almost seeming to stain it blood red: 'She was holding the flowers up to her face. It was awful, for you could see her mouth thicken and redden over its edges and shake.' Instead, with McBride, the sexual encounters are as vicious as they are explicit. She takes us back down the lane and stuffs the blood red in our face.

With *A Girl Is a Half-formed Thing*, McBride has ushered *Ulysses*'s Gerty MacDowell and Molly Bloom into the twenty-first century. The reader is not confronted, as in Joyce's Gerty MacDowell sequence, with a man on a beach masturbating to the mental tune of a limping woman. Nor is the book a tease, which would be one way of describing Molly Bloom's erotically charged monologue, on which *Ulysses* ends and which led Carl Gustav Jung famously to write to Joyce to congratulate him:

'I suppose the devil's grandmother knows as much about the psychology of women. I didn't.'[28] (Which, as a dear friend wryly observed to me long ago, simply shows how little Jung knew about women.) Precisely because the novel is so thick with allusions to modernism, *A Girl Is a Half-formed Thing* offers itself, I would suggest, as modernism's return of the repressed. To get a sense of what, linguistically and sexually, has happened, this is Leopold Bloom, the central character in *Ulysses*, musing on the beach as he watches MacDowell, who is both lost in thought and playing to his stares:

> O sweety all your little girlwhite up I saw dirty bracegirdle made me do love sticky we two naughty Grace darling she him half past the bed met him pike hoses frillies for Raoul to perfume your wife black hair heave under embon *señorita* young eyes Mulvey plump years dreams return tail end Agendath swoony lovey showed me her next year in drawers return next in her next her next.[29]

Famously this passage condenses more or less everything in the novel up to this point, or more precisely all of Bloom's women: Gerty MacDowell, the actress Anne Bracegirdle, Molly, Martha Clifford, *ad infinitum*, as one might say. This is writing that heaves under its own sensual weight, plumpness, embonpoint, girdles and swoons. The only possible response as a reader, one almost feels, is either to applaud or fall at his feet (notwithstanding that, as the novel also mercilessly narrates, he is a cuckold).

If we turn back to the passage from *A Girl Is a Half-formed Thing* cited in the last chapter (p. 196), it should be enough to get the measure of the difference, not only as a testament to the perils of sexual abuse, but now as a radical engagement with a whole history of modernist writing which it bends, unerringly, to its purpose.

This is language as a bloody mess, barely but always just about intelligible, as she splices words together and pulls them into shreds: 'I lie thisright place for me with my fingers ripped onthebody Mine is Lie in the ground faceWhere I Right for meyes [. . .] Smear the blood up is there any no no t reeeeelly.' McBride is presenting disenchantment with the world on behalf of women – 'Full of nothing. Full of dirt the. I am. My I can' – without ever losing faith in the capacity of language to recraft the worst of history: 'There there breath that. Where is your face off somewhere. Where am I lay down this tool. I fall I felled. I banged my face head I think. Time for somewhere. Isgoing home.'[30]

Almost immediately after, girl walks into the lake. As she slowly submerges herself, taking the reader into the water with her, it is impossible not to read McBride as paying tribute to Virginia Woolf, who drowned herself in the midst of the Second World War (an act which, given the real threat of Nazi invasion, was far more measured and worldly wise than crazy, which is how it is most often seen). How to write what the world might feel and look like as you drown?

o   o   o

As I suggested in Chapter Four, it is the energy of the writing which stops *A Girl Is a Half-formed Thing* from coming anywhere close to a chronicle of despair, even while the agony of the novel leaves us with the problem – as indeed did Woolf and Morrison – of how to survive the world's cruelties. In all of these books, literature appears repeatedly as the place in our culture where the worst of history, especially in relation to women, can be represented as it enters deep into the space of the mind. As we hear in relation to the daily revelations of sexual abuse, telling the story, however unbearable and awful, is one of the ways to survive. But having cast its deathly shadow over the page, violence at such a pitch of intensity also confronts us with the question of where and how such horrors can be endured and/or fought against. By the end of *Between the Acts*, Woolf restores a barely credible semblance of England which she clearly does not believe in herself. Morrison famously ends *Beloved* with the refrain and/or injunction: 'This is not a story to pass on' – hand down through the generations or pass over? preserve or refuse? or both? In *The Lesser Bohemians*, her second novel, McBride offers her response to the same question. The novel has been criticised for playing havoc with syntax once more – as if such experimentation is something you should only do once, and the linguistic disruptions of *Girl* were a tic she should be getting over (a bit like those who respond to the rising reports of sexual harassment with the helpful suggestion that women should just deal with it and move on).

Instead, I suggest, *The Lesser Bohemians* takes its exploration of literary form into a new domain. Sexual abuse is still an ever-present danger, but, for all that, the possibility of love, of sexual and human contact, is not seen as scuppered for ever. The novel can be read as its own precarious, only partial cure, since any redemption is troubled and incomplete. In *The Lesser Bohemians*, the violence of the modern world spreads across the psychological landscape. No one is exempt. It is impossible to dismiss the turbulence as the expression of one freak, damaged soul. At the same time, it explores the type of human communication necessary for the worst of modern times to be held, however gingerly, between individual people, and inside their own heads. And it goes further than *Girl* by daring to mix the reality of sexual abuse with the pleasures and unpleasures, the joy and potentially mortal danger, of sex (not perhaps since the writing of Georges Bataille have the two been released into such intimate proximity).

Speaking about the novel, McBride has lamented the dearth in past fiction of anything approaching an adequate exploration of sexual experience, even in the modernist tradition she rejoins and celebrates, especially in relation to the sexual experiences of women. Only when she first discovered Edna O'Brien did she understand that 'there was a part of women's lives that had been absent in everything I had read'.[31] Bored (her word) with the way sex is mostly written about, she has now given us two novels in which language falls apart under the pressure of sex. And violence. After all, sex and violence are two experiences which tend to leave people lost for words (remember that Hannah Arendt described violence as 'mute'). In McBride's hands, they re-find their natural affiliation, together precipitating a crisis of speech. With *The Lesser Bohemians*, coming on the heels of *Girl*, McBride has definitively established herself as the foremost writer of sexual abuse, now recognised as one of the hallmarks of the century in which we are living.

There are of course traces of dimly remembered abuse in Virginia Woolf, ghostly visions in corridors, shadows that fall across the page. The woman speaker of Beckett's *Not I* is haunted by some ugly, not quite spoken, event. And, as already touched on, something which is never named happens to May Sinclair's young Harriett Frean down the lane. With McBride, it is all up front. Seen in this light, the earlier accounts of modernism, with which this chapter began, once again look a bit limited, only this time not just too psychologically anodyne, instead coy or strait-laced. What fucks up language, *The Lesser Bohemians* suggests, is fucking – good, bad or indifferent. There is scarcely a page of the novel untouched by the linguistic fallout of sex. Joyce may have shown McBride that 'you could do whatever you wanted with language and that the rules didn't apply', but he does not go here.[32] Seen in this light, Molly Bloom's euphoric self-affirmation appears too lyrical, Gerty MacDowell's allusions to menstruation too seemly and quaint. McBride has said that her aim is 'to make language cope and more fully describe that part of life that is destroyed once it begins to get put into straightforward grammatical language'.[33] 'Destroyed' is crucial. Nearly all her characters are in recovery. They do not all make it. In contrast to *Girl*, *The Lesser Bohemians* ends on an up beat, but, given all that has gone before, the reader is left unsure. What, given half a chance, are bodies capable of doing to each other? More or less single-handed, McBride has taken us back to the experiment of modernism and ushered it into a new gut-wrenching phase: 'Guts to gorge', 'Flesh scraping fear against the Do of my brain.' 'Then I am back in the world and must understand again how to cover my bones with my skin.'[34]

The Lesser Bohemians is a love story narrated through the mind of an eighteen-year-old girl from Dublin who comes to London to take up a place at drama school, and falls wildly in love with an established actor more than twice her age. Readers of *Girl* would be forgiven for not expecting a tale of heterosexual passion to have been McBride's next move, especially a tale courting more than one cliché – man initiates girl into sex, older man with a girl the age of his own daughter, women who take pleasure in pain: 'I like of his upon me, whatever marks he's made' (early in their relationship he refuses her request to sodomise her and then finally relents).[35] Or even for seeing this as a betrayal of the first novel, especially the ending, when the narrator, after her lifetime of abuse and the sexual self-harm which is its consequence, took herself off to the river after her beloved brother's funeral and drowned; as one feminist paradigm would have it: the abuse of girls by men leads to death. Grief is key, taking its place alongside sex and violence as another experience that brings language shuddering to a halt (you choke on grief). McBride describes herself as a feminist – 'Decisively so.'[36] A thirteen-year-old allowing a forty-one-year-old 'to do what he wants to her will probably feel complicit in that act, but is not and cannot be.' But the victim narrative is misleading. The girl also goes on to choose her fate. McBride insists on her agency: 'Now the reader may not find that the girl has become – and I shudder to say it – "a better person" by the end of the book, but she has, undeniably, become herself.'[37] Nonetheless, by no stretch of the imagination can the end of the first novel be seen as a happy ending. The last line of *Girl* is: 'My name is gone.'

By contrast, from the very first page, *The Lesser Bohemians* makes its lilting bid for life: 'Here's to be for its life is the bite and would be start of mine.' These lines then track through the first part of the novel as a refrain: 'I will make myself of life here for life is this place and would be start of mine'; 'what this pleasant present lacks. I will it, hope and dream it. Fine my life'll be when it comes. When I am right. When I have made myself. When I have. When I.'[38] London is the scene, specifically the streets, pubs, clubs and letting houses of north-west London in the 1990s (with occasional references to the IRA, Pakis and the poor of the East End). One way of reading *The*

Lesser Bohemians would be as girl given a second chance: from the suffocating and fraudulent moralism of Catholic family life in Dublin to free-wheeling London where promiscuity, instead of incurring damnation, is more or less the norm. This shift of place, of tone and mood puts paid to the idea that, in her second novel, McBride was repeating herself.

What is constant is McBride's unswerving commitment to unplugged syntax as it veers between common and uncommon sense. But while *Girl* was virtually no commas and all stops, commas proliferate in *The Lesser Bohemians*, one of whose most striking syntactic features is elongated, unfilled spaces between words. It is the difference between a voice that does not pause for breath, stopping and starting in its tracks, and blanks as a way of registering what can barely be spoken. In such moments, the more conventional ellipses would, it seems, have cluttered the spaces too much: 'like not being fine was alright   was fine   was how it should be' (the repetition – 'alright', 'fine', 'how it should be' – underscoring that it was clearly not fine at all). Or again: 'But do not find so do not ask. Especially about the little girl who is not. And this greater swathe that she cuts through his life, what is its   what can it mean?' (At this point in the story she knows almost nothing about his relationship to his daughter.)[39] To the question of *Girl*: how to speak when the worst has happened? *The Lesser Bohemians* adds another: to whom do we tell our stories, especially those we cannot bear to tell ourselves? As we have seen, *Girl* is a type of inner monologue (with the proviso that she is also almost always addressing her brother). As if partly in response, *The Lesser Bohemians* sets a different challenge: how on earth does anyone ever manage to talk to somebody else? How close in language can, or should, you try to get? The issue of sexual and that of linguistic proximity turn out to be one and the same thing. McBride has said that in writing and rewriting the novel, she was most worried about the representation of sex: 'Actually,' she then qualifies, 'it was really about trying to maintain the connection between the inner life and the physical life.'[40] What makes this novel so powerful is the way she jams the bodies into the speech (we have never been given sex quite like this before). Sex is presented as intensely pleasurable, but it is never innocent. McBride has no interest whatsoever in purging her characters of their potential for violence, a move which – as I suggest throughout this book – is the precondition, under cover of a falsely regimented world, for projecting violence onto others and then enacting it.

Roughly halfway through *The Lesser Bohemians* Stephen tells his story to Eily (it takes seventy pages). Since they are named for the first time after he has done so, the message would seem to be that only when you can bring yourself to talk to another can you ever hope to find yourself. Critics who objected to the way the novel's voice divides at this point, or saw Stephen's narrative as 'hijacking' the narrative, or inconsistent with the novel's form, were therefore missing the point. For the reader of *Girl*, the only place to go was inside the mind of the narrator. *The Lesser Bohemians* is suggesting on the other hand that in order to survive, you must be more than one. Unlike the continuous present of *Girl*, the protagonists of *The Lesser Bohemians* arrive at something like a moment of truth, when 'the past sits forward and the cold comes pouring in.' They have each been warding off this moment for their own reasons but it marks the shift between the casual sex they had been enjoying and not enjoying up until then, and their full-blown love affair. This, we could say, is the unconscious contract between them (as indeed between many couples). It is what they have been gearing up for – and what the reader has been primed to expect – from the start: 'Mess is why we're here.' 'How were you fucked up? Let me count the ways!'[41]

According to one psychoanalytic theory, mother–son incest is worse than father–daughter, because somewhere in the great cosmic and social scheme of things, girls are meant to be wooed by their fathers into a heterosexuality to which their own deepest impulses would not otherwise take them. The dire heteronormative view of women's destiny, so often attributed to Freud, is therefore tinged with a radical streak, as I suggested in relation to abuse and trans in Chapter Three (nature has nothing to do with it, girls have to be more or less forced into their role). Mother–son incest, on the other hand, is catastrophic (psychosis-inducing), yanking boys beneath the social radar altogether since their psychological task is to break away from their mothers if they are to have any chance of becoming 'men'. Just to be clear, this does not mean that it is good for thirteen-year-old girls to be seduced by forty-one-year-old men, nor indeed eighteen-year-olds by men of thirty-eight. If the distance between thirteen and eighteen from *Girl* to *The Lesser Bohemians* makes all the difference, McBride must have been aware that she runs the ages of the protagonists in the two novels perilously close to each other. Like girl in the first novel, Eily has been abused as a young girl, in this case by a friend of her mother, who remains in denial even when Eily confronts her near the end of the book. Momentarily, she also tries on girl's response to trauma by seeking out sex as degradation and terror: 'Devil at my navel. Devil at my breast.' 'And why shouldn't I reject my scum-rid history and wherever I'm wanted, go?' 'And how much do I already know I can take.'[42]

But, alongside Eily's past, it is Stephen's shocking story of his repeated seduction as a young boy by a violent mother which takes up the most space (shocking not as in worse but less familiar or less often told). Although pretty much out of her head most of the time, the mother knew exactly what she was doing: 'I think she thought once she did that I'd never leave.' He nearly goes mad: 'And she hadn't counted on that   that there, in the fucked-up body getting fucked, was a person starting to come to life, starting to want to hurt her and do all the things to her body that she'd done to his. Do worse. Wanting to fucking fling her on the floor and stamp on her face and   I could tell I was starting to go off my head.'[43] Eventually he escapes only to destroy first himself (almost) and then his relationship to the mother of his daughter, from whom, when he first meets Eily, he is completely estranged (the mother takes the daughter to Canada to get her out of his reach). But the way this story erupts in the middle of the novel so unexpectedly and for so long is, as I read it, a way of asking: can this story be told, and, like the incest it narrates, once told, will it ever stop?

There is a formal problem – shades of Prospero telling Miranda the story of their past at the opening of *The Tempest*, stretching the reader's belief that Stephen never got round to telling Eily before. But in a stroke of genius, McBride transposes this age-old difficulty into a device for conveying the mind's resistance to horror: 'He dry retches again. Are you alright? He nods but the grey eyes black and the wall they stare through into that past has gone so eerily thin I can almost see her too.' 'So far so horrible. But not you I say It.' 'Sorry it's turned into an epic night. I'm not, I say.'[44] Critics who dismiss or gloss over Stephen's story are therefore, as I see it, complicit with a time-worn silence which makes the abuse of boys inaudible. The problem is global. In 2019, a study which examined rape laws in forty countries found that just under half of jurisdictions lacked legal protections for boys, and in many cases, laws specific to girls did not recognise boys as victims.[45] McBride has not only lifted an abused girl out of monologue into conversation. She also seems to be saying that the world will continue to run to its end if women only tell the stories of their own damage and refuse to listen to the tale of traumas lived by men. Mothers, it should be said, do not come out so well in *The Lesser Bohemians*. The second remarkable story Stephen has to tell is of the lengths Marianne, the mother of their daughter, has gone to make the daughter hate him, including, in a final bid for cruelty, telling her of the incest he was subjected to as a boy. It backfires as these things tend to do, turning the daughter's anger against the mother, and only making her pity, love and long for her lost father more.

There is therefore a type of redemption, although the novel studiously avoids any piety of the cure. 'I hate a moral,' McBride has stated, 'and I'm not much keener on an inspirational tale of survival against the odds.'[46] After Stephen tells his story, things get better between them, then worse – 'This is the start of the strange for us, of that long night's story doing its work in ways I now can see'; 'All the past now collating instead of forgotten. I suddenly misplace the best of myself, allowing a far worse in' – before getting better again.[47] We seem then to be living in cyclical time. To evoke the title of Freud's famous article 'Remembering, Repeating and Working Through', *The Lesser Bohemians* messes with the order of play ('working through' is usually evoked clinically to suggest the completion of the psychic process, as if matters move psychically to their resolution along a more or less straight line). Despite the euphoric ending, the debris and detritus of these stories will, one feels sure, track the lives of those who will continue to struggle against them. Like all novels with a happy ending, *The Lesser Bohemians* leaves you asking whether the finale is any match for the sheer magnitude of what has gone before.

Before she was a novelist, McBride was an aspiring actress, close to the one she portrays in her novel. Both of her novels are streaked with autobiography (in relation to *Girl*, she has described the death of her brother as the most devastating event in her life). The *Lesser Bohemians* of the title refers to the life of the jobbing actor, the artistic life less celebrated, those who never get to be stars and who struggle to pay the bills, carrying on simply because they love the work. But acting is also a pathway out of fear, providing an exit route from one life into another: 'Converting the self into flecks of form and re-form. Her. Into Her. Into someone else.' 'Excused of myself by the in out of words.'[48] In acting, you bring the other to life. It is, one might say, the perfect context and frame for a novel whose main drive is to get two people, finally, to talk to each other. We might note in passing how far this is from one current Hollywood ethos: 'I don't think that, as a creative person, you have that much to contribute when your life experiences are limited to those you have while you're emulating someone else,'[49] Renée Zellweger explained in a recent interview. In fairness she was trying to shed the idea that she *is* Bridget Jones, but the casual dismissal of the idea of emulating, entering into the body and soul of, someone else is striking.

Such is McBride's commitment to this project that at moments it drives the writing into a hallucinatory dimension which, as we saw in Toni Morrison's *Beloved*, intensifies mental space beyond endurance. As if to match the violence of the modern world, McBride has to force the screw of modernism's linguistic disorientation one more turn. It is no coincidence that for Morrison in relation to slavery, and McBride in relation to sexual violence, language goes off the rails. For example, in one of the most formally eccentric moments in the novel (there is nothing quite like it in *Girl*), Stephen's daughter, known only from a photograph in the room, starts addressing Eily when she is in the middle of sex: 'This is my father.' 'He made me doing this, what he'll do with you.' 'But he is my father. And your father taught me this, showed me how until I love to and know him like you never can. This is my father. Taking my knickers down.' In relation to those last two sentences, it is only by doing a double take and distinguishing the voices beyond what the writing quite permits – they are speaking in turn – that the reader can save the daughter from incest (although the form surely also invites the other reading). And only if we halt the flow will we recognise that Eily, rivalrous to the limit, is also trying to deflect the daughter from harm: 'And good to be hurt by him in ways you never will' (the fantasy seeming to be that submitting herself to sexual pain is a way of saving a child).[50] The punctuation gives you minimal guidance. You have to work it out for yourself; along with the suspended blank spaces, this is another repeated stylistic peculiarity of the book. Then, when Stephen tells Eily of meeting up with Marianne, the voice starts splintering to infinity: in Marianne's words – although it is Stephen speaking – we are given Stephen's stepfather's account, as told to Marianne, of Stephen's mother confessing as she lay dying what she had done to her son. Faced with all this, any reader would be forgiven for thinking they were going crazy but that, I would suggest, is the point. Formal decorum is hardly appropriate, or has its limits, in a tale of how people find and force themselves into each other's bodies and heads. In a world of such rampant licence, why on earth would you expect to know who or where you are?

McBride has said that her aim in her novels is 'to go in as close as the reader would reasonably permit' – a perfect aesthetic formula for the sexual problem that haunts her book. In a rare distancing from Joyce, she describes *Finnegans Wake*, alongside Gertrude Stein's *The Making of Americans*, as 'obscure' and 'obtuse' for the non-specialist reader ('kamikaze missions'). Instead, she uses the simplest vocabulary in the hope that this will allow readers to make the complexities of the syntax their own, as if the narrative was running inside their minds: 'from the inside out rather than the outside in.'[51] It is, then, hardly surprising that abuse, incest, passion have been her themes to date. In each case, closeness is the burning issue: whether desired, killing, too little or too much. Aesthetic form and story are twinned. 'Fright', Eily says when things are going badly, 'goes everywhere like losing blood.' Sometimes it feels that, as a writer, McBride is chasing her own fear. Without ever passing judgement, *The Lesser Bohemians* situates itself at that point of moral, sexual and grammatical uncertainty where, in Eily's words again, 'pure is indivisible from its reverse.'[52] If we are to face down the reality of violence in our times, violence thrust deep into the life of the mind, this is, I suggest, the only place to begin.

THE KILLING OF REEVA STEENKAMP,
THE TRIAL OF OSCAR PISTORIUS

Sex and Race in the Courtroom

On 3 March 2014, the first day in the trial of Paralympic champion Oscar Pistorius for the killing of law graduate and model Reeva Steenkamp, Judge Thokozile Matilda Masipa entered Courtroom GD at North Gauteng High Court in Pretoria, the courtroom used for high-profile cases involving intense security because it is closest to the exit. Riddled with severe arthritis, although this received little attention at the time, she sat on an orthopaedic chair during the trial, much smaller than the vast leather chairs of the two assessors on either side. Judge Masipa made her way across the courtroom slowly and haltingly, with greater difficulty than the defendant she was there to judge.[1] According to one observer, Pistorius 'strode' up to the dock.[2]

Depending on your opinion of her final judgement, Judge Masipa was either uniquely qualified or unsuited to her task. She found Pistorius not guilty of murder, guilty of culpable homicide – the equivalent of manslaughter in Anglo-American law. When the judgement was overturned on appeal by the South African Supreme Court, she increased his sentence by one year, a decision which, like her original judgement, was described by the prosecutors as 'shockingly lenient' and greeted with widespread dismay (after a subsequent appeal by the prosecutors in November 2017, the sentence was doubled to thirteen years and five months, i.e. fifteen years minus time already served).[3] Following her original verdict, Masipa had been the target of misogynistic and patronising vitriol; she was called 'an incompetent black woman', taunted with being 'blind and deaf' and required round-the-clock house protection from the court.[4] Many of those accusing her spoke in the name of justice for women.

Judge Masipa was a latecomer to the law, undertaking her pupillage in her forties. Admitted as an advocate in 1991 as one of only three black women at the Johannesburg bar, she was appointed judge in the Transvaal Provincial Division of the High Court of South Africa in 1998, the second black woman to be appointed to the bench. Despite her rulings in the Pistorius case, Judge Masipa is known for the harsh maximum sentences she metes out in cases involving violence against women. In 2009, she gave a life sentence to a police officer who shot and killed his wife: 'You deserve to go to prison for life,' she said in her sentencing, 'because you are not a protector, you are a killer.'[5] In May 2013, she sentenced a serial rapist to 252 years – fifteen years on each of eleven counts of robbery, twelve years for attempted murder and life sentences for each of three rape charges. Judge Masipa knows about violence. Born in Soweto, she is from a family of ten children, four of whom died young, one of them stabbed to death by unknown perpetrators when he was twenty-one.

As with many characters in this tale, Judge Masipa's life tracks violence from apartheid to its aftermath, uncovering the reality of South Africa's hidden and unhidden crimes. She has, as one could say, done her time. She knows what it means to be on the wrong side of the law (even if the law itself in apartheid South Africa was wrong). In the 1970s she was a crime reporter for the *World*, a paper banned in 1977 by Justice Minister Jimmy

Kruger with its staff detained. Before releasing the prisoners for a court appearance, four white court wardens demanded they clean out their toilets (they refused). In 1964, she had marched in protest with several female colleagues against the arrest of black male reporters from the white-owned newspaper the *Post*. When five of the women, including Masipa, were detained, locked in a cell and taken to court, they refused to enter a plea on the grounds that they did not recognise the authority of the apartheid state. At the *Post*, she had launched and headed a supplement on women.[6]

Judge Masipa is 'compassionate' – her word. She brings her history, the racial history of South Africa, into the court. You look at the law, she says in one interview, 'with different eyes', 'because you're compassionate.' Faced with a black woman on trial, she continued, 'you might make things easier for her by explaining things and not being too hard on her. But not everyone understands that.'[7] Not everyone understands the racially inflected care which, as one of South Africa's first black women judges, Masipa brings to the law. In another of her judgements she found in favour of a group of Johannesburg squatters on the grounds that the city had failed in its duty of care: the city, she said, was trying to 'distance itself' from the occupiers.[8] 'I sort of can identify with what these youngsters are going through,' she has commented on young offenders who pass through her court, 'because this is where I come from.'[9] Just how remarkable this is can be gauged by comparison with the instruction given by Susan Shabangu, minister of mines at the time of the 2012 police massacre of thirty-four workers who were part of a strike for an increase in pay at the Marikana platinum mine. As deputy minister for security, she had said to a meeting of police officers the previous year on how to deal with offenders: 'You must kill the bastards if they threaten you or your community. You must not worry about the regulations. That is my responsibility.'[10]

Some have argued that Masipa's compassion clouded her judgement: that she empathised too closely with Pistorius and his disability. Like a psychoanalyst, she should have put her feelings and preferences, even her own history, to one side (although it is arguable whether this is what a psychoanalyst can, or should, do). Throughout the trial, Masipa's voice was steady, unlike that of the defendant, who fell apart and broke down at every turn. But what does it mean to talk of the still, calm voice of the law in conditions of rampant racial and sexual violence and inequality?

o o o

Every four minutes in South Africa a woman or girl – often a teenager, sometimes a child – is reported raped and every three hours a woman is killed by her partner (the second figure, from a report of 2019, shows how fast this violence is accelerating, as it was every eight hours according to reports from the time of the Pistorius trial).[11] The phenomenon has a name in South Africa: 'intimate femicide', or, as Margie Orford calls the repeated killing of women across the country, 'serial femicide'. According to Cyril Ramaphosa, elected president in 2018, South Africa is 'one of the most unsafe places in the world to be a woman'.[12] On 2 February 2013, less than two weeks before Reeva Steenkamp was killed, Anene Booysen was raped and murdered in the Western Cape. If the two deaths are mentioned together it is mostly in terms of the cruel disparity between the neglected black woman's body and that of her glamorous white counterpart (graveyard racism, we might say). Steenkamp saw things rather differently. For her, violence against women knew no racial bounds. A week after Booysen's murder, she tweeted a report of her funeral, and posted on her Instagram feed a graphic of a man's hand silencing a screaming woman with the words: 'I woke up in a happy safe home this morning. Not everyone did. Speak out against the rape of individuals.'[13]

In the final year of her law degree, Steenkamp broke her back in a riding accident. On recovery, she returned to complete her degree and resolved to pursue her dream of becoming a model in the big city. 'I believe', she said in a blogsite interview, 'I have the ability to fall back into my legal mind under the pressure of my will to succeed.'[14] Her legal mind would always be there, even if on the surface she would start to look like and then be treated as a model and nothing else. The law would become the backdrop or invisible companion of her ambition, the joint riposte to a life that could have been – was nearly – spent in a wheelchair. This was not her first brush with brokenness. According to her cousin Kim Martin, at the sentencing of Pistorius (the only time during the whole trial that the Steenkamp family got to speak), when Reeva was a young girl, the family's pet poodle became paralysed and was going to have to be put down. Reeva saved the dog, 'became its legs', as Martin put it, carrying the animal with her everywhere.[15] Was Steenkamp prey to a fatal identification? Did her compassion for the underdog – 'underdog' literally in this case – play its part in what killed her? One of the most striking things about this trial is that wherever you look, you see bodies that are broken. Near the end of the trial, before the closing arguments, Pistorius's elder brother, Carl, was involved in a head-on car collision which crushed both his legs below the knees – the link to his brother surely as glaring as it appeared to remain unspoken – leaving it unclear whether he would live or ever walk again. In fact, he recovered speedily enough to make it into the courtroom in a wheelchair in time for the verdict.

Judge, victim, perpetrator: the lines of the case, the positions, could not be more clearly drawn. It was never in question that Oscar Pistorius had fired the four shots that killed Reeva Steenkamp. There was no judgement to be passed on whether he had committed the act. He had. Instead the question was, by Masipa's own account, entirely 'subjective'.[16] What was going on inside the mind of Pistorius when he shot through the bathroom door? Everything hung on that question. Did he know he was shooting Reeva Steenkamp? Or did he believe it was an intruder, as he claimed more or less from the moment it happened and certainly to the friends and the police who were the first at the scene of the crime? And *if* we believe him, then did he know he might kill the person on the other side of the door and shoot anyway? In the words of Masipa, 'Did the accused foresee the possibility of the resultant death, yet persisted in his deed reckless whether death ensued or not?'[17] If he did, he would be guilty under South African law of the crime of *dolus eventualis*, which falls short of premeditation but which still counts as murder because the possibility of death is foreseen. Masipa's dismissal of this possible charge against Pistorius was at the heart of the legal disputes around her verdict and formed the basis of the subsequent appeal.

This famous trial sits at the crux of violence in our times. First, because a woman was killed by a man in the privacy of a home. It is therefore a case of justice for women. Secondly, because it contains at its core questions of race and disability which have been the focus of so much discrimination and hatred. And finally, because the trial turned crucially on intent – by Masipa's own account, on what can only be 'subjective' – forcing the law to enter the deepest, most intransigent and sometimes deadly recesses of the mind.

o   o   o

A week before the killing of Reeva Steenkamp, I was in Cape Town, where I found myself reading *A Bantu in My Bathroom*, a book of essays by Eusebius McKaiser, a South African political and social theorist and radio talk-show host.[18] He is known for being provocative. He likes to challenge South Africans to confront their darkest thoughts (his collection is subtitled: *Debating Race, Sexuality and Other Uncomfortable South African Topics*).[19] In 2012, eighteen years after the end of apartheid, he was looking for a room to rent and lighted upon an advertisement from a woman willing to share her house but only, the ad stipulated, with a white person. On the phone, McKaiser got her almost to the point of sealing the deal before announcing that he was not white (she hung up when he suggested her choice might be racist). When he presented the question to the audience of his weekly radio programme, *Politics and Morality* on Talk Radio 702, two responses predominated. Either the listeners sided with the owner of the house (her property, her preference, no different from 'non-smokers only need apply'); or else they made a more subtle, but disquieting, distinction: if the room were in premises in her backyard, the choice would be racist, but clearly she had the right to share her house with whomsoever she pleased.

'Reasonable' as the second preference might seem, he concedes – we will return to the category of the 'reasonable' later – for McKaiser, it is no less 'morally odious', no less 'the product of our racist past':

This viewpoint is an acknowledgement (indeed, an expression) of a deep racial angst. Why else would you be fine with Sipho [the name McKaiser assigns to the fictional black tenant] sleeping in the flat outside but heaven forbid that you should wake up in the morning and the first thing you see on your way to the bathroom is the heart attack-inducing spectacle of Sipho smiling at you, a horror that just might elicit a scream of apartheid proportions, 'Help! There is a Bantu in my bathroom!'[20]

'Not one listener', McKaiser comments, 'grappled with how it is that eighteen years after our democratic journey [. . .] racialism's reach and endurance inside their homes and hearts dare not be spoken about.' Not one avoided the cliché – indeed they rehearsed it to perfection – that your private life is private and it is up to you what you do in your own home (a cliché whose potentially lethal consequences were of course long ago dismantled by feminism). In failing to do so, they 'betrayed dark secrets about themselves and our country' and 'a tragic lack of self-examination'. McKaiser is digging the dirt. He likes to tell things as they are. In another essay he refers to the Coloureds of Cape Town – he himself is a Coloured – as 'the dirty little secret' of the city (the term 'Coloured' is used to refer to South Africans of mixed European and Asian or African descent, mostly from the Western Cape). 'Cape Town, you see,' he elaborates, 'treats coloured people like dirt.' 'The dirty secrets ['dirty' again] of both Jozi [Johannesburg] and Cape Town are a stain on both cities' images, like mud on a kid's new white pants.'[21]

It soon became clear that a strange, racially charged and legally confused distinction would be at the heart of the trial. If Pistorius wasn't aware when he fired the shots from the bathroom that Steenkamp was in the toilet, but believed he was shooting an intruder, then the charge of premeditation would fall. There was no doubt that the second possibility was seen – or rather would be presented by advocate Barry Roux for the defence – as the lesser offence, and not just because of the category of 'putative private defence' (defending oneself against a presumed attacker, even if the presumption was wrong) which would present the shooting as the legitimate response to fear. In fact this would be one of a 'plethora of defences' put forward by Pistorius, to use Masipa's telling phrase and to which I will return.[22] What was largely unspoken, however, was that in the second case, we can be all but certain that the person killed in the bathroom would be – could only be – imagined as black. 'As the judge will not have failed to register,' writes South African journalist John Carlin, 'if his story were true – and even if it were not – the faceless intruder of his imagination had to have had a black face, because the fact was that for white people crime mostly did have a black face.'[23]

Margie Orford was one of the few to draw out the racist implications. 'It is', she wrote in an article for South Africa's *Sunday Times*, 'the threatening body, nameless and faceless, of an armed and dangerous black intruder' into what she calls 'the contemporary version of the laager', 'nothing more than the reclaiming of the old white fear of the *swart gevaar* (black peril)'. For Orford, there is something profoundly amiss – morally for sure and perhaps legally – if this is Pistorius's main defence. She continues: 'If Pistorius was not shooting to kill the woman with whom he had just been sharing a bed, those four bullets indicate that there is still no middle ground. Because whoever Pistorius thought was behind that door, firing at such close range meant that when he finished there would be a body on that bathroom floor.'[24] A Bantu in the bathroom. Or to elaborate McKaiser's point: in the white racist imagination, the only Bantu permitted in a white bathroom is a Bantu who is dead. Whichever way you look at it, the killing of Reeva Steenkamp was either a sex or a race crime.

If Orford's reasoning is correct, what this also means is that the charge of *dolus eventualis* – proceeding with a violent act reckless of whether 'death ensued or not' – should, from the outset, have been allowed to stand (Pistorius would be guilty of murder). In fact, Masipa's dismissal of that charge hangs on a distinction she herself is not quite able to make: 'How', she asks in her judgement, 'could the accused reasonably have foreseen that the shots he fired would kill the deceased? Clearly he did not subjectively foresee this as a possibility that he would kill the person behind the door, let alone the deceased, as he thought she was in the bedroom at the time.' For me, the issue here is not that she chose to believe him – as she rightly points out in law, the contrary cannot be proved. Rather it is the slippage between intruder and Steenkamp that is the giveaway: it is indeed clear that he couldn't have foreseen that he might kill Steenkamp if 'he thought she was in the bedroom at the time.' But how can that also apply to 'the person behind the door', whoever it was, given that he was shooting at that door with a 9mm handgun?[25] According to Masipa, however, if he did not know he was killing Steenkamp, then he is not guilty of murder. Never mind anyone else. The Bantu slips syntactically under the bathroom door.

o o o

Eusebius McKaiser's essay set me thinking about the trial – indeed about bathrooms – in the context of South Africa's past.

Under apartheid law, the rules for white private residences were explicit: servants' quarters had to be across the yard, 'mean little rooms with a sink and a toilet', in the words of South African journalist Mark Gevisser in his 2014 memoir *Lost and Found in Johannesburg*. No shared walls between white master and black servant, above all no shared ablution facilities across racial lines, which suggests that, for apartheid, it is above all the races' body fluids and matter that must not mix, especially if you bear in mind apartheid's ban on cross-racial sexual intercourse, which is so much better known and which might in fact be easier, as in cleaner, to talk about. McKaiser's fastidious respondents, who would make a white racist's bathroom preferences no more than a matter of personal liking and etiquette, are therefore enacting a form of memory as buried as it is historically precise. The white world, Mark Gevisser writes, was defined 'by what it had been walled against'.[26] To illustrate the insane lengths to which this project could be taken, Gevisser gives the example of the ten-foot-high fence built by the apartheid authorities across the rocky promontory off the shore of Cape Town where gay men of different races would congregate in the 1960s. To make sure that Coloureds could not cross into the neighbourhood of white residences at Clifton where his family lived, they extended the fence twenty feet into the Atlantic Ocean. Like the famous and ill-fated king, apartheid believed it could control the waves (unlike Canute, who is simply humbled by his misadventure, apartheid would eventually drown).

There is a politics of water, there is a politics of shit. Remember Masipa and her co-journalists in their prison cells asked to clean out the toilets before appearing in court. In the black township of Alexandra, where there was no sewage system, residents had to leave their shit outside their doors every night for collection (the basis of a protest poem by Mongane Wally Serote – 'What's in This Black "Shit"?'). All the more remarkable, then, as Gevisser observes, were those who carried their anti-apartheid struggle not just into the privacy of their homes, but into the water, allowing bodies to swim, touch and mix against the brute, squeamish hand of the law. Bram Fischer's pool on Beaumont Street was legendary for its parties of black and white men, women and children, photographed lovingly by *Drum* magazine in the 1960s, when Fischer was presenting the concluding arguments in the famous Treason Trial of 156 members of the ANC. Or the home offered by one of Gevisser's acquaintances, Roger, with his black lover, for interracial gay men and boys, a house protected from the prying eyes of the law by soaring cypresses, where the bath was always full so you could wash off someone else's bodily fluids if there was a raid. The Pistorius trial, writes Gevisser, 'coursed through the electoral season like a foul river carrying the country's legacies of fear and violence on its currents'.[27] The analogy is eloquent. Like a foul river, bringing pestilence in its wake, the killing in the bathroom both enacted and drew to the surface of the national psyche its deepest racial fears. What, Orford asks, is this 'irrational fear that has sunk deep into the psyche'? Or in the words of McKaiser, 'mud on a kid's new white pants'.

This is not of course unique to South Africa. Bodily racial insult is something at which regimes since the end of apartheid – regimes which might seem to be on the opposite end of the political scale – have excelled themselves. When President Obama was briefed on a 2015 CIA report on torture, he is recorded as expressing discomfort with the 'image of a detainee, chained to the ceiling, clothed in a diaper, and forced to go to the bathroom on himself'.[28] Commentators were quick to point out that it stretches belief that he didn't in fact already know. The state owns the monopoly on violence and masters the arts of the body to perfection. It is adept at breaking down the body's walls (waterboarding would then just be the most obvious such form of abuse). It is a common racist trope to see the black body – and most of the bodies at Guantánamo and Abu Ghraib were of course non-white – as always already stained. Blackness, Toni Morrison wrote in 1991, at the time of the Clarence Thomas/Anita Hill hearings, 'is already a stain and therefore unstainable'. If Thomas was to ascend to the Supreme Court Bench, if the bench were to be stain-free, 'this newest judge must be bleached, race-free.' The state on the other hand is slick and unctuous, dedicated to the smooth running of its own machine: 'To inaugurate any discovery of what happened', Morrison observes, 'is to be conscious of the smooth syrup-like and glistening oil poured daily to keep the machine of state from screeching too loudly or breaking down entirely as it turns the earth of its own rut, digging deeper and deeper into the foundation of private life, burying itself for invisibility, for protection, for secrecy.'[29]

Pistorius was surely not aware, at least not consciously, that, when he insisted the person he shot in the bathroom was an intruder, he was re-enacting one strand of his nation's cruellest past. Some excuse, we might say. At the very least, even if this defence stands, which finally it didn't, he can hardly be held to be innocent. 'Because', to repeat Margie Orford, 'whoever Pistorius thought was behind that door, firing at such close range meant that when he finished there would be a body on that bathroom floor.' Pistorius's gun was loaded with Black

Talon expanding bullets which mushroom on striking human tissue (removed from the market and then rebranded under the name Ranger). As Mandy Wiener and Barry Bateman point out in their book on the case, this is 'killer ammunition designed to cause as much damage to the target as possible'.[30]

o   o   o

So did Pistorius know that it was Steenkamp in the toilet? It is here that we move into the realm of speculation and dream, where the law hits against the buffer of what is at once screaming out for our attention and cannot be known. When I suggested to the writer Rachel Holmes that this was a case where knowing and not-knowing collide – we know he knew it was Steenkamp in the toilet, only of course we don't, we can think we know but our knowing has its limits, our knowledge, we could say, is not flush with our desire – she suggested that the correct and far simpler distinction to be drawn in this case is between knowing and having no proof. Legally she is of course right, as Masipa dismissed the charge of premeditated murder on the grounds that his intention to kill Steenkamp had not been proved beyond reasonable doubt. But, whichever way you read it, it is clear that, in the words of Masipa, 'there are a number of aspects in the case that do not make sense.' She then proceeded to list questions which, she stated, will 'unfortunately remain a matter for conjecture'.[31] Why, when Pistorius heard the bathroom window opening, as he claimed, did he

> not ascertain from the deceased [. . .] whether she too had heard anything? Why did he not ascertain whether the deceased had heard him since he did not get a response from the deceased

before making his way to the bathroom? Why did the deceased, in the toilet and only a few metres away from the accused, not communicate with the accused, or phone the police as requested by the accused?[32]

'It makes no sense', Masipa observed, 'to say she did not hear him scream "Get out"', since 'it was the accused['s] version that he screamed on top of his voice.' Why did the accused fire not one but four shots before he ran back to the bedroom to try, as he claimed, to find the deceased?[33] To which we can add the questions of Gerrie Nel, leading for the prosecution, and those of the judge at the original bail hearing. Why would someone who slept with a firearm under his bed and was apparently fearful of crime fall asleep with a sliding door to the bedroom wide open? Although Pistorius stated he had been the victim of violence and burglaries, there was no police record of his ever opening a case where he was the victim of a crime.[34] Why did he not see that Steenkamp was not in the bed at the time he unholstered his weapon? Why did he not ascertain the whereabouts of his girlfriend when he got out of bed? Why did he not verify who exactly was in the toilet? Why, in the circumstances of believing an intruder had entered the bathroom, would he not escape through the bedroom door rather than venturing down the corridor? And why, if he knew the intruder was in the toilet, would he further venture into danger, leaving himself open to attack before he shot?

None of these questions was ever fully answered (although Pistorius's defence would work hard to take them down one by one). The police officer on the scene, Hilton Botha, made no bones of the fact that he disbelieved the intruder story. The story does not make sense – as Masipa conceded, while arguing that Pistorius's confused, evasive and lying testimony was not in itself a proof of guilt, which is of course legally correct. Pistorius's former girlfriend Samantha Taylor put it most simply: 'It definitely didn't make sense to me. I would . . . I don't know, I find that kind of weird, I definitely wouldn't close the door, especially if it's not even connected to the bedroom. I don't know why someone would lock the door, even if they are at their boyfriend's house.'[35] Her comments have all the additional force of high-risk empathy – she is willing to imagine herself where she might have ended up, that is, in Reeva Steenkamp's place.

For anyone who reads this killing through the prism of domestic violence, and on behalf of the legions of women who have been its target, one question surely stands out from all the rest. Why did Steenkamp not speak or cry out, not from the bedroom if that is where she was, nor from the toilet? Why, the whole time the accused was screaming, even when he was in the bathroom, did she not utter a word? This is Pistorius in his final statement: 'I got to the entrance of the bathroom, at the end of the passage, where I stopped screaming.' 'At this point I started screaming again for Reeva to phone the police.' 'I kept on screaming.' 'I shouted for Reeva . . . I kept on shouting for Reeva.'[36] Why didn't she answer or call out? A dead woman becomes a silent witness in the courtroom, voiceless now, voiceless then. Twice over, Pistorius silenced Reeva Steenkamp, turned her into a ghost.

It is worth staying for a while with this question of voice because it produced one of the most extraordinary and unanticipated turns of the trial. Four witnesses – Michelle Burger and her husband Charl Johnson, Estelle van der Merwe and Dr Johan Stipp – testified that they heard the unmistakeable voice of a woman before the shots were fired: a woman, more than one of them insisted, who sounded as if she feared for her life. On the witness stand, each of them was adamant that the voice of the person 'screaming hysterically' was a woman's voice.[37] Their testimony was finally dismissed as inconclusive (largely owing to inconsistencies in timings). The argument for the defence was that the cries they heard came after, not before, the fatal shots were fired, and were those of Pistorius as it dawned on him what he had done: establishing the timeline between cry and shots was therefore crucial to the defence, as was the assertion that Steenkamp would have been so instantly and fatally wounded after the first shot that she would have been incapable of making any sound.

The cries, man or woman, came after. Masipa didn't seem to register that Pistorius's own claim that he was screaming 'on top of his voice' as he made his way along the corridor was inconsistent with his argument that the cries heard by the witnesses came after the shots were fired: 'It was the accused['s] version that he screamed on top of his voice, when ordering the intruders to get out.'[38] When you read Pistorius's statement, it seems pretty clear that his repeated insistence that he was shouting out was his means – under legal instruction, no doubt – of countering the witnesses who claimed to have heard a woman's screaming voice before the shots were fired (in which case all the time spent trying to establish that the screams came after the shots, and could therefore not have been Steenkamp, was a complete waste).

But if there was screaming before the shots, how to see off the charge that it could have been her voice? At this point, the trial suddenly became surreal as it turned on its head the perfect heterosexual narrative which accounts for so much of the seductive pull of this case. When he screams, the defence claimed, Oscar Pistorius – Blade Runner, stud, hero – *sounds like a woman.* At one point, in support of this argument, Roux asked two female witnesses to demonstrate the crying they had heard: unsurprisingly, they sounded like women, as would any woman letting out 'two long wails' (unsurprisingly, he did not repeat the experiment with any of the male witnesses, who presumably would have sounded like men). He also announced that decibel tests and an expert witness would establish that when Pistorius is anxious, he screams like a woman. In fact no such testimony was ever laid before the court and no audio of Pistorius screaming was ever played. Samantha Taylor stated that when Oscar screamed, 'it sounded like a man.' Roux dismissed her evidence on the grounds that she had never heard him in situations where he perceived his life to be in danger, which she had to concede.[39]

Better to sound like a woman than to have murdered one. Better a cross-gender identification than a killing masculinity (on that much, feminism, and not only feminism, would surely agree). To save his skin, Oscar Pistorius ventriloquised a woman, or was led by his legal team to do so. He took her place. Behind what might be seen as a moment of unanticipated and welcome gender confusion – since gender confusion is always, or nearly always, to be welcomed – we might also, or rather, see a man going to the furthest lengths he can go, including sacrificing the image of himself as a man, to make absolutely sure that no one hears the voice of a woman crying out in fear for her life.

o o o

Gender trouble has become one of the theoretical mantras of our time. But there are forms of gender uncertainty which add insult to injury and one of the most glaring instances I have come across was surely on display at this trial. We know that for the ANC women protesting outside the court and for women the world over, this case bore all the signs of lethal domestic violence (even if Steenkamp and Pistorius did not strictly share a home). We know that what often appears to be, indeed might be, the most intimate, loving relationship can fail to protect. We know that passionate attachment can be the riverbed of hatred, that, as many women discover too late, sex is often the bedfellow of crime – although, as I make clear throughout this book, I am not a feminist who believes all men, simply by dint of being men, are violent towards women. We also take note, as British journalist Suzanne Moore was the quickest to point out, after the first sentence imposed by Masipa, that Pistorius got less for killing Reeva Steenkamp than he would have got for killing a rhino (five years with parole possible after ten months).[40]

But the fact that this was a case where a man had killed his girlfriend did not stop the defence from arguing – incredibly and offensively – that, because of his disability, when Pistorius shot through that door he himself could best be understood by being compared with an abused woman who, after years of pressure, finally snaps and kills her abuser. When, as one would expect, the analogy was challenged by Masipa – 'how does [an abused woman's situation] apply to the accused in this case?' – Roux, as I see it, only makes matters worse:

I am not talking about abuse here. You know I cannot run away. I cannot run away. I do not have a flight response [. . .] His experience with that disability, over time you get an exaggerated fight response [. . .] That is the 'slow burn' effect. Not abuse . . . That constant reminder I do not have legs, I cannot run away. I am not the same . . . He can pretend . . . he can pretend that he is fine [. . .] because of the anxiety [. . .] it was in that sense that I say the abuse is different, but it is the same. Without legs, abuse, abuse, abuse. So ultimately when that woman picks up that firearm . . . we can use the common word, I have had enough, I am not shooting you because you have just assaulted me, not because of one punch with a fist in my face. I would never have shot you because of one punch with a fist in my face, but if you have done it 60, 70 times, that effect of that over time, it filled the cup to the brim that is . . . in that sense, My Lady.[41]

Now Pistorius does not just sound like a woman, he *is* a woman. This almost defies comment, but not quite. There is a kernel of truth in here, to which I will return, about Pistorius having to pretend he was fine for most of his life. But this mimicry of a woman, this claim yet again to be speaking in a woman's voice – 'I have had enough' – a woman who, we are to imagine, has just been, for the sixtieth or seventieth time, the target of physical abuse – while clearly beyond the pale, might at the same time be read as a veiled confession, the unconscious acknowledgement by the defence of the very version of this story which they are busy exerting their utmost skills to repudiate: that this is a story of a man enacting violence against a woman, a woman who – if statements by Steenkamp's friends and family are anything to go by – had had enough.

Here is part of a 518-word WhatsApp message Steenkamp sent Pistorius eighteen days before she died, as read out in court, which was one of the few moments when her own words were heard: 'you have picked on me incessantly since you got back from CT and I understand that you are sick but it is nasty [. . .]

I am scared of you sometimes and how you snap at me and of how you will react to me [. . .] I am not some other bitch, you know, trying to kill your vibe.'[42] 'Normal relationships', Masipa commented in her judgement, 'are dynamic and unpredictable most of the times, while human beings are fickle. Neither the evidence of a loving relationship, nor of a relationship turned sour can assist this court to determine whether the accused had the requisite intention to kill the deceased. For that reason the court refrains from making inferences one way or another in this regard.'[43] Again she is right – certainly about relationships. Yet for me this is perhaps the darkest moment in the judgement, when the law, when a woman judge, fails to give due weight to another woman, one who will not survive. For while I do not believe that all women are at risk from all men, I do believe that a woman does not say she is scared of a man without cause and that when she does so, we must listen. It is the 'how you *will* react to me' – 'I am scared of you sometimes [. . .] and of how you *will* react to me' – the fear in the future tense which, for me, is most loudly calling for our attention. In Afrikaans, 'will react' can also be understood as a continuous present, as in 'how you do react to me', but if anything that makes matters worse.[44]

None of which of course excludes the presence of love, as any abused woman will testify (her fear is not incompatible with her leaving him an unopened valentine's card). For the same reason, Pistorius's grief at Steenkamp's death – which must include the repeated moments of his weeping, retching and vomiting in the courtroom – surely cannot be taken as proof that he lacked the requisite intent to kill her. As if guilt cannot intensify grief. As if you cannot regret with all your heart what was your most fervent wish only seconds ago. As if love and murderousness are incompatible. Instead Masipa argued that Pistorius's grief would have had to be fake, which it clearly wasn't, if he had wanted to kill his girlfriend – just one more moment in the proceedings where, for me, we sorely needed Freud. Here is another. Interrogated by Nel as to why he thinks Steenkamp did not cry out, Pistorius replies: 'I presume that she would think that the danger was coming closer to her. So why will she shout out?'[45] Another veiled confession – although the moment appears to have received no commentary – in which Pistorius, trying to wriggle out of one corner (why did she not cry out?), lands himself in another by correctly, if unintentionally, identifying himself as the approaching danger against which Steenkamp was protecting herself ('the danger was coming closer').

And another: cross-examined by Nel on why he was screaming after firing the shots, Pistorius said, 'I slowly made my way back, tried to shout for Reeva, screaming.' 'Why did you scream?' 'I wanted to ask Reeva why she was phoning the police.' By this point Steenkamp was dead. The statement would have been even more damning had he made it with reference to the time before the shooting as he approached the bathroom. Nonetheless at the very least it gives us Pistorius confessing that Steenkamp was calling the police as he insists he asked her to do, which means they could hear each other; and suggesting that she was not in fact doing so at his instigation and, therefore, by implication, had her own reasons for calling them. The two reasons of course cancel each other out: he asked her to call the police, he did not know why she was calling them (what Freud would call the 'kettle logic' of the unconscious). Amazingly, his choice of words – 'why she was phoning the police' – wasn't picked up by the prosecutor or anyone else.[46]

o o o

Sex, race, disability, and that's not all, even if it is too much or certainly more than enough. So let's return to Roux's comment: 'He can pretend that he is fine.' They were of course the perfect couple. They both honed their bodies. On her left ankle, Steenkamp had a tattoo of the word 'Lioness' (she was a Leo), which she explained on Twitter: 'Abundance and power are yours, for you are the lioness.'[47] She had trained herself to 'flawless super-fitness', Hagen Engler, editor of *FHM* magazine, recalled in a column in the *Daily Maverick*, days after she was killed.[48] On Pistorius's upper back, these words from Corinthians are tattooed:

> I do not run like a man running aimlessly
> I do not fight like a man beating the air.
> I execute each strike with intent.
> I beat my body and make it my slave.
> I bring it under my complete subjection
> To keep myself from being disqualified
> Having called others to the contest.

The line about making my body my slave is not in most translations from Corinthians, nor is subjection described as 'complete'. Pistorius was raising the stakes. He was also punishing, or even indicting, himself. 'To keep myself from being disqualified' is telling. In 2007, he had been under investigation by the International Association of Athletics Federations to determine whether his prostheses gave him an unfair competitive advantage. (He eventually won his case and was allowed to compete in the Beijing Olympics in 2008.) We might contrast this with the May 2019 ruling of the IAAF, sport's governing body, against DSD (intersex) South African athlete Caster Semenya, that she would have to reduce her testosterone in order to compete, a decision seen as 'discriminatory' and greeted with an outcry.[49] As if, however accepted on the surface, there is always an aura of suspicion hovering over disabled and trans bodies, an unspoken demand that they not excel themselves too much.

Commenting on an interview he conducted with Bill Schroeder, headmaster of Pretoria Boys High School, Carlin observes that the lessons his mother imparted to Pistorius 'all boiled down to the same thing [. . .] to run as fast as he could.' We don't need Freud here to note the ambiguity and impossible weight of that demand: running to win, getting the hell out at any price. Schroeder recalls that when he tentatively asked Pistorius's mother about her thirteen-year-old son, 'But . . . is he going to cope?' referring to his prosthetic legs, she exchanged glances with her son and shrugged: 'I don't think I follow [. . .] What are you saying?' She then observed, 'There's no problem at all. He's absolutely normal.'[50] On the first page of his autobiography, written before the killing of Steenkamp, Pistorius explains the attitude integral to his family's philosophy: 'This is Oscar Pistorius, exactly as he should be. Perfect in himself.'[51] In fact his mother was a depressive and an alcoholic who died when Pistorius was fifteen. As Carlin points out, the words 'my mother' were the two words Pistorius repeated most in his testimony (his mother slept with a firearm under her pillow, Pistorius slept with a firearm under his bed).

For disability studies, indeed for anyone involved with disability, Sheila Pistorius's description of her son, and the Pistorius family philosophy, would surely be correct – in the eyes of any humane philosophy, all bodies are as they 'should be'. Today, under a Conservative government in the UK whose reasserted harshness towards disability seems to know no limits, it may be more important to insist on this than ever before. As feminist literary critic Cora Kaplan observed twenty years ago, the discourse of fiscal responsibility in both the United States and Great Britain has long had disability in its sights as an intolerable economic burden on so-called 'normal' citizenry.[52] Sheila Pistorius's 'He's absolutely normal' could then be read as a socially attuned riposte. The only response to such bureaucratic inhumanity must be to argue that need or frailty, alongside the human dignity – indeed 'normality' – of the disabled, should be recognised. We are talking about justice and human rights (which are the terms in which much recent disability studies defines its task).

But this in itself is something of a double bind. Insist on dignity and normality, the risk is that both physical and psychic suffering become invisible, denied, and then have to deny themselves (he is perfect). Worse, such a denial veers dangerously close to the repudiation of weakness and suffering that has historically licensed the sometimes genocidal cruelty directed towards the disabled themselves: because you suffer, because we have to see your suffering, we will not suffer you. 'In the context of recent disability theory,' writes Hilary Clark, '[the] experience of darkness – of suffering in disability and chronic illness – is not much emphasised [. . .] to talk about what one has suffered and lost no longer feels quite decent.'[53] She is writing in a book of essays on the life and writing of poet and literary critic Nancy Mairs, who was struck down with multiple sclerosis and whose best-known essay is called 'On Being a Cripple', now an unspeakable word but one which she reclaims for herself. 'Society is no readier to accept crippledness', Mairs writes, 'than to accept death, war, sex, sweat or disease.'[54] For Mairs it is emancipatory not oppressive, and the opposite of inhuman, to speak openly of a body that fails.

On these matters, the trial of Oscar Pistorius is truly a case book. Professor Merryll Vorster, the forensic psychiatrist called by the defence, was in no doubt that the amputation of both of Pistorius's lower limbs as a pre-verbal child under a year would have been experienced as a traumatic assault, that the family attitude had meant that he was never allowed to see himself as disabled, and that this had a significant detrimental impact on his development: 'By concealing his disability, it rendered him less able to access the emotional support he required.'[55] In a vicious cycle, she argued, his physical vulnerability made him more anxious, which then made him more intent on concealing his physical vulnerability from the world. We could say that his disability became the encrypted secret of his body and his life.

When the prosecution saw that Vorster's comments might lead to a defence based on General Anxiety Disorder, Nel immediately demanded that Pistorius undergo a full psychiatric assessment. It was a moment of high drama – leading to a one-month suspension of proceedings. Nel had taken a risk. Hoping to rule out a possible defence for Pistorius, he might instead have been opening the door to his being acquitted on grounds of mental incapacity. When the court resumed, however, the decision was unequivocal: Pistorius suffered no form of mental debility and showed no lack of criminal capacity, which would have prevented him from knowing the consequences of his act or from distinguishing between right and wrong. 'There was', Masipa comments in her judgement, 'no lapse of memory or any confusion on the part of the accused.'[56]

Strangely, and without anyone seeming to notice, the battle in the courtroom was now repeating the internal dilemma of Oscar Pistorius himself, as it split down the middle between the two ways of seeing disability in our time: Pistorius as crippled and vulnerable, Pistorius as perfect and empowered. If the first, then he shot Reeva Steenkamp out of his deep-seated fears; if the second, he shot because his physical prowess, and the acclaim that followed, had allowed him to nurture the illusion that he ruled the world and could take the law into his own hands. Ironically, it was the prosecution that had to believe unreservedly in Pistorius on his own terms, had – in effect – to side with him. 'For the prosecution to succeed,' Carlin writes, 'he needed Pistorius to be regarded by the judge as he had always portrayed himself prior to the trial [. . .] Nel had to deny the existence of the secretly vulnerable and fear-plagued amputee as vigorously as the Blade Runner himself had sought to do all his life until the night of the shooting.'[57] The defence, on the other hand, could only proceed by ruthlessly dismantling his lifelong, most carefully nurtured, image of himself: 'Without legs, abuse, abuse, abuse.'

It was therefore the defence that mutilated Pistorius's own defences, as it proceeded to uncover his disability in the eyes of the world. On two occasions during the proceedings, he was obliged to reveal his stumps to the courtroom (one might also see his weeping, retching and vomiting in court as his body spilling over its borders and revealing itself). In fact, he himself was more than ready to follow this line of his defence: 'The discharging of my firearm was precipitated by a noise in the toilet which I, in my fearful state, knowing that I was on my stumps, unable to run away or properly defend myself physically, believed to be the intruder or intruders, coming out of the toilet to attack Reeva and me.'[58] Note: 'the discharging of my firearm was precipitated' – no subject of the act, no agent, no responsibility, as if the gun had gone off all by itself.

Perfection is killing. We have to ask whether making heroes of the disabled – which of course in Pistorius's case, indeed in all cases, is somehow also right – might not at the same time exacerbate the anguish and violence of the soul. Banners at the 2012 London Olympics read: 'Paralympics. We are the super-humans.'[59] Not cripples but gladiators, as one commentator observed. Pistorius was the 'bullet in the chamber' (the strap line to the banner on his official website). Between Pistorius, his father, two of his uncles and his grandfather, his family owned fifty-five guns. In one notorious episode, Pistorius shot through the sun roof of a car after an altercation with a police officer about his gun when the driver was pulled over for speeding: 'You cannot just touch another man's gun,' he offered by way of explanation for his rage – his gun a body part, the most intimate piece of himself. Samantha Taylor spoke about his gun as a 'third party' in their relationship. A 9mm Luger bullet sat upright on his kitchen counter. At the time of the killing, he was waiting to take delivery of six firearms including a semi-automatic, the same as that used by the South African Police Service, and 580 rounds of ammunition.[60]

There is, again, a history of South Africa to be told here. The Afrikaner had conquered the southern tip of Africa with guns, a heritage of which, Carlin observes, the Pistorius clan were proud.[61] In Zakes Mda's 2014 novel *Black Diamond*, a white magistrate is under threat for her crackdown on crime. When she insists to her assigned black protector that she does not want guns in her home, he replies with a smirk on his face: 'You don't want guns? [. . .] What kind of Afrikaner are you?'[62]

As Gillian Slovo put it in her Ralph Miliband lecture at the London School of Economics in May 2014, the guns that supported and opposed apartheid are still too present in South Africa today.[63] 'In this vast and beautiful land of post-apartheid South Africa,' Jonathan McEvoy wrote on the trial in the *Daily Mail*, 'there is too often a gun at the end of their Rainbow.'[64] Pistorius was fearful of crime – no white South African, indeed no South African, can avoid being fearful of crime. Robberies in residential properties increased by seventy per cent between 2003 and 2012, although in nine out of ten cases the victims of such burglaries are unharmed, and it is the poor who are most often the victims of violent crime. In fact, the vast majority of South Africans do not own firearms (barely five per cent of the population, a figure that has stayed roughly stable since then).[65]

On this Masipa was unhesitant. Pistorius's actions could not be justified by his fears. 'I hasten to add that the accused is not unique in this respect,' she states, in for me one of the best moments in her judgement. 'Women, children, the elderly and all those with limited ability would fall under the same category.' 'But,' she asks, 'would it be reasonable if without further ado they armed themselves with a firearm if threatened with danger?' 'Many have been victims of violent crime but they have not resorted to sleeping with firearms under their pillows.'[66] Vulnerability is no licence to violence. You think you are unique in this regard? Think again. Disability or weakness is something you can suffer, but never own. It is no excuse. For that reason I am not persuaded by those who argue that Masipa's sympathy for Pistorius's disability swayed her judgement, although it is surely true that she refused to join in the hatred directed against him.[67] She is a universalist, moved by a compassion that manages at once to be specific to South Africa while taking in the vulnerable – women, children, the elderly, all those with limited ability – everywhere. Nor am I convinced that she was above all driven by the desire to avoid being seen as enacting revenge justice – that is black justice – on a rich white man (although it is surely the case that, as a black woman judge, she too was on trial).

o o o

Sex, race, disability, what's left? What's left is the life of the mind, the limits of human knowledge, the psychic and political imperative of thought. There are guns, and there is thinking. In his testimony, Pistorius repeatedly insisted that he wasn't thinking when he fired four shots through the door:

> [In] the split moment I believed somebody was coming out to attack me. That is what made me fire. I did not have time to think.
>
> I did not shoot at anyone. I did not intend to shoot at someone. I shot out of fear.[68]
>
> I fired my firearm before I could think.[69]

Or as Masipa replays in her summary of what she has heard him say: 'I am a gun enthusiast. I did not have time to think.'[70]

But if he did not intend to shoot anyone and was not thinking, then he cannot rely on an argument of putative self-defence (that he shot in response to a perceived threat). Whereas if he shot because he thought he was in danger of attack, then he clearly had time to think. As he himself explains, only making matters considerably worse, had he wanted to kill an intruder, he would have shot higher up, towards the chest. 'I pause to state', Masipa comments, 'that this assertion is inconsistent with someone who shot without thinking.'[71] Pistorius's 'plethora of defences' obey the logic of the unconscious, each one cancelling out the next. He was judged according to whether his behaviour was that of a reasonable person, but it is something beyond reason that the law found itself up against. 'What is this irrational fear that has sunk so deep into the psyche?' was Margie Orford's question. 'In that unyielding construct of threat and danger,' she elaborates, 'of your death or mine, there is no middle ground, no compromise and no space for thought or language.'[72] Not thinking does not render you innocent, any more than fear. It is in the split second between thought and non-thought that you kill.

Recall that in her dismissal of *dolus eventualis*, Masipa argued that Pistorius could not 'reasonably have foreseen' that the shots he fired could kill 'the person behind the door, let alone the deceased, as he thought she was in the bedroom at the time.' And yet, finding him guilty of culpable homicide, she asks: 'Would a reasonable person in the same circumstances as the accused, have foreseen the possibility that, if he fired four shots at the door of the toilet, whoever was behind the door, might be struck by a bullet and die as a result? Would a reasonable person have taken steps to guard against that possibility? The answer to both questions is yes.'[73] This is reason straining at its own leash: the accused could not have reasonably foreseen the death of the deceased, a reasonable person would have taken steps to guard against the death of the person behind the door. Who is this reasonable person? If Masipa is wrong – as the Supreme Court decided on appeal – it might be because the law cannot take full measure of the complexities of the human heart to which we, unreasonably, expect it to be equal. It might also be because its category of reason, not least in the realm of violent crime, is a shape-changer. 'The reasonable man', Masipa observes, quoting a legal precedent, 'of course evolves with the times. What was reasonable in 1933 would not necessarily be reasonable today.'[74]

There is also an issue of language involved, as the attribution of guilt hangs on the finest linguistic discriminations, in particular on the auxiliary verb. Some examples: 'I am not persuaded that a reasonable person with the accused's disabilities in the same circumstances, *would have* fired four shots into that small toilet cubicle.'[75] Criminal liability is attributed according to whether 'he *ought to have* foreseen the possibility of resultant death'.[76] The court, Masipa commented, citing another preceding judgement in relation to the charge of murder, 'should guard against proceeding from "*ought to have* foreseen" to "*must have* foreseen" and thence to "by necessary inference *in fact foresaw*" the consequences of the conduct being inquired into.'[77] '[The inference] of subjective foresight cannot be drawn if there is a reasonable possibility that the accused did not foresee, even if he *ought reasonably to have done so* and even if he *probably* did so.'[78] At which point, we appear to have entered the world of that first great experimental novel, Laurence Sterne's *Tristram Shandy*, of 1759. How, asks Tristram's Uncle Toby, can someone speak about a white bear if he never saw one? Whereupon Tristram's father produces this paean to the auxiliary verb and its power to conjure before our eyes what isn't there:

A WHITE BEAR! Very well. Have I ever seen one? Might I ever have seen one? Am I ever to see one? Ought I ever to have seen one? Or can I ever see one?

Would I had seen a white bear! (for how can I imagine it?)

If I should see a white bear, what should I say? If I should never see a white bear, what then?

If I never have, can, must, or shall see a white bear alive, – have I ever seen the skin of one? Did I ever see one painted? – described? Have I never dreamed of one?

Did my father, mother, uncle, aunt, brothers, or sisters, ever see a white bear? What would they give? How would they behave? How would the white bear have behaved? Is he wild? Tame? Rough? Smooth?

– Is the white bear worth seeing?

– Is there no sin in it? –

Is it better than a *black one?*[79]

This is language as speculative decay, losing its grip on reality, which – as we have known since the Swiss linguist Ferdinand de Saussure (and Sterne) – it never had anyway.

o o o

'What is this irrational fear that has sunk deep into the psyche?' (Orford's question.) So let us return to bathrooms. After all, it is not just in the South African imagination that they are the scene of the crime – the shower scene in Hitchcock's *Psycho* most obviously comes to mind. In one of the most famous passages in Proust's *A la recherche*, the narrator – at no small physical risk – hoists himself on a ladder and peers through a fanlight into the shop into which the Baron Charlus and the tailor Jupien have disappeared after a mutual seduction in the courtyard. Whereupon he hears sounds so violent that 'had they not constantly been taken up an octave higher by a parallel moaning, I might have thought that one person was slitting another's throat close beside me, and that the murderer and his resuscitated victim were then taking a bath to wash away the traces of the crime.'[80] A bathroom is a place of purity and danger. Not just the scene of a killing, but the first place you go in order to wash away the traces of the crime.

In Western culture bathrooms are places where we submit the roughage of our inner and outer worlds to the regimen of the controlled and the clean. 'There is no denying the cleanliness,' Junichirō Tanizaki laments of the Western toilet in his 1977 meditation *In Praise of Shadows*; 'every nook and corner is pure white.' Yet, '[t]he cleanliness of what can be seen only calls up the more clearly thoughts of what cannot be seen.' 'I suppose I shall sound terribly defensive,' he continues, 'if I say that Westerners attempt to expose every speck of grime and eradicate it, while we Orientals carefully preserve and even idealise it.'[81] Like the Nyakyusa, described by Mary Douglas in *Purity and Danger* (the first and still the last word on these matters), who make it part of the ritual of mourning to venerate their own detritus and sweep rubbish onto mourners, 'to welcome filth'. An obsessional culture, on the other hand – Western culture – is guilty, unsettled in the discriminations it most earnestly wishes to police (the distinction between men and women, or between black and white). As Douglas also points out, it is only around norms and behaviour which are contradictory or unstable – for instance, the attempt to subordinate women in a culture which partly recognises their autonomy as human – that pollution fears tend to cluster, and that they are rarely independent of sex (she gives the example of the husband 'needing to be convinced of his own masculinity and of the dangers thereof').[82] In the case of Pistorius, it was not just his body – 'I beat my body and make it my slave' – but also his mind that he wanted to subordinate: 'Every race is won or lost in the head, so you have to get your head right,' he responded to a question about his obsessional note-taking in an interview with the *Financial Times*. 'Writing things down helps you to control your thoughts.'[83]

But there is a limit to such control. After Mark Gevisser had been attacked in a private home with two close women friends, he started by believing that their lives were saved by the respect they paid to the black intruders. By the end of the process, he came to things rather differently: 'You have no control over what will happen to you. It is random and chaotic, and even if your reasonable behaviour lessens the odds of your being hurt or killed, it guarantees you nothing. You have no control over when, and how, you will die. Once you understand this, you accept that life is a gift.'[84] This is the opposite of obsessional thought which, as Freud puts it, endlessly returns to – because it cannot make peace with – 'those subjects upon which all mankind are uncertain and upon which our knowledge and judgement must necessarily remain open to doubt'; a form of thought which above all cannot bear human ambivalence.[85] On this, Gevisser's story is exemplary. He felt genuine empathy with his intruders, but this did not prevent him from pursuing one of them to court, a Zimbabwean migrant whose story of barely surviving in the city he unfolds with the utmost care. But he also hates him: 'I hated him for having made me hateful and I hated myself for hating him.'[86] This tale bookends *Lost and Found in Johannesburg*. Its psychic complexity is surely the perfect counterfoil to the idea that the only way to deal with an intruder in today's South Africa is to shoot four times through a locked door.

More than twenty-five years after the end of apartheid, South Africa is riddled with violence, still suffering the legacy of its history, 'that unfinished business buried in the South African body politic', which the Paralympic superhero Oscar Pistorius was called upon to help the nation deny and transcend.[87] We could say that it was his tragedy, although far more the tragedy of Reeva Steenkamp, that, prey to a fantasy of omnipotence in which the whole world colluded, he tried to take control of whatever he could: his body, his mind, his women, his guns. If there is a lesson to take from all of this, it is that we keep human injustice and suffering in our sights, while understanding that we too are the criminals; that we should not expel our own hatreds in a futile effort to make ourselves – to make the world – clean. 'The dark hole in the floor', Rebecca West observes of a toilet in old Serbia on her extraordinary 1930s journey through Yugoslavia, 'made it seem as if dung, having been expelled by man, had set itself up as a new and hostile and powerfully magic element that could cover the whole earth.'[88] Expelling dirt is as self-defeating as it is murderous. Someone – a race, a sex – has to take the rap. As I see it, our pressing task is to look at whatever cowers from the light, but without deluding ourselves that we can master it, without ever claiming to know too much.

POLITICAL PROTEST AND
THE DENIAL OF HISTORY

South Africa and the Legacy of the Future

Given the awfulness of the political moment, the ugly collective fantasies of nationhood being unleashed across the US and the UK, it seems urgent to turn to examples of political activism where a collective or group, together with its accompanying rage, has been spawned in the name of social and racial justice. All the more so where that same movement has been charged up with a visceral, affective energy which has made it the target of critique. The student protests which started in South Africa in 2015 have implications which reach way beyond their original complaint: witness their resurgence after the police killing of George Floyd in May 2020, the felling of the statue of slave dealer Edward Colston in Bristol and the revival of the Rhodes Must Fall campaign in Oxford. In this chapter, I suggest that, far from being an eruption of disorder to be met with an 'appropriately' firm, coercive, state response, this moment, in all its intense volatility, is best understood as bringing back to life a violent history which the nation was, and is, trying to transcend and forget. There is of course a long tradition of emotionally charged political struggles being mobilised on behalf of the oppressed: feminism, civil rights, Black Lives Matter, and a recurrent focus here, #MeToo and #AmINext. But what happens when such a movement carries an additional psychic burden, when it rises up in the name of a radically incomplete emancipatory project which is in danger of being undone?

Over a period roughly between 2015 and 2017, I found myself receiving a steady flow of information – news articles, commentaries, leaflets, statements, official and unofficial, counter-statements – from the University of Cape Town and beyond about the protest campaigns that had been taking place in universities across South Africa since March 2015 (Rhodes Must Fall and then Fees Must Fall). In March 2017 I arrived in Cape Town from Great Britain, which, as the mainly white metropolis of empire in the nineteenth and early twentieth centuries, has much to answer for in relation to the torn fabric of South African history. The 1913 Land Act, an act of sheer theft initiated by the British which laid the ground for segregation and then apartheid, would be a good enough place to begin, not least because the unresolved question of land – its still cruelly unequal distribution – is at the core of the continuing struggle in South Africa, one of the most enduring and troubling legacies of the past. In fact, my family were all Jewish migrants from Poland who travelled, under various forms of persecution and duress, to what was felt then to be something of a haven in the UK. Nonetheless, it is from this distance, and with this sense of historic responsibility and privilege, that I found myself immersed in the stories of the protests that had erupted across the educational landscape of South Africa – protests which initially arose within the universities, but which speak to, and drew so much more than, education in their train.

As I read the *Daily Maverick*, the *Daily Vox* and *The Conversation*, they seemed to me to constitute an alternative university space of their own. From their pages I heard voices speaking, analysing, protesting, voices calling for colloquia,

dialogue, workshops, debates, for a form of radical understanding that can be politically transformative without, in
the words of Dudu Ndlovu, black radical feminist and Fallist
(Rhodes/Fees Must Fall activist) who chaired many meetings,
'collapsing the space'.[1] That suggestive formula gave me pause.
I read her as calling for a space that somehow holds across the
fractures and fault lines it must also expose and create, a space
that emerges from a message of brokenness in both declara-
tory and imperative mode, a statement of fact and intent: this
is already broken, this *must* break. Or in the words of Petrus
Brink, farm worker and activist from Citrusdal, a township on
the Western Cape, interviewed by Simon Rakei in the student-
issued pamphlet *Pathways to Free Education*, 'This is . . . this
is . . . this is really not working.'[2] Brink is a member of the
Food Sovereignty Campaign and the Farm Workers, Dwellers
and Migrants Forum, just two of the groups to whom the
student protests reached out and who reached out to those
protests in turn. I was struck by how far building solidarity
nationally and internationally across struggles stood out as a
key aim of the protests: the campaign against outsourcing, the
challenge to the hierarchy between manual and intellectual
labour, the call, issued by Brian Kamanzi amongst other students, for a socially responsive university which would offer
asylum to fellow Africans and diasporas across the globe –
a call which, in the face of Trump's assault on migrants and
refugees, not to speak of the UK's own inhuman policies, has
never felt more relevant.[3]

So how to move forward without forfeiting either the disruptive force of Brink's deceptively simple statement ('this is
really not working') or the space for dialogue and understanding – without collapsing the space? Or to put it another way,

can politically motivated rage be generative, can it erupt and move us forward in the same breath? In her Ruth First memorial lecture on 'Violence and Rage', delivered in August 2016, Leigh-Ann Naidoo spoke of the 'violent, pathological' inequality which was scarring the nation.[4] When Lovelyn Nwadeyi addressed the top two hundred South Africans selected by the *Mail & Guardian* in June of the same year, she described the time as 'disjointed, out of sync, plagued by a generational fault line that scrambles historicity'.[5] 'Pathological', 'plagued' – these are powerful, evocative words, all the more so as they resonate with today's crisis of Covid-19. It is my argument in this chapter that the South African protests – subdued today in South Africa but by no means silenced – together with the outpouring of commentaries, was a unique political moment which raised the relationship between affect and politics to a new pitch.

As a young woman in the late 1960s and early 1970s, I was part of the student protests in Oxford and Paris. In fact, shortly before going to Oxford as an undergraduate, I had taken the last plane home out of Paris in May 1968 before the airports shut down, to the accompaniment of headlines: '*La France s'écrase*' – 'France is crumbling.' If the campaigns in South Africa evoked for me memories of those moments – the same hyperbole of destruction thrown at the protests (after all France did not crumble or fall apart in 1968) – the worlds could also not be more different. Up to that time, Oxford had been a site of unadulterated privilege, barely touched by questions of race, gender and class. Today it seems fair to ask if, or how far, any of that, at a deep level, has really changed. Taking their cue from UCT, students at Oxford initiated their own Rhodes Must Fall campaign in 2015, demanding first and foremost the removal of the statue of Cecil Rhodes from its prominent position at Oriel College as founding father and benefactor. Having first agreed to consider this demand, the college management revoked their offer when various alumni threatened to withdraw their donations and/or disinherit the college in their wills. A major donor whose legacy was rumoured to be in the region of £100,000 was reported to be 'furious'. 'Rhodes Will Not Fall' was the front-page headline of the right-wing *Daily Telegraph*, which could barely conceal its elation at this climbdown.[6] When, in response to the renewed protests in May 2020, the governors finally voted to have the statue removed, Husan Kuyai, tech entrepreneur and former Oxford student, pledged to make up the funds that 'any racist donors pull'.[7]

There is an irony here. After all, it was Britain that was one of the first countries to import into the African continent the brute force of capital whose continuing sway in post-apartheid South Africa is the cause of so much that is broken today. It was, then, somehow ironically appropriate that, faced with the petulant omnipotence of money, the Oxford University management should in the first instance, without a trace of historic self-consciousness, so promptly and cravenly buckle. Those who defended the presence of the statue on the grounds that it needed to remain as part of historical debate; or who argued more bluntly that students wishing to take it down rather than engage in such civilised discussion had no place at Oxford and should seek their education elsewhere (Oxford's chancellor, Sir Christopher Patten, no less); or that one of the main student organisers disqualified himself from any protest since, as a Rhodes scholar, he was indebted to Rhodes, of course never for one minute raised the question of the ongoing histories of material exploitation, of global capital shunted around an increasingly unequal world, in which the monies before which they prostrated themselves might be embedded.

As a young student, I was the beneficiary of a free state-provided education. Like many in the UK, I have watched appalled as the right to free higher education, a key demand of the protests in South Africa, has been systematically dismantled, while an increasingly instrumental version of learning, wedded to 'impact' and quantifiable forms of knowledge in tune with the calculations of capital, has spread across universities. That these fees impact disproportionately on the disadvantaged goes without saying (a manageable loan for the middle class being an insurmountable debt for the poor). So it seemed to me crucial to start by expressing my solidarity with the basic demand for no fees – whether in the form of free education for all or free education for the poor which was also a subject of often fierce debate. I have witnessed the deleterious effects on the house of critical thought of any whittling down of that fundamental right in the so-called free world. Certainly in the UK, the introduction of university fees has been accompanied by an increasing impatience, bordering on contempt on the part of the Conservative government, for the questioning attitude which is the lifeblood of the humanities.[8] In South Africa, subsequent to my visit, the demand for free university education appeared just for a split second to have been met, a progressive parting gesture of then President Zuma, although it later turned out that nothing would happen and that he had not even consulted the Treasury. Students marching on the government buildings to make this demand in October 2015 chanted one of the famous 'revolting songs' of the apartheid era, a song which they pelted 'like a rock at the glass house now run by those erstwhile radicals of the 1970s, '80s, and '90s'.[9]

o o o

The question of this chapter, which the reality in South Africa has so sharply helped and obliged me to focus, is: what, in moments of historical crisis, is being passed down from one generation to the next? In a struggle which is also a reckoning with the past – as all political struggles may be, but this one surely was – what both can, and cannot, be borne? What do we not want to know about the past? What do we not want to know about ourselves? What forms of anger and recrimination might one generation be carrying on behalf of the generation that came before, a generation which believed and still believes in – which yearns above all for – a world that could resolve the injustices of the past and put an end to violence? In everything I read about the situation in South Africa, the word 'free' was central, first in the context of the demand for free education, and then again in the concept of the 'born free', the term applied to the generation born after the legal and political dismantling of apartheid in 1994. When the journalist Eve Fairbanks visited South Africa to investigate the protests for the UK's *Guardian* in November 2015, she was driven from the airport to UCT by a fifty-year-old black man from the township of Langa who, without prompting, told her how he had reacted when his fourteen-year-old son had asked him what apartheid had done to him: '"I don't want you to know about the past," he responded angrily, "you are free of all that!"' Sociologist Xolela Mangcu told her that he tries to avoid conversations about black history with his daughter who is attending a privileged mainly-whites school: 'I'm afraid of how she'll process it. How she'll relate to her friends. So I haven't had the courage to do it.' The historic and persisting division between black and white must not be spoken. I assume he fears that if he told her, she would from that point onwards see her white school friends only through the lens of apartheid and that she would hate them.[10]

At their most simple, both these parents were simply expressing the desire of all parents for their children to have a better life, a desire raised to the highest pitch in South Africa. But they also carry a subliminal message or instruction: This is not your story; do not hark back to or think about it; forget. Such an injunction is impossible for any human to obey, and in fact coils the recipient even more tightly inside the rejected legacy of the past. During the course of her investigation, Fairbanks found that many people who expressed outrage about the police killings at Marikana in 2012, when officers turned on striking miners, killing thirty-four, were more hesitant and wary in response to the student protests, a difference she read not just in terms of the greater quotient of violence of the former, but also in generational terms. There is a history in relation to the miners, whose demands recalled the days of apartheid when their brute exploitation was the hallmark of the regime (that their condition is still so appalling underscores the persisting class and race inequalities of the nation). For many, Marikana was a turning point, the moment when belief in the new dispensation collapsed – remember the minister, Susan Shabangu, instructing her police officers on how to deal with offenders the previous year: 'You must kill the bastards if they threaten you or your community.'[11] Whereas the students, the 'born frees', often privileged – as in the UK, the most deprived never make it to university in the first place – were meant to be coming from a new place. They 'were not supposed to feel that degree of historical pain'. 'How South Africa's Youth Turned on Their Parents' Generation' was the title of Fairbanks's article.[12]

'A kind of poignant switch had therefore been flipped,' observes Neo Muyanga, musician and cultural activist, 'transposing a new band of revolutionaries at the door – in this case, the *kids* – out where the *parents* once revolted.'[13]

The crisis in South Africa seemed, therefore, to be driven by a logic, or rather illogic, of generational time: disjointed, out of sync. According to Nwadeyi, the term 'illogical' has more than once been thrown at the protesting students in order to discredit them. 'The challenge of being young in South Africa,' she observes, 'perhaps, is having a past that you can never know enough about and having a future that was prescribed for you by those who themselves weren't sure of what that future would look like.'[14] This formula stood out for me. It defies the normally understood temporal state of things while also touching on the limits of human knowledge. Neither the past nor the future can be fully known. The passage from the one to the other, which is the time we are living, can therefore only be hesitant, messy and unsure (Leigh-Ann Naidoo's lecture had the title: 'The Anti-apartheid Generation Has Become Afraid of the Future'). However much we yearn to know the past, our legacy, like the psychoanalytic unconscious, one might say, escapes our mental grasp. The problem therefore is not just denial, but the false mastery it tries to exert on what will be, and on what has gone before.

But, although the past is not fully knowable – or rather for that very reason – it is no less part of who we are, shadowing the future it beckons. One cannot control the future any more than one can leave the past behind. We cannot, ever, just wrap the events of history under our belts and move on. Or in Nwadeyi's words again, 'South Africans, young and old, are now being forced to deal with the ghosts of our very present past.'[15] The legacy of the born frees is the 'present past'. Their task, although they were not thanked for it, was to bring back to the surface what the previous generation, in sway to unspeakable anguish, thought, prayed, was buried and done with. Writing in the 1970s, psychologist Chabani Manganyi had already described his 'chronic, silent, secret anguish'. Refused employment in South African universities on grounds of political activism, Manganyi left South Africa to take up a post at Yale University in the US. 'You and your society', he said as he walked out on his therapist at the time, 'have exhausted the revolutionary possibilities of your life.' 'You will never know what my people have to go through in the land of their birth.' Manganyi was apartheid's exile. He described himself as a 'pilgrim turned refugee in search of a gaping grave'.[16]

It is of course different now – how different, to what extent, and in what ways is the question. But this new generation were not meant to rise up against today's iniquities:

– the racially unequal dispensation;

– the crushing of the poor under the weight of a lawless, criminal capitalism which Sampie Terreblanche traces back to Reagan's licensing of transnational corporations across the world in the 1980s, giving them entry into the global south (a move he describes as 'pure madness');[17]

– the stranglehold of the Mineral Energy Complex (MEC), the mining and energy sectors of the economy, over South Africa's economic development, which, as students have pointed out, extends its reach into many university Electrical Engineering departments;

– the ambiguity – although this is contested – of the Constitution's property clause on the key issue of redistribution of land;[18]

– the deal struck by the ANC to secure political victory which, many argue, was at the cost of a potentially more radical, fairer, economic agenda; an agenda that had to be dropped from the historic agreement with the National Party in 1994 (as I was told more than once during my visit, a white army ready to provoke a civil war was standing at the door).

Finally, most crucially for the universities, there is the incomplete project of decolonisation, which democratisation has not secured (it has been a central contention of the student campaign that decolonisation has barely begun). 'The neo-liberalisation of universities', writes South African literary scholar Victoria Collis-Buthelezi, 'produced a set of silences in the production of their histories.' She was making her remarks in response to this chapter when it was first delivered as the VC Open Lecture at the University of Cape Town in 2017. Black suffering, she continued, citing Jamaican novelist and philosopher Sylvia Wynter, 'angrily denied by many', became the 'victim of a version of historical amnesia and bad faith'. This was the deal which the students had broken. For Collis-Buthelezi, the problem is therefore 'the how of history-making', the challenge therefore not so much the future ('a precarious continuum on which to set our hope') as the *here and now*.[19] To put it most simply, the next generation were not meant to cry foul, or claim that apartheid had not ended, or that their future was blighted by a past that had not gone away. They were meant to embody a new ideal of progress; although not of course the distorted version of progress, the foil to so-called 'barbarity', through which the colonisation of Africa had historically been justified. None of which is to minimise the radical, in many ways revolutionary, constitutional, political, legal transformation of 1994, nor the human struggles of those who made it possible.

For Hannah Arendt, the idea of progress was dangerous in so far as it allows rulers of the present dispensation to pretend that everything is just fine when it is not, and provides a licence for those in power to rule the world (a critique she mounts most forcefully in her essay 'Lying in Politics').[20] It can also be said to rob the people of their inalienable right to history by relegating history to a backwater, casting a smokescreen over the past. In her article for the *Guardian*, Fairbanks reported that in the mid-1990s, the government's curriculum-redesign committees eliminated history as a standalone subject, folding it into 'human and social sciences'. During a previous visit to UCT in 2013, Jane Bennett of the humanities department and Gender Institute told me that even in humanities departments, history – above all South Africa's immediate and still pressing history – was becoming harder and harder to teach. Today this story is still unwelcome. It is only recently that some of the hidden, often horrific, tales of apartheid – of secret policemen and state spies – have started to be told.[21] These protests were about enduring racial discrimination, poverty and inequality. But it also struck me that it was this deal, or no-deal, with history, a history that implicates the young so profoundly and which will not go away, that raised the temperature, precipitated the rage, made the situation feel at moments unmanageable.

o   o   o

In South Africa of all places this way of dealing with the past surely makes no sense. The ancestors revered in African culture are there to remind us that no one is ever born free – something understood far better and more deeply than in the metropolitan Western world. In his 2001 article 'An African

Perspective on Justice and Race', South African philosopher Mogobe B. Ramose described African communal life as consisting 'in a triadic structure of the living, the living-dead (the supernatural forces) and the yet-to-be-born'.[22] Note that the yet-to-be-born do not arrive from nowhere like visitants from a new world, but are cyclically folded into the triad. You cannot redeem your past any more than you can transcend or forget it. Legal and feminist scholar Drucilla Cornell has vividly described the extraordinary complex reckonings, the forms of obedience and disobedience, of anger and teasing humour, which the transgendered sangoma, healer and diviner Nkunzi Zandile Nkabinde, whom she met in KwaZulu Natal, conducts with her ancestors, female and male.[23] The legal implications, specifically in relation to temporality, of this cross-generational way of thought – which both she and Ramose draw from the African collective ethic of uBuntu, for which to be human is to exist through and for others – are far-reaching. 'To the African,' Ramose writes, citing Kéba M'Baye of the International Court of Justice, 'there is nothing so incomprehensible or unjust in our system of law as the Statute of Limitations, and they always resent a refusal on our part to arbitrate a suit on the grounds that it is too old.'[24] Can an ancestor who has survived the death of the body be too old?[25] The Statute of Limitations is unjust because it enshrines in law the repudiation of the past (its use to block rape complaints on the grounds that they happened too long ago has become a notorious part of the legal landscape in the US and the UK). 'The African believes', M'Baye insists, 'that time cannot change the truth.'[26] Nothing is over. You pay tribute to the past and usher in your future by remaining open to a conversation, however difficult and tetchy, with those who were here before you. In fact you are commanded to do so. Though it receives far less attention, this temporal dimension of honouring the forebears is the companion and complement to the openness towards others which is the most familiar understanding of the term uBuntu.

Perhaps, then, it might be fair to conclude, it is the poverty of insight in Western culture as regards these forms of frail but indomitable linkages across time that can help explain why psychoanalysis erupted, unwelcome, into Western thought, which has been so much less attuned to, indeed mostly pathologises, the idea that we are blessed by the voices of our foremothers and forefathers still guiding and chiding us in our heads. For psychoanalysis, nothing perishes in the mind. As subjects we are always haunted. Struggling for a suitable analogy, Freud compared the mind to a city whose layers of history all exist simultaneously, every earlier stage persisting alongside the later stage which appears to have buried it or left it behind.[27] Seen in this context, psychoanalysis is a counter-history, channelling what we have repressed from the past forward into a future struggling to find its own knowledge. Freud always insisted that the patient, rather than the analyst, holds the key to her or his unconscious truth. Writing after the Second World War in the 1950s, D. W. Winnicott described a patient who had gone looking for a piece of his lost past in the future, the only place he might possibly hope to find it.[28] This is the future perfect tense in which, for Lacan, the experience of psychoanalysis unfolds, as we have seen before in relation to modernist writing which also undercuts the dominant temporal logic of the West: what I will have been in the process of what I am becoming.[29] This formula of disjointed, generative temporality might, I suggest, also do for the political time in which South Africa has been living. Above all, our most fiercely guarded self is a palimpsest, peopled by those who have struck a chord, for better or worse, deep inside our heads.[30] It is the primary task of analysis to uncover these hidden histories which inhabit us, prompting and fleeing our consciousness in one and the same breath. For psychoanalysis, for uBuntu – for a moment to permit the bridge – the idea of being born free is meaningless. To be born free is not to be born at all.

In the opening essay of her collection *Breaking Inter-generational Cycles of Repetition: A Global Dialogue on Historical Trauma and Memory*, South African psychologist Pumla Gobodo-Madikizela tells a distressing story which might cast light on this idea of history in time (the Historical Trauma and Transformation Centre which she directs is the subject of the chapter that follows here).[31] A group of girls between seven and ten years old, '*not yet born* when the event they were enacting took place', restaged an act of necklacing from 1980s South Africa in the township of Mlungisi in the Eastern Cape. Necklacing involved the killing of suspected collaborators whose bodies were encircled by a burning tyre. It was an act which they could not have witnessed and which their parents most likely would not have talked about. 'It was strange, even surreal,' she writes,

> to see a group of young girls seven to ten years old laughing and cavorting in the streets of Mlungisi, the same township that between 1986 and 1988 had been the scene of so much misery, a tinderbox of inflamed emotions against the inhumanities of apartheid. *But that was before the children were even born.* The squeals and cries were the very embodiment of joy. They looked

like little tender shoots of foliage – little blades of life – poking out from under the cooled lava of the township once utterly devastated by apartheid's volcano.[32]

Note the repetition: 'not yet born', 'before the children were even born'. Only the idea of an unconscious legacy transmitted through the generations – what psychoanalysis terms 'transgenerational haunting' – can, I think, help us to grasp what then unfolded so shockingly before her eyes.

As she watched, the ringleader took on one by one all the roles of this saga – bystander, driver of the vehicle from which the tyre is seized, perpetrator and victim. Then, slowly but surely, she relinquished all roles but the last, pretending to strike a match as if the baying crowd of executioners had forced her to set herself alight, flailing and waving her arms, until her screams faded to a whimper and she lowered herself to the ground where she 'died'. It was a ghoulish performance, a memory of violence – of which this child can in fact have had no memory – enacted with glee. Gobodo-Madikizela suggests the children, in time-honoured fashion, were using their play in order to try and master something as intolerable as it was unspoken (violence as child's play). What struck me was, first, the sheer detail of the enactment, as if every component of the awful hidden memory was carried deep inside the body of this child. In fact this accords with today's neuroscientific concept of epigenetics which allows for one generation's lived experience, even when unspoken, to slip into the bloodstream of the next.[33] And then the fact that, for all the frantic circulation of parts, it was the role of dying victim that finally claimed her. Any mastery was therefore as perverse as it was self-defeating, since it could only proceed by snuffing out the life of the chief player, the mistress of ceremonies of her own deathly game. So, this story seems to say, it is when memory is buried or silenced by one generation that it erupts at its most virulent in the next. You cannot 'grass over the past': a Xhosa expression also from the writing of Gobodo-Madikizela.[34] These tender shoots of foliage poking out of the cooled lava of a devastating history were faced with only two options: ending their own lives or killing; setting themselves on fire or placing a burning necklace around somebody else's neck.

Critics of Rhodes Must Fall and Fees Must Fall who accused the university protests of being too 'visceral' would do well to look here. As would those who accused the movement of illogicality, or of being unreasonable or of rejecting conventional notions of reason, of going too far, not playing by the rules of the game (what or whose game? we might ask). It is as if affect, or unreason, instead of forming a constituent part of being human, were a slur on the political scene, like a dirty smudge on a scrubbed and scrupulously clean white plate. There is, however, nothing reasonable about the dispensation of the world we are living in today, a world in which Michael Flynn, before he had to resign as Trump's national security adviser in February 2017, could tweet: 'Fear of Muslims is RATIONAL', a tweet he did not delete after his appointment (nor as far as I know after he subsequently resigned). A Palestinian friend, appalled as so many by the presidency of Donald Trump in the US and Brexit in the UK, is nonetheless noticing that people who have not wanted to acknowledge the dire, steadily worsening predicament of her oppressed people over decades are at least now picking up that there is something wrong in the world. To repeat the words of Petrus Brink, 'this really is not working'.

What is reasonable in an unreasoned world? A world in which – to cite Manganyi again – the oppressed are expected to sport a 'mask' of sanity to veil the inhuman reality of their subordination, while pretending that the future and prosperity of the mask 'depends upon a negation of the past'?[35] Writing in the 1970s, he could be talking about today. The more you claim to own the house of reason in an unjust world, the louder and messier the clamour will come in reply. Manganyi is interested in what exploitation, racial inequality and oppression under colonialism do to the experience of being human, especially in the form of their denial. In his remarkable 1977 meditation *Mashungu's Reverie*, part memoir, part fiction, Manganyi, in response to such crushing of body and soul, called for a psychic space of 'violent reverie' – two terms not normally found together but which could be a perfect description for the game of the Mlungisi girls. This is a space of the deepest self-knowledge, where he encounters the most frightening aspects of himself: the 'incubated beast', a 'killer [. . .] demanding recognition', the fantasy of 'killing and being killed' (again the resonance with the fantasy enacted by the girls in Mlungisi is striking).[36]

Manganyi shares with psychiatrist and political philosopher Frantz Fanon a belief in the infinite complexity of who we are (Fanon, a key figure in post-colonial studies worldwide, was much debated on South African campuses during the protests). Under conditions of extreme oppression, Fanon wrote in *The Wretched of the Earth*, 'you are forced to come up against yourself.' 'We are forever pursued by our actions [. . .] Can we escape becoming dizzy? And who can affirm that vertigo does not affect the whole of human existence?' Engaged as they both were with the most uncompromising reckoning with injustice, neither Manganyi nor Fanon was interested in false innocence, in a whitewash of the mind. In the midst of the Algerian war of independence, Fanon treated victim and torturer alike. 'You must therefore weigh as heavily as you can upon the body of your torturer,' he wrote in the chapter on the mental disorders of colonialism, 'in order that his soul, lost in some by-way, may finally find once more its universal dimension.'[37] In discussions of Fanon as the revolutionary thinker he surely is, this call for radical empathy is rarely talked about.

There is a violence in the human heart, perhaps implanted, but certainly hugely aggravated, by social injustice and cruelty. And there is a violence in the world which buries its own ruthless logic deep inside the norm, and nowhere more so than when it boasts – vainly in a violent, unfree world – its own commitment to freedom. At the end of his preface to *Mashangu's Reverie*, Manganyi, with striking prescience, cites French philosopher Maurice Merleau-Ponty: 'We must remember that liberty becomes a false ensign – a "solemn complement" of violence – as soon as it becomes only an ideal and we begin to defend liberty instead of free men.' He then continues to cite words that chillingly anticipate and resonate with the neoliberal order under which so much of the world, including South Africa, continues to suffer: 'An aggressive liberalism exists,' Merleau-Ponty states, 'which is a dogma and an ideology of war [. . .] Its nature is violent, nor does it hesitate to impose itself through violence in accordance with the old theory of the secular arm.'[38] Rather than calling for reason as the only acceptable face of protest, therefore, we should be exposing how reason, masquerading as sanity, can itself be a form of violence and the bearer of unspeakable crimes. In the midst of the Algerian war, Fanon treated a twenty-one-year-old student whose lucidity, he realised, 'precisely by its rationalism' was a decoy. A mask of sanity, it was her way of trying to cover over the anguish she experienced at the funeral of her father, a high-ranking civil servant who had thrown himself into the 'Algerian man-hunt with frenzied rage'.[39] His death allowed her, or rather forced her, to rip the cover from her own reasoned illusion and to fully recognise the violence of state power.

There comes a moment, Freud suggested in the midst of the First World War, when the people realise that the state has outlawed violence to its citizens, not because it wants to abolish it, but because it desires to monopolise it 'like salt and tobacco'.[40] Margie Orford appeared in the last chapter as one of the journalists who wrote most powerfully on the trial of Oscar Pistorius. Known in South Africa as the 'queen' of crime fiction, she has publicly stated that, following the Marikana mining massacre of 2012, she has felt unable to write in this genre, since crime writing depends on being able at least to foster the illusion that the arm of the law is on the side of justice. It makes for a 'very different plot, a very different country,' Orford writes, 'when the moral centre of one's world can only exist outside state institutions.' Already in her 2009 crime novel *Daddy's Girl* she found herself exploring a 'feral society [. . .] in which the very institutions and individuals that should protect the vulnerable, are criminal.'[41]

It is Orford who has also named the systemic violence against women in post-apartheid South Africa 'serial femicide'. The issue of gender was the subject of sometimes acrimonious dispute during the protests, including the sidelining and isolation of black feminist organising blocs and, in one case brought to my attention, sexual assault.[42] In her address, Lovelyn Nwadeyi started by channelling her remarks to those among the black recipients of the award 'who identify as women': 'We cannot live our lives in fear of rapists neither should we live our lives in the kind of reductionism that forces us to make ourselves smaller.' There is the deepest link between racial and sexual oppression. In *Mashangu's Reverie*, which is also a sort of unhappy love story, Manganyi tracks the line from his own political impotence and rage – his 'chronic, silent, secret anguish' – to the obsession, the over-excitement, the casual disregard and denigration with which women are treated by himself and his African male friends exiled in America, where 'whoring' is a replacement for the lost struggle. Even thousands of miles away, 'the South African gloom gathered slowly around them. Like a bad dream.'[43] There is no political struggle that is not fed by and does not rebound on the social arrangements of gender and sexuality – tackling the oppression of women can never be some kind of political afterthought. There is no politics without affect and fantasy. The idea that the struggle of the students has 'recycled' emotions back into politics where they do not belong is, for me, meaningless, however high the temperature has been raised (the silencing of affect is the cause, not the solution, to the problem). There is no politics that does not tap into the subterranean core of who we are, no politics without the nightmare and the dream.

o   o   o

For South Africa, the dream was, of course, not just freedom but reconciliation, the latter to be effected through the manifold pathways of truth.[44] That was the challenge and the new dispensation which was intended to create a better world. The answer in protest has been that you can have neither freedom nor reconciliation in a world which still disproportionately oppresses black people and the poor (on this the pages upon pages of statistics circulated by the campaigners were truly eloquent). But there is another element – no less powerful and not finally detachable from the rest – which is the enduring obduracy with which historic injustice is registered in the deepest annals of the mind. Throughout this book, literary writing has been presented as the place where these annals have been stored, a record of deep history, and a rejoinder to what the worst of history can do, from Nagaland, to Belfast, to Haiti and the UK. So finally, I turn here to two literary texts which have helped me think through these dilemmas, first casting my net wider, away from South Africa, before returning there at the end.

Published in 2016 to enormous acclaim, winner of the 2017 Pulitzer Prize, Hisham Matar's *The Return* recounts his search for knowledge of his father, who disappeared in 1995 and was almost definitely killed by Libyan leader Colonel Gaddafi's henchmen in the notorious Abu Salim prison massacre of dissidents in 1996. The search seems interminable, endlessly thwarted by the remnants of Gaddafi's fallen regime – no truth commission to solve the enigma or to lay, or at least attempt to lay, the historic ghost to rest. What matters, however, is not the outcome of a search, which is in fact allowed some type of closure by the end of the book, but the process, and what it teaches him about the cunning ruse of the perpetrators, the gamble they take on the malleability of the human spirit in the face of the most corrupt, deadly forms of political power. As the news about the massacre started to dribble out into the open, the threatened grief was so intense that no one really wanted to know (unrelenting as he was in his search, Matar realises that this is no less true of himself). 'Power', he writes, 'must know this [. . .] Power must know that, ultimately, we would rather not know.' 'Power must believe, given how things proceed, that the world was better made for the perpe-trator than for those who arrive after the fact, seeking justice, or accountability or truth.' This was one of the critiques of South Africa's Truth and Reconciliation Commission, the fact that so many of the perpetrators lost nothing and got off scot-free. On this Matar is eloquent. As they try 'to make reason of the dia-bolical mess', the bereaved, the witness, the investigator and the chronicler rush every which way, 'like ants after a picnic, attending to the crumbs.'[45]

And yet, as time rolls on, and the chance of ever fully knowing what happened dwindles with every passing day, something happens to bring the thwarted, agonised past – a past on the brink of extinction – back to life: 'the point from which life changed irrevocably, comes to resemble a living presence, hav-ing its own force and temperament.'[46] For me, this is one of the most powerful evocations of what Nwadeyi described as the 'ghosts of our very present past'. In the face of impossible knowledge, the mind retreats. But that very same mind is also the place where such knowledge finds its most palpable, endlessly beating incarnation. Matar is writing about forms of psychic endurance, for better or worse, to which no Truth Commission could possibly expect to be equal. And he is writ-ing about the perpetrator for whom – against every fibre of our being, every impulse to justice – the world, we are shock-ingly told, is 'better made' ('The world was better made for the perpetrator than for those who arrive after the fact, seeking justice, or accountability or truth').

It is this mortal gamble of the perpetrator that leads to the award-winning South Korean writer Han Kang's *Human Acts*, also published in 2016, and which unexpectedly allowed me to make the link back to South Africa. I read the novel on the recommendation of South African novelist and playwright Gillian Slovo, when I told her about my visit to Cape Town and the difficulty I was having trying to think of the process of reconciliation and whether, as the protests might be taken to assert, history would judge that reconciliation had finally failed. She suggested that Han Kang's book might be helpful on that topic in relation to the healing of the past. What followed I was utterly unprepared for. *Human Acts* is one of the most disturbing novels about atrocity – if not *the* most disturbing – that I have ever read (the Zimbabwean writer Yvonne Vera's *The Stone Virgins* would be another[47]). It tells the story of the massacre of students in the southern city of Gwangju in the summer of 1980 at the command of Chun Doo-hwan, the army general who had replaced the dictator Park Chung-hee the previous year. Using the excuse of rumoured North Korean infiltration, Chun had extended martial law across the whole country, closed universities, banned political parties and further curtailed freedom of the press, provoking mass student demonstrations in response.

This is a novel that spares its readers nothing – the translator, Deborah Smith, describes the immense difficulty she had faced with the constant slide between 'corpse', 'dead body', 'dead person' and 'body'.[48] It begins with a young boy volunteering to lay out the bodies – corpses, dead persons – for identification in the morgue. He is looking for his best friend, pretending he is one of hundreds of students to have gone missing, although, as we slowly uncover, he was there with him when he was gunned down at the demonstration and saw him die. One of the novel's worst moments comes when a young woman, the victim of sexual torture – it is crucial that this is a novel written by a woman – is asked blandly and coercively by an academic researcher to 'face up to those memories', 'to bear witness', so she, the investigator, can write her report. The victim responds by repeating the question: 'Is it possible to bear witness to the fact . . .' before recounting in harrowing detail what was done to her.[49] With this format of question and chilling counter-reply, Han Kang seems to have found the perfect literary form for reluctantly disclosed knowledge, for memory and its repression lived in the same moment.

Slowly it dawned on me that I had misunderstood what Gillian Slovo was telling me, and that reconciliation and healing were the last thing that this novel was about: 'What is humanity?' 'Some memories never heal.' '"Forgive us our trespasses as we forgive those who trespass against us." I forgive nothing and no one forgives me.'[50] When I expressed my bafflement to her, she directed me to the open letter she had recently written, partly in response to Kang's novel, to her mother, the anti-apartheid activist Ruth First, who was murdered by a letter-bomb in Maputo, Mozambique in 1982.[51] What Han Kang's novel had confronted her with was the perpetrator. She then recounts a story, which she heard many years after her mother's death, of a young woman who, like First, had been detained and tortured, in this case not just mentally but also physically and for longer periods of time. Arriving in Maputo, she described her experiences to First, having sought her out, because of her unique quality of listening and the way she asked questions (unlike the blunt investigator in Kang's novel). And then, when the woman reflected that her torturers could not have possibly known what they had done and still be human, First unhesitatingly replied: 'They knew exactly what they were doing.' So, I understood, the point of Han Kang's novel, what I should have picked up above all else, was the title – *Human Acts* – its unflinching depiction of what human beings, in the fullest knowledge of what they are doing, are capable of. As the novel itself tells us, this is the hardest issue, not just personally but also politically, to face: the question – 'What is humanity?' – appears inside a book on the student movement in lines that were scored through by the censors.[52] 'You were able', Slovo addresses her mother, 'to tell this victim that her torturers had done what they did to her deliberately and your words helped release her from their thrall.' This is not reconciliation, but it is a way of confronting impossible knowledge. That was, she told me, what she had seen in Kang's novel. You have given me my lecture, I said.

And yet, there is a thread running through the novel which opens up a different imaginative possibility, not counter to the horror, but which grows out of it, like tender shoots of foliage or blades of life poking out from the cooled lava of an atrocious history, to evoke Gobodo-Madikizela's poetic description of the girls from Mlungisi once more. We are inside the mind and body of the dying friend, dumped from the back of a lorry with a pile of other corpses – it is here that the ambiguity of 'corpse', 'body', 'dead person' comes into its own – when he feels a presence, 'that breath-soft slip of incorporeal something, that faceless shadow, lacking even language, now, to give it body.' It is an intangible, barely imaginable, form of connection between two bodies, one dead, the other not quite alive: 'Without the familiar bulwark of language, still we sensed, as a physical force, our existence in the mind of the other.' 'My shadow's edges became aware of a quiet touch; the presence of another soul.' This is not a flight into false lyricism or religious sentiment. It is rather a form of linkage across space, bodies and time (Nwadeyi's 'ghosts of our present past' again, or maybe ancestors on the cusp of being born). Perhaps, in a world of such cruelty, human and inhuman, the only place where we can envisage such Utopian being – the idea of really existing, without let or discrimination, in the mind of the other – is the world of the dead. Or else in the fleeting moments of recognition between those who have survived, but only if they are able to look fully at each other without the faintest intent of wiping the shadows from the other's face: 'As we each enquired how the other had been, something like transparent feelers reached tentatively out from our eyes, confirming the shadows held by the other's face, the track marks of suffering which no amount of forced jollity could paper over.'[53] I see these transparent feelers, the breath-soft slip, the touching at a shadow's edge, as this novel's answer to the rigidity of the bodies in the morgue. In such moments, only if we entertain our ghosts, will we have the remotest chance of moving forward into the next stage of historical time.

So what, to conclude, is the tentative message of this chapter? To hold in the mind what is hardest. To acknowledge that the past has not gone away. Write it, breathe it, because we *are already* doing so. Stare straight in the eye of the perpetrator still at large who knows, but takes no responsibility for, what he has done (weigh on the body of the torturer, as Fanon would say). Above all do not blame those who erupt because they were burdened with an injunction to transcend history, an impossible demand that can have no place in any attempt to build a better world. In the end what I heard most loudly in the student protests was a plea to the previous generation which might go something like this: Reopen your minds, even if, perhaps especially if, it means returning to where you never wanted to tread once more. Not least because that is where we, the next generation, are still living. None of it has gone away. Such knowledge is the only way to understanding, the only path to justice.

8

ONE LONG SCREAM

Trauma and Justice in South Africa

In the afterlife of atrocity, two faces of injustice call out for redress. The student protesters of the last chapter were 'alerting' the nation to ongoing inequality, the persistence of racism, the failure of government to bring corruption to an end. Tearing down statues, they were felling illusions: for many, the much-loved concept of the 'rainbow nation' – or 'post-racial' world – was an affront, a mantra of hope draped over the cruel schisms of the new South Africa. Even more harrowingly, some declare, in an image resonant of apartheid atrocity, that the corpse of justice is lying in plain sight on the roadside for those willing to see. At the same time, they were presenting the authorities with a form of political anger, all the more powerful for bringing back to the surface the pain of the past. They were carrying a double burden. How to acknowledge grief and cry freedom?

In December 2018, I returned to South Africa for a gathering of apartheid survivors and perpetrators, psychiatrists and thinkers to try and understand more deeply the cross-generational persistence of trauma, just how far and in what insidious ways it entrenches itself in body and soul. In the process I learnt how taking a political stand in the present can be a way of remembering, how healing is an interminable process that can never be taken for granted, that political and psychic struggle can be one and the same thing. To accept responsibility for the past is agonising. We should never underestimate the lengths human subjects, governments and nations, will go to turn their back on a violent history and to silence disaster.

On 27 June 2016, Lukhanyo Calata issued a public statement on corruption at the South African Broadcasting Corporation where he had worked as a journalist for several years. He knew that it would probably result in his dismissal. The Corporation had succumbed to what has come to be known in South Africa as 'state capture': working in the interests of Jacob Zuma's government, in itself allegedly prey to big business. Zuma had especially close ties to the notorious Gupta brothers who face possible extradition from the UAE to answer criminal charges in South Africa, charges which they deny. Calata had dared to speak out against the 'despotic rule' of the chief operating officer, Hlaudi Motsoeneng. On the day of his disciplinary hearing, he also joined a picket outside SABC opposing the Corporation's decision not to report on a rising wave of violent 'service delivery' protests across the country. The aim of the protests was to secure better housing, job opportunities, municipal governance and social services, and to force the ANC government to reverse policies – far from the vision which had first brought it to power – that were manifestly failing those citizens, mainly black, who were most socially vulnerable. In fact the writing had been on the wall for Calata since February 2014 when, following Zuma's annual State of the Nation Address, he was grabbed by the scruff of his jacket by the head of news, Jimi Matthews. Matthews told Calata not to get him 'into shit' and ordered him to cut positive soundbites of reactions from opposition parties to Zuma's speech. Calata refused (even had he wished to, he could hardly have complied as no such soundbites existed). Motsoeneng was subsequently dismissed from the SABC. The resonances with the apartheid era were, however, chilling. Under the regime of P. W. Botha, the SABC had been known as 'his master's voice'.[1]

Calata had chosen his moment carefully. The day he spoke out was the thirty-first anniversary of the 1985 state-ordered murder of the anti-apartheid activists from the Eastern Cape known as the 'Cradock Four' – his father, Fort Calata, Matthew Goniwe, Sparrow Mkonto and Sicelo Mhlauli. In South Africa, the killing of the Cradock Four is legendary. Its brutality – torture by blowtorch, as well as multiple stabbings – provoked a national and international outcry. The fingers on Fort Calata's left hand were severed. He had been wearing the wedding band of his wife, Nomonde, which she had removed when her fingers became swollen during her pregnancy with their third child. This was not torture, anti-apartheid activist Allan Boesak recalled, but a 'demonstration'.[2] Most likely the attackers were from the Security Police, specifically the notorious 'Hammer Unit' whose members used their own personal weapons and who, by their own account, would drive into the townships 'dressed as kaffirs, with our faces and heads blackened'.[3] Sixty thousand people defied banning orders to attend the funeral, along with dignitaries from all over the world. In response, President Botha declared a national state of emergency, granting 'complete indemnity against any civil or criminal proceedings' to the state and all its functionaries. Lawyers working in London with the anti-apartheid United Democratic Front and the Cradock Residents Association issued a statement to alert the international community: the South African government's failure 'to contain the people's anger', they said, had 'given rise to a new phase of terror against the people'.[4] Today it is generally recognised that Botha's move was an act of desperation that signalled the beginning of the end of apartheid.

Lukhanyo Calata was three at the time of the murders; his elder sister, Dorothy, was ten; his younger sister, Tumani, was born a few weeks after the funeral. Though Lukhanyo grew up with no conscious memory of his father, he is convinced he became the journalist he is today as a result of years watching journalists flocking to his family home in an attempt to uncover the truth behind the killing of the Cradock Four. The full story has never been told. At the end of *My Father Died for This*, the remarkable book he has co-written with his wife, Abigail Calata (they took turns to write different sections), he can offer only an imaginative reconstruction of the murders. He pieces the story together from partial records, from conversations with people who had first-hand knowledge of the security apparatus, and from the inconclusive legal hearings which have prevented both the family and the nation from achieving any kind of closure on this case. At the first judicial inquest in 1989, any state involvement was denied, but in 1992 the *New Nation* newspaper published on its front page a copy of the 'signal' sent by Colonel Lourens du Plessis ordering the 'permanent removal from society' of Matthew Goniwe, Fort Calata (two of the Cradock Four) and Mbulelo Goniwe (another ANC activist). Du Plessis now says that, when he was called to Pretoria after the story broke, he had the impression that the state attorneys wanted him 'to say what I didn't think was the truth'.[5] At the second inquest in 1994, Judge Zietsman ruled that the killers were members of the security forces but declared himself incapable, on the basis of the evidence before him, of identifying the murderer or murderers, who have never been named.[6] It has become a truism of post-apartheid South Africa to say that, in order to secure the transition to democracy, the new nation opted for truth rather than justice. In the case of the Cradock Four, there has been neither.

I met the Calata family in December 2018 at a conference on 'Recognition, Reparation and Reconciliation' in Stellenbosch, organised by Pumla Gobodo-Madikizela at the Historical Trauma and Transformation Centre which she chairs at Stellenbosch University.[7] Having served on South Africa's Truth and Reconciliation Commission, Gobodo-Madikizela, who we encountered in the last chapter, has worked ceaselessly over the past two decades to keep its best spirit alive.* The title of the conference gestures towards healing, but a closer glance suggests that all three of its terms touch an open wound. Any call for recognition has to start from the premise that there are things which we cannot bear to know and see. Reparation remains one of the sore points in relation to the Commission, as substantive reparations for past wrongdoing fell outside its brief (the Thabo Mbeki government effectively rejected the recommendations it did make). And what are the chances of reconciliation in conditions of rampant racial inequality which have barely diminished – some would say have worsened – since the first democratic elections of 1994? In the words of Mark Solms, psychoanalyst, neuroscientist and owner of a farm in nearby Franschhoek, who also attended the conference, the question for the white beneficiaries of apartheid is 'how we had sort of got away with it' (not the outcome he personally had

---

* The Centre extends its brief to consideration of trauma across Africa and beyond to include Zimbabwe, Nigeria/Biafra, Rwanda and Israel-Palestine. Following objections to their presence from members of the Palestine Solidarity Committee in support of BDS (the campaign in support of Boycott, Divestment and Sanctions in relation to the Israeli government), the Israeli participants withdrew from the conference.

sought as over the past seventeen years he has tried to initiate a new racially inclusive model of land ownership on the farm neighbouring his own).

In fact the Calata story, as told in *My Father Died for This*, would suggest that, in the transition to democracy, truth was not the alternative to justice, but just as much a casualty. The 'once glorious liberation movement of the ANC', Lukhanyo concludes in a final bitter chapter, 'A Life Betrayed', 'has not honoured the pain of our people in its politics'. Interviewed by Lukhanyo in September 2017, John Jeffrey, the current Deputy Minister of Justice, admitted that turning a blind eye to the murder of the Cradock Four and others like Steve Biko (Bantu Stephen Biko) 'was the price that had to be paid'. Partly for budgetary reasons, he explained, there would be no further investigation, as he had to prioritise present-day crimes. Such frank admissions are surely rare, most likely drawn out of Jeffrey as his way of honouring Lukhanyo Calata as his father's son. Even those who see the forfeit of criminal justice by the Commission as a historic error, or who argue, in the face of that critique, that amnesty was the only way of averting civil war, do not put it quite like this. For Allan Boesak, old comrade and family friend, there can be no doubt that the Cradock Four would have been part of the secret negotiations between the ANC and the apartheid leaders: 'The generals and architects of apartheid had negotiated themselves out of murder.' This brings the case of the Cradock Four crashing into the present. 'The perpetrators', Father Paul Verryn writes in his foreword to the book, 'should meet this family face to face.' 'I don't know', Boesak told Calata, 'how any leader in the ANC can look your mother in the eye, without feeling they must be damned to hell for what they did and continue to do . . . How can people walk through this country, how can we walk our streets, how can we walk through our townships and not see the blood still on the soil.'[8]

Calata devoted a central part of *My Father Died for This* to his great-grandfather Canon James Calata, president of the Cape ANC and National Secretary General from 1936 to 1949, who famously brought his politics to the pulpit and was central in making Cradock the politically conscious and active community for which it was still being punished in the early 1990s (he was also a dedicated musician who made it part of his politics to infuse the harsh early years of apartheid in the 1950s with song). Fort, James Calata's grandson, was named after the Old Fort Prison where James was imprisoned for treason in 1956. The book feeds the voices from the past through the new generation, as a way of enacting its core belief – one shared today by many across South Africa – that the past has not been assuaged and that the present dispensation or social order is a form of treachery. South Africa has been transformed, above all, legally and constitutionally, but the need for vigilance is unending as aspects of the apartheid era are starting to repeat themselves. In what must be a deliberate allusion to the Cradock Four and the Gugulethu Seven (another group of ANC activists, killed by the security forces in March 1986), the SABC protesters have come to be known as the 'SABC8'. Having been dismissed by the Corporation for 'disrespect' and for undermining 'the authority' of its management, they were all finally reinstated on appeal (bar one on a technicality, although on appeal the Corporation had to pay his legal costs). 'How', Lukhanyo asks on the opening pages of the book, do the former leaders of the liberation movement 'watch as the rights and freedom [which] the "Cradock Four" were brutally murdered for are systematically being undone?'[9]

As the SABC story makes clear, freedom is indivisible, meaningless without freedom of expression and of knowledge. By refusing to broadcast the protests, the Corporation was trying to render silent and invisible the fault lines in post-apartheid South Africa (another historic instance of the violence of those in power taking cover from the light). The picket outside the Corporation was organised by the Cape Town advocacy group Right2Know. Silencing social protest and not naming the state functionaries who killed the Cradock Four are reverse sides of the same coin (truth and social redistribution are not bargaining chips to be weighed against each other in the scales). Both are acts of censorship, sinister forms of quietism, negating the mind's capacity for judgement in a bid to make the world feel easier with itself. The year before the conference, I had attended a public lecture given by Gobodo-Madikizela at the Gordon Institute of Performing and Creative Arts at Cape Town University, in which she used the word 'perpetrators' to refer to the beneficiaries of the current economic regime. Barely before she had finished speaking, a member of the Helen Suzman Trust, the South African NGO for human rights, rose to her feet to object. But Gobodo-Madikizela's allusion had been neither casual nor sloppy. She knows more than most what a perpetrator looks like. Outside South Africa, she is best known for her book of interviews with Eugene de Kock, the apartheid death squad chief who was called 'Prime Evil' by his own men, and who she believed was at least partly rehumanised by their encounter.[10] Naming today's beneficiaries as 'perpetrators' was a way of bringing violently to the surface, with deliberate provocation, I imagine, the failure and corruption of South Africa's present social order. 'To insist that the public should not see the effects of the anger of service delivery protests,' writes Verryn, 'but should somehow be protected from what our reality is, is a denial of our fundamental right to know.'[11] This too has its historical echo. On the night of the killing, Fort Calata and his comrades would almost definitely have been transported to the notorious municipal training college called uMtombolwazi, which means 'the fountain of knowledge'.[12] The title of the book – *My Father Died for This* – is ironic. Underscore 'This', add a question mark, and its despair becomes palpable.

o o o

It felt both strange and appropriate that such a conference should be held in Stellenbosch, whose resonance in South African history could not be more different from that of Cradock. For a long time, Cradock was a small and relatively poor service centre for the surrounding white-owned farms, before becoming a pivot of black migration in the face of forced removals and a by-word for sustained political agitation and resistance to the apartheid regime. Cradock is recognised as the 'Cradle of the Freedom Charter', an idea first mooted at an ANC conference hosted there in 1953 (in fact its history of political resistance to racial injustice is generally dated back way before, to the arrival in the town of Canon James Calata in 1928).[13] Today unemployment in Cradock is above fifty per cent, poverty is endemic, especially in the squatter camps that ring the townships, and education is underfunded as black residents who can afford it send their children to formerly whites-only schools.[14] Stellenbosch, on the other hand, is a fiefdom of Afrikaner and, increasingly, expatriate wealth. Nestling in the heart of vineyard country, the town has an aura of unreality. Chic cafes and restaurants, with mainly white English- or Afrikaans-speaking clientele, spill onto the pavements of streets lined with stores selling fine art and jewellery, mohair scarves and garments, handbags made of antelope. African goods hover in dark recesses or are cluttered on stands as you pass. As Gobodo-Madikizela pointed out in her opening remarks at the conference, squatter homes, mainly built today by the young generation, are growing in number and creeping closer and closer to the vineyards of Stellenbosch. Needless to say, the next generation of Africans were not meant to be living in squatter homes.

At one of these vineyards, Lanzerac, described on its website as 'the ultimate experience in the Cape Winelands', a celebration was held on the last night of the conference to mark twenty years since the publication of the Report of the Truth and Reconciliation Commission and to honour Archbishop Desmond Tutu and his wife, Leah Tutu, both in attendance along with commissioners, the conference delegates, activists from Ireland, and the Calata family. Anyone who wanted could have their photo taken standing behind Desmond and Leah Tutu in their wheelchairs, who generously smiled for the camera, even though there was no reason why they should know who many of us were.

Earlier in the week, we had gathered in the evening at Dornier, another vineyard, where Albie Sachs, ANC freedom fighter and retired justice, who played such a key role in drawing up the new Constitution, gave an impromptu speech on the hillside in the fading light. He reminded us why 'soft vengeance', as he himself had coined the term – the achievement of a non-racial democracy – had had to be the priority, at the same time as he recognises the harsh, unresolved, injustices confronting the nation today.[15] Sachs is an eternal optimist. Perhaps that is why the beautifully incongruous landscape and his speech did not finally jar. He defends the Constitution, fiercely critiqued for failing to deliver its promise, as an 'activist Constitution', which now demands a ceaseless struggle to ensure that its clauses on everything from non-discrimination to redistribution of land and resources are put into effect. Drawn up by 490 people – mostly black, many of whom had been in prison – it was far from the stitch-up between de Klerk and Mandela that it is often reputed to be.[16]

Way beyond the remit of the Truth and Reconciliation Commission, the Constitution had called for the prosecution decades later of a policeman who had covered up the murder of anti-apartheid activist Ahmed Timol in 1971, and for any prosecutions dampened by political interference to be resumed, although this clearly did not happen in the case of the Cradock Four.[17] Above all, Sachs describes how the new dispensation is demanding radical changes in the practice and spirit of the law: the 'interpretative dance' it initiates, the challenge to traditional modes of legal reasoning (all this is the 'agony of law').[18] In a famous 2004 judgement – Port Elizabeth Municipality versus various occupiers – Sachs, writing for a unanimous Constitutional Court, ruled against the eviction of fifteen African families squatting on vacant ground close to an upmarket suburb of the city, on the grounds that the task of the court was to introduce 'grace and compassion into the formal elements of law'.[19]

But it was above all the university's history that made the location of the conference in the Theology School of Stellenbosch so meaningful for our theme. Hendrik Verwoerd, the architect of apartheid, had been a theology student at the university in the 1920s. He was unable to join the School of Theology itself because the minister of his home town, Brandfort, with a foresight of which he can hardly have been aware, felt unable to provide the requisite statement on his suitability (Brandfort would later become famous as the town to which Winnie Mandela was banished and placed under house arrest from 1977 to 1986). After a few years studying in Europe and the US, he returned to Stellenbosch in 1928 as a professor, first of applied psychology and psychotechnics (*sic*), then of sociology and social work. By 1937 he had left to pursue a career in politics, becoming editor of the Afrikaner nationalist newspaper *Die Transvaler* and committing himself to the Nationalist Party.

Prime Minister of South Africa from 1958 until his assassination in 1966, as Minister of Native Affairs before that, Verwoerd had been responsible for some of apartheid's most inhuman laws: the Pass Laws of the 1950s, the 1953 Reservation of Separate Amenities Act and the 1953 Bantu Education Act whose purpose, by his own account, was to ensure that blacks only had enough education to work as skilled labourers (he famously described apartheid as 'good neighbourliness'). Not until May 2015, in response to the Rhodes Must Fall student protests, was a large plaque honouring Verwoerd removed from the campus.

It is this university to which Gobodo-Madikizela's Historical Trauma and Transformation Centre has recently moved from the University of the Free State. Since 2006, the Centre has hosted a conference every three years on its topic in increasingly sombre mood, apart from 2015 at the height of the student protests. Not quite singlehandedly – the feeling is of the widest imaginable co-operation of disparate voices – she has set herself the task of trying to understand the persistence of historical pain, the cross-generational psychic legacy of apartheid. The space felt as fragile as it was resolute. If I was there to present my work and thoughts on these matters, the stories told over the five days of the conference by those still living the aftermath soon established that thinking was not enough. Not that 'feeling' will do it either, a term deeply suspect in this context where expressions of empathy – 'I feel your pain' – can be the best pretext for doing nothing.

Everyone was friendly. The project of understanding and transformation was held in common. Some of the most famous dignitaries of the anti-apartheid struggle mingled and shared platforms with young activists and students, treating them as the comrades and friends that they clearly were. I never felt I was not included, even when a black caucus was called to give the Africans and African-Americans attending the conference more room for their own collective voice. And yet, one reason this conference was different from any other academic event I have ever attended was the way it pushed in your face suffering which was meant to be over and done (trauma studies made flesh). Whether to do so, whether giving and continuing to give a voice to a family such as the Calatas can be redemptive, was a question the conference raised but did not pretend to resolve.

Perpetrators and the sons and daughters of perpetrators were welcome and given the space to speak – unsurprisingly given Gobodo-Madikizela's experience with De Kock. Hendrik Verwoerd's grandson, Wilhelm Verwoerd, a political philosopher also based at Stellenbosch, has loudly disowned his grandfather's legacy to become an ANC supporter and social activist working with former combatants in Northern Ireland who are now advocates for peace (he supported and was present at the removal of the plaque honouring Verwoerd). To his family – his own father proudly collects the memorabilia of the illustrious Hendrik's legacy – Wilhelm is a bloodline traitor to the dead.

In his presentation, he used the vocabulary of 'thick relation-ships' to designate the pressure on him to embrace his repellent family history and the effort of repudiation he has had to make. 'I don't take for granted', he said about talking in public, 'that I will be able to speak' (this did not feel like special pleading or pathos but a statement of fact). The overriding question for him is what whites 'are willing to do by way of white work?'

This was the question that pretty much every white per-son attending the conference had to ask of themselves. Poet and artist Eliza Kentridge, also present, is the daughter of the leading anti-apartheid lawyer Felicia Geffen, who died in 2015 (her father is Sydney Kentridge, who defended Nelson Mandela in the 1956 Treason Trial). In the middle of her poetic grief-sequence, *Signs for an Exhibition*, a voice pronounces in a capitalised one-liner: 'YOU ARE NOT FIT TO TOUCH THE HEM OF AFRICA.'[20] Unlike other moments in the poem, it does not seem here as if this is the voice of the mother speaking to her daughter, but the daughter, punishingly, addressing herself. When I look back on the conference, in fact pretty much whenever I write about or visit South Africa, it is a version of this voice that I hear resounding, or that I think should be resounding, in my own head.

Articulate, poised, Verwoerd made a stark contrast to Ste-faans Coetzee, one of the bombers of the Worcester shopping mall in 1996, who came across as a wrecked man. Four peo-ple died in the blast and sixty-seven were injured, many se-riously. Coetzee had been a member of the white Afrikaner Weerstandsbeweging ('Afrikaner Resistance Movement') and an admirer of 'Wit Wolf' Barend Strydom, who in 1988 massacred seven black people and injured more than a dozen others at Strijdom Square in the centre of Pretoria. (A few weeks earlier he had randomly killed a black woman in an informal settlement in De Deur, outside Johannesburg, to test his resolve.) Coetzee had felt unable to accept the new ANC government: 'I was filled with hatred and I still don't know why.' He was seventeen at the time.

In 2016, Coetzee ran the Comrades Marathon in KwaZulu-Natal with the number 67 – the number of the injured – tattooed on his arm (at the end of the run, he handed his medal to one of the victims). Before he spoke, we were shown a film clip in which, head bowed, he muttered compulsively 'I apologise.' A failing sound system gave the impression of someone more or less talking to himself. But 'saying sorry', he also insisted, was not enough: 'There must be doing of sorry.' His suggestion might usefully be communicated to the killers of the Cradock Four, who have faced neither accountability nor justice. 'Our theology', he stated from his time deep within the Christian far right of the country, 'taught us a cheap form of forgiveness.' Only legislation, he suggested, will enforce responsibility. Asked by a member of the audience if he had found love – a brutally intrusive question which also felt like the question we all wanted to ask – he replied that he takes humility, patience and friendliness as his ethos of love from the Bible, but that marriage was impossible as he was not the kind of guy that any woman would ever want to introduce as her boyfriend.

Can you touch a perpetrator, or their descendants? Several people who I spoke to after Wilhelm Verwoerd's session said that, moved as they were, they could not bring themselves to shake his hand (an odd idea in itself as there had been no hand-shaking at the end of any of the other sessions I had attended). The day after she touched the hand of De Kock, Gobodo-Madikizela woke up to find that she could not lift her right forearm, which had gone completely numb, 'as if my body were rejecting a foreign organ illegitimately planted'. At their next meeting, De Kock too seemed panicked after the physical contact as though, she thought, he were struggling to split off from his body his 'killer hand'.[21] The vocabulary – frozen limbs, splitting – makes more than a gesture to the language and history of psychoanalysis which began with the case of hysteria of Anna O, the patient whose arm froze into the petrified shape of a snake as she sat with it wrapped round the back of her dying father's chair; while terms like splitting, scotomisation or derealisation (mental self-blinding), which were discussed in Chapter Five, slowly crept into Freud's late vocabulary as he began to confront minds whose only recourse in the face of mental pain was to take complete flight from themselves.[22] No surprise that such a conference should find itself skirting the worst of psychic trouble – from hysterical paralysis to psychotic modes of defence. In her presentation, Cathy Caruth, a leading figure in the study of trauma, seemed to be shifting her ground, away from trauma as a story that defies representation – an idea which not uncontroversially has almost become orthodoxy – to trauma as a tale which shatters the very basis of human communication because there is no one either inside or outside the head to address, no one there to listen. In perhaps his best-known essay, written in 1959, W. R. Bion, one of the first psychoanalysts to bring psychoanalysis into the world of psychosis, called this 'attacks on linking'.[23]

As the conference skirted this hallucinatory dimension, it was as if all of us, in the face of past atrocity and the ever-receding horizon of social justice, were scrambling for a language of sanity. Lindiwe Hani, who also spoke, is the daughter of Chris Hani, one of the most famous ANC activists and the much-loved leader of the South African Communist Party. He was murdered in 1993 by a hired killer, migrant Janusz Waluś, in flight from Polish Communism, in the countdown to the first democratic elections as part of an attempt to provoke a civil war: 'an explosion of carnage and race war', as Joe Slovo said at his funeral, 'a massive spilling of blood and the end of negotiations' (instead the almost immediate consequence was that the ANC secured the date, 27 April 1994, for the elections).[24] Lindiwe Hani was twelve years old. In the months after his death, every time someone asked her how she was doing, she would reply 'robotically': 'Fine.' As she puts it in her 2017 memoir, *Being Chris Hani's Daughter*, it took years for her to realise that 'fine' is an acronym for 'Fucking Insane'.[25]

Madness can be generative (which does not mean that it is a condition to be either welcomed or sought). In an attempt to confront her demons, Lindiwe Hani visited Waluś several times in prison; she had already met Clive Derby-Lewis, the 'mastermind' behind the killing who provided Waluś with the gun. She had, she writes, been living in a 'shroud of death'.[26] In the years after her father's murder her first serious boyfriend, with whom she had been planning her future, died after accidentally crashing his car into a wall; her sister, Khwezi, who had heard the shooting and was the first to discover her father's body, died of a cocaine overdose in 2001 (Lindiwe is adamant that drugs were involved even though the autopsy stated asphyxiation from an asthma attack). Lindiwe herself was in recovery from years of major addiction to alcohol and cocaine. One of the things Waluś disclosed to her, she told us at the conference, was that the summer before the killing he had gone to see his own twelve-year-old daughter, who was living in Norway, because he knew he would never see her again (in the event his death sentence was commuted when the death penalty was declared unconstitutional by the South African Constitutional Court in June 1995). Why, Hani found herself asking, in what seemed like an act of astounding generosity, should another twelve-year-old daughter lose her father as she had lost hers? 'I would wish for five minutes with my father, so why should not this little girl have five years with hers?'

Waluś was reapplying for parole, which had been granted and then overturned. He remains in prison to this day. His and Derby-Lewis's applications to the Truth and Reconciliation Commission for amnesty were refused on the grounds they had not shown they were acting for a political organisation and had not fully disclosed the background to their crime. Lindiwe Hani, on the other hand, accepted Waluś's apology, even began to like him, although she was not inclined to forgive. Hatred and forgiveness would come over her in waves. 'Don't forget you killed my father,' she would throw into the conversation with Waluś whenever things got too cosy – at one point, he weirdly asked permission to be able to say he was 'proud of her'. But she did not want to 'perpetrate the anger'. Like 'doing of sorry', the wording struck me with its sheer inventiveness (a state of mind can surely be perpetrated as much as any deed).

o o o

Where is trauma meant to house itself when the mind, like the body, in shreds or shot to pieces, is no longer recognisable, no longer bears the faintest resemblance to anything that might remotely be called home? The very persistence of horror in South Africa tells us that thinking about trauma in relation to language, circling endlessly round whether or not it can be spoken, which has tended to dominate academic discourse, is not enough. In South Africa, Nomonde Calata is famous for the wailing, almost inhuman cry she emitted at the start of the proceedings of the Truth and Reconciliation Commission which momentarily brought the hearing to a complete halt (Tutu asked for a ten-minute break). The cry has become iconic. Gobodo-Madikizela's March 2017 lecture was called 'The Cry of Nomonde Calata'. For poet Antjie Krog, who had been sent by the SABC to report on the Commission's proceedings, the cry marked its true beginning. She felt she was witnessing the 'destruction of language'. 'To remember the past of this country is to be thrown back into a time before language [. . .] to be present at the birth of language itself' (way before a time when individual speech is even an issue).[27]

We need to redraw the cartography of the mind, to venture beyond the paths on which Freud, safely and unsafely, was willing to tread. We need insane visionary moments, including the world of dream and hallucination, to be credited as part of the landscape of trauma – the psychic equivalents of 'upsurge' and 'turbulence', evocative terms used by the South African literary and cultural critic Sarah Nuttall to capture the increasing outbursts of rage and protest that are spreading across South Africa today.[28] Such moments arrive unbidden, erupting from what feels like another world. Abigail Calata tells a story that when she was dating Lukhanyo but had not yet met her future mother-in-law, Nomonde, she felt the presence of Fort Calata in her bathroom. Without hesitating, she picked up the phone to tell Nomonde, at that point a complete stranger, that she had a message to give her from her dead husband: he had never intended to leave her in that way. The same night, it emerged, he had also appeared to Nomonde in a dream (a genius mode of introduction, as it turned out, for the two women). On another occasion, when Fort appeared in a dream telling Nomonde to go home, she rushed back to Cradock to find that his grave had been vandalised. Impossible links across the geographic landscape, or between people barely known to each other, these moments of cross- and inter-generational transmission will not be held to normal protocols of space and time. In the end the simplest message of the whole conference was perhaps the most far-reaching premise of psychoanalysis and also its most banal. Nothing perishes inside the body or the mind, which is why the suggestion that South Africa has left apartheid behind is as psychologically as it is politically inept.

Allan Boesak is convinced that the political faith of Canon Calata, Lukhanyo's great-grandfather, played a decisive role in the challenge Lukhanyo mounted to the SABC and in every political move or protest any member of his family has ever made: 'Otherwise you would not have made that decision. Your father would not have made that decision, otherwise your mom would not have made that decision. It's in your DNA.'[29] Today epigenetics tells us that such forms of ghostly transmission, traces of history in the bloodstream, are biologically possible. Oddly, in the context of South Africa, this might be grounds for the very optimism that has so visibly faltered. In one of the best-received papers I attended, Jaco Barnard-Naudé, legal scholar and activist on freedom for sexual minorities and same-sex marriage, offered a rereading, after Jane Harrison, of the classic story of Pandora in which the evils that spill from her box are the ghosts of past wrongs unavenged and forgotten. The one item left in her box, when evil has thus been exhumed, is hope. Ghosts stalked the corridors of this conference. Perhaps its most important task was to give them room to do so.

But it was not just the ghosts who were calling out for recognition, or the story of the Cradock Four that lingered like a body uncased. The ethos of the heroic freedom fighter and his family has also played its part in clamping down on psychic pain. Lindiwe Hani's mother, Limpho, saw it as a slur on the family honour when she checked into rehab under her real name (owning the name in fact played a key part in Lindiwe's recovery). At one point in *My Father Died for This*, Lukhanyo calls Nomonde 'a mighty soldier of a woman'. Abigail describes her as the 'true hero' of the whole story.[30] At the conference, Siyah Mgoduka, whose father, Warrant Officer Mbalala Glen Mgoduka, was one of many killed under instruction from Eugene de Kock, described his mother, Doreen, as 'a better man than I could ever be'. As if, in each of these cases, lack of frailty – of 'woman's' frailty – was the highest possible praise, though Siyah Mgoduka also repeated three times that, as the years have passed, he has slowly become 'softer' as a man (Doreen forgave De Kock, who designed the bomb placed under her husband's car; Siyah refused). By staging their dialogue for us to hear, they seemed to be demonstrating that in today's South Africa, such barely perceptible, momentous shifts of the heart can only be spoken in front of a witness. A conversation between the two has also been made into a split-screen film, a technique which perfectly conveyed the barrier, the slowly moving closeness and distance between them (the film had one of its first screenings at the conference).[31] By means of this strange format, they were summoning a symbolic 'third' presence into the room. For the psychoanalyst Jessica Benjamin, speaking of her work with perpetrators and victims in Gaza, such a 'third' is the only possible basis for any non-violent form of political recognition, whereas in a direct encounter, identities tend to entrench themselves.[32]

As the widows of fighters, Nomonde Calata and Limpho Hani were never allowed to show grief. 'One does not cry for a hero,' Nomonde was told: 'I had to put up the face.' Again, 'put up *the* face' feels right (as opposed to the more familiar version of 'put *on a* face'). Even in the presence of her children, only one mask of unwavering courage and fortitude was acceptable. Nor has she been offered therapy, or indeed anything close. 'I would love', she said in conversation with Gobodo-Madikizela, 'to have a one-to-one conversation. I want someone to listen.' She is famous for her role in the Truth and Reconciliation Commission, but it was another type of listening that she was asking for here (the lack of any such follow-up is seen as one of the Commission's most serious failings). Some time later, I discovered that Nomonde's remark had provoked in both Eliza Kentridge and me the same wild fantasy or wish: that someone would step out of the audience to offer her their services, or at the very least guide her to someone who could.

In South Africa, psychoanalysis came to a shuddering halt in 1949, the year after apartheid was established, with the death of its only training analyst, the Lithuanian Wulf Sachs, who had come to the country from the UK (a flourishing psychoanalytic community of South African exiles has been present in London ever since). Mark Solms and Tony Hamburger, the two figures who have done most to give psychoanalysis new life post-apartheid, both spoke at the conference. But like pretty much everywhere else in the world, and despite best efforts to the contrary – notably the Ubelele psychotherapy centre – psychoanalysis as an option remains out of reach for the many – in South Africa, the racial majority and the poor.[33]

'To establish psychoanalysis in South Africa', Solms remarked, 'without confronting its elite status is to create a still-birth.'

o   o   o

When Abigail Calata first heard on 27 June 2016 that Lukhanyo had released his statement on corruption at the South Africa Broadcasting Company, she was not happy. She felt she should have been consulted before he took such a momentous step in her life and in the life of their four-year-old son, Kwezi. Once she let him know her feelings, and his statement had gone viral, followed by numerous media interviews, she felt proud. From that point on, Lukhanyo involved her in every political decision that he made. But by allowing us that glimpse of anger at the start of their book, Abigail Calata briefly opens the window on a long history, one that also resonated across the conference, of wives, often themselves activists, who were nonetheless left behind while their husbands engaged in undercover work, were imprisoned, fled into exile. James Calata's wife Miltha was a leader in her own right, an equal partner whose bravery, according to the memory of a close friend, matched that of her husband – they were awarded the Silver and Gold Luthuli medals for their part in the struggle respectively (Fort also receiving the Silver).[34] But she rarely saw him because he was always on the move. After her marriage, Limpho Hani became involved with the ANC and in 1977–8 was detained for several months for her role in ferrying recruits across the border to Swaziland. But the family hardly ever saw Chris Hani. Dedicated to armed struggle, he had crossed the border and lived for long stretches of time in Zambia, Lesotho, Tanganyika (now mainland Tanzania), Bechuanaland (now Botswana), Angola and

Rhodesia (now Zimbabwe).[35] Lindiwe Hani describes how her mother raised her three daughters more or less single-handed.[36] When her husband was in prison, Nomonde Calata had to scrape together a living for her family. She had been working in the canteen at Cradock Provinicial Hospital, but was sacked after being reported by a police officer who spotted her on a bus wearing a T-shirt bearing the slogan 'Free Mandela'. Her husband had never talked to her about his activities in the ANC underground.[37] In this context, the killing of these men can be understood as a sinister type of continuity, enshrining an absence that was already at the core of so many of these women's lives. 'I do want my time,' Nomonde stated as she sat there with her three children, 'all the time I lived for others, for fear, for protection.' As if the most basic feminist demand – to be able to live one's own life, without fear, and not just for others – had been soaked in the blood of a whole people.

Of these stranded, abandoned wives the most famous is of course Winnie Mandela, who, though barely ever mentioned at the conference, also seemed to be stalking the halls. Sometimes this was explicit: Winnie Mandela was a family friend, heroine and role model for Lindiwe Hani, someone she 'channels', to use her own term. 'The Hani girls with Big Mummy Winnie at Mama's 50th' is the caption for one of the photographs in her memoir. But she was also there implicitly and far more awkwardly in the fact that Lukhanyo and Abigail chose Father Paul Verryn – a family friend since the 1980s, when he had visited Fort Calata in Diepkloof Prison – to write the foreword to their book. Verryn is the Methodist minister Winnie Mandela charged with paedophilia, on the basis of no evidence, as the net started to close around her infamous team of bodyguards, the Mandela United Football Club, who terrorised the township of Soweto, where she had moved after Brandfort. In 1988, members of the club kidnapped four teenage boys who were living at Verryn's manse, including Stompie Moeketsi, also known as Stompie Seipei, who was murdered by Jerry Richardson, 'Chief Coach' and Winnie Mandela's bodyguard. In 1991 she was sentenced by a Johannesburg court to six years in prison for ordering the kidnap and for her active part in the assault, commuted on appeal to a fine and two-year suspended sentence. No South African reading the Calatas' book is likely to miss the reference.

And yet, one of the most surprising things I discovered during my visit is that in today's South Africa, blighted by persistent, glaring social, economic and racial injustice, the star of Winnie Mandela is once again on the rise. For many it has never waned: not for those who always considered the historic 1994 compromise between Nelson Mandela and De Klerk a betrayal which sacrificed justice at the altar of freedom and which has turned out to be a travesty of freedom for the oppressed; nor for those of the new generation who believe decolonisation was bartered for democracy. This was at the core of the student protests of the past years, the charge that the halls of learning, as bastions of white privilege, had been left intact; until, that is, as we saw in the last chapter, the Rhodes Must Fall campaign took matters into their own hands. Seen in this light, Winnie Mandela's obduracy, her refusal to bow to the Commission, becomes her foresight. Only when Tutu pleaded with her did she offer a paltry apology, her parting gift to proceedings for which she had never hidden her contempt (a moment which, in its own way, has also become 'iconic').

Like the hysteric who ushers in the birth of psychoanalysis, and who so often carries the malaise of a whole family,

Winnie Mandela might then be seen as a figure who, on behalf of everyone, sported in Technicolor the unhealed sickness of the nation. With almost uncanny links to everything raised at the conference, Sisonke Msimang concludes her 2018 book *The Resurrection of Winnie Mandela*: 'The past must be opened, not just to grief, but to the structural nature of racism.' 'Just there, in the recent past, like the body of a wounded animal hit by a speeding car, there lies the corpse of justice.' Whatever her crimes, Msimang argues, Winnie Mandela will remain on a pedestal 'until there is a harder, sterner form of justice [. . .] until all the apartheid murderers are named on a public roster so that they are known to the world.'[38] Remember Verryn in relation to the Calatas: 'The perpetrators should meet this family face to face.' Thus neatly and troublingly, although I imagine unknowingly, Msimang aligns her defence of Winnie Mandela with the grief at the heart of the conference and with the call for justice and accountability which is the driving premise of Lukhanyo and Abigail Calata's book.

The Resurrection of Winnie Mandela was pressed into my hands by Mervyn Sloman, the owner of the Cape Town Book Lounge – renowned independent bookstore and venue for cultural events – where I had been invited to talk about mothers. In the discussion, I had been asked what I made of Winnie Mandela as 'Mother of the Nation', a crushing idealisation, I responded, which, it can be no surprise, she failed so spectacularly to live up to. Certainly, in those days running up to the conference, I was completely unprepared for the latent affiliation – lines of potential if not actual solidarity – between the life of Winnie Mandela and the lives of the women I listened to throughout the week as they described the personal and political horrors they had experienced under apartheid. In fact

Winnie Mandela has already been granted, at least symbolically, re-entry into a communal world in Njabulo Ndebele's 2003 novel *The Cry of Winnie Mandela*, in which she narrates her own story after four other women, each one abandoned by her husband for a distinct reason, have offered their story to her (a huge success in South Africa, the book was republished in a new edition in 2013). One of the men is a disappeared mine worker, others leave in search of educational or marital advancement (a new white wife) or sexual freedom. The women embrace Mandela for her brazen flouting of the myth of the ever-patient, virtuous Penelope, waiting for Ulysses to return – a cruel centuries-old European hoax, Ndebele implies, against African women. The novel ends with all five women welcoming Penelope, in the modern guise of a hitchhiker, into the car in which, joyously and with fierce independence, they have taken to the road together (definite shades of the 1991 feminist road movie *Thelma and Louise*). 'You personify extreme political perception unmediated by nuance,' the third narrative voice of Mamello Molete, aka Patience Mamello Letlala, addresses Winnie, 'nuance having been drained out of us by the blatant obscenity of apartheid, which reduced life to one long scream.'[39] Impossible to know if these lines are deliberately evoking the cry of Nomonde Calata.

Even if the apartheid era ranks as one of the ugliest chapters of the twentieth century, we should expect no thanks from those who suffered if we reduce them to mere victims of history. One of the things that I came away with from the conference is just how far that applies to the women caught up in the struggle – which must include Winnie Mandela – whether despite or because of the enforced passivity and subjugation they endured. The random violence of the security forces whenever they raided activists' homes was notorious. It did not stop Nomonde Calata from refusing to leave her house when ordered to do so by a police officer, or from telling him to get off her bed: '"You will have to take your gun and shoot me, and take me out of the house." Well, they stood up and left.' Their vulgar sexual taunting also failed to deter her: 'Hau [*sic*] . . . you've got a baby without a father,' one of them mocked at sight of her pregnancy, 'don't you want us to be the father of your baby?'⁴⁰

In 1969–70, Winnie Mandela was held in detention without charge for 491 days, subject to beatings and torture, often in solitary confinement, sleeping on a blood-soaked mat in her cell next to the assault chamber, and for periods in a death cell. These details have only recently emerged with the publication of her prison diaries and letters in 2013. She is eloquent on how much better conditions are for a prisoner – read her husband – compared with a detainee. 'I'd communicate with the ants,' she recalls in her epilogue to the book, 'anything that has life. If I had had lice, I would even, I would even [*sic*] have nursed them [. . .] There is no worse punishment.' 'You are going to talk against your will,' Major Ferreira, one of her interrogators, told her (the other was the notorious torturer Major Swanepoel). 'We can go to the torture room now,' she replied. 'My defence has my instructions on my prospective inquest.' She also snubbed a request to address her captors in Afrikaans, telling them she preferred to use the language of 'her first oppressors'.⁴¹

'You know what is so bad?' Ferreira responded. 'She means what she says and no one can do anything about it.' Like Nomonde Calata, she was the target of sexual innuendo. 'The bloody bitch has sucked the saliva of all the white communists,' Swanepoel snaps during one of his interrogations. '[She would have] seduced the Pope if she had wanted to use him politically' ('they roar with laughter'). This is a prisoner who suffered frequent blackouts, palpitations, breathlessness, who regularly woke up screaming in the night, would mutter the names of her children, and at one point almost starved herself to death. For political reasons she did everything possible to conceal the fact that this was an attempted suicide. 'And they wonder', she comments in her epilogue, 'why I am like I am.'[42] A statement I see as undiminished in its impact by the fact that she is clearly trying to exonerate herself.

She has been the target of the most vicious sexual hatred, her refusal to retire as a sexual being seeming at moments to be the worst of her crimes. In the early 1990s, I went to visit a well-known writer on South Africa then based at Oxford University. My plan had been to discuss his take on the violence spreading across the country in the run-up to the 1993 elections. Instead, I found myself being regaled with endless stories of Winnie Mandela's sex life as I gazed out at the college lawns while we sat sipping tea. She was meant to be carrying the flag for her husband's and the nation's freedom. Instead she became the sinner to his saint. 'That Winnie began her fall from grace just as Nelson was beginning his ascent to sainthood', Msimang writes, 'is both a tragedy and another sort of fiction.'[43] Or in the words of her character in *The Cry of Winnie Mandela*: 'Whereas imprisonment had prepared him for the language of transcendence, I was too grounded in the muck of folly' (both, surely, tragic outcomes).[44]

Why do we expect, in situations of vicious political injustice, that virtue accumulates on the side of the oppressed? At the very least Winnie Mandela does us the favour of demonstrating the folly of that belief. But why, we might still ask, do we rush to divest the downtrodden of the ethical ambiguity which is surely the birthright of everyone? It is a truism of psychoanalysis that nobody's thoughts are pure. We are all traitors inside our heads. Lindiwe Hani is a model of giving in relation to the man who shot her father, but the day after meeting his mastermind she had woken up with 'the pure and clear urge to kill'.[45] Even De Kock is permitted ambiguity and not only in Gobodo-Madikizela's book. Siyah Mgoduka told us that his feelings started to soften when De Kock stepped forward to say that he had issued the command to kill his father, just when the presiding magistrate, for lack of evidence, had been about to close the case. Only the woman, it seems, has to be one thing or the other. Only she is hurled into the vortex of her collapsed moral grace. 'The woman who greeted [Nelson Mandela] on that sunny day in February 1990', Msimang comments on the day of his release from prison, 'was morally ambiguous [. . .] she spoiled the picture of the perfect revolution that the ANC was intent on creating. She was a reminder that the country was burning.' 'Just look', Msimang writes on the final pages, 'at where we are.'[46] Unlike Winnie Mandela, neither P. W. Botha nor F. W. de Klerk have ever been convicted in law for any crime.

By the end of the conference, I was still texting home that I was not sure I could stand any more. I had taken to walking in and out of the Stellenbosch Botanical Gardens at every available opportunity, even when there was only a ten-minute break. The gardens are another jewel in the area, established no doubt on the back of dubiously acquired wealth (and who was I, in any case, to go in search of solace?). So it struck me as nothing short of miraculous that, in one of the last plenary lectures, Cameroonian philosopher and activist Achille Mbembe managed to talk of beauty. He was not being sentimental. 'The

Trauma of the World and the World as Trauma' was the title of his paper. Mincing no words, he spoke of the 'traumatogenic' institutions of capitalism and liberal democracy which to this day have never delivered racial equality, of the 'genocidal unconscious' which turns humans, foremost the racial 'other', into disposable commodities (violence under so-called 'quiet conditions', as Rosa Luxemburg would say, which is where this book begins).[47] A more viable future will only emerge, he suggested, out of rupture, only if we begin by recognising the brokenness all around; only from here might we light on the potential beauty in everyone. We need a new political subject, no longer in flight from interiority, who deploys multiple selves, inhabits the cracks and crevices of the world, who knows how to be nobody, knows when she has nothing to hide, and when to rush to the other side to meet her double.

At first I thought that this version of political hope, grounded in brokenness, belonged to a different universe from that of Tumani Calata, the youngest daughter of Fort Calata with whom Nomonde had been pregnant when he was killed. While growing up, she had wanted to know nothing about her father, a stranger whom she never grieved. Then, slowly, she started down the path which finally allowed her to begin again, to take possession of the utterance, 'I am the daughter of a hero. I know who I am.' In the end, despite the apparent contrast between self-affirmation and breakage, it seemed to me that both of them were saying the same thing. Something unprecedented still has to happen. There will be no political emancipation for anyone until we all recognise the corpse still lying on the road, the continuing injustice, the work that remains to be done.

9

AT THE BORDER

In March 2018, 120 women detainees went on a one-month hunger and work strike at Yarl's Wood Immigrant Removal Centre in the UK. Several received letters from the Home Office informing them that their deportation would not be paused by their action, in fact it would more likely accelerate. Serco, the private company running the centre, denied that the hunger strike was taking place. Serco is best known for its policy of changing locks on its properties as a means of evicting asylum seekers living in the community. Despite being fined £6.8 million for its treatment of asylum seekers, its contract to house asylum seekers was renewed by the Home Office in June 2019. (A year later, at the height of the Covid-19 pandemic, it was also awarded the private contract for test-and-trace in the teeth of objections based on its past conduct.) The women were demanding that asylum seekers, minors, pregnant women and survivors of torture, rape and trafficking should not be detained. They were calling for an end to indefinite detention, a practice which is sanctioned in no other European country apart from the UK; in the US, it was first introduced under the post-9/11 Patriot Act and then signed into law under President Obama (the most notorious example being Guantánamo Bay). They were also protesting the conditions under which they were held. Three years previously, the non-profit London-based organisation Women for Refugee Women had published a pamphlet describing those conditions under the title *I Am Human*.

325

Both the pamphlet and the strike exposed to public view the cruel and degrading treatment that characterises the detention of migrant women in the UK. Why, for example, were women in detention being watched in intimate situations – naked, partly dressed, in the toilet or shower, or in bed – by male guards? Why were they being routinely touched and searched by men: 'Men touch your knickers . . . A man touches your knickers and leaves them on the bed?'[1] Given that detention is expensive – estimated at £35 million per annum – and that asylum claims could just as easily be processed while the women lived in the community, why in fact were they being detained at all?[2] Today legal entry for refugees, asylum seekers or unskilled workers has been made virtually impossible in the UK. Migrant women who try to enter specifically as refugees or asylum seekers are increasingly being criminalised.[3] In 2002, the 'feminisation of irregular migration' was already being described as 'perhaps the most significant [migration] phenomenon of recent decades'.[4] Out of thirty-one women whose cases were investigated in 2012 by the Cambridge Institute of Criminology, twelve of the fourteen whose outcomes were known had been refused asylum. Although most of them had been trafficked, they were treated as illegal migrants, rather than as the targets of abuse.

These women are being punished, often viciously, for already being the victims of crimes. When one woman was moved to Yarl's Wood after seven months in prison on charges which were dropped, she said that it felt as if she was being punished 'for being a foreigner'.[5] The fact that conditions at the centre included being exposed to watching men – there were also reported cases of sexual assault by the guards – suggests that these detainees were no less being punished for being women. This reality is by no means restricted to the UK. In July 2019,

New York Congresswoman Alexandria Ocasio-Cortez was the object of sexually explicit Facebook posts by Customs and Border Protection guards – 9,500 current and former guards are members of a secret Facebook group – after she had reported the horrifying conditions in US border detention centres where detainees described being abused by officers and where women were being forced to drink out of toilets. The posts also questioned the authenticity of images, which had gone viral, of a drowned man, Oscar Alberto Martínez Ramírez, and his twenty-three-month-old daughter, Angie Valeria, who had tried to cross the US–Mexican border. 'Nine thousand five hundred CBP officers sharing memes about dead migrants,' wrote Ocasio-Cortez, 'and discussing violence and sexual misconduct towards members of Congress. How on earth can CBP's culture be trusted to care for refugees humanely?'[6]

Migration has become one of the most urgent political issues of our time. A politics purportedly founded on reason and utilitarian logic – the need to get numbers under control for the benefit of all – reveals itself as drenched in sexual hatred. Though the harsh realities of migration make no sexual distinctions (the sea is gender-indiscriminate in who it drowns), in this chapter I will be exploring the special pleasure which migration policy appears to take in targeting women. In the Ocasio-Cortez story, scorn of women and of migrants were visibly fuelling each other, spewed out in the same over-excited, violent run of memes (the posts also included Photoshopped pictures of Ocasio-Cortez performing oral sex on migrants and on Donald Trump).[7] At Yarl's Wood, a woman from Kenya, beaten by her family and forced to undergo FGM as 'punishment' for being lesbian, was dragged across a room at the centre: 'They were taunting me . . . they were pulling on my legs.' When she took refuge in the bathroom, they laughed at her, put her in a headlock, and bound her wrists and feet 'like a goat'.[8] A Nigerian rape survivor described how she was thrown on the floor 'like a bag of cement'.[9] Another detainee, who had been coming to the UK from St Vincent since she was nine, had been raped at gunpoint at fifteen by three men as a way of settling financial scores with her father. Disowned by her grandfather who first brought her to England, she then took to prostitution and, after a prison sentence, found herself at Yarl's Wood as part of an immigration crackdown: 'I thought prison was bad but Yarl's Wood pushed me to the point of wanting to commit suicide.' Male officers would enter her room behind her back, go through her bed, her underwear: 'I felt raped all over again.'[10] Serco dismissed the accounts as 'uncorroborated', insisted that this wasn't their practice and said they would fully investigate the complaints.[11]

Exposed to sexual and physical insult, the women are also radically disempowered by being cut off from all knowledge. Anyone in indefinite detention enters a hallucinatory, interminable world, since the whole point is that you never know for how long you will be held: 'In prison you know what's your release date . . . But in Yarl's Wood, you don't know.'[12] Although there has been some reduction in detention times in the past couple of years, Home Office data going back to 2010 show cases where people were held for as long as four years (cases of multiple detention, or detention and re-detention, which was routine for the opponents of South Africa's government under apartheid, are known but not reflected in the statistics).[13] 'Everything is pending,' writes poet David Herd in his afterword to *Refugee Tales*, a collection of stories gathered from refugees by campaigners on a solidarity walk from Canterbury that has taken place annually since 2015: 'We are deep here within the logic of suspension.'[14] No point in etching the number of days on the walls if at any moment you might be deported (with no prison sentence or release date, you 'count up' rather than 'count down' the days).[15] In the literature on migration, the commonly used technical term for the forcible return of migrants to their country of origin is 'refoulement' (literally, pushing back or repulsing), which also happens to be the French word for the psychoanalytic concept of repression. As if somewhere it is being acknowledged that returning a migrant to the country from which they fled is not only inhumane, and most likely illegal under international law; it also straitjackets the detainees' mental access to their own experience, makes it impossible for them to take the measure of their world. It is also an attempted cover-up, a way of pretending there is nothing ugly going on at either end of the journey. A Chinese woman trafficked for cannabis production, who found herself caught up in the UK criminal justice system, makes the direct parallel between here and there: 'I just felt I was in their hands – like being in the hands of the people who brought me here' – 'hands' in this case no metaphor.[16]

These women are being slammed by the system into positions of unwilled ignorance: 'I didn't know where I was going', 'They don't explain anything to you.' 'Can *you* tell me what is happening?' – this last addressed as a plea to one of the Cambridge researchers given access to a detainee in the course of her investigation (normally, anyone visiting a detention centre is not allowed to bring a pen and paper into the building).[17] Often, the forced ignorance takes them right back to the place of unknowing where their journey began. In the words of a trafficked detainee who had been promised a new life: 'We were not allowed to ask questions.'[18] They are being held, writes Herd, outside 'the skin' of language, since, with no record of their appeal – there is only a written determination – whatever they may have said or tried to say leaves no trace (a key reason for the project of *Refugee Tales*).[19] Not just repressive, what these women experience is closer to a wipe-out of identity in which all self-knowledge or self-recognition is lost: 'I did not know who I was anymore', 'I do not appear to exist', 'It is as if you are inside a grave.'[20] The alienation is then matched by the world outside the walls of the centre, where little is known of these stories. There are exceptions. In a recent interview, campaigning journalist Amelia Gentleman, who has played such a key role in bringing the Windrush scandal into the public eye, tells the story of a woman who arrived in the UK from Jamaica in 1974 aged one, but was classified as an illegal immigrant decades later and sent to Yarl's Wood, after which she killed herself.[21] For the most part, a situation of 'knowing and unknowing' permits the rest of the world to continue blithely on its path through the 'cultural production of ignorance'.[22] Hence the felt urgency of the Canterbury tales project to undertake its criss-crossing of national spaces – Kent, Surrey, Sussex – to make visible a group of people around whom the nation has organised itself 'in order precisely that they be kept from view'.[23] One more instance of violence unseen as it has littered the pages of this book.

In the twenty-first century, Kafka's Joseph K has taken on the trappings of a migrant woman as she tries and fails to make sense of an impenetrable, gratuitously unjust, foreign law. Everything seems to be arranged to ensure the maximum degree of befuddlement, to shrink to an absolute minimum the asylum seeker's pathway to and through her own mind. Communication from the UK Border Agency's Criminal Casework Directorate, to which many of these women are referred, is almost uniformly in English. Access to interpreters is minimal to non-existent, and notification of a hearing is rarely given far enough in advance to allow time for preparation (twenty minutes with a barrister is typical). Women who have been trafficked, and whose papers and passports are confiscated by the traffickers, find themselves arrested on arrival for false or missing documentation, or for fraud. The sentence for false documentation is twelve months' imprisonment, which also happens to be the period after which deportation is automatic, which means that they may just as well have been turned around at the port of entry and sent directly back home. The Cambridge report records the story of one victim of trafficking who was sentenced to two consecutive periods of twelve months for using a false document with intent and making a false statement for the purpose of marriage. Although eventually a Conclusive Grounds decision was made confirming her victim status, two weeks before her release date she received a letter from the UKBA stating that she was 'considered to have committed a particularly serious crime and to constitute a danger to the community in the United Kingdom' and would not be granted asylum (on appeal her sentence was reduced, which meant she was not automatically deported).[24]

'Serious crime', 'a danger to the community'; as if such women were the agents of their own abuse, and then, in a senseless twist, a threat to the presumed-to-be law-abiding citizens of the UK. At any given moment the number of victims is likely to exceed the numbers of convicted traffickers in UK prisons (a statement to that effect with reference to Scottish prisons was made in the House of Lords in 2014).[25] Most of the traffickers get off scot-free. In the UK and US prison systems, women are already being incarcerated at an ever-increasing rate – since 1978 the number of women and girls locked up in the US has been growing at double the rate of men and boys.[26] Most often, the prison sentences are being handed down for low-level non-violent offences, despite repeated recommendations to the contrary by official bodies, such as the Corston report commissioned in 2006 after the deaths of six women at Styal prison, and published the following year.[27] This is especially true of foreign nationals. Figures released in 2010 for example showed a twenty-seven per cent growth in the female prison population in the UK, but the growth in the number of foreign nationals was forty-nine per cent.[28] There isn't the slightest evidence that this increase reflects the increasing seriousness of the offences. A 2007 report from the Prison Service Women and Young People's Group for dealing with foreign national offenders described 'the low rate of violent offences as particularly noteworthy'.[29] Instead women seeking asylum are immediately treated as culpable, even when, as in the case of trafficking, it is their handler who has committed the crime. 'Why did they not try and arrest the man who had stolen my passport? Why did they do nothing about it?' asked a woman asylum seeker from Iran, handcuffed at the airport and taken to a police station holding cell.[30] She had been trafficked after her father had just managed to get her out on temporary release from a notorious prison where she had been held in solitary confinement, abused and subject to daily threats of rape.

Yet what is expected – indeed legally required – of these women, if they are to have the faintest chance of being granted entry, is the fullest co-operation with every aspect of a system rigged in advance to oppress and exclude them. When a migrant is referred as a potential victim of trafficking, there follows a mandatory forty-five-day period of 'reflection and recovery' (as if recovery from trauma is something that can be mandated in forty-five days). After this time, a decision to prosecute will be taken if the evidence – mostly hard, often impossible, to establish – is conclusive. Leave to remain may then be extended to one year if the victim has agreed to assist the police in their criminal investigation.[31] 'Reflection' in this case clearly has nothing to do with the idea of freedom or the capacity for independent thought. During a performance organised by Women for Refugee Women at the South Bank in June 2019 as part of UK Refugee Week, one of the women refugees, caught in the net of the system, apologised: 'I'm sorry I'm thinking too much.' Another simply asked, 'What will happen to my mind?'[32]

No one, including visitors (rare) or investigators (even rarer), is spared. 'We will do as we are told,' the writer Ali Smith intones to herself as she makes her way through the four security checks to the cell of the detainee she has been given permission to meet as part of the project of *Refugee Tales*.[33] When one trafficked woman refused to respond under questioning (presumably in English with no legal support), the UKBA, as the designated Competent Authority (CA) on behalf of the National Referral Mechanism (NRM) for potential victims of trafficking, used her failure to do so as evidence that her claim to have been trafficked most likely was false.[34] Even as I write them, the acronyms are enough to drive anyone insane (CA for 'Competent Authority' presumably not intended as a cruel tautology or a joke). 'What you've told me today', one investigator observed to a woman arrested for cannabis production, 'does not make a great deal of sense.' She was refusing to disclose the names of the people who had trafficked her into the UK.[35] But it is common knowledge that to name names puts the one trafficked, together with their entire family – whether accompanying them to the UK or back in their originating country – at mortal risk: 'If you tell, pool of blood.'[36]

Somewhere there always seems to be an assumption that the asylum seeker is never acting under duress (she is a criminal manipulator, not someone who might have been manipulated herself). One trafficked woman was asked if she had wanted to come to the UK, and when she replied that yes, she had, was told that she therefore must have come 'willingly', so no trafficking can have been involved.[37] Another had been given a false passport when she was thrown onto the streets after being held and made to work as a prostitute for seven years. Despite the fact that she did not even know it was a fraud case, the judge concluded that she had 'knowingly' used a false document and imprisoned her for six months (when he commented that he presumed she was also guilty of illegal entry, he had to be reminded that this was not one of the indictments in the case).[38] Another woman had been invited to join an acquaintance on a holiday with friends who were arrested on the return journey and found in possession of cocaine. Even though she was not caught in possession of any drugs herself, she was charged with being 'knowingly' concerned in their importation and received a fifteen-year sentence.[39] 'Willingly', 'knowingly' – the law moves in on the foreign plaintiff on the grounds that they acted with volition, knowledge, awareness, consent, under conditions which mostly make such states of being and mind impossible. As a consequence, many of these women are advised to plead guilty so as to reduce their sentence and avoid the twelve months which bring automatic deportation.

'Knowingly' might in any case give us pause. One of the

hardest things in law is to prove that the defendant's actions pass the test of intent needed for a criminal charge. As we have seen, this indeed was the key, legally undecidable, issue in the Oscar Pistorius case. Lawyers involved in asylum cases, on the other hand, seem to have no compunction in attributing intent and foreknowledge with remarkable ease, despite the utter tenuousness of the evidence and the drastic legal and human consequences which follow. We might note the gulf which separates this process – or lack of due process – from the way the law treats those in power. Thus Robert Mueller's investigation into Trump's possible collusion with Russian interference in the 2016 election tied itself in knots when concluding that there was a lack of strong enough evidence to prove beyond a reasonable doubt that Trump and his team had acted 'with general knowledge of the illegality of their conduct' (not that acting without such knowledge in this case would have made things a lot better).[40]

What image of the mental life of the vulnerable and underprivileged is being pieced together with such ugly dedication out of the debris of their lives? And if, from outside the penitentiary and detention centre, we go along with these assumptions or fail to question them, what psychic damage are we being asked at once to ignore and be complicit with? On the far side of will and knowledge are experiences which the mind cannot bear to countenance, which throttle the voice and muddle the tongue. But the last thing you will find in this system is the barest tolerance for an asylum seeker who might be so traumatised as to be confused in their narration of events. The minutest inconsistency between one version of their story and the next will disqualify their case. One woman whose case was included in the Cambridge report stated at first that she had been separated from her companion before she was raped; subsequently she said that it was after the rape that he was taken to a different place. The refusal letter, seizing the moment, jumping – again – to the wrong conclusion, stated that her conflicting accounts made it 'difficult to accept that this is a true account of a real event'.[41]

And yet blurred recollection can be a sign of authenticity, of the heart and mind faltering as it attempts to retrieve, and also push away, a truth which it cannot tolerate. In this context, the perfectly honed story is the one not to be trusted (in one episode of the 1970s US TV series *Perry Mason*, the detective nailed the child culprit because of the impeccable word-to-word precision with which the young boy repeated three times under questioning his fabricated account of the crime). In the world of asylum, you will look in vain for the faintest sign of sympathetic treatment when, as is often the case, the one seeking asylum cannot even begin to speak. Many of those held start having nightmares and flashbacks as detention, alongside their earlier experiences, comes to be lived as a trauma in itself. But the idea that silence might not derive from a deliberate withholding of evidence, might instead be an expression of trauma, which has become a truism of our times, seems not to be on the radar of this reality. Before the law, trauma is a troublemaker, like a stubborn, wilful child.

Before the law, or outside it? 'How', asks Herd, 'is the institution of the removal centre legal? Or rather, since, in conventional terms, it plainly offends legal principles, what relation does such a site have to the law?'[42] There are for the most part no legal, let alone human, grounds to justify these policies or for the legal decisions of disqualification, imprisonment or deportation that are made. 'Who decides what happens to someone cross-ing the border?' asks Madeleine Schwartz in her investigation of US detention centres (not one of the lawyers she spoke to could point to any written rules laying down why a migrant should face deportation, arrest or custody).[43] Today, migration has become a tipping point for the law's relationship to itself. The more this system turns asylum seekers, who are after all among the most vulnerable people in the world, into criminals, the more the law flounders, as it runs the risk of exposing the criminality of the state. 'Criminalisation by the state', Michael Grewcock writes with reference to equally dire migration pol-icies in Australia, 'is integral to legitimising criminal activity by the state.'[44] Mopping up the migrant population, hoarding them into detention centres, the prisons and the courts – in Australia onto the notorious island camps of Nauru and Manus, where migrants are more or less caged – a government sweeps its own stables. Of course, criminal activity is integral to capitalist economies, whose increasing neoliberal ruthlessness is one of the key drivers of migration in our time. 'Behind the sublimated cloak of legality', observes Marxist geographer David Harvey, 'lie overt violence and outright theft.'[45]

Political philosopher Howard Caygill goes so far as to argue that violence at the borders of the modern nation state has been the chief means by which modernity has contained and denied the violence of its own civility: 'The possibility of feats of extravagant and unrestrained violence at and beyond the border [have historically] contrasted with the constraints of rational management of violence within the borders of the nation states' (what he calls 'the scission of civility and the vio-lence which sustains it').[46] To invoke Arendt again, the border is the place where the ideal of progress, to which the so-called

civilised nations make their appeal, is placed under the se-
verest strain. To put it simply, violence at the border serves a
purpose, as indeed does the shock it provokes. It obscures
the violence of colonial expansion and of the internal social
arrangements of modern nations which fight to preserve the
privilege of the few against the many. 'The rational management of violence within the nation state', Caygill continues,
'was only possible when potential and actual violence had
been displaced to the border.'[47]

We should therefore recognise violence against migrants at
the border not as the exception, but the rule. This too can be
traced back in time. Christian moral freedom, Caygill observes
after Hegel, could 'only become certain of itself and its inner
spiritual possessions by means of the violent subjugation of
the infidel at the borders of Christendom'.[48] 'Become certain'
is crucial: what is being secured by these policies is the futile
attempt of unjust regimes to justify themselves. And who,
exactly, decides what we are allowed to understand as violence?
– one of the questions with which this book began. As Judith
Butler has long maintained, the exercise of such decisions is in
itself a form of violence.[49] Binding migrants into the legal process with no hope of exit (other than prison or return) obfus-
cates the violence of the state. It is the perfect way to distract
the rest of us from the corpses lying on the shore.

One thing seems clear. For a migrant to be successfully criminalised, it must be that, at each stage of their perilous journey,
they acted with full knowledge of consequences, even when
these were unknowable in advance and therefore beyond the
bounds of their consent. Which amounts to saying that, contrary to the living testimony of any and every refugee, they only
wished the worst for themselves. The system is as crazy as its

own claim to reason is intemperate. Nestled within its perverse logic, we can see the traces of a central feminist demand – that women should determine their own destiny – which the system twists and turns against itself: 'You knew what you were doing. You asked for what you got. You are dispensable.'

Across the contemporary terrain of crime and punishment, women are either being assigned punishing forms of human agency or being deprived of agency altogether. In British prisons, a relatively new ethos of 'responsibilisation' (*sic*) is ostensibly intended to give women a greater sense of control over their lives. But it also serves to make women – as opposed to inequality, poverty or domestic violence – wholly accountable for what are most often petty, low-level, non-violent 'survival' crimes, crimes for which most, if not all, of them should never have been incarcerated in the first place. These inmates have way more in common with women struggling with their daily lives outside the prison walls than with the often violent criminals inside them (in the past few years, the number of UK women recorded as homeless on entering prison has increased by seventy-one per cent).[50] At the other pole, an increased focus on trafficking, which in a just world should secure a woman's right to asylum, makes alleviating women's lives conditional on their being 'rescued'.

According to a similar logic, the surest way to get a woman acquitted of, say, killing an abusive partner is 'diminished responsibility', which robs women of any notion that they may have had rational motives for their act, that, provoked beyond endurance, they acted with due consideration, under duress or in self-defence. 'We are still a long way from recognising the retaliation of an abused woman,' writes journalist Sophie Elmhirst on the case of Farieissia Martin, who stabbed her violent partner to death after years of abuse, 'as a desperate bid to escape, rather than an act of murderous insanity.' In 2019 Martin won the right to appeal against her conviction of murder, on the grounds that years of abuse had led to post-traumatic stress disorder which substantially impaired her ability to exert self-control.[51] In the words of feminist criminologist Hilary Allen, this has the dubious advantage of rendering such women, and by implication all women, 'harmless', never the fully conscious agents of their own deeds: 'What is potentially oppressive to women – criminal or otherwise,' she writes, 'is for the frailties and disadvantages that do tend to characterise their position in society to be treated as exhaustive of their condition as social or legal subjects.'[52] How are these women to be thought about? What perverse, normative ethical agenda trails their ongoing mistreatment by the state? Either women are handed the keys to mental freedom only to find themselves stranded and accused with no moral or legal recourse to justice, or they are turned into subjects with no control over their own lives. As if there were no middle position, and no get-out clause. Women are always guilty, either of having too much human agency, or not enough.

o   o   o

In the UK, most of the cases I have described so far are the logical outcome of Theresa May's call for a 'hostile environment' for so-called illegal migrants which she issued as Home Secretary in 2012.[53] The instruction was then translated into government policy in the Immigration Acts of 2014 and 2016. Despite widespread objections and protest – including a call by Tory rebels in June 2020 for a twenty-eight-day limit on detention – it is still in place as I write.[54] Glyn Williams, architect of the policy as head of the Home Office department of migration at the time, was made a Knight Commander of the Order of the Bath in the June 2019 Honours list. If anything, for May, the policy would seem to have been a visible source of pride. The nastier things get, the more it could be seen to be fulfilling her brief. Under May's guardianship, the safe haven has turned into an inferno. What she doubtless did not intend was that the brutishness of her own policy would rip the cover from the civility of the state, thereby undermining the cherished distinctions between civilised countries and the rest of the world on which the whole of today's Western migration policy relies and without which it becomes meaningless. How hostile can the UK be towards migrants in flight before it begins not just to criminalise those seeking safety, but to tarnish and incriminate itself? Put more simply, for the refugee, the host country – not that anyone is exactly being 'hosted' – was meant to be a 'better place'.

Of course, hostility towards refugees and asylum seekers in Europe long predates the aggressive policies of Theresa May. Indeed, it has been one of Europe's hallmarks, notably in the second half of the twentieth century, a type of postwar consensus where inhumanity, which was thought to have been assigned to the past after the Second World War, quietly and then unquietly festers. Hatred of migrants can even be seen as a direct consequence of that war. As historian Tony Judt describes it, the relative ethnic purity that settled over Europe after the war was the surreal fulfilment of Hitler's legacy. Today's migrants clamouring at the door of Europe are its ghosts.[55] Many of them are also trying to exchange the crushed and/or exploitative economies of former colonies by 'building a nest' in the gaps of the economies of their former oppressors (claiming a place which, to say the least, might be seen as rightfully theirs).[56] In 1994, migration and human rights lawyers Jacqueline Bhabha and Sue Shutter described the dire record on migration of European countries as a whole, or 'Fortress Europe', as it was then termed (we could say that Brexit has merely contracted the space). One point three million refugees were living in Europe, as compared with two million at the time in Sudan, one of the poorest countries in the world. In May 1993, the German parliament voted to amend the constitution and revoke the right of asylum in response to a dramatic escalation in xenophobia and racist violence, coupled with the resurgence of the far right, following an influx of migrants over the previous eighteen months. A betrayal by Western governments of the post-war commitment to human rights was, write Bhabha and Shutter, becoming 'increasingly harsh, not to say hysterical'.[57] The tightening of immigration policy is always accompanied by frenzy.

Today the violence inherent in such policy is if anything more blatant. In June 2019, a legal submission to the International Criminal Court argued for the prosecution of the EU and member states for intentionally allowing thousands of deaths of migrants at sea – with 'foreknowledge and full awareness of the lethal consequences' – in order to deter others.[58] These decisions expose the lunatic undercurrents of the so-called reason of state. Their irrationality seems to know no bounds. When states across Europe announce that they are suspending all rescue boats for migrants at sea in order to deter them from an unsafe crossing, they surely know that, as a result of this policy, more migrants will drown.[59] When the French and British governments agree to shut down the Calais 'Jungle' camp, on the grounds that it is unruly and dangerous, they must be aware that the numbers of minors attempting the perilous Channel crossing in flimsy dinghies and boats will rise.[60]

In August 2015, Angela Merkel stunned the world by opening the doors of her country to a million migrants with her famous utterance '*Wir schaffen das*' ('We will handle this' or even 'Yes we can'). To many, it felt like an act of atonement, or at least the sign of a wish that Germany appear humane. The fact that only a few months before she had screwed Greece financially by refusing to forgive the country's debt as the German debt had been forgiven after the war – which if anything she seemed to forget – simply shows how much more comfortable it is for a political leader (for anyone) to feel magnanimous than to be absolved of a crime. In relation to Greece it was also the Federal Minister of Finance, Wolfgang Schäuble, who bore down on her, not to speak of the banks. But even if she has never explicitly made the link to the nation's past, there is surely an inverted echo: making room for the wretched of the earth as the opposite of Hitler's land seizure policy of *Lebensraum* which sent millions on the move.

Merkel must also have been conscious of the political danger she was courting. In 2017, the far right entered the Bundestag for the first time since 1945 in the form of the AfD ('Alternative for Germany') which is calling for the borders to be closed – its supporters have cited the arrival of the refugees as their top concern. This was the context for the death of Walter Lübcke, who was found dead with a gunshot wound to his head in June 2019. Several of her allies and cabinet members who have publicly stood up for refugees have received death threats.[61] The AfD is also demanding an end to the country's preoccupation with public memory – the 'culture of atonement' for Second World

War atrocities – and a restoration of national pride. Memory and borders shut down. 'As the harmonisation process gathers steam,' write Bhabha and Shutter of the tightening policy across Europe, it 'obliterates the past'.[62] The defence – and we know historically that most fortifications turn out to be useless – goes to work on two levels, on the land and in the head. Such panicked entrenchment suggests that it is the vulnerability of migrants that makes them so hated. A sudden, highly visible influx of refugees, observed British-Polish sociologist Zygmunt Bauman in one of his last interviews, draws to the surface the dim suspicion that our fate lies with forces beyond our mastery and control, feelings we try to 'stifle and hide' (a theme that has been constant here).[63] These migrants are the pitiful reminder of the most shameful moments of European history, and also of the fragility with which in the end all human subjects, regardless of nation, race, wealth or status, hold on to the ramparts of life. Just as it seems to be the vulnerability of the women at Yarl's Wood that provokes the next stage of violation, the touching, the taunts, the jibes.

o   o   o

The 1951 Geneva Convention on the status of refugees did not include gender as a ground of persecution: race, religion, nationality, membership of a particular social group or political opinion were the only categories recognised. The implications for women refugees and asylum seekers have been momentous and have surely played their part in what was to come. In a much-discussed case from 1984, Sofia Campos-Guardado, a Salvadoran woman, fled to the US and applied for asylum after being forced, together with her female cousins, to witness her uncle and male cousins, activists in the agrarian reform movement, being hacked to death. The women were then raped and told to leave on pain of death. Her case was rejected by the US Board of Immigration Appeals on the grounds that her account had failed to prove that the harm she feared might come to her was based on her political opinion or membership of a particular group (despite the fact that the attackers chanted political slogans during the assault).[64] In the same year, Olimpia Lazo-Majano, also from El Salvador, failed to persuade the Board that the repeated rapes and beatings she had suffered at the hands of a military sergeant, who threatened to expose her as a subversive as a post facto justification for killing her, qualified as political (his actions were ruled as 'strictly personal'). In this case, a majority on the Ninth Circuit Court disagreed and overturned the decision, but according to the one judge who produced a dissenting opinion, the sergeant – in uniform and carrying a gun which he used 'to vent upon her his rapacious assault' – was displaying a 'pathological display of a lover's wooing'.[65]

Since the 1990s rape has been seen as a violation of human rights and a persecutable offence under international law. Since the Rwandan genocide of 1994, it has been defined as a crime of genocide. As feminists have long pointed out, the rape of women pertains to the group since one of the things it does is to enforce a woman's place in the subordinate category of women (always containing an element of display, it is the great ugly performative of gender). In the twentieth century its collective dimension has never been more clear. In countries ranging from Chile and Argentina in the 1970s to Haiti and Turkey in the 1980s and 1990s, rape has been used as an instrument of national security. Under the 1990s post-Marcos government of Corazon Aquino in the Philippines, the government, which had lifted martial law, continued military operations against the New People's Army, breaking into homes and raping women suspected of being insurgents or of working on their behalf.[66]

In Bosnia, women were systematically raped by the nationalist military on grounds of ethnicity. Mixed-ethnic marriages, relatively common in Serbia, were seen as 'factories of bastards' and the female body a spoil of war, a territory whose borders 'spread through birth of enemy sons'. When the Belgrade feminist group Women in Black visited the refugee camps they found that the women who had been raped were being pressured to 'suppress their own subjective understanding of their experiences'. They were being prepared as 'fodder' for the next war which would be waged to overcome the 'national shame'.[67] These rapes are political, although the rape victim is permitted neither access to her own experience nor any control over the consequences of the act. The irony is that the assault on the woman can fuel over-masculinised identities which will in turn make rape – as an act of national vindication – more likely. Anti-rape campaigners in situations of military conflict or foreign occupation – the rape in 1995 of a twelve-year-old girl in Okinawa by American troops is a famous instance – always run the risk of inflaming nationalist military swagger.[68] Viewed in this light, classifying rape as purely personal in relation to any asylum seeker in flight from a situation of military conflict is a form of daylight robbery. It strips of all significance an experience which, as numerous survivors testify, already works to blank out the mind.

Despite the shifts in international law, women migrants raped in their home country can still not be confident of asylum in the liberal democracies of the West. Violence against migrant women, whether perpetrated in the country of origin or after their arrival, is simply not sufficient cause. The number of women immigrants refused leave to remain after being subject to domestic violence in the UK more than doubled from twelve to thirty per cent between 2012 and 2016 (a direct outcome of the hostile environment policy).[69] 'What we are doing in these cases is saying we care about domestic violence,' observed Thangam Debbonaire, Labour MP for Bristol West in August 2019, 'except if you have insecure immigration status and then we don't.'[70] 'From the point of view of the government,' writes gender historian Eithne Lubhéid of the situation in the United States, 'the rapes of undocumented women remain largely unrepresentable.'[71] This is at least partly due to the silence surrounding the systematic rape by border guards of migrants and those seeking asylum in the US.[72] Across Europe, the same story applies. In September 2019, asylum seekers from North Africa claimed to recognise the captors who had systematically raped women at a migrant registration centre in Messina (three men were arrested by detectives on charges of torture, kidnapping and human trafficking).[73]

Whether or not asylum will be granted appears to be something of a lottery. In the US, for example, evidence of the woman's resistance to subordination has been the condition for her to be potentially eligible for asylum based on her 'political opinion' (one of the categories recognised by the Geneva Convention). In one case from 1999, the judge ruled in favour of a Guatemalan woman who had undergone years of domestic violence, including rape and assault, on the grounds that she was opposed to male domination and had therefore been attacked in retaliation for her political views (this would make all resistance to domestic violence a political act, as feminists have long insisted it is).[74] The Board of Immigration then overturned the decision. In the same year, agents from the Immigration and Naturalization Service in the States came to the house of 'Ana Flores' and arrested her for deportation because she had bitten (*sic*) a habitually abusive husband.[75] In 1990, the Canadian authorities granted refugee status to a woman and her two daughters on the grounds of a well-founded fear of persecution based on their membership of the social group 'consisting of women and girls who do not conform to Islamic fundamentalist norms'.[76]

But if these decisions in favour of the women applicants are humane, the logic – the grounds of recognition – remain suspect. What does it mean to make resistance a condition of freedom from oppression? What hidden, or not so hidden, Islamophobic agenda might be lurking behind the generic category of 'Islamic fundamentalism', or behind the idea that women can be seen as belonging to the legally requisite status of a group only on the grounds that they are resisting it? Why should trashing one's home country and culture be one of the necessary conditions of asylum? 'Some of us,' remarks Saeed Rahman, a woman from Pakistan who was granted asylum because of persecution based on her sexual orientation, 'as people of color and immigrants in this country, do not buy completely into the discourse of freedom and rights.'[77] She grew up, she adds, under a military dictatorship in Pakistan strongly backed by the US. 'Are we willing', asks Judith Butler, 'to have our claims to freedom instrumentalised for the purpose of a racist European national identity through restrictive and coercive immigration policies?'[78]

And what is being implied by the suggestion that men may sometimes have political, sometimes purely personal, reasons for assaulting their wives, with the corresponding implication that in the second case, flight by the assailed woman, and hence the woman's asylum claim, is not justified? Again, it is as if the fragility of the woman's status, the unstable ground – literally as well as metaphorically – that she treads, is then reproduced by the uncertain and unpredictable legal apparatus which is meant to be protecting her. Despite the voice of feminism over more than half a century, it would seem that, as far as migrant women are concerned, what goes on in private, the world of domestic intimacy, however violent, still falls outside the purview of the law. In July 2020, MPs in the UK were told that migrant women with no recourse to public funds would be excluded from the forthcoming domestic abuse bill. 'The state', observed Jess Phillips, the Labour shadow minister for domestic violence and safeguarding, 'is continuing the threat of the perpetrator who says "no one will believe you, you won't have anywhere to go and no support" – and right now the abuser is absolutely right.'[79] In 2018, then US Attorney General Jeff Sessions passed an interim order that ruled out domestic abuse as grounds for granting refuge.

In what has become a notorious case, Vilma Carrillo, a Guatemalan mother whose husband had beaten and almost killed her, was separated from her eleven-year-old child, Yeisvi, at the border. When she flew to Georgia to be reunited with her daughter, she was taken to a detention centre and threatened with deportation, while her child, who had US citizenship, was put out to care in Arizona two thousand miles away. A legal petition to release Carrillo on humanitarian grounds was turned down, even though it was clear that it would be impossible for her to avoid her violent husband if she returned to Guatemala. 'She faces certain death', stated Shana Tabak, the executive director of the immigrant advocacy group Tahirih Justice Center, 'if she returns.' Lawyers appealing her deportation claimed she was not given a fair hearing as her papers were in a backpack confiscated on entry to the US and because her first language was a Mayan dialect different from that spoken by her interpreters. In December 2018, a Washington, DC District Court judge ruled Sessions's decision unlawful for having imposed 'an arbitrarily heightened standard to credible determinations of fear'.[80]

In October 2018, months after Trump announced that he was ending his policy of forced separation, a five-year-old Honduran girl, Helen, was seized from her grandmother, Noehmi, who had fled along with several other relatives after her teenage son was threatened by gangs. Helen's mother, Jeny, had migrated to Texas four years before. Arrested at the South Texas border, the family passed through several detention centres, at the last of which the child was taken and placed in a cage. 'The girl will stay here,' the Border Guards told Noehmi, 'and you will be deported.' It took months for Noehmi and Jeny to track the child down. Eventually they traced her to a Baptist shelter contracted by the federal government, where she was being taught to develop '*SMARTgoals*' – goals that are 'Specific, Measurable, Achievable, Relevant, and Time-bound' – as if at five years old she had been hired by an upmarket commercial firm. Although she had known enough, even at that young age, to assert her legal right to have her custody reviewed, when it came to filling out the requisite Flores Bond form, she ticked the box withdrawing her previous request for a hearing (border officials had helped her to fill out the form). The form also declared its right to determine 'whether you pose a danger to the community' (she was five years old). In her backpack was found a sketch of 'Lady Liberty' with the instruction that the students 'draw one of the most representative symbols of the United States'.[81]

It would seem that the power to separate mothers from their children excites especial venom. Visiting the Port Isabel Detention Center in Los Fresnos, Texas, Schwartz tells the story of one woman who was forced into solitary confinement and 'subject to starvation' when she tried to tell a visiting official that she had been separated from her child.[82] This too has a history. From as far back as the 1970s, border patrollers regularly engaged in beatings, torture, murder and rape including of girls as young as twelve, using the children of migrants either as bait or to extract confessions. Mothers, one border agent is reported as boasting, 'would always break'.[83] By 2016, the year of Trump's election, more was already being spent by the US on immigration and border control than on all other federal law-enforcement agencies combined. Children would often try to cross the border alone because increased militarisation made it too dangerous for families to travel together.[84] In July 2020, it emerged that two years previously Deputy Attorney General Rod Rosenstein had advised attorneys during a conference call that there could be no ban on prosecuting migrant parents with children under the age of five, which effectively meant that no child was too young to be separated from his or her parents.[85]

The UK fares little better. A 2020 Amnesty Report described the government as 'deliberately and destructively' preventing child refugees from being with their families (adult refugees have the right to bring their families to the UK but not the other way round).[86] In relation to migrants, the dictum – 'women and children first' – is bypassed or turned on its head. In 2008, the Secretary of State's first recommendation in relation to mother and baby units in prisons was that pregnant women or women with young children should only be imprisoned when there are no suitable alternatives to custody, a recommendation more or less systematically ignored or overridden in relation to migrant women from the point of arrest.[87] The average age of the ten children separated from their asylum-seeking mothers in the Cambridge investigation was three: 'They came at six o'clock in the morning. There were five, four police officers and one woman from DWP [Department for Work and Pensions]. They were not nice. They gave me no time to say goodbye to my children [aged four and two].' Two women were separated from their babies while still breastfeeding; by the time they were reunited they had stopped lactating. Another woman, after being arrested, heard nothing of her children for three weeks. Her 'manager' told her she would not be able to see them until she had been to court: 'WHY. I had done nothing to hurt them and I am not even yet found guilty.'[88]

In Ireland, as Luibhéid has documented, mothers and children found themselves at the heart of a storm over migration, and its pawns. Until 1 January 2005, Ireland granted citizenship rights to anyone born on Irish soil or seas, the aim being to increase the birth rate of the true Irish-born. The provision was overturned in response to a large influx of immigrants, mainly seeking work, in the 1990s. Ireland had entered the global economy, rapidly changing from a country of emigration to one of immigration. It became known as the 'Celtic Tiger', with growth figures that outpaced the rest of Europe. The atmosphere started to shift. Pregnant asylum seekers, or those who gave birth in Ireland, especially African women, were now characterised as parasites and scroungers. 'Pregnancy rates and childbearing patterns became the primary form of knowledge about migrant women,' Luibhéid writes, 'that was produced and disseminated in ways that reduced them to their sex organs' (this of course had been no less true before, when giving birth on

Irish soil had conferred automatic citizenship on their babies).[89] In 2002, a woman became pregnant as the state was trying to deport her. Her right to remain relied on Article 40.3.3 of the Constitution, which guaranteed the right to life of the unborn. 'It is obvious', the Supreme Court stated in its ruling against her, 'that the rights of the born, in this context, cannot be less than those of the unborn.'[90] Clearly 'rights of the born' was a euphemism for anti-migrant voters and for the state's right to enforce its deportation policies unobstructed.

In such cases, a barely concealed revulsion towards migrant sexuality comes very close to revealing itself. This too has a history. The earliest 'undesirable' immigrants to the US under the Page Act of 1875 were Chinese women suspected of being prostitutes.[91] During debates over the British Nationality Act of 1948, which remained in force up to 1983, it was argued by MPs from both major parties that alien women were entering the country 'for immoral purposes' or as spies and that they were paying British subjects to marry them so they could qualify as British subjects themselves: 'We do not want people in this country who can do a great deal of harm by being British citizens,' the Labour MP Barbara Ayrton-Gould said in a House of Commons debate on 13 July 1948, 'and who have no loyalty at all to Britain or to the things in which we believe.'[92]

o   o   o

As I have been writing this chapter, I have become steadily more aware that the very fact of recounting these cases – a true litany of horrors – is risky. That to describe what is being done to these women might seem to re-enact their status as victims, embedding them further inside an unjust world with no – or only a forced, one-way – exit; even if not to do so is to be complicit with their invisibility, the carefully cultivated 'cultural production of ignorance' which works to hold national identity in place. As this book argues throughout, strange and fetid undercurrents of fascination pulse through the worst stories of our time. Think of the images of weeping and drowning children which have become iconic: the little girl wailing at the Mexican border; or three-year-old Syrian Alan Kurdi cradled in the arms of the stricken man who in September 2015 discovered the boy's body washed up on a beach in Turkey. Or that image of Oscar Alberto Martínez Ramírez and his daughter, drowned as they tried to cross the river into the US from Mexico (the image whose authenticity was denied by the Texan border guards). In 2015, versions of the *Guardian* headline – 'Shocking images of drowned Syrian boy show tragic plight of refugees' – spread across news outlets across the world. 'Tragic' and 'plight' might give us pause. They render the agony timeless, turn the drowned child into an object of raw pity, obfuscate the human agency, the historical choices and wilful political decisions, that lie behind them. We must be wary of the lure of pathos.

When Trump announced in June 2018 that he had ended the practice of separating migrant children from their families at the border, it seemed for a brief moment that these images might have worked. But they might just as well have pushed the problem in deeper. As anticipated, the outrage at the images of Ramírez and his daughter have been accompanied by no softening of US policy towards migrants whatsoever (in July 2019, immigration officers were granted the power to deport without appeal).[93] Surreptitious cruelty, it would seem, is OK. In the end, it doesn't matter what a politician does provided he brings the art of lying to perfection (Trump in the US, Boris

Johnson in the UK). In fact these tales might suggest that the opposite is more likely or equally likely to be the case. Trump was not exactly lying. Rather, he knows that everyone will know only too well that the idea of ending the practice has never truly entered his calculations (the nod and the wink to his followers which are the backbone of his presidency). The problem is therefore not so much or only that he is a liar – the most consistent ever to have occupied the White House, as has been amply documented. Far more sinister and dangerous is just how reliably he can be trusted to do the worst. Trump has granted new freedom to trample on the most vulnerable, which, in the final analysis, all human subjects, including – or perhaps especially – Trump himself, fear themselves to be. The unspoken contract is to give licence to the shared unconscious pleasures of hatred. Loyal retainer to the pits of the psyche, on that component of his behaviour he will never let you down. Brett Kavanaugh's testimony against Christine Blasey Ford, and the whipping up of fear towards the caravan of Central American migrants heading to the US border, are generally acknowledged to have fired up Trump's base during the 2018 mid-term elections. Rage against women and migrants never fails.

Finally, we must be careful not to render the rest of the world innocent, not even those who suffer most, or to rush from privilege to rescue in a way that simply redistributes the share of blame, of good and evil, in our own favour – especially when the display of virtue has hardened into a core facet of the internet. 'Posting photos from a protest against border family separation, as I did while writing this, is an expression of genuine principle,' comments *New Yorker* journalist Jia Tolentino, 'and also, inescapably, some sort of attempt to signal that I am good.'[94] Trafficking is mostly invisible but when it rises to the consciousness of the world as an open wound, it just as quickly mutates, a mere itch on our compassion. Or else it turns into a unique object of horror which serves to obscure the wider world's iniquities.

So, to end then with what must be the most vulnerable migrant category of all, the child trafficked into prostitution, target of what has become known as CSEC (the commercial sexual exploitation of children). Provoking what feels like righteous outrage, this child can then also be used, in a further twist of exploitation, to reinforce the self-serving rhetoric of what we have seen to be the corrosive powers of state: 'The law must have an iron fist to smash those who prey on children' was a *Sun* newspaper headline of 2003. The fact that these forms of childhood abuse are often a direct consequence of the state's own racist migrant policies is of course unspoken or else seen as irrelevant. In Athens in the late 1990s, for example, riot police were used for mass deportations of ethnic Albanians, forcing many of them into a clandestine world, which made the sexual exploitation of children more likely. In the UK, child asylum seekers are being subject to abuse after being wrongly classified as adults by Home Office officials, even though assessing a person's age based on their appearance is unlawful, and means, amongst other things, that they can be forcibly deported.[95]

At the start of *Children in the Global Sex Trade*, Julia O'Connell Davidson almost apologises for not viewing this form of child exploitation as 'uniquely terrible'. Hers is one of several books I read on this topic where it felt as if the author would have been far happier not having to write it in the first place (although such reluctance felt to me her most important qualification for doing so). 'The belief that children are harmed by sexual abuse', she writes on the opening pages, 'is not enough, in itself, to explain the ferocity and turbulence of the emotions it arouses.' What does the pitch of heady excitement over these particular victims do to all the rest? What purpose of distraction does it also serve? 'Most Westerners know', writes Davidson, 'that vast numbers of the world's children live and die in wretched circumstances' (starving, without medical attention or education, labouring inhuman hours).[96] And why is it impossible to accept that someone under eighteen – the legal definition of childhood – might be able to make a decision about their own life? Even if, as is the case in pretty much every story documented here, these young people are being presented with an impossible choice between 'grief and nothingness': the hardship and aggravation that awaits them as migrants in nations whose pull has turned out to be a colossal deceit; versus the emptiness, violence or simple lack of human and economic prospects which rules over their lives at home.

In their treatment of migrants, the Western powers are chasing their own tail, drawing lines in the sand in the shape of their own vile cunning. This is a cautionary tale of what has already been, and, in this worsening political scenario, of what is likely to come. Targeting women refugees and asylum seekers, turning them into criminals, lays bare the pleasure in sexual hatred, alongside the increasingly violent forms of inequality for which women have always been punished – both of which continue to fuel gender injustice across the globe. Today's migrants have become the ultimate scapegoats of a social order whose ever-expanding greed is on course to destroy the very air we breathe. As if they were the cause of it all, the perfect cargo for blindness, the best way not to see what is truly happening.

AFTERWORD

The idea of an 'afterword' on the topic of violence seems misleading, though 'conclusion' would surely be worse. Violence is not a subject about which any one can believe, other than in a state of delusion, that everything has been said and done. One of the traumatic aspects of the Covid-19 pandemic is that it has so often felt like an act of violence that has fallen without warning from the skies. We might call it gratuitous except that, for those living in a godless universe, the idea of gratuitous violence rained down from the heavens sounds empty. It is hard to imagine an entity or agent vast enough to match the horror, one for whom inflicting such untold cosmic torment might be an act of judgement or even a source of pleasure. Covid-19 threatens the possibility that we might be living in a senseless world.

Who gains from Covid-19? The richest of the super-rich in the US who have made $845 billion in additional profit since the pandemic began; the rulers who use the justified fear of their people to seize increasingly demotic powers; the abusers for whom the enforced intimacy of lockdown gives them a new licence to kill. If for a second anyone allowed themselves to think that the virus is indiscriminate – the 'great equaliser', as some commentators put it in the early days – it has rapidly become clear that this virus, like the boils of the ancient bubonic plague, is scratching at the skin of our cruellest social arrangements, bringing the putrid sores of a viciously unequal world to the surface and hence more vividly to life. In fact, the pandemic is far from random, but most likely the result of human acts.

The destruction of biodiversity allows – and, unless the devastation is halted, will go on allowing – microbes to leap from animals into humans across a broken, desolate, species chain (several such pandemics a year from now on is one scientific prediction). A key lesson to be learned from the pandemic might be that violence, like a virus, is an opportunist. It persists because it is so familiar with the ways of the world, knows how to seize its moment, driving home its capacity to endure, return, mutate and survive. The struggle against violence must therefore continue because, as long as the world continues to be scarred by the fault lines of injustice and inequality, the fight against violence has not been won.

When Derek Chauvin killed George Floyd by kneeling on his neck for eight minutes and forty-six seconds in May 2020, one of the most striking things about the moment was the way he stared unfailingly, without a glimmer of awkwardness, straight at the camera. As if he was announcing to the whole world: 'See this.' The new tragedy of the pandemic had, it seemed, emboldened him, allowing him to display a racism that in 'normal', that is non-pandemic, times operates more under cover, doing everything it can in order to hide itself, even if street killings of mainly black men in the US have become increasingly commonplace. In the case of Chauvin, I think we can be fairly sure that he reckoned neither with the charges that would be brought against him (raised within days to murder in the second degree in response to the ensuing protests, although still not to first-degree murder as the family demands), nor with the public outpouring which, across the world, brought the cry for an end to racist injustice and state-sanctioned violence spilling onto the streets. Something which, despite the history of civil rights struggle, continues to be at least partially obfuscated and denied became unavoidable, not least as the demonstrations brought the mostly silenced legacy of slavery back onto the stage of politics. Hence too the counter-rage that seemed to follow those protests with such indecent haste, when a white couple was photographed pointing their guns at black protestors as a way of proclaiming, behind the bastion of their enclave, that theirs were the lives under greatest threat. Perhaps, then, the racist backlash was not just a counter-attack, a defence of white privilege, or an attempt to put violence back on the other foot by casting the protestors as thugs, looters, arsonists, a danger to the peace – although it was undoubtedly all of these – but the result of a dawning, not fully conscious, recognition. Racist violence – institutional and at the heart of the law – which never wants to admit its own existence, let alone assume its own name, was now out there, in your face, in the proud, unflinching gaze of Derek Chauvin. In a time of pandemic, we see the world anew.

This tension between the increasing visibility and the invisibility of violence has trailed the path of this book. Violence likes to boast. On a BBC Panorama programme in August 2020, an abused woman trapped by lockdown in her home described how her husband folded his arms, puffed out his chest and pronounced, 'You think it was bad before? Let the games begin.' But violence is also canny; the thing it appears to hate most is having to take responsibility for itself. We are living in a moment in which the capacity for denial appears to have reached new heights. Over this past year, more than one politician has persistently denied the reality of the pandemic, downgrading it, for example, to 'mere flu'. And then, when the same politicians have been struck by the virus, they have used their own recovery – massively subsidised by lavish combinations of drugs and medical attention way beyond the reach of the many – to downplay it even more. Not a tremor of guilt for the thousands of deaths for which their own negligent policies are responsible. In fact, the toll has been the consequence of sheer government ineptitude: flagrant errors of judgement; procrastination; former policies of austerity that have decimated health care; more recently in the UK, a categorical first refusal by the government to follow the plea of its own scientific advisers for a circuit-breaking full lockdown to stop the spread of the virus in its second wave; the decades-old neglect of preventable diseases – obesity, type 2 diabetes – which have fuelled the pandemic, driven up the markers of poverty and inequality and stalled life expectancy across the globe. This is violence 'under quiet conditions', to re-evoke Rosa Luxemburg's suggestive phrase, or, in Toni Morrison's words, the violence that is 'swallowing' the dispossessed. And yet I for one have not heard a single politician acknowledge for a split second that their decisions have been deadly. It is true that no one can get a full grip on what is happening. But there is a world of difference between recognising that reality and ignoring the extent to which self-blinding incompetence is leading so many unnecessarily to their graves.

For psychoanalysis, which has also accompanied me throughout these pages, it is more or less axiomatic that violence is the mental property or portion of everyone. But it is also something that is cast off like a discarded children's toy, an aspect of the inner world which nobody wishes to own or have ever owned. One of the most obdurate forms of violence, therefore, is the one we call upon in order to stamp out our living, anguished, relationship to violence itself. Repression, suppression, denial, negation, projection, foreclosure, sublimation are just some of the terms deployed by psychoanalysis to convey the extent to which our minds are endlessly engaged in the business of tidying up the landscape of the heart so that, to put it at its most simple, we can feel better about ourselves. It is a losing battle. Although, as witnessed on a daily basis, this fact does not diminish by one jot the havoc and destruction that such a battle can create. Throughout this book I argue that it is the multiple strategies deployed in repudiation of one's own psychic violence that grants violence its licence to roam, since it then becomes essential that someone else bear the responsibility, shoulder the burden, pay the price. Someone who, then, in an 'ideal world' – a dangerous notion, to be distinguished from the idea of a world you can struggle to improve – we can with impunity make it our task to subdue or eliminate (as if we are all engaged in a holy war).

Again, the pandemic is offering up the spectacle of the rampant lengths, not only in terms of denial but also of false self-idealisation, to which those in power will go to burnish their sense and image of themselves. From the present incumbent of the White House post his brush with Covid-19 – I am writing this mid-October in the run-up to the US election when all the chips are down – describing himself as 'the perfect specimen', 'extremely young', running against 'stone-cold crazy' people 'with big issues' (the last of these a flagrant act of projection if ever there was one); to the UK prime minister being cheered by his foreign minister as a 'fighter', implying that his recovery was the result of unique moral courage and personal mettle; to the Brazilian leader declaring that the virus represented no danger, since his people could bathe in excrement and emerge unscathed (if not so deadly serious, this would be a joke which, no doubt unintentionally, gives the idea of 'toxic masculinity' a whole new gloss). For these male leaders, it seems, the only way to respond to a disease that is mowing down people in their hundreds of thousands is to proclaim their immortal perfection; to deny, amongst other things, that death is always stalking in our midst. This is masculinity bloated with an inhuman capacity over life and death. It is then hard not to make the link to the silent domestic abuser, charged up by his new lockdown powers, puffing out his chest, force-feeding his partner, forbidding her to leave the house for her hospital pregnancy scan, stopping her from washing her hands so that there is nowhere, inside or outside the home, where she can feel safe (all examples that have come to light).

Whether on the political stage or behind closed doors, it is the presence of death that ratchets up the prowess, although it is not hard to discern its shadow behind the masquerade. The forty-fifth US President's grandfather died of the Spanish flu. The loss was brushed under the carpet, which might help explain his father's, and then his own, utter abhorrence of human frailty. Nothing quite like a pandemic, one might say, for confronting man with those realms in which he 'cannot change and cannot act and in which, therefore, he has a distinct tendency to destroy'; lines from Hannah Arendt that have been my refrain. These are not the only kinds of men who appear in these pages (I also know I am not alone in praying the three just alluded to will be out of their jobs by the time you are reading this book). As I argue throughout, not all men are the violent embodiments of their worst selves. There are men, though not enough, who recognise the lethal farce of the masculinity on offer, and want none of it – otherwise there would be no hope. Again it is the wager of psychoanalysis, one of its most radical, that both men and women have to be mentally straitjacketed into their allotted sexual roles. In the unconscious and in their deeds, everyone is capable, even under duress, of being more flexible in their identifications, less obdurate in their hatreds, always potentially other to themselves. Even while the fine, tenacious, threads which run from men in positions of political power to the silent abusers of women in their homes have perhaps never been so glaring.

When I made violence against women my main theme, I could never have predicted the cruel shape it would assume under the weight of Covid-19. Although more men than women worldwide are dying from the virus, violence against women has dramatically intensified, a 'shadow pandemic' according to one UN report, or even a new 'femicide'. In a non-pandemic world, fear of mortality and life's fragility is more easily pushed to the back of our minds, stuffed into the mental closets through which we organise and protect ourselves. It has been the task of women through the ages – against such unconscious knowing – to make their partners, children and dependents feel secure in a messy and uncertain world, to sweep the dirt and debris away. As we have seen in these pages, this arrangement goes back at least as far as the Greek city-state when the drudgery of women and slaves was the precondition of political freedom for men who ruled as tyrants in the home. But in a time of pandemic, the expectation that women should clean up the world and the mind is one to which no woman can possibly be equal (nor at any other time, it should be said). Meanwhile the burden of care is falling back on their shoulders, as gains for women in the workplace and in relation to childcare and domestic labour in the home are in danger of being lost. The options for women are stark: back to the 1950s, the 'Great Leap Backwards' as it is being termed; or straight into the eye of the storm.

Today women are being punished – sometimes paying with their lives – for a death that has become too visible, for the bodies that are failing and falling all around, as psychic defences start to crumble in the face of unbearable fear and grief. I find myself asking whether they are in double jeopardy, subject to a form of violence which, before lockdown, they at least had a chance to escape; but perhaps also the targets of something else, a type of revenge – 'backlash', as it is called – for the fact that, for many though by no means all women, in today's world being shut in and isolated in the home is no longer the norm. These women are first and foremost scapegoats for the awfulness of the hour. But they are also being murdered for their hard-won freedom. To which one might add that women are being assaulted by men who, as they too find themselves confined to the home, feel as if they are being turned into women. It is not only our hold on life that is uneasy, an unease repudiated at any cost, but, as also seen throughout these pages, our most entrenched sense of who – men or women, both or neither – we are.

I did not expect to be ending this book at such a time. But given how grim the world has turned, it is then all the more remarkable to witness the forms of resistance and fierce clarity to which the ugly new dispensation has also given rise. There are women who, in the midst of pandemic, escape their abusers even though the funds promised to the UK refuge sector barely match the cuts of the past decade. There are victims of traffickers who risk their lives to document in secret every single detail of their journey and find solicitors who, despite the hostile racist and misogynist environment stacked against them, make and win their anti-deportation case. There are the movements – Black Lives Matter, #MeToo, trans activism, Rhodes Must Fall, who have figured throughout this book – whose courage in unearthing buried wrongs seems to be limitless and who go on alerting the world to its historic and ongoing injustices in their struggle for a better life. There is the renewed attention to care, its life-saving process, its gifts and its necessary costs – whose place at the core of human life feminism has been urging for decades – as the emerging ethic for our times.

Last but not least, there are the leaders – mostly, significantly, women leaders – who, according to a survey of 194 countries conducted by the Centre for Economic Policy Research and the World Economic Forum in summer 2020, are proving to be so much more effective against Covid-19: Germany's Angela Merkel, New Zealand's Jacinda Ardern, Denmark's Mette Frederiksen, Taiwan's Tsai Ing-wen, Finland's Sanna Marin and Mia Mottley of Barbados – although the fact has received little attention. These women are more risk-averse with regard to fatalities, more willing to take risks with the economy which, for the majority of male leaders, is the inviolable domain. Perhaps it is because they are able to acknowledge the necessity of dying that they know a needless death when they see one. Taking the true measure of death, it would seem, is paradoxically the only way to prevent it carrying off thousands before their time. Mass testing in Barbados began before the first case had even been identified.

It has been a core argument of this book that violence will not diminish, let alone cease, if violence continues to be something which people turn away from, blot from their minds, prefer – at least as far as they personally are concerned – not to talk or think about. Everything in these pages suggests that violence surely has to be included in our understanding of the 'density' of being human, which Arundhati Roy has recently stated is the only antidote to the crass, mind-numbing and crushing simplifications of resurgent fascism. The message of this book is finally twofold. To struggle against the forms of violence that are spreading with added virulence across the globe and which the pandemic is making daily more visible for everyone. And to understand the inner force of violence, to resist the deadly temptation to make violence always the problem of somebody else. Meanwhile we keep our ears to the ground, as I have tried to do here, listening out for voices that travel the unsteady path between these two endeavours – those who show that reckoning with the violence of the heart and fighting violence in the world are inseparable.

October 2020

ACKNOWLEDGEMENTS

Many occasions and voices inspired and provided the germ of these essays.

Chapter Four was first delivered as the Diane Middlebrook/ Carl Djerassi lecture at the Centre for Gender Studies, Cambridge University, on 3 November 2014. Thanks to Director, Jude Brown, Founding Director, Juliet Mitchell and Deputy Director, Lauren Wilcox, for hosting me so warmly in Michaelmas Term 2014. An earlier version was published in the thirtieth anniversary issue of *Cultural Critique* 94, Fall 2016.

My thanks to the hosts of the Modernist Studies Association Conference held in London on 26 June 2014 and to *Critical Quarterly* 60, no. 2, July 2018, where part of Chapter Five was first published.

Chapter Six was delivered as my inaugural lecture at Birkbeck, University of London, on 11 June 2015. Thanks to my Birkbeck colleagues for invaluable conversations at the Psychoanalytic Working Group. The Birkbeck Institute for the Humanities continues to be a space of freedom where I learn and think.

Thanks to Juliet Jacques, Roz Kaveney, Jay Prosser for crucial input into Chapter Two.

My thanks to Richard Sacks, Tracy Morgan and their colleagues for welcoming me so generously to the New York Centre for Modern Psychoanalytic Studies where I first presented a version of Chapter Three on 17 November 2018.

Chapter Seven was first delivered as the VC Open Lecture at the University of Cape Town on 16 March 2017. My thanks to

Max Price for inviting me, to Jaco Barnard-Naudé for initiating and organising the visit, to Victoria Collis-Buthelezi for formally responding to the lecture, and to all those – Antje Krog, Karin van Marle, Nombuso Mathibela, Njabulo Ndebele, Nigel Patel and the UCT Trans collective, Deborah Posel, Albie Sachs, Mark Solms, Pierre de Vos – who made my time so memorable.

Thanks to all the participants at the Stellenbosch Conference on 'Recognition, Reparation, Reconciliation', held from 5–7 December 2018 at the Centre for Historical Trauma and Transformation under its inspirational director Pumla Gobodo-Madikizela. The remarkable stories told at the conference led me to write Chapter Eight. Thanks to Mervyn Sloman of the Cape Town Book Lounge for inviting me to speak during this visit and to Lou-Marie Kruger for the discussion.

The essays on South Africa have also benefitted from the experience and guidance of Rachel Holmes, Margie Orford and Gillian Slovo. Thanks to Natasha Walter of Women For Refugee Women and Amelia Gentleman for bringing the treatment of women refugees and asylum seekers in the UK to public attention. Any errors of fact or judgement are of course my own.

Early drafts of several of the essays first appeared in the *London Review of Books*, which continues to be a vital intellectual home (40: 4, 22 February 2018; 38: 9, 5 May 2016; 38: 18, 22 September 2016; 37: 22, 19 November 2015; 41: 10, 23 May 2019; 41: 19, 10 October 2019). Thanks again to Mary-Kay Wilmers, to Paul Myerscough, Daniel Soar and to Deborah Friedell. As the pace of change has been so dramatic over the past years, each of these essays has demanded new attention and they have been substantially revised and updated for this collection.

Some details in the Afterword are drawn from my essay

on Camus' *The Plague*, published in the *London Review of Books* 42: 9, 7 May 2020, and from 'Living Death', published in *Gagosian Quarterly* 16, Winter 2020, special edition guest edited by Jamieson Webster and Alison Gingeras. I am grateful to Jamieson Webster for inviting me to contribute.

Thanks to Laura Hassan at Faber and Mitzi Angel at Farrar, Straus and Giroux for being such insightful and supportive editors.

Tracy Bohan always knows how to anticipate my concerns, encourage my thinking, and keep me confident in a project to which she has contributed much over these past years.

For loving support, friendship and understanding: Sally Alexander, Judith Butler, Sam Frears, Cora Kaplan, Elizabeth Karlsen, Margaret Reynolds, Alison Rose, Mia Rose, Jon Snow, Diana Stone and Clair Wills. In your unique ways, you all enrich me more than I can say.

The book is dedicated to my cousin Braham Murray – a guiding spirit of my life.

NOTES

Introduction: On Violence and On Violence Against Women

1. Lucy Rahim, 'Donald Trump Cuts Abortion Funding . . . Surrounded by Men', *Daily Telegraph*, 24 January 2017.
2. Jessica Glenza, 'Anti-abortion Bill Says Ectopic Pregnancies Must Be Reimplanted', *Guardian*, 30 November 2019.
3. Liz Ford, 'US Abortion Policy Amounts to Torture – UN Commissioner', *Guardian*, 4 June 2019.
4. Conrad Duncan and Lizzie Dearden, 'Reynhard Sinaga: Most Prolific Rapist in UK History Jailed for Life for Manchester Attacks', *Independent*, 7 January 2020.
5. Virginia Woolf, *Three Guineas*, London: Hogarth, 1938.
6. Sigmund Freud, 'Our Attitude Towards Death', Essay 2 of 'Thoughts for the Time on War and Death', 1915, *The Standard Edition of the Complete Psychological Works*, Vol. 14, London: Hogarth, 1957, p. 297.
7. Hannah Arendt, *The Origins of Totalitarianism*, New York: Harcourt, Brace, Jovanovich, 1951, p. 301.
8. On the disposal of bodies, see Wendy Brown, *Undoing the Demos – Neoliberalism's Stealth Revolution*, New York: Zone, 2016. On the drive of capital, anything by David Harvey.
9. Rosa Luxemburg, *Redner der Revolution*, Vol. 11, Berlin, 1928, cited in Peter Nettle, *Rosa Luxemburg*, abridged edition, Oxford University Press, 1969, p. 250.
10. Patrick Butler, 'Plan to Redirect Cash to Tory Shires from Urban Councils a "Stitch-up"', *Guardian*, 20 January 2019.
11. Helen Pidd, 'Why Duncan Smith Award Was "a Slap in the Face"', *Guardian*, 4 January 2020.
12. Alexandra Topping, 'Brexit Poses Threat to Rights of Women, Report Warns', *Guardian*, 23 July 2019; Patrick Butler, 'Universal Credit is Forcing Women into Sex Work, MPs Told', *Guardian*, 30 July 2019; Sarah Marsh, 'Actor's Plea to Government: Stop Austerity Forcing Women into Sex Work', *Guardian*, 30 July 2019.
13. Dennis Campbell, 'Thousands Die Waiting for Hospital Beds – Study', *Guardian*, 10 December 2019.

14. Gabriel Pogrund, George Greenwood and Emanuele Midolo, 'Richard Desmond, "Boris Johnson Promised to Alter Gambling Rules for Me"', *Sunday Times*, 28 June 2020.

15. For example, Catharine A. MacKinnon, *Feminism Unmodified – Discourses on Life and Law*, Cambridge: Harvard University Press, 1987, and *Are Women Human? and Other International Dialogues*, Cambridge: Harvard, 2006; Andrea Dworkin, *Pornography – Men Possessing Women*, London: Women's Press, 1981.

16. Jodi Kantor and Megan Twohey, *She Said – Breaking the Sexual Harassment Story that Helped Ignite a Movement*, London: Bloomsbury, 2019, p. 63

17. Ibid., p. 111.

18. Ed Pilkington, 'Weinstein Faces Jail After Being Convicted of Rape', *Guardian*, 25 February 2020.

19. Kantor and Twohey, *She Said*, p. 62.

20. Lauren Aratani, 'Former Actor Tells Court How Weinstein Coerced and Threatened Her', *Guardian*, 1 February 2020.

21. Deanna Paul, 'Harvey Weinstein Says He Feels "Like the Forgotten Man." His Accusers Are Furious', *Washington Post*, 17 December 2019.

22. Anne Enright, 'Diary', *London Review of Books*, 24 October 2019.

23. Lanre Bakare, 'Two Years On, Storyline is Far from Simple in Entertainment Industry', *Guardian*, 14 October 2019.

24. Kim Wilsher and Simon Murphy, 'I Stand by My Verdict on Boycott, Says Judge', *Guardian*, 18 September 2019.

25. Susan McKay, 'Belfast Rape Trial Verdict Does Not Erase Players' Horrific Sexism', *Irish Times*, 29 March 2018.

26. Decca Aitkenhead, 'I've Had Vitriol Thrown at Me for as Long as I Can Remember', Interview with Chelsea Clinton, *Guardian Weekend*, 26 May 2018.

27. McKay, 'Belfast Rape Trial Verdict'.

28. Cited in Jonathan Freedland, 'John Bolton Deserves Not Thanks, But Fury and Scorn', *Guardian*, 20 June 2020.

29. Simon Murphy, '"I'm Still Waiting for an Apology." The Journalist Who Boris Johnson Conspired to Have Beaten Up', *Guardian*, 15 July 2019.

30. David Smith, 'We're Not Going to Give Liars a Platform', *Guardian*, 24 January 2020.

31. Hannah Arendt, *Eichmann in Jerusalem – A Report on the Banality of Evil*, New York: Viking, London: Penguin, 1963, p. 150.

32. Simon Jenkins, 'It Wasn't the Senate that Saved Trump', *Guardian*, 7 February 2020.

33. Philip Oltermann, 'Germany Slow to Hear Alarm Bells in Killing of Walter Lübcke', *Guardian*, 2 July 2019.

34. Annie Karni, Kevin Roose and Katie Rogers, 'Trump Fans Spice Memes with Violence', *New York Times*, 15 October 2019.

35. Tom Phillips and Dom Phillips, 'Bolsonaro Wins First Round of Brazilian Election', *Guardian*, 8 October 2018.

36. Anna Jean Kaiser, 'Lawmaker Insulted by Bolsonaro Fears Rise of Rape Culture', *Guardian*, 23 December 2018.

37. Phillips and Phillips, 'Bolsonaro Wins First Round'.

38. Kaiser, 'Lawmaker Insulted by Bolsonaro'.

39. Judith Butler, *Gender Trouble – Feminism and the Subversion of Identity*, New York and London: Routledge, 1990.

40. Thais Bessa, 'Judith Butler, "Gender Ideology" and the Rise of Conservatism in Brazil', https://feministacademiccollective.com/2017/11/17/judith-butler -gender-ideology-and-the-rise-of-conservatism-in-brazil/, 17 November 2017.

41. 'Poland's Bishops Have Shamefully Fostered Rightwing Homophobia', Lead article, *Guardian*, 10 October 2019.

42. Grant Barrett (ed.), *The Oxford Dictionary of American Political Slang*, Oxford University Press, 2006.

43. 'Spanish Ultraconservative Group Launches Bus Campaign against "Feminazis"', *El Pais*, English version by Melissa Kitson.

44. Ibid.

45. Angela Giuffrida, 'Femicide – Italian Women Fight to Halt Growing Number of Attacks', *Guardian*, 20 November 2019; Kim Wilsher, 'New Measures to Tackle Domestic Violence in France after Protests', *Guardian*, 26 November 2019; Benjamin Haas, 'South Korea – "I Can't Even Tell My Mother, and She's My Best Friend"', *Guardian*, 12 November 2019; Hannah Ellis-Peterson, 'Protests Escalate in India over Gang-rape and Murder of Woman', *Guardian*, 2 December 2019; Hannah Ellis-Peterson, 'Calls for Death Penalty Grow in India as Protests Spread over Rape and Murder', *Guardian*, 3 December 2019; AFP, 'Tens of Thousands March in Rome to Protest the Murder of Women', *Local*, 2 December 2019; Robin-Lee Francke, 'Thousands Protest in South Africa over Rising Violence against Women', *Guardian*, 5 September 2019.

46. Associated Press, 'Meghan Starts African Visit with Message "as Woman of Colour"', *Guardian*, 23 September 2019.

47. Meaghan Beatley, 'The Shocking Rape Trial that Galvanised Spain's Feminists and the Far Right', *Guardian*, 23 April 2019.

48. Vox, *Envios Postales de Propaganda Electoral*, Catalunya, Barcelona, 2018.

49. 'The Rise of Christian-nativist Populists is a Worry for Us All', lead article, *Guardian*, 26 December 2019; 'Hungary: Asylum Seekers Denied Food', *Human Rights Watch*, 22 August 2018.

50. Mark Townsend, 'Revealed: 10,000 Child Refugees Have Risked Their Lives to Get into Britain in the Past Decade', *Observer*, 12 January 2020.

51. Tom Phillips, 'Waiting in Hell – Trump's Border Policies Force Asylum Seekers into Deadly Gamble', *Guardian*, 20 December 2019.

52. Ibid.

53. Edouard Louis, *History of Violence*, 2016, translated from the French by Lorin Stein, New York: Farrar, Straus and Giroux, 2018, p. 65.

54. Enright, 'Diary'.

55. Stephen Pinker, *The Better Angels of Our Nature: Why Violence has Declined*, New York: Viking, 2011.

56. Graeme Armstrong, 'I Bashed Out the First Draft Without Withdrawal', Books Interview, *Observer*, 23 February 2020.

57. Arendt, *Origins of Totalitarianism*, p. 203.

58. Ibid., p. 124.

59. Margie Orford, 'Nostalgia for the Future', PhD thesis (unpublished), University of East Anglia, 2020.

60. Rosa Lyster, 'The Death of Uyinene Mrwetyana and the Rise of South Africa's "#AmINext Movement"', *New Yorker*, 12 September 2019.

61. Rosa Lyster, Twitter.com/rosalyster, 13 September 2019.

62. John Rawls, *A Theory of Justice*, Cambridge University Press, 1971.

63. Jason Burke and Vincent Lali, 'We Are a Special Country and an Extraordinary People', *Guardian*, 4 November 2019.

64. Sampie Terreblanche, *Lost in Transformation – South Africa's Search for a New Future Since 1986*, Johannesburg: KMM Review, 2012, p. 20.

65. Gillian Rose, *The Broken Middle – Out of Our Ancient Society*, Oxford: Blackwell, 1992.

66. Hannah Arendt, *The Human Condition*, London: University of Chicago Press, 1958, p. 5.

1. I Am a Knife – Sexual Harassment in Close-up

1. Kantor and Twohey, *She Said*, p. 168.

2. Vanessa Grigoriadis, *Blurred Lines – Rethinking Sex, Power, and Consent on Campus*, Boston, New York: Houghton Mifflin Harcourt, 2017, p. 100.

3. Rebecca Solnit, 'The Fall of Harvey Weinstein Should Be a Moment to Rethink Masculinity', *Guardian*, 12 October 2017.

4. Ann Sedley and Melissa Benn, *Sexual Harassment at Work*, NCCL Rights for Women Unit, 1982, p. 17.

5. Molly Redon, 'Top Hollywood Women Back Commission on Harassment',

Guardian, 18 December 2017; Rory Carroll, 'Hollywood Sees a New Hope after Weinstein Scandal', *Guardian*, 1 January 2018; Bakare, 'Two Years On'.

6. Dayna Tortorici, 'Reckoning with a Culture of White Male Resentment', *Guardian*, 19 December 2017.

7. Edward Helmore, 'You Are Not Qualified to Speak About Abuse We Suffer Every Day, Driver tells Damon', *Guardian*, 18 December 2017.

8. Redi Tlhabi, *Khwezi – The Remarkable Story of Fezekile Ntsukela Kuzwayo*, Johannesburg and Cape Town: Jonathan Ball, 2017, p. 244.

9. Grigoriadis, *Blurred Lines*, p. 78.

10. Jennifer Doyle, *Campus Sex, Campus Security*, South Pasadena: Semiotext(e), 2015, p. 27.

11. Grigoriadis, *Blurred Lines*, pp. 67–8, 71.

12. Ibid., p. 82.

13. Ibid., pp. 194–7.

14. Roxane Gay, 'Blurred Lines, Indeed', *Bad Feminist*, New York: HarperCollins, London: Corsair, 2014, p. 191.

15. Sophie Elmhirst, 'No Way Out', *Guardian*, 31 October 2019.

16. Louis, *History of Violence*, pp. 30, 171.

17. Martha Hayes, 'I Don't Have that Kind of Fame Now', *Guardian*, 2 September 2019.

18. Louis, *History of Violence*, pp. 171–2.

19. Sabrina Siddiqui and Amanda Holpuch, 'Trump Berates Critics as Harassment Furore Grows', *Guardian*, 13 December 2017.

20. Grigoriadis, *Blurred Lines*, p. xxv, 104.

21. Doyle, *Campus Sex*, pp. 17, 30.

22. Philip Oltermann and Pádraig Collins, 'German Far-right MPs Facing Race Crime Inquiry over Tweet', *Guardian*, 3 January 2018.

23. The Reynoso Task Force, 'UC Davis November 18, 2011, "Pepper-Spray Incident" Task Force Report', March 2012, p. 8, cited in Doyle, *Campus Sex*, p. 16.

24. Doyle, *Campus Sex*, p. 11.

25. Grigoriadis, *Blurred Lines*, p. 77.

26. On the US student debt crisis, see Jia Tolentino, 'The Story of a Generation in Seven Scams' in *Trick Mirror – Reflections on Self-Delusion*, New York: Random House, 2019.

27. See Grigoriadis, *Blurred Lines*, pp. 72–4.

28. Catharine A. MacKinnon, *Sexual Harassment of Working Women*, Yale University Press, 1979, p. 220.

29. Alexandra Topping, 'Gender Pay Gap Widening for Women in their 20s, Data Shows', *Guardian*, 10 November 2017.

NOTES TO PAGES 47–57

30. Sam Levin, 'More Women Join Lawsuit Accusing Disney of Gender Pay Discrimination', *Guardian*, 19 September 2019.
31. MacKinnon, *Sexual Harassment*, p. 221.
32. Jordan Stephens, 'The Pain of Young Boys that Creates This Toxic Masculinity', *Guardian*, 24 October 2017.
33. Grigoriadis, *Blurred Lines*, p. 57.
34. For a summary of recent literature on this topic, see Arlie Russell Hochschild, 'Male Trouble', *New York Review of Books*, 11 October 2018; Pippa Allen-Kinross, 'GCSE Results 2019 – Girls Still Lead the Way over Boys', *School Week*, 22 August 2019.
35. Grigoriadis, *Blurred Lines*, p. 151.
36. Ibid., p. 275.
37. Ibid., p. 55.
38. Catherine Porter, 'All-Boys Catholic School in Toronto is Disrupted by Reports of Hazing', *New York Times*, 24 November 2018.
39. Sean O'Hagan, 'Animal House', *Guardian*, 10 December 2019.
40. Grigoriadis, *Blurred Lines*, p. 230.
41. Ibid., pp. 269–70.
42. Ibid., p. 276.
43. Alexandra Topping, '"The Police Laughed at Me" – Anger over Rape Case Failings,' *Guardian*, 6 January 2018.
44. Grigoriadis, *Blurred Lines*, pp. 36, 265, 133, 271, 71.
45. Ibid., p. xxxi.
46. Freud, 'The Dissection of the Psychical Personality' in *New Introductory Lectures*, 1933, Lecture 31, *The Standard Edition of the Complete Psychological Works*, Vol. 22, London: Hogarth, 1964, p. 79.
47. Gay, *Bad Feminist*, pp. 187–91.
48. Grigoriadis, *Blurred Lines*, p. 74.
49. Ibid., pp. 273, 174.
50. US Department of Education, 'Dear Colleague Letter on Sexual Misconduct', 22 September 2017, https://content.govdelivery.com/accounts/USED/bulletins/1b8ba66.
51. Grigoriadis, p. xxxi.
52. Greta Anderson, 'Attorneys General Sue DeVos, Education Department Over Title IX Rule', *Inside Higher Education*, 5 June 2020.
53. Grigoriadis, pp. 83, xxi.
54. bell hooks, *Teaching to Transgress – Education as the Practice of Freedom*, London: Routledge, 1994, p. 2.
55. Ibid., p. 207.

56. Jane Gallop, *Feminist Accused of Sexual Harassment*, Durham: Duke University Press, 1997, pp. 34, 57, 42, 53–4, 87, 92–3.

57. Laura Kipnis, *Men – Notes from an Ongoing Investigation*, New York: Picador, 2014, p. 14.

58. Ibid., p. 6.

59. Grigoriadis, *Blurred Lines*, p. 56.

60. Laura Kipnis, *Unwanted Advances – Sexual Paranoia Comes to Campus*, New York: Harper, 2017, p. 85.

61. Kayla Schierbecker, 'Professor Broke the Law by Writing Book on "Sexual Paranoia," students claim', University of Missouri, 27 April 2017, www.thecollegefix.com/post/32326/.

62. Sara Ahmed, feministkilljoys.com/2016/07/12/evidence/.

63. Ilza Veith, *Hysteria – the History of a Disease*, University of Chicago Press, 1965, p. 229.

64. Kipnis, *Unwanted Advances*, p. 75.

65. Kantor and Twohey, *She Said*, p. 119.

66. David Brown and Alexi Mostrous, 'Rape Case Scandal is Just "Tip of the Iceberg"', *The Times*, 16 December 2017; Hannah Quirk, Letters, *The Times*, 20 December 2012.

67. Caelainn Barr, 'Revealed: Police Flaws that Betray Rape Victims', *Guardian*, 20 September 2019.

68. Caelainn Barr, 'Children Reporting Rape Being Told to Give All Mobile Phone Data to Police', *Guardian*, 27 September 2019.

69. David Batty, Sally Weale and Caroline Bannock, 'Sexual Harassment "at Epidemic Levels" in UK Universities', *Guardian*, 5 March 2017.

70. Merril D. Smith, *The Encyclopedia of Rape*, Westport CT: Greenwood Press, 2004, p. 167, cited in Grigoriadis, *Blurred Lines*, p. 46.

71. Grigoriadis, *Blurred Lines*, p. 45.

72. Sara Ahmed, Twitter.com/SaraNAhmed, 30 May 2016.

73. Ahmed, 'Feminist Killjoys', 17/34.

74. 'We Want Truth', blog, https://wewanttruthgoldsmiths.wordpress.com/.

75. Anemona Hartocollis, 'Lawsuit Accuses Dartmouth Professors of Sex Abuse', *New York Times*, 16 November 2018; 'Dartmouth Reaches $14 Million Settlement in Sex Abuse Case', *New York Times*, 6 August 2019.

76. Sally Weale, 'Whistleblower Calls on Universities to Do More to Safeguard Students', *Guardian*, 7 March 2017.

77. Sally Weale and Caroline Bannock, '"We Felt Inferior and Degraded": Reporting Sexual Harassment at University', *Guardian*, 5 March 2017.

78. David Batty, 'Warwick Accused of Not Being a "Safe Place" for Women', *Guardian*, 15 July 2019.

79. Cited in Leila Whitley and Tiffany Page, 'Sexism at the Centre: Locating the Problem of Sexual Harassment', *New Formations* 86, special issue on sexism, 2015, p. 35.

80. Sara Ahmed, *Living a Feminist Life,* Durham: Duke University Press, 2017, p. 141.

81. Ahmed, Twitter.com/SaraNAhmed, 3 June 2016.

82. Personal communication, Lisa Blackman, 24 November 2017.

83. David Batty, Helena Bengtsson and Sally Weale, 'University "Complacency" Revealed over Harassment Survey', *Guardian*, 9 December 2017.

84. Richard Adams, 'Universities Told to Hire Specialist Staff to Address Harassment', *Guardian*, 12 June 2019.

85. Batty, 'Warwick Accused'.

86. David Batty, 'University Refuses to Investigate Alleged Rapes of Students Off Campus', *Guardian*, 18 November 2019.

87. Ahmed, feministkilljoys.com/2016/06/02/speaking-out/.

88. Rachel Cooke, 'Sexual Paranoia on Campus – and the Professor at the Eye of the Storm', *Observer*, 2 April 2017.

89. https://wewanttruthgoldsmiths.wordpress.com/2016/07/23/we-want-truth/.

90. Freud, 'Femininity' in *New Introductory Lectures*, 1933, Lecture 33, *The Standard Edition of the Complete Psychological Works*, Vol. 22, London: Hogarth, 1964, p. 115.

91. Ahmed, https://feministkilljoys.com/2016/07/12/evidence/.

92. Brown and Mostrous, 'Rape Case Scandal'.

93. Helena Kennedy, *Eve Was Shamed – How British Justice is Failing Women*, London: Chatto and Windus, 2018, p. 132.

94. Cited in Grigoriadis, *Blurred Lines*, p. 103.

95. Kipnis, *Unwanted Advances*, p. 102.

96. Jamie Grierson, 'Survey Reveals Impact of Proposed Spending Cuts on Women Fleeing Abuse', *Guardian,* 28 November 2017; Peter Walker, 'Legal Aid Cuts Leave More Abuse Victims Without Lawyers', *Guardian*, 27 December 2017.

97. Amanda Taub, 'A New Covid-19 Crisis: Domestic Abuse Rises Worldwide', *New York Times*, 6 April 2020, revised 14 April 2020.

98. Jamie Grierson, 'Domestic Abuse Killings "More than Double" During Covid-19 Lockdown', *Guardian*, 15 April 2020.

99. Rowena Mason, 'PM Criticised over Plan to Toughen Up Westminster Sexual Harassment Policies', *Guardian*, 15 November 2017.

100. Rowena Mason and Heather Stewart, 'Speaker Tells Tories to Reveal Their Policies on Misconduct', *Guardian*, 3 November 2017; Mason, 'PM Criticised over Plan to Toughen Up Policies'; Aamna Mohdin, 'New Code for

Employers on Sexual Harassment "Does Not Go Far Enough"', *Guardian*, 18 December 2018.

101. PA Media, 'Ex-minister Who Sent Lewd Texts Cleared of Wrongdoing', *Guardian*, 9 September 2019.

102. Trades Union Council, *Still Just a Bit of Banter? Sexual Harassment in the Workplace in 2016*, London: TUC Publications, 2017.

103. 'Tarana Burke', portrait, https://www.americanswhotellthetruth.org/portraits/tarana-burke.

104. Rebecca Nicholson, 'Jessica Chastain', *Guardian*, 20 December 2017; '#MeToo Was Only a Beginning. Time to Decide What Comes Next', *Guardian*, 1 January 2018.

105. Annie Kelly, 'Fashion's Dirty Secret', *Guardian,* 20 August 2020.

106. Roxane Gay, *Hunger – A Memoir of (My) Body*, New York: HarperCollins, London: Corsair, 2017, pp. 13, 20.

107. Ibid., pp. 18–19, 35.

108. Roxane Gay, 'The Careless Language of Sexual Violence', *Bad Feminist*, p. 135 (emphasis original).

109. Sandra Newman, 'Bold Feminist Stories', *Guardian*, 10 February 2017; Gemma Sieff, 'No Shrinking Violets', *New York Times*, 3 January 2017.

110. Gay, *Hunger*, p. 132; see also pp. 150, 162, 172, 197, 249, 273.

111. Ibid., p. 172.

112. Roxane Gay, 'Florida', *Difficult Women*, New York: Grove Atlantic, London: Corsair, 2017, p. 47.

113. Gay, *Hunger*, p. 222.

114. Roxane Gay, 'North Country', *Difficult Women*, pp. 92, 93.

115. Roxane Gay, 'Break All the Way Down', *Difficult Women*, pp. 144–5.

116. Roxane Gay, 'I Am a Knife', *Difficult Women*, pp. 179, 185, 187.

117. Jessica Benjamin, *Beyond Doer and Done To – Recognition Theory, Intersubjectivity and the Third*, London: Routledge, 2018.

2. Trans Voices – Who Do You Think You Are?

1. April Ashley with Douglas Thompson, *The First Lady*, London: John Blake, 2006, pp. 262, 276.

2. Mark Rees, *Dear Sir or Madam: The Autobiography of a Female-to-male Transsexual*, London: Cassell, 1996, pp. 157–9.

3. Women and Equalities Committee, *Transgender Equality – First Report of Session 2015–2016*, 14 January 2015, Summary, p. 3.

4. Ashley, *First Lady*, p. 284.

5. Corbett v. Corbett (otherwise Ashley), Judgement by Justice Ormrod, February 1970, p. 18.

6. Corbett vs. Corbett, pp. 18, 2.

7. Ibid., p. 19.

8. Kate Bornstein, *A Queer and Pleasant Danger, A Memoir – The True Story of a Nice Jewish Boy Who Joins the Church of Scientology and Leaves Twelve Years Later to Become the Lovely Lady She Is Today*, Boston: Beacon Press, 2012, p. 251.

9. Jennifer Finney Boylan, 'Loving Freely', *New York Times*, 24 October 2015.

10. Robert Stoller and Ralph Greenson, 'Gender Identity: Origins and Vicissitudes', unpublished draft, prob. 1964, courtesy of John Forrester.

11. Robert Stoller, 'Near Miss', 1982, courtesy of John Forrester; Robert Stoller, *Sex and Gender*, London: Hogarth, 1968, p. 140.

12. Stoller, *Sex and Gender*, p. 136.

13. Ibid., p. viii; Vol. 2, *The Transsexual Experiment*, London: Hogarth, 1975.

14. Ashley, *First Lady*, p. 161.

15. Ibid., pp. 178–9.

16. Ibid., pp. 161, 178–9, 277.

17. Viviane K. Namaste, *Invisible Lives – The Erasure of Transsexual and Transgendered People*, University of Chicago Press, 2000, p. 1.

18. Juliet Jacques, *Trans – A Memoir*, London: Verso, 2015 (unless otherwise specified, all references to Jacques are to this text).

19. Harold Garfinkel, 'Passing and the Managed Achievement of Sex Status in an "Intersexed" Person', 1967, in *The Transgender Studies Reader*, edited by Susan Stryker and Stephen Whittle, London: Routledge, 2006, p. 60.

20. Susan Stryker and Aren Z. Aizura, *The Transgender Studies Reader 2*, London: Routledge, 2013, p. 6.

21. Buzz Bissinger, 'He Says Goodbye, She Says Hello', *Vanity Fair*, July 2015, p. 120.

22. Jacques, *Trans*, p. 190, original italics.

23. Bissinger, 'He Says Goodbye', p. 66.

24. Namaste, *Invisible Lives*, Chapter 6, 'Queer Bashing.'

25. David Valentine, *Imagining Transgender – An Ethnography of a Category*, Durham: Duke University Press, 2007, see especially Chapter 6, 'The Calculus of Pain: Violence, Narrative and the Self', p. 212.

26. Ibid., p. 209.

27. 'How We'll Remember US Trans Women Killed in 2015', http://www.advocate.com/transgender/2015/11/20/how-well-remember-us-trans-women-killed-2015. See also 'Rebecca Nicholson Meets Laverne Cox' ('Now

I have the money to feminise my face, I don't want to. I'm happy with this face'), *Guardian*, 15 June 2015.

28. Review of 'Transcripts', Edinburgh Film Festival, *Guardian*, 17 August 2015.

29. 'AMA Adopts New Policies on First Day of Annual Meeting', https://www.ama-assn.org/press-center/press-releases/ama-adopts-new-policies-first-day-voting-2019-annual-meeting.

30. 'The Quest for Transgender Equality', full-page leader, *New York Times*, 4 May 2015.

31. Susan Stryker '(De)Subjugated Knowledges – An Introduction to Transgender Studies', *Transgender Studies Reader*, p. 10.

32. Jacques, *Trans*, p. 34.

33. National Center for Transgender Equality, 'Trump Administration Announces Beginning of Transgender Military Ban on April 12', https://transequality.org/press/releases/trump-administration-announces-beginning-of-transgender-military-ban-on-april-12.

34. Moriah Balingit, 'Education Department No Longer Investigating Transgender Bathroom Complaints', *Washington Post*, 12 February 2018. https://www.washingtonpost.com/news/education/wp/2018/02/12/education-department-will-no-longer-investigate-transgender-bathroom-complaints/.

35. Lauren Gambino and Erin Durkin, 'LGBT Groups Outraged over Trump Proposal to Remove Trans Rights', *Guardian*, 23 October 2018.

36. Jacques tells her story in 'Trans Eye View', a column she wrote for *one80news*, a free LGBT newspaper handed out in Brighton clubs, before writing her online *Guardian* column on transitioning (she retells the story in *Trans*).

37. Jacques, *Trans*, p. 262.

38. Roz Kaveney, *Tiny Pieces of Skull or A Lesson in Manners*, London: Team Angelica, 2015, p. 95.

39. 'Rebecca Nicholson Meets Laverne Cox'.

40. 'AMA Adopts New Policies'.

41. Jayne County with Rupert Smith, *Man Enough to Be a Woman*, London and New York: Serpent's Tail, 1995, p. 30.

42. Patricia Gherovici, *Please Select Your Gender: From the Invention of Hysteria to the Democratizing of Trangenderism*, London: Routledge, 2010, p. 238.

43. Jan Morris, *Conundrum*, London: Faber, 1974, pp. 137, 147.

44. Margaret Talbot, 'About a Boy', *Vanity Fair* special edition, *Trans America*, August 2015, pp. 17, 103.

45. Virginia Goldner, 'Editor's Note,' *Psychoanalytic Dialogues* 21:2, 2011, special issue: 'Transgender Subjectivities: Theories and Practices', p. 153.

46. Stryker, '(De)Subjugated Knowledges', p. 11.

47. Bissinger, 'He Says Goodbye', p. 120.

48. Mark Brown, 'Leibovitz: Most People Would Rather Be at Dentist than Before a Camera', *Guardian*, 14 January 2016.

49. Jacques, 'He to She', *Aeon*, 15 January 2014, http://aeon.co/magazine/culture/before-and-after-the-makeover-industrys-favourite-trope/.

50. Susan Stryker, 'My Words to Victor Frankenstein Above the Village of Chamounix', *GLQ – A Journal of Lesbian and Gay Studies* 1:3, 1994, www.annelawrence.com/mywords.html 4/15.

51. Garfinkel, 'Passing', pp. 62, 84.

52. Melanie McDonagh, 'Changing Sex is Not to Be Done Just on a Whim', *Evening Standard*, 5 January 2015.

53. Chris Johnston, 'Ian McEwan Criticised by Campaigners over Transgender Remarks', *Guardian*, 2 April 2016.

54. 'Rebecca Nicholson Meets Laverne Cox'; Bissinger, 'He Says Goodbye', p. 67.

55. Jessica Cartner-Morley, 'Modern Family: How the Kardashians Became a Force for Good', *Guardian*, 3 June 2015.

56. Stryker, 'My Words'.

57. Ibid.

58. Garfinkel, 'Passing', p. 64.

59. Personal communication for which thanks to Roz Kaveney.

60. Family Division and Administrative Court, High Court of Justice, Case FD1800035, Before The Rt Hon Sir Andrew McFarlane, President of the Family Division, between The Queen (on the application of TT) and The Registrar General for England and Wales, 25 September 2019, p. 60 – my thanks to Jeremy Rosenblatt for bringing this to my attention. See also Robert Booth, 'Transgender Man Loses Court Battle to Be Registered as Father', *Guardian*, 25 September 2019.

61. McFarlane, p. 1, clause 40.

62. Re M (Children), 2017, England and Wales Court of Appeal civ., 2164. My thanks to Jeremy Rosenblatt for sending me these details.

63. Talbot, 'About a Boy', p. 16.

64. Niels Hoyer (ed.), *Man into Woman – An Authentic Record of a Change of Sex – The true story of the miraculous transformation of the Danish painter Einar Wegener (Andreas Sparre)*, translated from German by H. J. Stenning, London: Jarrolds, 1933, London: Blueboat, 2004 with Foreword by Helen Parker, pp. 6, 7; David Ebershoff, *The Danish Girl*, London: Weidenfeld and Nicholson, 2000.

65. Morris, *Conundrum*, p. 138; Ashley, *First Lady*, pp. 33, 112.

66. Chelsea Manning, 'The Five Years Since I Was Jailed over War Diaries Have Been a Rollercoaster', *Guardian*, 28 May 2015.

67. Bornstein, *Queer and Pleasant Danger*, p. 251.

68. Jay Prosser, *Second Skins – The Body Narratives of Transsexuality*, New York: Columbia, 1998, pp. 1, 6.

69. Melanie Suchet, 'Crossing Over', *Psychoanalytic Dialogues* 21:2, 2011, special issue: 'Transgender Subjectivities: Theories and Practices', p. 184.

70. Prosser, *Second Skins*, p. 88.

71. Sandy Stone, 'The Empire Strikes Back – A Posttranssexual Manifesto', *Transgender Studies Reader*, p. 228.

72. Jay Prosser, 'A Palinode on Photography and the Transsexual Real', *a/b: Auto/Biography Studies* 14:1, 1999.

73. Prosser, *Second Skins*, p. 49.

74. Carol S. Vance, *Pleasure and Danger – Exploring Female Sexuality*, London: Routledge, 1984.

75. Frances J. Latchford, 'Sexed Life is a Cabaret: The Body Politics of Nina Arsenault's *The Silicone Diaries*' in Judith Rudakoff (ed.), *Trans(per)forming Nina Arsenault: An Unreasonable Body of Work*, Chicago and Bristol: Intellect, 2012.

76. Ibid., pp. 75, 219.

77. Jacques, *Trans*, p. 288.

78. Amia Srinivasan, 'He, She, One, They, Ho, Hus, Hum, Ita', *London Review of Books* 42:13, 2 July 2020.

79. Juliet Jacques, 'On the "Dispute" Between Radical Feminism and Trans People', *New Statesman*, 6 August 2014, https://www.newstatesman.com/juliet-jacques/2014/08/dispute-between-radical-feminism-and-trans-people.

80. 'Why the Trans Community Hates Dr Janice G. Raymond', *Transgriot*, 20 September 2010, https://transgriot.blogspot.com/2010/09/why-trans-community-hates-dr-janice-g.html.

81. Germaine Greer, *The Whole Woman*, London: Doubleday, 1999, pp. 64–74.

82. Steven Morris, 'Transgender Protest Fails to Stop Greer Delivering Lecture at Cardiff University', *Guardian*, 18 November 2015.

83. Germaine Greer, 'On Why Sex Change is a Lie', *Independent*, 22 July 1989, cited in Paris Lees, 'Germaine Greer and the Hypocrisy of the "Left"', 20 November 2015, https://www.vice.com/en_uk/read/germaine-greer-paris-lees-hypocrisy-left-free-speech.

84. Janice Raymond, *The Transsexual Empire – The Making of the She-Male*, New York: Athene, 1979, cited in Jacques, *Trans*, p. 105.

85. On this debate, see correspondence from Beatrix Campbell, Moira Dustin, Jay Prosser, Victoria Dutchman-Smith, Rachael Padman, and reply by Jacqueline Rose in *London Review of Books* 38:11–15, 2 June, 16 June, 14 July, 28 July 2016.

86. Moustapha Safouan, Cambridge talk, part of a series organised by Colin MacCabe, 1980.

87. A. Finn Enke, 'The Education of Little Cis – Cisgender and the Discipline of Opposing Bodies', *Transgender Studies Reader 2*, p. 235.

88. Catherine Millot, *Horsexe – Essai sur le transsexualisme*, Paris: Point Hors Ligne, 1983, p. 32.

89. Juliet Mitchell, 'Sexuality, Psychoanalysis and Social Changes' in Anthony Molino and Christine Ware (eds), *Where Id Was – Challenging Normalization in Psychoanalysis*, London: Continuum, 2001, pp. 108, 97.

90. Ashley, *First Lady*, p. 280.

91. Rees, *Dear Sir or Madam*, pp. 176–7.

92. Valentine, *Imagining Transgender*, pp. 114–15.

93. Stryker, 'My Words'.

94. County, *Man Enough*, p. 139.

95. Bornstein, *Queer and Pleasant Danger*, pp. 199, 240.

96. Jacques, *Trans*, pp. 115, 227.

97. Ibid., p. 251, emphasis original.

98. Bornstein, *Queer and Pleasant Danger*, pp. 203, 236.

99. Paris Lees, 'Why I'm Trans . . . and a Feminist', *Guardian*, 18 January 2013.

100. Letters, *Guardian*, 18 October 2018, see also replies, 18, 23 October, 2 November. The correspondence started in response to a *Guardian* editorial of 17 October 2018, on the proposed changes to the Gender Recognition Act.

101. Stryker, 'My Words'.

102. Liam Coleman, 'Ladies Pond Changes Rules for Trans Women', *Evening Standard*, 23 May 2019.

103. So Mayer, 'Ah! To fleet/Never fleets móre' in *At the Pond: Swimming at the Hampstead Ladies' Pond*, London: Daunt, 2019, pp. 55–6.

104. Bornstein, *Queer and Pleasant Danger*, p. xiv.

105. Cited in Latchford, 'Sexed Life is a Cabaret', p. 79.

106. Morris, *Conundrum*, pp. 70–1, 73, 87, 126.

107. John Gregory Dunne's 1997 article on the killings, 'The Humboldt Murders', was reprinted in the August 2015 special edition of *Vanity Fair* on *Trans America*.

108. Jack Halberstam, *In a Queer Time and Place*, NYU Press, 2005, pp. 45, 65.

109. Dunne, 'The Humboldt Murders', p. 110.

110. Ibid., p. 95.

111. Talbot, 'About a Boy', p. 14.

112. *Transsexual Stories*, BBC1, 24 August 2015.

113. Suchet, 'Crossing Over', p. 186.

114. Ibid.

115. Goldner, 'Editor's Note', p. 153.

116. Mary Mehl, cited in Sandy Stone, 'The Empire Strikes Back', *Transgender Studies Reader*, p. 229; Goldner, 'Editor's Note', p. 168.

117. R. Nick Gorton, 'Transgender as Mental Illness – Nosology, Social Justice, and the Tarnished Golden Mean', *Transgender Studies Reader 2*.

118. Valentine, *Imagining Transgender*, p. 220.

119. Goldner, 'Editor's Note', p. 154.

120. Jacques, *Trans*, p. 160.

121. Ken Corbett, 'Speaking Queer: A Reply to Richard C. Friedman', *Gender and Psychoanalysis* 2, 1997, p. 499, cited in Goldner, 'Editor's Note'.

122. Jacques, 'On the "Dispute"'.

123. Jacques, 'He to She'.

124. Jacques, *Trans*, pp. 252, 280.

125. Hoyer (ed.), pp. 231, 260.

126. Judith Butler, *Frames of War: When is Life Grievable?*, London: Verso, 2009.

127. Avgi Saketopoulou, 'Mourning the Body as Bedrock: Developmental Considerations in Treating Transsexual Patients Analytically', *Journal of the American Psychoanalytical Association* 62:5, 2014, pp. 781, 792. My thanks to Richard Sacks and colleagues at the Center for Modern Psychoanalytic Studies in New York for drawing this article to my attention.

128. Stone, 'The Empire Strikes Back', p. 230.

129. Dean Spade, 'Mutilating Gender', *Transgender Studies Reader 2*, p. 322.

130. Stone, 'The Empire Strikes Back', p. 231.

131. David Willets, 'Officer and a Gentlewoman', *Sun*, 19 January 2015; Rachel Williams, 'Gay, Bisexual and Transgender Parents and Adopters Step Forward', *Guardian*, 4 March 2015; Diane Taylor, '100% Surge in Children Seeking Gender Change', *Guardian*, 6 November 2016; Jenny Kleeman, 'Boys Will Be Girls Will Be Boys', *Guardian Weekend*, 12 September 2015; Tavistock and Portman NHS Foundation Trust, 'GIDS Referrals Increase in 2017/2018', 17 May 2018, https://tavistockandportman.nhs.uk/about-us/news/stories/gids-referrals-increase-201718/.

132. Kristina R. Olson, Lily Durwood, Madeleine DeMeules and Katie A. McLaughlin, 'The Mental Health of Transgender Children Who Are Supported in Their Identities', *Pediatrics* 137:3, 2016, p. 1.

133. Kleeman, 'Boys Will Be Girls'; Lancashire County Council v TP (2019), England and Wales Family Court, 30, para. 58; Vickie Pasterski, 'What Is the Essence of Gender?', TED, April 2019.

134. See for example Jon Brooks, 'The Controversial Research on "Desistance" in Transgender Youth', *KQED Science*, 23 May 2018.

135. Kleeman, 'Boys Will Be Girls'.

136. Talbot, 'About a Boy', p. 102.

137. Ibid., p. 101.

138. Kleeman, 'Boys Will Be Girls'.

139. Michael Savage, 'Gender Identity Treatments for Young to Get Expert Review', *Observer*, 2 February 2020.

140. Lucy Bannerman, 'Calls to End Transgender "Experiment on Children"', *The Times*, 8 April 2019.

141. Ibid.; see also Jamie Doward, 'Governor of Tavistock Foundation Quits over Damning Report into Gender Identity Clinic', *Guardian*, 23 February 2019; The Christian Institute, 'NHS Trans Clinic Governor Quits over "Serious Ethical Concerns"', 28 February 2019, www.christian.org.uk.

142. Leslie Feinberg, 'Transgender Liberation – A Movement Whose Time Has Come', *Transgender Studies Reader*.

143. Stephen Whittle, 'Foreword', *Transgender Studies Reader*, p. xv.

144. Afsaneh Najmabadi, 'Reading *Transsexuality* in "Gay" Tehran (Around 1979)', *Transgender Studies Reader 2*; Gayatri Reddy, *With Respect to Sex – Negotiating Hijra Identity in South India*, New Delhi: Yoda Press, University of Chicago Press, 2006.

145. Ashley, *First Lady*, p. 12.

146. Editors' note to Magnus Hirschfeld, 'The Transvestites – The Erotic Drive to Cross-Dress', *Transgender Studies Reader*.

147. Ashley, *First Lady*, pp. 2, 17.

148. Casey Quackenbush, 'Caitlyn Jenner Says Voting for Trump Was "a Mistake"', *Time Magazine*, 26 October 2018.

149. Bissinger, 'He Says Goodbye', pp. 66–7.

150. County, *Man Enough*, pp. 30, 69, 177, 184.

151. Sarah Lamble, 'Retelling Racialized Violence, Remaking White Innocence – The Politics of Interlocking Oppressions in Transgender Day of Remembrance', *Transgender Studies Reader 2*, p. 33.

152. Morgan Bassichis, Alexander Lee and Dean Spade, 'Building an Abolitionist Trans and Queer Movement with Everything We've Got', *Transgender Studies Reader 2*, pp. 653, 663.

153. Wesley Yang, 'The Revolt of the Feminist Law Profs', *Chronicle Review*, 7 August 2019.

154. Katy Steinmetz, 'The Transgender Tipping Point: America's Next Civil Rights Frontier', *Time Magazine*, 29 May 2014.

155. Margot Sanger-Katz and Noah Welland, 'Trump Administration Erases Transgender Civil Rights', *New York Times*, 12 June 2020.

156. Margot Sanger-Katz and Erica L. Green, 'Supreme Court Expansion of Transgender Civil Rights Undercuts Trump's Restrictions', *New York Times*, 15 June 2020.

3. Trans and Sexual Harassment – The Back-story

1. Sigmund Freud, 'Katharina', *Studien über Hysterie*, 1895, *Gesammelte Werke* 1, Frankfurt: Fischer-Verlag, London: Imago, 1952, p. 195n, 1924; 'Case 4 – Katharina', *Studies on Hysteria*, 1893–1895, *The Standard Edition of the Complete Psychological Works*, Vol. 2, London: Hogarth, 1955, p. 134n.

2. Christopher Bollas, 'The Trauma of Incest', *Forces of Destiny*, London: Free Association Books, 1999, pp. 48–9.

3. Sigmund Freud, *Moses and Monotheism*, 1939, *The Standard Edition of the Complete Psychological Works*, Vol. 23, London: Hogarth, 1964.

4. Sigmund Freud, *Beyond the Pleasure Principle*, 1920, *The Standard Edition of the Complete Psychological Works*, Vol. 18, London: Hogarth, 1955.

5. Sigmund Freud, 'Female Sexuality', 1931, *The Standard Edition of the Complete Psychological Works*, Vol. 21, London: Hogarth, 1961, p. 239; '*Über die weibliche Sexualität*', 1931, *Gesammelte Werke* 14, Frankfurt: Fischer-Verlag, London: Imago, 1948, p. 533.

6. Sigmund Freud, *Civilisation and Its Discontents*, 1930 (1929), *The Standard Edition of the Complete Psychological Works*, Vol. 21, London: Hogarth, 1961, p. 104; *Gesammelte Werke* 14, Frankfurt: Fischer-Verlag, London: Imago, 1948, p. 464.

7. Helene Deutsch, 'The Significance of Masochism in the Mental Life of Women', 1930, and 'The Psychology of Women in Relation to the Functions of Reproduction', 1925, in Robert Fliess (ed.), *The Psychoanalytic Reader – An Anthology of Essential Papers with Critical Introduction*, New York: International Universities Press, 1969.

8. Suchet, 'Crossing Over', p. 177.

9. Sigmund Freud, 'Hysterical Phantasies and Their Relation to Bisexuality', 1908, *The Standard Edition of the Complete Psychological Works*, Vol. 9, London: Hogarth, 1959, p. 166.

10. Sara Ahmed, *Cultural Politics of Emotion*, Edinburgh: Edinburgh University Press, 2014, p. 35.

11. Kate Bornstein, *Gender Outlaw*, cited in Jacques, *Trans*, p. 108.

12. Esi Edugyan, *Washington Black*, London: Serpent's Tail, 2018, p. 367.

13. My thanks to Deborah Friedell for bringing this tweet to my attention.

14. See also Eliot Weinberger, 'Ten Typical Days in Trump's America', *London Review of Books* 40:20, 25 October 2018, in particular, the thirty-one alleged instances of perjury in his testimony compiled by the activist group Demand Justice.

15. Bob Woodward, *Fear: Trump in the White House*, New York: Simon and Schuster, 2018, p. 37.

16. Benjamin Margolis, 'The Object-oriented Question: a Contribution to Treatment Technique', *Modern Psychoanalysis* 8:1, 1983, p. 35.
17. Freud, 'Case 4 – Katharina', p. 132.
18. Ibid., p. 127.
19. Sigmund Freud to Wilhelm Fliess, 30 May 1893, in Freud, *The Origins of Psychoanalysis: Letters to Wilhelm Fliess, Drafts and Notes, 1887–1902,* edited by Anna Freud, Marie Bonaparte and Ernst Kris, translated by Eric Mosbacher and James Strachey, London: Imago, 1954, p. 73 and note.
20. Freud, 'Case 4 – Katharina', p. 132.
21. Butler, *Gender Trouble.*
22. All references in this section taken from Philip Kuhn, 'In "The Dark Regions of the Mind": A Reading for the Indecent Assault in Ernest Jones's 1908 Dismissal from the West End Hospital for Nervous Diseases', *Psychoanalysis and History* 17:1, 2015.
23. T. D. Savill, 'A Clinical Lecture on the Psychology and Psychogenesis of Hysteria and the Role of the Sympathetic System', *The Lancet*, 13 February 1909, p. 29, cited in Kuhn, 'In "The Dark Regions"'.
24. Ellen Pinsky, *Mortal Gifts – Death and Fallibility in the Psychoanalytic Encounter*, Abingdon and New York: Routledge, p. 63.
25. Ibid.
26. Juliet Mitchell, *Mad Men and Medusas – Recalling Hysteria and the Effect of Siblings on the Human Condition*, London: Penguin, 2000.
27. Robin Pogrebin and Kate Kelly, *The Education of Brett Kavanaugh – An Investigation*, New York, Random House, 2019.
28. Women and Equalities Committee, *Transgender Equality – First Report*, p. 3.
29. For a full discussion of this history, see Moustapha Safouan, *Jacques Lacan and the Question of Psychoanalytic Training*, translated with an introduction by Jacqueline Rose, London: Macmillan, 2000.
30. Kristina Harrison et al., 'Standing Up for Transsexual Rights', *Guardian*, Letters, 5 May 2018.
31. Alexandra Topping, 'Prison Assaults Reignite Debate over Transgender Inmates in Women's Jails', *Guardian*, 10 September 2018; Jamie Grierson and Jessica Elgot, 'Justice Minister: Women's Safety Key When Placing Transgender Prisoners', *Guardian*, 20 October 2018.
32. Nazia Parveen, '"It Was a Terrifying Time." Neighbours Recall "Manipulative and Controlling" Trans Offender', *Guardian*, 12 October 2018.
33. Bornstein, *Queer and Pleasant Danger*, p. xiv.
34. Suchet, 'Crossing Over'; Sandra Silverman, 'The Colonised Mind: Gender, Trauma, and Mentalization', *Psychoanalytic Dialogues* 25, 2015.
35. Saketopoulou, 'Mourning the Body'.

36. André Green, 'The Neuter Gender', 1973, in Rosine Jozef Perelberg (ed.), *Psychic Bisexuality – A British-French Dialogue*, London: Routledge, The New Library of Psychoanalysis, 2018, p. 254.

37. Moustapha Safouan, *La Civilisation post-oedipienne*, Paris: Herman, Collection 'Psychanalyse', 2018, p. 128.

38. Grigoriadis, *Blurred Lines*, p. 56.

39. Stryker, 'My Words'.

40. Gambino and Durkin, 'LGBT Groups Outraged over Trump Proposal'.

41. Spade, 'Mutilating Gender', p. 320.

42. Audre Lorde, 'The Uses of Anger', *Your Silence Will Not Protect You*, London: Silver Press, 2017, p. 113.

43. Freud, 'Why War?', 1933 (1932), *The Standard Edition of the Complete Psychological Works*, Vol. 22, London: Hogarth, 1964, p. 210; 'Warum Krieg?', *Gesammelte Werke* 16, Frankfurt: Fischer-Verlag, London: Imago, 1950, p. 21.

44. Freud, 'The Disillusionment of the War', Essay 1, 'Thoughts for the Time on War and Death', *The Standard Edition of the Complete Psychological Works*, Vol. 14, London: Hogarth, 1957, p. 282.

45. Kantor and Twohey, *She Said*, p. 244.

46. Sigmund Freud, *Three Essays on the Theory of Sexuality*, 1905, *The Standard Edition of the Complete Psychological Works*, Vol. 7, London: Hogarth, 1953, p. 146n; *Gesammelte Werke* 5, Frankfurt: Fischer-Verlag, London: Imago, 1946, p. 44n.

47. Daisy Johnson, *Everything Under*, London: Jonathan Cape, 2018.

48. Safouan, *La Civilisation post-oedipienne*, p. 40.

49. For a searching critique of the concept of happiness in our times, see Sara Ahmed, *The Promise of Happiness*, Durham and London: Duke University Press, 2010.

50. Weinberger, 'Ten Typical Days'.

51. Anna Burns, *Milkman*, London: Faber, 2018, p. 1.

52. Bollas, 'The Trauma of Incest'.

53. Burns, *Milkman*, pp. 5, 178, 166.

54. Ibid., pp. 303, 171, 193, 282.

55. Ibid., p. 127.

56. Ibid., pp. 76, 128, 264.

57. Ibid., p. 112.

58. Ibid., pp. 147, 45, 314.

59. Ibid.

60. D. W. Winnicott, 'Transitional Objects and Transitional Phenomena', *Playing and Reality*, London: Routledge, 1971.

4. Feminism and the Abomination of Violence

1. See Diane Wood Middlebrook, *Anne Sexton – A Biography*, Boston: Houghton Mifflin, 1991; Jacqueline Rose, *The Haunting of Sylvia Plath*, London: Virago, 1991.

2. For an account of these disputes, see Jacqueline Rose, 'This is Not a Biography', *On Not Being Able to Sleep – Psychoanalysis in the Modern World*, London: Chatto and Windus, 2003.

3. Catharine A. MacKinnon, 'Human Rights and Global Violence Against Women', *Are Women Human? and Other International Dialogues*, Cambridge: Harvard, 2006, p. 28.

4. Subsequently printed in Robbie Duschinsky and Susan Walker, *Juliet Mitchell and the Lateral Axis – Twenty-first-century Psychoanalysis and Feminism*, Critical Studies in Gender, Sexuality and Culture, London: Macmillan, 2015, pp. 207–27.

5. Christina Lamb, '50,000 Women Raped and the World Shrugs', *Sunday Times*, 9 December 2018.

6. European Union Agency for Fundamental Rights, 'Violence Against Women – an EU wide survey', March 2014, http://fra.europa.eu/en/publication/2014/violence-against-women-eu-wide-survey-main-results-report; see also Beatrix Campbell, *The End of Equality*, Manifestos for the 21st Century, University of Chicago Press and Seagull, 2014.

7. World Bank, *Gender-based Violence* (*Violence Against Women and Girls*), 2 April 2019, https://www.worldbank.org/en/topic/socialdevelopment/brief/violence-against-women-and-girls.

8. 'Rape Has "Effectively Become Decriminalised", Women's Rights Activists Warn', *Morning Star*, 12 September 2019; Caelainn Barr, Alexandra Topping and Owen Bowcott, 'Rape Prosecutions Fall to 10-year Low in Spite of Sharp Rise in Complaints', *Guardian*, 13 September 2019; see also Caelainn Barr and David Pegg, 'Prosecutions for Rape at Lowest Level for Five Years, New Figures Reveal', *Guardian*, 6 March 2019.

9. www.cps.gov.uk/sites/default/files/documents/publications/cps-vawg-report-2019.pdf; 'A Sharp Rise in Domestic Killings Must Lead to Action, Not Despair', *Guardian*, leader article, 14 September 2019.

10. Caelainn Barr and Owen Bowcott, '"Secret Targets" Could Explain Plunge in Rape Convictions', *Guardian*, 13 November 2019.

11. Caelainn Barr and Owen Bowcott, 'CPS Faces Legal Action for "Failing to Pursue Rape Cases"', *Guardian*, 25 September 2019.

12. Caelainn Barr and Alexandra Topping, 'Downing Street Plans Rape Prosecution Targets for Police and CPS', *Guardian*, 9 August 2020.

13. Andrew Van Dam, 'Less than 1% of Rapes Lead to Felony Convictions', *Washington Post*, 'Wonderblog', 6 October 2018.

14. 'A Sharp Rise in Domestic Killings'; Laith Al-Khalaf and Alexandra Topping, 'Women Killed by Men Knew Assailant in 94% of Cases', *Guardian*, 20 February 2020.

15. Jamie Grierson, 'Number of Female Homicide Victims Reaches 14-year High', *Guardian*, 14 February 2020.

16. Arkadi Gerney and Chelsea Parsons, 'Women Under the Gun', *Center for American Progress*, 18 June 2014, also reported in *Social Solutions*: https://www.socialsolutions.com/blog/domestic-violence-statistics-2018/.

17. Jane Martinson, 'Extent of Violence against Women in EU Revealed', *Guardian*, 5 March 2014.

18. Hannah Summers, 'Women's Refuges Turn Away Victims Who Speak No English', *Guardian*, 9 August 2020.

19. MacKinnon, 'Human Rights and Global Violence Against Women', p. 28.

20. Hannah Arendt, 'Lying in Politics', *Crises of the Republic*, New York: Harcourt, Brace, Jovanovich, 1972, p. 34.

21. Arendt, *The Human Condition*, pp. 5, 6.

22. Arendt, *On Violence*, New York: Houghton Mifflin Harcourt, 1970, pp. 3, 14.

23. Seyla Benhabib, 'Feminist Theory and Hannah Arendt's Concept of Public Space', *History of Human Sciences* 6:2, 1993; Mary Dietz, 'Hannah Arendt and Feminist Politics', *Hannah Arendt – Critical Essays*, Albany: Suny University Press, 1994.

24. Arendt, *The Human Condition*, p. 27.

25. Ibid., pp. 31, 34.

26. Judith Butler, *Precarious Life – The Powers of Mourning and Violence*, London: Verso, 2004.

27. Arendt, *On Violence*, p. 53.

28. Ibid., pp. 53, 55, 87.

29. Catharine MacKinnon, 'Desire in Power', *Feminism Unmodified*, p. 53.

30. Arendt, *The Human Condition*, pp. 62–3.

31. Ibid., pp. 244, 191.

32. Hannah Arendt, *One/Thinking*, Vol. 1, *The Life of the Mind*, New York: Harcourt, Brace, Jovanovich, 1971, 1978, 1977, p. 57, 61, 55, 122.

33. Ibid., p. 199.

34. See Lyndsey Stonebridge, *Stateless People – Writing, Rights and Refugees*, Oxford University Press, 2018.

35. Arendt, *The Life of the Mind*, p. 198.

36. Ibid., p. 198; Lacan, *The Four Fundamental Concepts of Psychoanalysis*, translated by Alan Sheridan, London: Penguin, 1973, Karnac, 2004, p. 76.

37. Arendt, *The Life of the Mind*, p. 150.
38. See Arendt's essay 'Rosa Luxemburg: 1871–1919', *Men in Dark Times*, London: Jonathan Cape, 1970, and also my discussion of Luxemburg, 'Woman on the Verge of Revolution: Rosa Luxemburg', *Women in Dark Times*, London: Bloomsbury, 2014.
39. Arendt, 'Willing', *The Life of the Mind*, p. 136.
40. Luxemburg to Hans Diefenbach, 1917 (complete date not given), cited in Elzbieta Ettinger, *Rosa Luxemburg: A Life*, Boston: Beacon Press, 1986, p. 213.
41. Elliott Jaques, 'Foreword', Melanie Klein, *Narrative of a Child Analysis – The Conduct of the Psycho-Analysis of Children as Seen in the Treatment of a Ten-year-old Boy*, London: Hogarth, 1984.
42. Ibid., pp. 22, 194, 347 (my italics).
43. MacKinnon, 'Introduction – Women's Status, Men's States', *Are Women Human?*, p. 2.
44. MacKinnon, 'Women's September 11th – Rethinking the International Law of Conflict', *Are Women Human?*, pp. 260–1, 272.
45. Julia Kristeva, *Melanie Klein*, translated by Ross Guberman, New York: Columbia University Press, 2001.
46. Klein, *Narrative of a Child Analysis*, pp. 34, 25, 111.
47. Ibid., p. 426 (my italics).
48. See Jacqueline Rose, 'War in the Nursery', *Why War? Psychoanalysis, Politics and the Return to Melanie Klein*, Oxford: Blackwell, 1993.
49. Klein, *Narrative of a Child Analysis*, p. 100n
50. Ibid., p. 466.
51. Juliet Mitchell, 'The Law of the Mother – Sibling Trauma and the Brotherhood of War', *Canadian Journal of Psychoanalysis* 21:1, 2013.
52. See Luingam Luithui and Nandita Haksar, *Nagaland File – A Question of Human Rights*, Delhi: Lancer International, 1984.
53. Temsula Ao, *These Hills Called Home – Stories from a War Zone*, New Delhi: Zubaan, Kali for Women, 2006, p. x. My thanks to Akshi Singh for bringing Ao to my attention.
54. Ibid., p. 33.
55. Ibid., pp. 92, 93, 97.
56. Ibid., pp. 96, 108, 113.
57. Sam Jordison, 'Eimear McBride's Publisher Gives the Inside Story', *Guardian*, Saturday Review, 7 June 2014.
58. Eimear McBride, *A Girl Is a Half-formed Thing*, Norwich: Galley Beggar Press, 2013, p. 3.
59. Ibid., p. 95.

60. Virginia Woolf, *A Room of One's Own*, 1929, Oxford University Press, 1992, pp. 126–7, 62.

61. McBride, *Girl*, pp. 162, 95.

62. Anne Enright, reviewing McBride, *Guardian*, 20 September 2013.

63. McBride, *Girl*, p. 96.

64. Ibid., p. 194.

65. For a fuller discussion of critical responses to the novel, including an account of the lecture in which I first discussed McBride – 'Modernism: The Unfinished Legacy', delivered at the British Association for Modernist Studies (BAMS) on 26 June 2014 – see David Collard, *About a Girl – A Reader's Guide to Eimear McBride's* A Girl Is a Half-formed Thing, London: CB Editions, 2016.

5. Writing Violence – From Modernism to Eimear McBride

1. Will Self, 'Journey to the End of the Night', *Guardian*, 3 August 2012; Gabriel Josipovici, *What Ever Happened to Modernism?*, New Haven and London: Yale University Press, 2010.

2. John Gray, *Al Qaeda and What It Means to Be Modern*, London: Faber, 2003.

3. Theodor Adorno and Max Horkheimer, *The Dialectic of Enlightenment*, 1944, London: Verso, 1979, pp. xvii, xii.

4. Josipovici, *What Ever Happened to Modernism?*

5. Eric Hobsbawm, *The Age of Extremes: The Short Twentieth Century, 1919–1941*, London: Michael Joseph, 1994.

6. Sigmund Freud, 'A Disturbance of Memory on the Acropolis', 1936, *The Standard Edition of the Complete Psychological Works*, Vol. 22, London: Hogarth, 1964, pp. 237–48.

7. Ibid., pp. 244, 245.

8. Virginia Woolf, *Between the Acts*, 1940, Oxford University Press, World's Classics edition, 2008, p. 160.

9. Ibid., Introduction by Frank Kermode, pp. xiii–xv.

10. Jacques Lacan, 'The Function and Field of Speech and Language in Psychoanalysis', 1953, *Ecrits*, translated by Alan Sheridan, London: Tavistock, 1977, p. 86 (my italics).

11. Woolf, *Between the Acts*, p. 89.

12. Woolf, *Three Guineas*, 1938, Oxford World's Classics, 1992.

13. Rosa Luxemburg, *Rote Fahne*, 18 November 1918, cited in Tony Cliff, *Rosa Luxemburg*, London: Bookmarks, 1959, p. 31.

14. Walter Benjamin, 'Theses on the Philosophy of History', *Illuminations*,

edited with an introduction by Hannah Arendt, translated by Harry Zohn, London: Collins/Fontana, 1970, p. 259.

15. Josipovici, *What Ever Happened to Modernism?*, p. 106.

16. Rosalind E. Krauss, *The Picasso Papers*, Massachusetts: MIT Press, 1998, p. 33.

17. Ibid., p. 34.

18. Toni Morrison, 'Unspeakable Things Unspoken: the Afro-American Presence in American Literature', presented as the Tanner Lecture on Human Values, University of Michigan, 7 October 1988, p. 3. tannerlectures.utah.edu/ _documents/a-to-z/m/morrison90.pdf.

19. Toni Morrison, *Beloved*, London: Chatto and Windus, 1987, p. 3

20. Morrison, 'Unspeakable Things Unspoken', p. 31.

21. Morrison, *Beloved*, p. 36.

22. Steve Dow, '"Such Brutality": Tricked into Slavery in the Thai Fishing Industry', *Guardian*, 21 September 2019; Royal Borough of Kensington and Chelsea, *Modern Slavery*, 2020, www.rbkc.gov.uk/community-and-local-life/ community-safety/modern-slavery.

23. https://www.ucl.ac.uk/lbs/.

24. 'Write Good Books and Try Not to Die – Interview with Eimear McBride' in David Collard, *About a Girl*, p. 140.

25. Eimear McBride, 'My Hero: James Joyce' in ibid.

26. McBride, *Girl*, pp. 28, 33, 131.

27. May Sinclair, *The Life and Death of Harriett Frean*, 1922, London: Virago, 1980, p. 18.

28. Carl Gustav Jung to James Joyce, August 1932, cited in Richard Ellmann, *James Joyce*, Oxford University Press, 1959, p. 642.

29. James Joyce, *Ulysses*, 1922, Harmondsworth: Penguin Modern Classics, 1971, p. 379.

30. McBride, *Girl*, p. 194.

31. McBride, 'My Hero, James Joyce'.

32. Alice O'Keeffe, 'Eimear McBride: "I Was Really Bored with the Way Sex is Written About"', *The Bookseller*, 8 July 2016.

33. Ibid.

34. Eimear McBride, *The Lesser Bohemians*, London: Faber & Faber, 2016, pp. 39, 26, 231.

35. Ibid., p. 57.

36. Collard, *About a Girl*, p. 137.

37. Ibid., pp. 137–8, 133.

38. McBride, *Lesser Bohemians*, pp. 3, 4, 14.

39. Ibid., p. 110.

40. O'Keeffe, 'Eimear McBride'.

41. McBride, *Lesser Bohemians*, pp. 70, 110.

42. Ibid., pp. 105–6.

43. Ibid., pp. 165, 166.

44. Ibid., pp. 166, 169, 186.

45. Rebecca Ratcliffe, 'Sexually Abused Boys Often Overlooked by State Laws, Global Study Warns', *Guardian*, 16 January 2019.

46. Collard, *About a Girl*, p. 139.

47. McBride, *Lesser Bohemians*, pp. 241, 243.

48. Ibid., pp. 137, 263.

49. Vanessa Thorpe, 'There is So Much More to Her than Bridget Jones', *Observer*, 4 September 2016.

50. McBride, *Lesser Bohemians*, pp. 124–5.

51. Collard, *About a Girl*, p. 137.

52. McBride, *Lesser Bohemians*, pp. 107, 114.

6. The Killing of Reeva Steenkamp, the Trial of Oscar Pistorius – Sex and Race in the Courtroom

1. John Carlin, *Chase Your Shadow: The Trials of Oscar Pistorius*, London: Atlantic Books, 2014, pp. 198, 221.

2. 'Oscar Pistorius Murder Trial: as it happened', *Daily Telegraph*, 4 March 2014.

3. Jamie Grierson, 'South Africa Court Doubles Oscar Pistorius's Prison Sentence', *Guardian*, 24 November 2017.

4. Carlin, *Chase Your Shadow*, p. 361; Johnny Steinberg, 'Pistorius Has Become a Source of Racial Shame', *Business Day Live*, 19 September 2014. For comments on the verdict, see also Leon Louw, 'Ignorance Fuels Feeding Frenzy over Pistorius', *Business Day Live*, 17 September 2014; Trudi Makhaya, 'Masipa's Pistorius Ruling Puts Judicial Error in the Spotlight', *Business Day Live*, 16 September 2014; Kim Ludbrook, 'Judge Masipa Got It Wrong', *IOL News*, 11 September 2014; Eusebius McKaiser, 'Oscar: Fair Sentence But for Unjust Reasons', *IOL*, 21 October 2014; Kim Hawkey, 'Masipa Got Pistorius Judgement Right – on the Law', *Business Day Live*, 18 September 2014; Jonathan Burchell, 'Masipa's Decision to Acquit Oscar of Murder Justified', *Business Day Live*, 17 September 2014.

5. Carlin, *Chase Your Shadow*, p. 189.

6. Mandy Wiener and Barry Bateman, *Behind the Door: The Oscar Pistorius and Reeva Steenkamp Story*, London: Macmillan, pp. 206ff.

7. Cited in ibid., p. 213.

8. Ibid.

9. Ibid., pp. 212.

10. Nick Davies, 'Who Was the Man in the Green Blanket?', *Guardian*, 19 May 2015

11. Aislinn Laing, 'A Chime Every Four Minutes for the Victims as South Africa Radio Stations Join Rape Outcry', *Telegraph*, 8 February 2013; Ashraf Hendricks, 'Every Three Hours a Woman Is Murdered in South Africa', *Al Jazeera*, 3 September 2019, https://www.aljazeera.com/indepth/ inpictures/3-hours-woman-murdered-south-africa-190905103533183.html.

12. Associated Press, 'Meghan Starts African Visit'.

13. Cited in Wiener and Bateman, *Behind the Door*, p. 39.

14. Ibid., p. 34.

15. Greg Nicholson, 'Pistorius Trial: Reeva Steenkamp Emerges on Day 46', *Daily Maverick*, 15 October 2014. Thanks to Rachel Holmes for sending me this link.

16. Cited in Wiener and Bateman, *Behind the Door*, p. 543.

17. Masipa Judgement, 'In the matter between the State and Oscar Leonard Carl Pistorius', High Court of South Africa, Gauteng Division, Pretoria, Judgement, Vol. 42, pp. 3280–351, 3328.

18. Thanks to Rachel Holmes, who has long been a key informant on South Africa, for alerting me to this book.

19. Eusebius McKaiser, *A Bantu in my Bathroom: Debating Race, Sexuality and Other Uncomfortable South African Topics*, Johannesburg: Bookstorm and Pan Macmillan, 2012.

20. Ibid., p. 25.

21. Ibid., pp. 26, 25, 43.

22. Masipa, Judgement, p. 3311.

23. Carlin, *Chase Your Shadow*, p. 233.

24. Margie Orford, 'Oscar Pistorius Trial: the Imaginary Black Stranger at the Heart of the Defence', *Guardian Africa*, 6 March 2014, also cited in Wiener and Bateman, although they attribute the article to the *Sunday Times* (p. 453).

25. Masipa, Judgement, p. 3328.

26. Mark Gevisser, *Lost and Found in Johannesburg*, Johannesburg and Cape Town: Jonathan Ball, 2014, pp. 82, 36.

27. Ibid., pp. 136, 199, 36.

28. 'Report of US Senate Select Committee on Intelligence covering the period from January 3, 2013 to June 5, 2014', 31 March 2015, p. 40 of 499, http://www.intelligence.senate.gov/study2014/sscistudy1.pdf.

29. Toni Morrison, 'Introduction: Friday on the Potomac', *Race-ing Justice,*

En-gendering Power, Essays on Anita Hill, Clarence Thomas, and the Construction of Social Reality, New York: Pantheon, 1992, pp. xi–xviii.

30. Wiener and Bateman, *Behind the Door*, p. 255.

31. Masipa, Judgement, p. 3320.

32. Ibid.

33. Ibid.

34. Wiener and Bateman, *Behind the Door*, p. 142

35. Ibid., p. 353.

36. Pistorius, Final Statement, cited in ibid., pp. 399–401.

37. Ibid., pp. 231–2.

38. Masipa, Judgement, p. 3320.

39. Wiener and Bateman, *Behind the Door*, pp. 234, 328, 342.

40. Suzanne Moore, 'Reeva Steenkamp Was a Victim of Male Violence. That is the Real Story', *Guardian*, 22 October 2014.

41. Wiener and Bateman, *Behind the Door*, p. 516.

42. Ibid., p. 368.

43. Masipa, Judgement, pp. 3304–5.

44. Thanks to Gillian Slovo for pointing this out to me.

45. Wiener and Bateman, *Behind the Door*, p. 424.

46. Thanks to Zeina Ghandour for sending me the link: https://www.youtube.com/watch?v=l_hle5shsDY. The moment comes at 17.00 minutes into the footage. As Ghandour also points out, it is pretty amazing this was not picked up by Nel nor indeed it seems by any commentator (we were hoping Nel would read this and it would change everything).

47. Wiener and Bateman, *Behind the Door*, p. 37.

48. Ibid., p. 35.

49. Sean Ingle, 'Semenya Loses Landmark Case against IAAF over Testosterone Levels', *Guardian*, 1 May 2019.

50. Carlin, *Chase Your Shadow*, pp. 53, 48.

51. Oscar Pistorius, *Blade Runner – My Story*, first published as *Dream Runner*, Milan: Rizzoli, 2008, London: Virgin, 2009, p. 11.

52. Cora Kaplan, 'Afterword: Liberalism, Feminism, and Defect' in Helen Deutsch and Felicity Nussbaum (eds), *'Defects': Engendering the Modern Body*, Ann Arbor: University of Michigan Press, 2000, p. 304.

53. Hilary Clark, 'On Depression Narratives: "Hence, into the Dark, We Write. . ."' in Merri Lisa Johnson and Susannah B. Mintz (eds), *On the Literary Non-Fiction of Nancy Mairs, a Critical Anthology*, Palgrave, 2011, p. 64.

54. Nancy Mairs, 'On Being a Cripple', *Plaintext: Essays by Nancy Mairs*, Tucson: University of Arizona Press, 1986, p. 10.

55. Wiener and Bateman, *Behind the Door*, p. 471.

56. Masipa, Judgement, p. 3314.

57. Carlin, *Chase Your Shadow*, p. 320.

58. Wiener and Bateman, *Behind the Door*, p. 217.

59. Carlin, *Chase Your Shadow*, p. 204.

60. Wiener and Bateman, *Behind the Door*, p. 430, 22, 450.

61. Carlin, *Chase Your Shadow*, p. 102.

62. Zakes Mda, *Black Diamond*, Calcutta: Seagull, 2014, p. 119.

63. Gillian Slovo, 'Barrel of a Gun? The Armed Struggle for Democracy in South Africa', Ralph Miliband Lecture, LSE, 5 May 2014.

64. Wiener and Bateman, *Behind the Door*, p. 84.

65. Ibid., p. 454.

66. Masipa, Judgement, pp. 3317, 3332–3.

67. Steinberg, 'Pistorius Has Become a Source of Racial Shame'.

68. Masipa, Judgement, p. 3315.

69. Wiener and Bateman, *Behind the Door*, p. 464

70. Ibid., p. 355.

71. Masipa, Judgement, p. 3310.

72. Orford, 'Oscar Pistorius Trial', also cited in Wiener and Bateman, *Behind the Door*, p. 453.

73. Masipa, Judgement, p. 3334.

74. Ibid., p. 3330. Masipa cites S v Ngema (1992) (2) SACR 651 (d).

75. Ibid., p. 3333.

76. S v Mithiza 1970 (3), SA 747A, cited in Masipa, Judgement, p. 3324 (my italics).

77. S v Bradshaw, 1977 (1) PH 860 (A) Wessels, cited in Masipa, Judgement, p. 3348.

78. S v Sigwatia, 1967 (4) SA 566 (A) Holmes JA, cited in Masipa, Judgement, p. 3349.

79. Laurence Sterne, *The Life and Opinions of Tristram Shandy, Gentleman*, 1759, edited by James Aiken Work, New York: Odyssey Press, 1940, pp. 406–7.

80. Proust, *In Search of Lost Time*, Vintage edition, Volume 4, *Sodom and Gomorrah*, p. 10; Penguin, Vol. 4, p. 13; Pléiade, 3 vols, Vol. 2, p. 609 (translations modified or rather merged).

81. Junichirō Tanizaki, *In Praise of Shadows*, London: Vintage, 2001, pp. 11, 20.

82. Mary Douglas, *Purity and Danger*, London: Routledge and Kegan Paul, 1966, pp. 208, 166, 186.

83. Carlin, *Chase Your Shadow*, p. 112.

84. Gevisser, *Lost and Found*, p. 283.

85. Sigmund Freud, 'Notes upon a Case of Obsessional Neurosis' (The 'Rat Man'), 1909, *Standard Edition of the Complete Psychological Works*, Vol. 10, London: Hogarth, 1955, p. 233.

86. Gevisser, *Lost and Found*, p. 294.

87. Hedley Twidle, 'The Oscar Pistorius Case: History Written on a Woman's Body', *New Statesman*, 7 March 2013.

88. Rebecca West, *Black Lamb, Grey Falcon: A Journey through Yugoslavia*, 1942, London: Canongate, 1997, p. 896.

7. Political Protest and the Denial of History – South Africa and the Legacy of the Future

1. Rouen Thebus, 'In Conversation with Dudu Ndlovu: Useful Tips When Chairing Plenaries/Meetings', *Pathways to Free Education* 2, *Strategy and Tactics*, 2018, p. 63.

2. Simon Rakei, 'Community and Struggles and the Tactics of Land Occupations in Conversation with Petrus Brink', *Pathways to Free Education* 2, *Strategy and Tactics*, 2018, p. 20.

3. Brian Kamanzi, 'Decolonising the Curriculum: The Silent War for Tomorrow', *Daily Maverick*, 28 April 2016.

4. Leigh-Ann Naidoo, 'The Anti-apartheid Generation Has Become Afraid of the Future', *Mail & Guardian*, 17 August 2016.

5. 'Lovelyn Nwadeyi's Empowering Message: We All Have Agency and We Must Use It to Disrupt the Status Quo', *Mail & Guardian*, 29 June 2016, https://mg.co.za/article/2016-06-29-we-all-have-agency-and-we-must-use-it-to-disrupt-the-status-quo/. Thanks to Albie Sachs for bringing Nwadeyi's speech to my attention.

6. Javier Espinoza and Gordon Rayner, 'Rhodes Will Not Fall', *Daily Telegraph*, 29 January 2016.

7. Ben Quinn and Richard Adams, 'Rhodes Statue: Tech Boss Pledges to Cover Funds Pulled by "Racist Donors"', *Guardian*, 20 June 2020.

8. See Stefan Collini, 'Inside the Mind of Dominic Cummings', *Guardian*, 6 February 2020. Cummings is currently Boris Johnson's chief adviser.

9. Brad Evans, interview with Neo Muyanga, 'Songs in the Key of Revolution', *Violence*, edited by Brad Evans and Natasha Lennard, London: City Lights, 2018, p. 190.

10. Eve Fairbanks, 'How South Africa's Youth Turned on Their Parents' Generation', *Guardian*, 18 November 2015.

11. Davies, 'Who Was the Man in the Green Blanket?'

12. Fairbanks, 'South Africa's Youth'.

13. Muyanga in Evans and Lennard (eds), *Violence*, p. 190 (italics original).

14. 'Lovelyn Nwadeyi's Empowering Message'.

15. Ibid.

16. N. Chabani Manganyi, *Mashangu's Reverie and Other Essays*, Johannesburg: Ravan Press, 1977, pp. 65, 44, 6.

17. Terreblanche, *Lost in Transformation*, p. 20.

18. Lungisile Ntsebeza, 'Land Distribution in South Africa: the Property Clause Revisited', in Lungisile Ntsebeza and Ruth Hall (eds), *The Land Question in South Africa: The Challenge of Transformation and Distribution*, Cape Town: HSRC, 2007.

19. Victoria Collis-Buthelezi, 'Response to "The Legacy, or, What I Have Learnt From You"', University of Cape Town VC Open Lecture, 16 March 2017, published in Jaco Barnard-Naudé, *Decolonizing the Neoliberal University: Law, Psychoanalysis and the Politics of Student Protest*, London: Birkbeck Law Press; London: Routledge, 2021.

20. Arendt, 'Lying in Politics', *Crises of the Republic*, pp. 1–48.

21. Paul Erasmus, *Confessions of a Stratcom Hitman*, Johannesburg: Jacana, 2020; Jonathan Ancer, *Betrayal: The Secret Lives of Apartheid Spies*, Cape Town: Tafelberg, 2020; for a discussion of these books see Jason Burke, 'Yet to Be Reconciled – Books Expose Secret History of Apartheid that Many Don't Want to Hear', *Guardian*, 13 July 2020.

22. Mogobe B. Ramose, 'An African Perspective on Justice and Race', *Themes*, 2001, p. 1, https://them.polylog.org/3/frm-en.htm.

23. Drucilla Cornell, 'Rethinking Ethical Feminism through uBuntu', *Law and Revolution in South Africa: uBuntu, Dignity, and the Struggle for Constitutional Transformation*, New York: Fordham University Press, 2014, pp. 141–7.

24. Ramose, 'An African Perspective', p. 7.

25. Cornell, 'Rethinking Ethical Feminism', p. 206 n. 11.

26. Kéba M'Baye, cited in Ramose, 'An African Perspective', p. 3.

27. Freud, 'The Disillusionment of the War', p. 285.

28. D. W. Winnicott, 'Fear of Breakdown', *International Review of Psychoanalysis*, 1974.

29. Lacan, 'The Function and Field of Speech and Language in Psychoanalysis', p. 86.

30. I discuss this more fully in Jacqueline Rose, Introduction, Sigmund Freud, *Mass Psychology and Other Writings*, translated by J. A. Underwood, London: Penguin Classics, 2004.

31. Pumla Gobodo-Madikizela, 'Introduction – Breaking Intergenerational Cycles of Conflict' in *Breaking Intergenerational Cycles of Repetition: A Global Dialogue on Historical Trauma and Memory*, edited by Pumla Gobodo-Madikizela, Opladen, Berlin, Toronto: Barbara Budrich, 2016 (conference at UFree State, 2012), pp. 1–11.

32. Ibid., p. 1 (my italics).

33. The literature on this is now extensive and not without controversy but see, for example, Leon Mutesa et al., 'Transgenerational Epigenomics of Trauma and PTSD in Rwanda', *Human Heredity and Health in Africa,* https://h3africa.org/index.php/consortium/transgenerational-epigenomics-of-trauma-and-ptsd-in-rwanda/; Natan P. F. Kellerman, 'Epigenetic Transmission of Holocaust Trauma: Can Nightmares Be Inherited?', *Israel Journal of Psychiatry* 50:1, 2013; Rachel Yehuda, 'Intergenerational Transmission of Trauma Effects', *World Psychiatry* 17:3, October 2018. For a discussion of the transmission of trauma in relation to psychoanalysis, see Catherine Malabou, *The New Wounded – From Neurosis to Brain Damage*, translated from the French by Steven Miller, New York: Fordham University Press, 2012. The key text on the psychic transmission of trauma remains Nicolas Abraham, 'Notes on the Phantom' in Nicolas Abraham and Maria Torok, *The Shell and the Kernel*, edited by Nicholas Rand, University of Chicago Press, 1994. For one of the most valuable discussions of the psychic transmission of trauma, see Ilse Grubrich-Simitis, 'From Concretism to Metaphor: Thoughts on Some Theoretical and Technical Aspects of the Psychoanalytic Work with the Children of Holocaust Survivors', *Psychoanalytic Study of the Child* 39, 1984.

34. Pumla Gobodo-Madikizela, 'Memory and Trauma' in Jillian Edelstein, *Truth and Lies – Stories from the Truth and Reconciliation Commission in South Africa*, London: Granta, 2001, p. 29.

35. Manganyi, *Mashangu's Reverie*, pp. 20, 44.

36. Ibid, Preface, p. ii, p. 43, p. iii.

37. Frantz Fanon, *Les Damnés de la terre*, 1961, *The Wretched of the Earth*, 1961, Penguin edition, pp. 249–50, 203n., 238.

38. Manganyi, Preface, *Mashangu's Reverie*, p. iv.

39. Fanon, *The Wretched of the Earth*, Penguin edition, pp. 222–3.

40. Freud, 'The Disillusionment of the War', p. 279.

41. Margie Orford, 'The Grammar of Violence: Writing Crime as Fiction', *Current Writing: Text and Reception in Southern Africa* 25:2, 2013, pp. 220–9.

42. Brian Kamanzi, '#FeesMustFall: The Eye of the Hurricane', *Daily Maverick*, 10 October 2016.

43. Manganyi, *Mashangu's Reverie*, p. 22.

44. There is now an extensive literature on South Africa's Truth and Reconciliation Commission, unique at the time for holding its hearings in public. One of the most justly celebrated is Antjie Krog, *Country of My Skull*, Johannesburg: Random House, 1998. I discuss the Commission in 'Apathy

and Accountability – the Challenge of South Africa's Truth and Reconciliation Commission to the Intellectual in the Modern World' in *The Public Intellectual*, edited by Helen Small, Oxford: Blackwell, 2003.

45. Hisham Matar, *The Return*, London: Random House, 2016, p. 247.
46. Ibid., p. 248.
47. Yvonne Vera, *The Stone Virgins*, New York: Farrar, Strauss and Giroux, 2002.
48. Deborah Smith, 'Introduction' to Han Kang, *Human Acts*, translated from the Korean by Deborah Smith, London: Portobello, 2016, p. 2.
49. Kang, *Human Acts*, p. 274.
50. Ibid., pp. 100, 140, 158.
51. Slovo's letter is available on the website of the UK arts organisation, Artangel, originally as part of their 'Inside Prison' project of 2016, *Inside – Artists and Writers in Reading Prison*, www.artangel.org.uk/project/inside/.
52. Kang, *Human Acts*, p. 100.
53. Ibid., pp. 51–3, 131.

8. One Long Scream – Trauma and Justice in South Africa

1. Lukhanyo Calata and Abigail Calata, *My Father Died for This*, Foreword by Paul Verryn, Cape Town: Tafelberg, 2018, pp. 25, 34–5.
2. Ibid., p. 226.
3. Ibid., pp. 213, 216.
4. Ibid., pp. 240, 225.
5. Ibid., p. 245.
6. Ibid., p. 246.
7. All unacknowledged quotes in this chapter are taken from this conference.
8. Ibid., pp. 250, 248, 249, 12, 251.
9. Ibid., p. 18.
10. Pumla Gobodo-Madikizela, *A Human Being Died that Night – Forgiving Apartheid's Chief Killer*, Preface by Nelson Mandela, Cape Town: David Philip, 2003, London: Portobello, 2006.
11. Calata and Calata, *My Father Died for This*, pp. 11–12.
12. Ibid., p. 217.
13. Michael Stanley Tetelman, *We Can! Black Politics in Cradock, South Africa 1948–1985*, Rhodes University: Institute for Social and Economic Research, Crory Library, 2012, p. 3; Calata and Calata, *My Father Died for This*, pp. 91–2, 123.
14. Tetelman, *We Can!*, p. 197.
15. Albie Sachs, *The Soft Vengeance of a Freedom Fighter*, revised and updated

with Foreword by Desmond Tutu, and Introduction by Njabulo S. Ndebele, Cape Town: David Philip, 2011.

16. Albie Sachs, 'A New African Jurisprudence: From Abstract Judicial Rulings to Purposive Transformative Jurisprudence', *We The People – Insights of an Activist Judge*, Johannesburg: Wits University Press, 2016, p. 161; see also Sachs, *Oliver Tambo's Dream*, Cape Town: African Lives, 2017, especially Lectures 3, 'Does the Constitution Stand in the Way of Radical Land Reform', and 4, 'The Constitution as an Instrument of Decolonialisation and Achieving True Equality'; also personal communication.

17. Albie Sachs, personal communication.

18. Sachs, 'A New African Jurisprudence', p. 163.

19. Constitutional Court of South Africa, Port Elizabeth Municipality v Various Occupiers (CCT 53/03) [2004] ZACC 7; 2005 (1) SA 217 (CC); 2004 (12) BCLR 1268 (CC) (1 October 2004).

20. Eliza Kentridge, *Signs for an Exhibition*, Cape Town: Modjaji Books, 2015, p. 91.

21. Gobodo-Madikizela, *A Human Being Died*, pp. 40–1.

22. Freud, *Studies on Hysteria*.

23. W. R. Bion, 'Attacks on Linking', 1959, *International Journal of Psychoanalysis* 40.

24. Hugh Macmillan, *Chris Hani*, Auckland: Jacana, 2014, p. 9.

25. Lindiwe Hani and Melinda Ferguson, *Being Chris Hani's Daughter*, Johannesburg: MF Books, 2017, p. 69.

26. Ibid., p. 91.

27. Krog, *Country of My Skull*, p. 42.

28. Sarah Nuttall, 'Upsurge' in Catherine Boulle and Jay Pather (eds), *Acts of Transgression – Contemporary Live Art in South Africa*, Johannesburg: Wits University Press, 2019.

29. Calata and Calata, *My Father Died for This*, p. 170.

30. Ibid., pp. 38, 103.

31. Penny Siopsis, *This Morning Comes*, video installation, 2018.

32. Jessica Benjamin, 'Non-violence as Respect for All Suffering: Thoughts Inspired by Eyad El Sarraj', *Psychoanalysis, Culture and Society* 21:1, 2016.

33. An attempt to create a non-elite psychoanalysis in South Africa has been the ongoing project of the Ububele South African Psychotherapy Resource and Training Centre, which combines Western psychoanalysis with indigenous systems of knowledge in the treatment of children, and was founded by Tony and Hillary Hamburger on the outskirts of Alexandra township in 2009.

34. Calata and Calata, *My Father Died for This*, pp. 74–5.

35. Hani and Ferguson, *Being Chris Hani's Daughter*, p. xii.

36. Macmillan, *Chris Hani*, pp. 25, 57–8.

37. Calata and Calata, *My Father Died for This*, p. 195.

38. Sisonke Msimang, *The Resurrection of Winnie Mandela*, Cape Town: Jonathan Ball, 2018, pp. 151, 157.

39. Njabulo S. Ndebele, *The Cry of Winnie Mandela*, Cape Town: David Philip, 2003 (revised edition, Picador Africa, 2013), p. 62.

40. Krog, *Country of My Skull*, pp. 39–44.

41. Winnie Madikizela-Mandela, *491 Days, Prisoner Number 1323/69*, Foreword by Ahmed Kathrada, Athens: Ohio University Press, 2013, pp. 57, 38.

42. Ibid., pp. 39, 80, 234.

43. Msimang, *The Resurrection of Winnie Mandela*, p. 146.

44. Ndebele, *The Cry of Winnie Mandela*, p. 109.

45. Hani and Ferguson, *Being Chris Hani's Daughter*, p. 172.

46. Msimang, *The Resurrection of Winnie Mandela*, pp. 148, 151.

47. Rosa Luxemburg, *Redner der Revolution*, Vol. 11, Berlin, 1928, cited in Nettle, *Rosa Luxemburg*, p. 250.

9. At the Border

1. Marchu Girma, Isabelle Kershaw, Gemma Lousley, Sophie Radice and Natasha Walter, *I Am Human*, London: Women for Refugee Women, 2015, p. 10.

2. Jamie Grierson, 'Putting a Time Limit on Detaining Immigrants "Could Save £35m a Year"', *Guardian*, 8 May 2019; see also Diane Taylor, 'Home Office Held More than 500 Trafficking Victims in Detention Centres', on the report of data-mapping project After Exploitation that, contravening its own guidelines, the Home Office was locking up hundreds of trafficking victims in detention centres, *Guardian*, 9 July 2019.

3. Liz Hales and Lorraine Gelsthorpe, *Criminalisation of Migrant Women*, Cambridge Institute of Criminology, 2012, p. 28.

4. Jackie Turner, 'Root Causes, Transnational Mobility and Formations of Patriarchy in the Sex Trafficking of Women' in Margaret Malloch and Paul Rigby (eds), *Human Trafficking: The Complexities of Exploitation*, Edinburgh: Edinburgh University Press, 2016, p. 201.

5. Hales and Gelsthorpe, *Criminalisation of Migrant Women*, p. 80n.

6. Tom McCarthy, '"Horrifying" Conditions Revealed at US Border Detention Centres', *Guardian*, 3 July 2019.

7. Eliot Weinberger, 'One Summer in America', *London Review of Books* 41:18, 26 September 2019.

8. 'Emma's story' in Girma et al., *I Am Human*, p. 8.

9. Diane Taylor, 'Nigerian Rape Survivor "Flung to Floor like a Bag of Cement'', *Guardian*, 17 January 2020.

10. 'Rechel's story' in Girma et al., *I Am Human*, p. 13.
11. See Amelia Gentleman, 'Female Detainees at Yarl's Wood Routinely Humiliated, Claims Report', *Guardian*, 14 January 2015; Black Women's Rape Action Project, Women Against Rape, *Rape and Sexual Abuse in Yarl's Wood Immigration Removal Centre, 2005–2015*, London, Crossroads Women's Centre, 2015.
12. 'Rechel's story' in Girma et al., *I Am Human*, p. 13.
13. Grierson, 'Putting a Time Limit on Detaining Immigrants'.
14. David Herd, Afterword, in David Herd and Anna Pincus (eds), *Refugee Tales*, Manchester: Comma Press, 2016, p. 135.
15. Kamila Shamsie, 'The UK Once Welcomed Refugees. Now We Are the Only Country in Europe to Detain Them Indefinitely. It's Time to End this Costly, Cruel and Unjust System', *Guardian*, 4 July 2020.
16. Hales and Gelsthorpe, *Criminalisation of Migrant Women*, p. 62.
17. Ibid., pp. 63, 65; Herd, Afterword, p. 140.
18. Hales and Gelsthorpe, *Criminalisation of Migrant Women*, p. 32.
19. Herd, Afterword, p. 140.
20. Hales and Gelsthorpe, *Criminalisation of Migrant Women*, pp. 65, 96; Girma et al., *I Am Human*, p. 18.
21. Amelia Gentleman, 'In the Eye of the Story', *Guardian Weekend*, 14 September 2019.
22. Kiril Shaparov in Malloch and Rigby (eds), *Human Trafficking*, p. 18.
23. Herd, Afterword, p. 138.
24. Hales and Gelsthorpe, *Criminalisation of Migrant Women*, p. 88.
25. Margaret Malloch, 'Criminalising Victims of Human Trafficking' in Malloch and Rigby (eds), *Human Trafficking*, p. 175.
26. Heather Ann Thompson, 'An Enduring Shame', *New York Review of Books*, 25 October 2015.
27. Home Office, *Corston Report – Review of Women with Particular Vulnerabilities in the Prison Justice System*, Prison Reform Trust, 2006.
28. Prison Reform Trust, *No Way Out*, 2012, p. 2.
29. Ibid., p. 3.
30. Hales and Gelsthorpe, *Criminalisation of Migrant Women*, p. 61.
31. Ibid., p. 14.
32. 'A Day in Our Lives', Women for Refugee Women, Queen Elizabeth Hall foyer, 23 June 2019. The performance was part of UK Refugee Week. To convey the unique experience they were providing for participants and audience alike, they repeated throughout, 'This is my life but also a performance, this is a performance but it is also my life.'
33. Ali Smith, 'The Detainee's Tale' in Herd and Pincus (eds), *Refugee Tales*, p. 58.

34. Hales and Gelsthorpe, *Criminalisation of Migrant Women*, p. 61.

35. Ibid., p. 59.

36. Ibid., p. 57.

37. Ibid., p. 74.

38. Ibid., p. 75.

39. Prison Reform Trust, *No Way Out*, p. 3.

40. Cited in David Runciman, 'How to Get Screwed', *London Review of Books* 41:11, 6 June 2019, p. 15.

41. Hales and Gelsthorpe, *Criminalisation of Migrant Women*, p. 85.

42. Herd, Afterword, p. 138.

43. Madeleine Schwartz, 'Inside the Deportation Courts', *New York Review of Books*, 10 October 2019.

44. Cited in Malloch and Rigby (eds), *Human Trafficking*, p. 187.

45. Cited in Bill Munroe, 'Human Trafficking: Capitalist Exploitation and the Accursed Share' in Malloch and Rigby (eds), *Human Trafficking*, p. 237.

46. Howard Caygill, Chapter 3, 'Violence, Civility and the Predicaments of Philosophy' in *Force and Understanding: Writings on Philosophy and Resistance*, edited by Stephen Howard, afterword by Jacqueline Rose, London: Bloomsbury, 2020, p. 42; and Chapter 4, 'Politics and War: Hegel and Clausewitz', p. 66.

47. Caygill, 'Violence, Civility', p. 42.

48. Caygill, 'Politics and War', p. 72.

49. Judith Butler, 'Contingent Foundations' in Judith Butler and Joan Scott, *Feminists Theorise the Political*, New York: Routledge, 1992, p. 18.

50. Jamie Grierson, 'Women's Prisons Report Big Rise in New Arrivals Registered as Homeless', *Guardian*, 4 July 2019.

51. Elmhirst, 'No Way Out'; Damien Gayle, 'Woman Wins First Stage in Battle to Overturn Murder Conviction', *Guardian*, 4 December 2019.

52. Hilary Allen, 'Rendering Them Harmless: The Professional Portrayal of Women Charged with Serious Violent Crimes' in Pat Carlen and Anne Worrall (eds), *Analysing Women's Imprisonment*, Devon: Willan Press, 2004, p. 93.

53. See Maya Goodfellow, *Hostile Environment – How Immigrants Became Scapegoats*, London: Verso, 2019.

54. Toby Helm and Mark Townsend, 'Tory Rebels Call for a 28-day Limit on Migrant Detention', *Guardian*, 27 June 2020.

55. Tony Judt, *Postwar – A History of Europe since 1945*, London: Heinemann, 2005, p. 9. See also Peter Gatrell, *The Unsettling of Europe – The Great Migration 1945 to the Present*, London: Penguin Random House, 2019.

56. Brad Evans, 'The Refugee Crisis is Humanity's Crisis', interview with Zygmunt Bauman in *Violence: Humans in Dark Times*, London: City Lights, 2018, p. 55.

57. Jacqueline Bhabha and Sue Shutter, *Nationality and Refugee Law*, Stoke-on-Trent: Trentham Books, 1994, p. 231.

58. Owen Boycott, 'EU Intentionally Sacrificed Migrants at Sea to Deter Others, Legal Papers Claim', *Guardian*, 3 June 2019.

59. Michael Peel, 'EU Poised to Order Migrant Rescue Ships Back to Port', *Financial Times*, 27 March 2019.

60. Aamna Mohdin, 'One Year On, Child Migrants Still Risk All to Cross the Channel', *Guardian*, 30 December 2019.

61. Philip Oltermann, 'Death Threats to German Politicians Who Back Refugees', *Guardian*, 21 June 2019; '"Why Are We Not Flooding to the Streets in Disgust?"', *Guardian*, 3 July 2019.

62. Bhabha and Shutter, *Nationality and Refugee Law*, p. 218.

63. Evans, 'The Refugee Crisis', p. 57.

64. The case is discussed in Bhabha and Shutter, *Nationality and Refugee Law*, p. 246 and in Eithne Luibhéid, *Entry Denied – Controlling Sexuality at the Border*, Minneapolis: University of Minnesota Press, 2002, pp. 106–7.

65. Luibhéid, *Entry Denied*, pp. 107–8.

66. Cynthia Enloe, *Maneuvers – the Systematic Politics of Militarising Women's Lives*, University of Chicago Press, 2000, pp. 123–32.

67. Ibid., p. 147.

68. Ibid., p. 121.

69. Jessica Elgot, 'How May's "Hostile Environment" for Migrants Brought Anguish to a Generation with Every Right to Live Their Lives in Britain', *Guardian*, 18 April 2018; Niamh McIntyre and Alexandra Topping, 'Abuse Victims Increasingly Denied Right to Stay in UK', *Guardian*, 16 August 2018.

70. Niamh McIntyre and Alexandra Topping, 'Abused Women Let Down by "Hostile Environment" Policy', *Guardian*, 16 August 2019.

71. Luibhéid, *Entry Denied*, p. 104.

72. Ibid., Chapter 5.

73. Lorenzo Tondo, 'Three Held over "Rape and Torture" in Migrant Camp', *Guardian*, 17 September 2019.

74. Luibhéid, *Entry Denied*, pp. 110–14.

75. Ibid., p. xvi.

76. Bhabha and Shutter, *Nationality and Refugee Law*, p. 250.

77. Cited in Luibhéid, *Entry Denied*, p. 114.

78. Judith Butler, *State Violence, War, Resistance – For a New Politics of the Left*, lecture delivered at the Barcelona Centre for Contemporary Culture, 7 April 2010, Barcelona: CCCB, 2010, p. 65.

79. Alexandra Topping, 'Migrant Women "Left out of" UK Domestic Abuse Bill, MPs Told', *Guardian*, 6 July 2020.

80. Miriam Jordan, 'Guatemalan Mother Could Lose Custody of Daughter, Because She's an American', *New York Times*, 23 November 2018; Massoud Hayoun, 'After 247 Days Vilma Carrillo, an Immigrant Woman Separated from her Daughter, Has Been Released from ICE Custody', *Pacific Standard*, 11 January 2019.

81. Sarah Stillman, 'The Five-Year-Old Who Was Detained at the Border and Persuaded to Sign Away Her Rights, *New Yorker*, 11 October 2018.

82. Schwartz, 'Inside the Deportation Courts'.

83. Greg Grandin, 'The Battle at the US Border', *Guardian*, 28 February 2019.

84. Ibid.

85. Stephanie Kirchgaessner, 'Senior US Official Said There Was No Age Limit on Child Separations', *Guardian*, 24 July 2020.

86. Diane Taylor, '"Destructive" Child Refugee Policy Keeps Families Apart Deliberately', *Guardian*, 11 January 2020.

87. Hales and Gelsthorpe, *Criminalisation of Migrant Women*, p. 109.

88. Ibid., pp. 101–2, 107.

89. Eithne Luibhéid, *Pregnant on Arrival – Making the Illegal Immigrant*, Minneapolis: University of Minnesota Press, 2013, p. 17.

90. Cited in ibid., p. 140.

91. Luibhéid, *Entry Denied*, p. 41.

92. Proceedings of the British Nationality Bill, *Hansard*, 7 and 13 July 1948, cited in Bhabha and Shutter, *Nationality and Refugee Law*, p. 26.

93. US protection has also been withdrawn from all Central American migrants who have passed through another country where they did not seek asylum; and, in a move generally seen as ending the founding vision of the US as an immigrant nation, a new rule came into effect on 15 October 2019 barring migrants if they fail to cross a poverty threshold, are in need of medical care, or can be construed in any way as being a burden on the state. Associated Press, 'Immigration Officers in US Given Powers to Deport Without Appeal', *Guardian*, 24 July 2019; Daniella Silva, Julia Ainsley, Pete Williams and Geoff Bennett, 'Trump Administration Moves to End Asylum Protection for Most Central American Migrants', *NBC News*, 15 July 2019; Daniel Trotta and Mica Rosenberg, 'New Rule Targets Poor and Could Cut Legal Immigration in Half, Advocates Say', Reuters, *World News*, 12 August 2019.

94. Jia Tolentino, 'The I in the Internet', *Trick Mirror: Reflections on Self-Delusion*, New York: Random House, 2019, p. 9.

95. Diane Taylor, 'Child Asylum Seekers Tell of Abuse After They Were Classified as Adults', *Guardian*, 30 May 2019.

96. Julia O'Connell Davidson, *Children in the Global Sex Trade*, London: Polity, 2005, pp. 5, 6.

INDEX